Assembling the Marvel
Cir

Assembling the Marvel Cinematic Universe

Essays on the Social, Cultural and Geopolitical Domains

Edited by JULIAN C. CHAMBLISS,
WILLIAM L. SVITAVSKY
and DANIEL FANDINO

McFarland & Company, Inc., Publishers
Jefferson, North Carolina

ISBN 978-1-4766-6418-7 (softcover : acid free paper)
ISBN 978-1-4766-3285-8 (ebook)

LIBRARY OF CONGRESS CATALOGUING-IN-PUBLICATION DATA

BRITISH LIBRARY CATALOGUING DATA ARE AVAILABLE

Front cover image of spinning film reel in the dark © 2018 iLexx/iStock

Printed in the United States of America

McFarland & Company, Inc., Publishers
  Box 611, Jefferson, North Carolina 28640
    www.mcfarlandpub.com

Table of Contents

Acknowledgments

The editors would like to thank the many writers, actors, producers, and crews who have created the Marvel Cinematic Universe. Their creativity, vision, and passion have inspired established comic book readers and fascinated new fans. We would also like to thank the comic book writers and artists (first and foremost Jack Kirby, along with others too numerous to mention) who inspired those filmmakers.

In addition, we would like to thank family for their support and understanding for this project. When we were unsure, Beth King, Betty Svitavsky, Emily Shea Harris, Denise Redmond-Smith, Nikki Redmond, and Ernest Redmond provided perspective.

Professional colleagues in a variety of fields offered their perspective and advice for this project. We would like to thank Martin Lund, Nicholas Yanes, Jennifer Rea and Will Brooker for their insight and feedback. We give special thanks to Thomas C. Donaldson for his assistance with this volume.

Introduction

The Marvel Cinematic Universe is an unprecedented series of inter-linked films that have mirrored the deeply interconnected nature of their comic book predecessors, pushed the boundaries of transmedia and mined the anxieties present in early 21st century American society and culture to fuel their storylines. However, while scholars have examined Marvel characters in print, less consideration has been given to the implications of live action adaptions. Despite the recent success of Marvel Studios and the rising academic interest in superheroes, no one has yet offered a comprehensive examination of the Marvel Cinematic Universe. This omission is surprising since the transition to film has provided new energy for comic book super-heroes in American society. Looking beyond box office achievements, Marvel's establishment of its own movie studio has increased its cultural impact in the United States and around the world.

This collection of essays examines the ways the Marvel Cinematic Universe represents, constructs, and distorts American culture. For decades, Marvel Comics' emphasis on socially relevant characters and plots has generated fan engagement and popular appeal. In the new millennium, the success of Marvel Studios' films (and subsequent reactions) represent a new and unique engagement with social, political, and economic concerns that challenge established values and call into question cherished beliefs. This book seeks to unravel the myriad threads that wind throughout the Marvel Cinematic Universe and ask if the whole is greater than the sum of its parts. The assembled essays of this volume suggest that the Marvel Cinematic Universe is not merely a popular set of materials convenient for analysis, but a significant phenomenon in its own right that is worthy of scholarly attention.

As befits a collaborative effort offering a far-reaching exploration of the Marvel Cinematic Universe, the essays in this collection are rooted in a variety of disciplines and theoretical approaches, and hence draw from a wide variety of previous work. A comprehensive bibliography at the end of this book lists the works cited herein. No other works at the time of this writing have the same scope as this collection: a multidisciplinary volume focused on the phenomenon of the Marvel Cinematic Universe. However, our work consciously exists in the context of a booming broader scholarship examining superheroes.

Several general studies of superheroes in comic books and other media are worth noting; they underlie the work of this volume's editors and contributors. Peter Coogan's *Superhero: The Secret Origin of a Genre* offers a useful definition of a superhero and traces the evolution of superhero stories; this approach is echoed in this volume's first section examining questions of genre, structure, and cultural context in the MCU.[1] In contrast, Bradford Wright's *Comic Book Nation: The Transformation of Youth Culture in America* is a historical examination of social context, an approach that dominates the second and third sections of this book.[2] The concept of this volume also has roots in the previous collection by editors Julian C. Chambliss, William L. Svitavsky, and Thomas Donaldson: *Ages of Heroes, Eras of Men: Superheroes and the American Experience.*[3] In that book we examined comic book superheroes with a sampling of approaches but with a comprehensive historical framework; in this volume we turn another sampling of approaches to a more current and tightly defined selection of texts.

While scholarship devoted to superheroes in comic books has grown abundantly in the last two decades, superhero films have been a minor genre until recently and critical examinations of them have been relatively rare. *Superhero Movies* by Liam Burke (a contributor to this volume) was an early effort in 2008; though primarily a reference guide aimed at fans and general movie viewers, it offers some thoughtful analysis of films that had appeared by that point and includes an interview with Stan Lee that mentions the forthcoming *Iron Man* and hints at other MCU movies with typical Stan Lee bombast.[4] Marc DiPaolo's *War, Politics and Superheroes: Ethics and Propaganda in Comics and Film* uses a variety of literary and historical approaches to analyze the political values expressed by a number of selected superheroes.[5] Covering many different media, no particular iteration of any character in a specific film is covered at great length; the MCU movies that had appeared by the time of publication get only brief mention. Richard J. Gray II and Betty Kaklamanidou's *The 21st Century Superhero: Essays on Gender, Genre and Globalization in Film* explores issues of globalization, gender, and genre in superhero films in the first decade of the 21st century.[6] Published when the MCU was still in its early stages, only the first two *Iron Man* movies and *The Incredible Hulk* are included among its coverage of superhero movies, and little attention is paid to the nature of the shared universe.

Some recent books have started to recognize the significance of the shared universe in Marvel movies. Matthias Stork and James Gilmore's *Superhero Synergies: Comic Book Characters Go Digital* examines the current era of superhero movies, arguing the centrality of digital technologies in shaping the genre; Stork's essay on *The Avengers* addresses at length the MCU phenomenon, asserting that the film reinvented the superhero movie as a self-promoting framework for a sustainable franchise.[7] *Marvel Comics into Film: Essays on Adaptations Since the 1940s* by Matthew J. McEniry, Robert Moses Peaslee, and Robert G. Weiner has a broader scope than this book, defining its subject as what the editors refer to as the "Cinematic Marvel Universe" as opposed the Marvel Cinematic Universe.[8] It includes a wide range of screen adaptations including Marvel live action and animated television shows, productions from other studios such as Elektra, Blade, and Ghost Rider, and even films based on properties with licensing links to Marvel such as Transformers, G.I. Joe, and Conan. Multiple essays discuss MCU films and the nature of the MCU itself, including Brian Cogan and Jeff Massey's essay on *Thor* and Julian C. Chambliss's essay on *Black Panther*. Several contributors to this book contributed to that effort as well. Most comparable to this book in its selection of films for examination is *The Marvel Studios Phenomenon: Inside a Transmedia Universe* by Martin Flanagan, Mike McKenny and Andy Livingstone.[9] Its approach is grounded in film studies and its focus is on Marvel Studios in the context of the film industry, rather than an explication of particular texts. Chapters address such topics as the history of Marvel Studios' formation and position within the Walt Disney Company, Marvel's principles of storytelling, genre tactics, use of minor properties within Marvel's rich catalogue of characters, and the power of Marvel's transmedia empire.

This study is informed by the recognition that Marvel Studios represents a distinct voice that leverages elements of the Marvel Comics print universe to inform and excite a new audience. In this way, we extend the point made in *The Marvel Studio Phenomenon*, by recognizing that the MCU's extended narrative replicates the excitement generated by Marvel Comics published in the 1960s. As the authors of that volume indicate, it was Marvel's "commitment to the 'shared universe' concept" that lent the company identity to the reading public.[10] Guided by a small cadre of writers and talented artists, Marvel Comics coordinated the roll out of characters and created a coherent experience for readers that encouraged greater involvement. As Bradford Wright illustrated, Stan Lee saw this as a marketing tool that gave Marvel "a certain personality ... where readers would identify with us and care about us."[11] The legacy of this approach shapes the MCU.

Yet, Marvel was not the first (or only) shared universe. As we consider the MCU we recognize the framework identified by Henry Jenkins in his seminal 2003 essay defining transmedia storytelling.[12] Jenkins argued that modern media was defined by expanding their narrative across platforms and that while "the technological infrastructure is ready" and "kids who have grown up consuming and enjoying Pokemon across media" were going to expect that same experience as adults, the media producers were not ready. Marvel Studios has seemingly mastered this form and the reason for their success is connected to the print form that gave rise to the MCU. The link between a tradition of transmedia storytelling rooted in the pulp adventure of Tarzan, Conan, and adventure heroes of the 1920s and 1930s shaped comic books. As Carlos A. Scolari, Paolo Bertetti, and Matthew Freeman demonstrate in *Transmedia Archaeology: Storytelling in the Borderlines of Science Fiction, Comics, and Pulp Magazine* the fan cultures that celebrated pulp heroes created narrative communities that mirror contemporary culture.[13] This heritage of deep fan involvement went beyond consumption. As Jenkins points out, transmedia architecture offers the opportunity to expand the narrative universe, not simply repeat the story in the original product. Thus, the success of *Star Wars* rested on the books and games moving background characters to the foreground, filling in the gap between films and providing context events before and after the film that birthed the universe. These actions were pioneered in comic book publishing. Thus, the idea that Marvel Comics characters and stories could be the basis of shared universe that existed across platforms should come as no surprise.

The structure and culture of comic book storytelling is infused into the Marvel Cinematic Universe. This structure relies on strong editorial control and collective narrative momentum that propels fans from one element within the shared universe to the next. With enough autonomous elements to allow the viewer to concentrate on one character, but integrated enough to reward fans, the knowledge of character and story that is key to the print universe has been reconfigured to create the Marvel Cinematic Universe. It is unquestionably a marketing exercise, yet the shared narrative empowers participation and generates new creative opportunities that can reflect changing social, political, and economic circumstances that previous transmedia narrative could not.

To investigate the breadth of the Marvel Cinematic Universe this book is divided into three parts, each concentrating on major associated elements found within the films. Our first section explores the relationship between the MCU and the rise of the transmedia experience. The filmmakers working within the Marvel Cinematic Universe have done far more than capitalize on the superhero craze in film to the fullest. They have introduced a new mode of filmmaking, one in which the franchise, the existing model of multi-installment narrative, has become subsumed into a larger conglomerate storytelling entity, the shared universe. In doing so, Marvel simply adapted the marketing and storytelling strategy that the company, along with DC Comics, had made standard operating procedure in the comic industry in the 1960s. By creating a shared universe encompassing a growing number of individual filmic franchises, Marvel Entertainment is on the cusp of revolutionizing the film industry. Because of the financial success of films such as *The Avengers, Captain America: The Winter Soldier,* and *Guardians of the Galaxy,* other companies have begun development of their own multi-franchise shared universe concepts, notably Warner Bros.' superhero universe featuring the characters of their subsidiary, DC Comics, and Universal's new effort featuring the monsters that brought the studio to prominence in the 1930s and 1940s. Disney, Marvel Studios' parent company, has also adopted a transmedia approach with the *Star Wars* franchise by announcing a slate of upcoming films featuring new and old characters while continuing the story in canonical video games and books. Beyond making the shared universe a new industry standard, Marvel is also transforming how audiences consume this growing agglomeration of characters by presenting them through a variety of media outlets other than traditional theatrical movies. In developing linked properties transmitted through venues such as exclusive DVD/Blu-Ray features, broadcast television, and streaming programming, as well as through theatrical releases, filmmakers are presenting the Marvel Cinematic Universe as a truly transmedia experience.

Starting our investigation into transmedia, Perry Dantzler argues that the Marvel Cinematic Universe requires a new literacy of continuity and expects a high level of sophistication on the part of a participant. Liam Burke then explores differences between transmedia storytelling and traditional adaptation, identifying along the way how Marvel succeeded where the studios had failed. Lisa K. Perdigao examines *Agents of S.H.I.E.L.D.,* uncovering a narrative informed and directed by its source material in a manner that suggests new ways of conceiving adaptation across mediums. Derek R. Sweet positions *The Avengers* as a kind of therapeutic public memory that not only conjures the perceived social and political failures surrounding 9/11 but also offers an opportunity to rehabilitate those failures. Concluding Section I, William L. Svitavsky looks at how the "shared universe" of the films differs from sequel-based franchises of the past as the basic assumptions of the narrative setting can change from story to story.

The book's second section focuses on the Marvel Cinematic Universe and the American social order in the 21st century. Since the early days of the genre, superheroes have been defenders of the American Way, regardless of their origin. Creators have traditionally associated this phrase with ideal abstractions such as "truth" and "justice," believing it to embody the positive virtues of U.S. culture. As the growing scholarship on comics points out, creators have made choices over the genre's history that have privileged particular races, ethnicities, classes, and genders over others. In doing so, creators have codified the status quo on the basis of social difference and made superheroes that defended this vision of the American way in order to perpetuate social inequality. Filmmakers of the Marvel Cinematic Universe have, whether they realize it or not, inherited this subtextual aspect of the genre from their print predecessors. While they have created parallels to some of the existing tropes that evolved in print adventures of Marvel superheroes, filmmakers have also created their own distinctive vision of the United States and how it should be in regards to the relationship between social distinction and differences in status.

In this section Sarah Zaidan addresses the current cinematic representation of Iron Man as the construct of a post–financial crisis, post–9/11 world and explores the factors that elevated Iron Man to the status of the iconic 21st century superhero. The uses of music in the MCU occupies the thoughts of two of our contributors, as James Rovira argues that the way *Guardians of the Galaxy* pits aggressive and murderous males against nurturing and protective females reveals how gender relationships work and Masani McGee considers the role of popular music and nostalgia. Elizabeth D. Blum reveals how the early 1960s origin stories of the Avengers and the early 21st century Marvel Universe films provide a look into the changes in environmental values and attitudes over 50 years. Finally, shifting to questions of violence and spectacle, Antony Mullen investigates the ways in which human, superhuman, post-human and non-human bodies are represented in Marvel films.

The connections between the Marvel films and modern American geopolitical anxieties are the focus of the third section of this volume. Paralleling the rise of the superhero genre during World War II, the creators of the Marvel Cinematic Universe developed their works in the wake of the September 11, 2001, terrorist attacks and the ensuing War on Terror. Filmmakers have utilized this geopolitical context as a frame of reference for the audience in order to ground their tales of superheroic fantasy in a reality with which viewers can relate. In doing so, creators have articulated major concerns of the American public about the foreign threats faced by the United States, while at the same time offering critiques as to how American policy makers have gone about defending the country from its external foes and existential crises.

Jason Bainbridge argues that a side effect of Marvel Studios' critical and commercial success has been the confirmation of the Marvel superhero as the exemplar of justice, law and authority. Sasha-Mae Eccleston discusses the characterization of villains in the Marvel Cinematic Universe and the nationalist and nativist anxieties of post–9/11 America. Jennifer A. Rea uncovers parallels between *Captain America: The Winter Soldier* and Virgil's *Aeneid*, asking why ancient Rome remains relevant in our modern post-war narratives and if the American ideal of individual freedom still exists in post–9/11 America. Jennifer Beckett's essay examines the way that the changing status of S.H.I.E.L.D. in films and on television mirrors current debates about the role and oversight of America's intelligence agencies. Finally, Samira Shirish Nadkarni finds the complicated identity politics at work in *Agents of S.H.I.E.L.D.* tied to a narrative of colonization and non-white ethnicity connecting to a depiction of an American neo-imperialist and neo-colonial stance regarding global security.

Each of the essays in this collection delves into specific elements of the Marvel Cinematic Universe, approaching their subjects from different perspectives and disciplines. Taken together, as with the assembling of the Avengers, they represent sometimes more: a joint exploration into an ambitious and multifaceted media phenomenon, pulling disparate threads into a conversation with each other. The need for such a collection as we have gathered here is evident with the increasing complexity, topical subject matter and deep cultural impact of the Marvel Studio films. The Marvel Cinematic Universe shows no sign of slowing down, continually evolving and emerging as no mere imitation of the comics but instead developing its own narrative and place in popular culture. As Marvel Studios continues to expand, etching their heroes into the popular consciousness and projecting reflections of American society onto the silver screen, so too does the need for academic inquiry into this cinematic universe.

NOTES

1. Peter Coogan. *Superhero: The Secret Origin of a Genre* (Austin, TX: MonkeyBrain Books, 2006).

2. Bradford W. Wright, *Comic Book Nation: The Transformation of Youth Culture in America* (Baltimore: Johns Hopkins University Press, 2003).

3. Julian C. Chambliss, William L. Svitavsky, and Thomas C. Donaldson. *Ages of Heroes, Eras of Men: Superheroes and the American Experience* (Newcastle upon Tyne: Cambridge Scholars Publishing, 2013).

4. Liam Burke. *Superhero Movies.* Harpenden: Pocket Essentials, 2008.

5. Marc DiPaolo. *War, Politics and Superheroes: Ethics and Propaganda in Comics and Film* (Jefferson, NC: McFarland, 2011).

6. Richard J. Gray II and Betty Kaklamanidou. *The 21st Century Superhero: Essays on Gender, Genre and Globalization in Film* (Jefferson, NC: McFarland, 2011).

7. James Gilmore and Matthias Stork. *Superhero Synergies: Comic Book Characters Go Digital* (Lanham, MD: Rowman & Littlefield, 2014).

8. Matthew J. McEniry, Robert Moses Peaslee, and Robert G. Weiner. *Marvel Comics into Film: Essays on Adaptations Since the 1940s* (Jefferson, NC: McFarland, 2016).

9. Martin Flanagan, Andrew Livingstone, and Mike McKenny. *The Marvel Studios Phenomenon: Inside a Transmedia Universe* (New York: Bloomsbury Academic, 2016).

10. Flanagan, Livingstone, and McKenny, *The Marvel Studios Phenomenon*, 2.

11. Wright, *Comic Book Nation*, 218.

12. Henry Jenkins, "Transmedia Storytelling," *MIT Technology Review*, January 15, 2003, https://www.technologyreview.com/s/401760/transmedia-storytelling/.

13. Carlos Scolari, Paolo Bertetti, and Matthew Freeman, *Transmedia Archaeology: Storytelling in the Borderlines of Science Fiction, Comics and Pulp Magazines* (Palgrave Macmillan, 2014), http://www.palgrave.com/page/detail/transmedia-archaeology-carlos-scolari/?K=9781137434364.

The Marvel Cinematic Universe Filmography

For the purposes of this book, the Marvel Cinematic Universe, or MCU, refers to the shared fictional universe featured in the films, television shows, and video short features ("Marvel One-Shots") produced (or coproduced) by Marvel Studios starting with *Iron Man* in 2008. We contend that these works are worth examining collectively not simply because they share a fictional setting, but because they are a distinct group of texts sharing common assumptions, values, and influences. The setting might also be considered to include various video and other online materials used for online marketing as well as comic books specifically tying into the MCU continuity, but there is minimal discussion of those items in this collection. For the sake of clarity and ease of reference, the works of the MCU released or scheduled as of this writing are listed here by medium and U.S. release date.

Feature Films

Phase One

Iron Man (2008)
The Incredible Hulk (2008)
Iron Man 2 (2010)
Thor (2011)
Captain America: The First Avenger (2011)
Marvel's The Avengers (2012)

Phase Two

Iron Man 3 (2013)
Thor: The Dark World (2013)

Captain America: The Winter Soldier (2014)
Guardians of the Galaxy (2014)
Avengers: Age of Ultron (2015)
Ant-Man (2015)

Phase Three

Captain America: Civil War (2016)
Doctor Strange (2016)
Guardians of the Galaxy vol. 2 (2017)
Spider-Man Homecoming (2017)
Thor: Ragnarok (2017)
Black Panther (scheduled for 2018)
Avengers: Infinity War (scheduled for 2018)
Ant-Man and the Wasp(scheduled for 2018)
Captain Marvel (scheduled for 2019)
Untitled *Avengers* film (scheduled for 2019)

Phase Four

Untitled *Spider-Man Homecoming* sequel (scheduled for 2019)
Guardians of the Galaxy vol. 3 (TBA)

Television Series

ABC

Marvel's Agents of S.H.I.E.L.D. (debuted 2013)
Marvel's Agent Carter (debuted 2015)
Marvel's The Inhumans (debuted 2017)
Marvel's Damage Control (TBA)

Netflix Series

Marvel's Daredevil (debuted 2015)
Marvel's Jessica Jones (debuted 2015)
Marvel's Luke Cage (debuted 2016)
Marvel's Iron Fist (debuted 2017)
Marvel's The Defenders (debuted 2017)
Marvel's The Punisher (debuted 2017)

Freeform

Marvel's Cloak & Dagger (scheduled for 2018)

Marvel One-Shots

The Consultant (2011)
A Funny Thing Happened on the Way to Thor's Hammer (2011)
Item 47 (2012)
Agent Carter (2013)
All Hail the King (2014)

Digital Series

Agents of S.H.I.E.L.D.: Slingshot (2016)

Section I

"In order to form a more perfect union": The Cultural Context of the Transmedia Universe

The filmmakers on the Marvel Cinematic Universe have done far more than capitalize on the superhero craze in film to the fullest. They have introduced a new mode of filmmaking, one in which the franchise, the existing model of multi-installment narrative, has become subsumed into a larger conglomerate storytelling entity, the shared universe. In doing so, Marvel simply adapted the marketing and storytelling strategy that the company, along with DC Comics, had made standard operating procedure in the 1960s.

By creating a shared universe encompassing a growing number of individual filmic franchises, Marvel Entertainment is on the cusp of revolutionizing the film industry. Because of the financial success of films such as *The Avengers*, *Captain America: The Winter Soldier*, and *Guardians of the Galaxy*, other companies have begun development of their own multi-franchise shared universe concepts, notably Warner Brothers' superhero universe featuring the characters of their subsidiary DC Comics, and Universal's new effort featuring the monsters that brought the studio to prominence in the 1930s and 1940s.

Beyond making the shared universe a new industry standard, Marvel is also transforming how audiences consume this growing agglomeration of characters by presenting them through a variety of media outlets rather than traditional film. In developing linking properties transmitted through venues such as exclusive DVD/Blu-Ray features, broadcast television, and streaming programming, as well as through theatrical releases, filmmakers are presenting the Marvel Cinematic Universe as a truly transmedia experience.

Multiliteracies of the MCU

Continuity Literacy and the Sophisticated Reader(s) of Superheroes Media

PERRY DANTZLER

Introduction

The Marvel Cinematic Universe (MCU) has emerged from decades of comic book narratives that created complex, intersecting storylines, but the recent media developments have pushed the entire conglomeration into further intricacy as the MCU continues to add more movies and television shows to its canon. At present count, the MCU media has amassed eleven films, two television programs, and multiple comic tie-ins. Marvel Studios has announced plans for more films to continue the world, characters, and storylines in locations ranging from American cities to the far corners of the galaxy.[1] In his synopsis of the MCU's success in establishing high-quality narratives and an expanding audience base, Aaron Taylor notes that "The narrative continuity of Marvel Studios' output from 2008 to the present is certainly not the film industry's first attempt at installment narratives [...] but it is certainly their most ambitious (and expensive) effort."[2] "Ambitious" seems like an understatement as their efforts to sustain continuity range from the minuscule, such as Captain America's shield emblem in *Iron Man 2* (2010), to the trans-modal with *Captain America: The Winter Soldier's* (2014) outing of HYDRA inside S.H.I.E.L.D. as the plot-point for most of the second season of *Agents of S.H.I.E.L.D.* (2013–).

These levels of development and interplay/intertextuality require a literacy of continuity that reflects the MCU's expectations of a sophisticated reader. A participant in this universe has to track individual characters through multiple films such as Tony Stark through *Iron Man 1* (2008), *Iron Man 2*, and *Iron Man 3* (2013), and *The Avengers* (2012) and *The Avengers:*

Age of Ultron (2015); plot devices through various histories, as in the case of the Infinity Stones through *Captain America: The First Avenger* (2011), *Thor* (2011), *Avengers, Thor 2: The Dark World* (2013), *Guardians of the Galaxy* 2014), and *Age of Ultron*; and established components beyond the movie theater with HYDRA in television's *Agents of S.H.I.E.L.D.* and the animated *Avengers Assemble!* (2013–). While other collections of visual texts have maintained stories over several modes, notably DC's success with Christopher Nolan's *Dark Knight* film trilogy and the television programs *Arrow* (2012–) and *Flash* (2014–), only Marvel has managed to expand its storylines into a web of interconnecting narratives that continue to amass more intrinsic stories that garner a wider and wider audience base.

The MCU has created a literacy of continuity through its stories and the necessity of a close-reading, erudite audience that develops this literacy in order to enjoy the multimodal texts of the MCU. The audience's literacy can expand or narrow as the individual reader/viewer requires in order to enjoy one film or multiple films. Audiences of superhero media have consistently developed continuity literacy as the stories they encounter are serial as in their original modes as comics and graphic novels, and these stories were prone to displaying variations of the same characters and even the same plots throughout the runs of multiple authors/artists.[3] The MCU films take this niche of specialized interest and develop narratives that require audiences to link and sustain stories over multiple texts to continue enjoying the story and characters.

The concept of continuity literacy for readers of comics is not new, as most readers of such texts—comic books and graphic novels—had to develop this particular literacy to keep engaging with superheroes and their stories. In particular, the MCU has created three specific changes that result in altering reader/viewer perceptions and engagements with the texts: first, the importance of continuity literacy allows for better-developed, more-complex stories told to their fullest capability; secondly, the viewers move from passive participants into active readers that must work to keep up with demanding webs of interrelated stories; and finally, this shift in storytelling reflects a fragmented postmodern understanding of fiction in that readers will start to gravitate towards a multiliterate conception of superhero stories, a state which many invested in multimodalities have already experienced but which the MCU has now made necessary by its continued expansion.

Continuing Narratives

Before expanding further on multiliteracies in the context of continuity, the complexities that extended narratives or serializations have had and the scholarship that has already explored their story arcs and audiences should be noted. Continuous narratives have been a commonality since the serialization of novels in magazines during the Victorian era with authors such as Dickens, Elliot, and Thackeray. Comics in the early 1900s appeared in similar fashion—short episodes of heroes that were published frequently and cheaply. According to Elliott Gaines, "The power of narrative extends the continuity of ideas across genres of representations. Good writing necessarily draws strength from logical connections; characters in a story function and develop in relation to other characters and significant events."[4] The concepts and criteria of "good writing" have been debated through the years, as comics and superhero stories as well as the pulp fiction of the first half of the 1900s were very much disposable entertainment, meant for younger audiences to enjoy and then toss aside.[5]

In the 1980s and '90s, superhero media gained credibility as their stories moved towards stronger narrative arcs and character development that allowed the serial comics to feel more literary and climactic in tone rather than simply episodic flashes of physical feats and overly dramatic storylines. According to Jason Dittmer, "National [American] narratives can also be understood as serialized" because they exhibit "a continually shifting storyline in which certain fundamentals remain the same even as the characters may grow, change, establish relationships, or disassociate from each other."[6] The growth of an audience's familiarity and continued interest in the medium or multimodal media becomes the strengths of these narratives and maintains the essence of the story's appeal: characters evolving and participating in their own worlds to the extent that they feel comfortable and normal to the audience.

In the latter half of the 1900s, continued narratives through film offered new opportunities to tell more in-depth stories that would sustain themselves of multiple texts, but they also presented challenges in terms of establishing an audience and then keeping that audience. In "Wait for the Next Pictures," Josh Lambert stresses that the success of continued narratives depends on three separate but equally important factors: "the availability of which depends on the synchronization of distribution networks of the medium in which a story is being told, that medium's capacity to handle summaries, and the feasibility of providing intertextual supplements."[7] The chances of synchronization, summarization, and intertextuality happening together effectively is rare, and their success is further complicated by the popularity of the art because, as Lambert adds, "Cliffhanger continuity can be successfully employed only after these [three] elements, and reliable audiences and patterns of consumption, are already in place."[8] Unsuccessful attempts at merging the three criteria are witnessed in book series made into films that flop at the box office, resulting in the end of their franchises after the first installment:

Lemony Snicket's A Series of Unfortunate Events (2004), *Sahara* (2005), and *Beautiful Creatures* (2013).

Some of the blame for their failure rests on the feasibility of transforming a book audience into a film audience or simply turning a book and its literary, alphabetic intricacies into a film with visual components. Often the pace of the novel or the comic book tells a story languidly over hundreds of pages that is not practical for a two-hour movie. As Henry Perritt, Jr., stresses, "Writing good narrative is art, not engineering. Each subplot and character has its own arc of exposition, complication, climax, and denouement. In effective narrative, these are intertwined and unfold at their own pace."[9] However, to draw out the stories into longer arcs and to create continuity from one text to another or between multiple texts requires careful navigation on the creator's part to balance out satisfaction and desire on behalf of the audience. For the story to continue past the end of one text and not frustrate the audience, Perritt insists, "Some kind of resolution must occur or be promised in future episodes. Suspending resolution is, of course, the key to serialization."[10] Audiences will come back for the next film only if they have felt that the film at hand has satisfied their needs as viewers.

For superhero media, continuity has played a significant role as most of the earlier comics were episodic and did not reach a final conclusion in and of themselves. Artists in the later decades of the '70s, '80s and '90s would create short runs of comics with beginnings, middles, and ends like normal narratives, including the X-Men's *Dark Phoenix Saga* (1980) and Batman's *Knightfall* (1993–1994). For the most part, the worlds of the superheroes have remained open to the possibilities of new narratives or character development, and these possibilities helped superheroes transfer to the small screen and then the silver screen, thus expanding upon an existing base of comic book readers and superhero fans. Mila Bongco discusses the paradoxes of superhero stories inside of cultural studies, mainly in that "the superhero comic book is a popular art form traditionally known for its apparently hegemonic and sometimes overly authoritarian texts" which often leads to comics being disdained by "the literary establishment, and has yet to build up its own juristic critical discourse through what is still rather misleadingly known as the fan press" and finally because comics offer an array of "contemporary mythology from which television and Hollywood have plundered and distributed material."[11]

Superhero media changed emphatically to become more sophisticated, intricate entertainment over recent decades even while explaining the same characters. For example, even though both tell stories of Batman, the difference between the 1960's *Batman* and Nolan's *Dark Knight Trilogy* is striking: goofy, melodramatic, biweekly episodes for kids produced cheaply vs. dark, intense, sometimes brutal films for action-adventure-seeking adults produced with an enormous budget. Yet, the changes in superhero media occurred over time, shifting gradually in direction or popularity; literacy of film is a connectivity of stories through visual, comic, and alphabetic texts that continues to unravel.[12] Through serialization and connectivity, characters and story arcs of the MCU feature changes and developments that do not happen in a bubble of exclusivity limited to a single visual text; such extensive storytelling needs multiple texts to extend the narratives.

One aspect of the superheroes' appeal are their roots in a historical narrative formation that reflects Judeo-Christian allegories intermeshed with American cultural values and strains of mythology that have been repeated and popularized in art and narratives. As Marco Arnaudo states in the *Myth of the Superhero*, "From the very beginning, the superhero comic has maintained such a strong relationship with myth and religion. [...] Ancient mythology offered an exhaustible reserve of superhero personalities and adventurous deeds that weren't the exclusive property of anyone."[13] From the Marvel Universe, Thor is the first obvious character who fits these criteria as he is himself a mythic god, but there are further extrapolations of characters that fits Joseph Campbell archetypes—Iron Man as the Reluctant Hero, Black Widow as the Hero of Action, Captain America as the Hero as Saint. Each superhero undergoes the descent and ascent arc in nearly every film: a dive into despair or catastrophe which he or she must fight against in order to become heroic, a binary of failure and triumph that satisfies audiences because "The deeds of the hero in the second part of his personal cycle will be proportionate to the depth of his descent in the first."[14] Yet, the relationship of superheroes to classical and ancient myths is more than just similar narrative arcs: Arnado notes that "It is unlikely that mythological heroes would have remained a constant source for superhero comics if there had not been particular narrative or symbolic affinities between the ancient stories and the new ones."[15] The retelling of stories through similar arcs or tropes helps to familiarize viewers/readers with the narrative and thus create better connection and sympathy with characters' choices, plights, and desires, as most studies of mythology and storytelling have demonstrated.

Films of the MCU follow patterns of Joseph Campbell's Hero's Journey in terms of self-improvement and growth, both which appeal to the films' audiences. Despite postmodern angst, existentialism, or twists that now characterize current superhero films, the heroes still work under traditional expectations of the hero/villain paradigm. *Iron Man 3* changed the viewers' expectations of the Mandarin villain when the Mandarin was exposed as a false front to mask the real villain, Aldrich Killian. This change from the original Iron Man comic book story (the Mandarin first appeared in 1964 and was depicted as a villainous Chinese Yellow Peril stereotype) demonstrated a need for current political correctness. Despite this shift, the hero's quest changes only from an objective to defeat a military warlord to an objective to defeat a military tech genius. Perceptions of appropriate cultural values and corresponding demonization of unpopular groups may change, but the driving impetus that draws audiences to sympathize with MCU superheroes and invest in their continued narratives remains strong. Part of the hype around *Avengers: Age of Ultron* and the success of the film may be due to its stylized action, special effects, and blockbuster cinematography, but a large part is the appeal of seeing these established superheroes have their world torn apart (Campbell's descent) and then work together to right the wrongs against them and their world (Campbell's ascent).[16] The reader/viewer does not need to create a new context to understand a new medium of narrative or new characters; the reader/viewer does have to draw on continuity literacy to ascertain each character from earlier films and throughout the film at hand.

Unlike the obvious or notable heroes of mythology, superheroes often appeal the most to audiences when they spend time as their human selves and their alter egos. According to Will Brooker, "Superhero mythology is about escape, about creating an alternative identity and becoming someone different, someone better. Arguably, superheroes are at their finest when they are the alter-ego creations of geeks and loners, not handsome hunks."[17] Even for MCU heroes who are hunks, some element of the hero is lacking or flawed: Steve Rogers is out of sync with American culture, Tony Stark has an addiction/control disorder, and Bruce Banner has rage issues that alienate him from others. Their flaws make the heroes relatable to their audiences; in "Heroes of the Superculture," Richard Reynolds asks, "In this brave new digital landscape, where are the myths to lend universality to our experience? Where are the heroes who will give visible dimensions to our complex identities?"[18] In answer of this new problem of identity and identification in an age of cynicism, he states, "The mythic heroes of our information age are the costumed superheroes. The superhero is a protagonist in the cycle of mythology that has to evolve to express and mediate the expansion of human action and identity in the postindustrial age."[19]

A portion of the MCU's success lies in its close relationship and portrayal of American culture, mainly in ideals of what constitutes heroism.[20] Alex Romagnoli defines this close connection as fundamental to creating a perpetual link between audiences and superhero media: viewers respond to well-crafted superheroes that "evolve with audiences and that reaffirm what is important to the collective, cultural consciousness. The heroes in these stories have conquered death, censorship, relegation, and creative strife only to come out stronger and more socioculturally relevant than ever."[21] The depth and intricacies of MCU superheroes have consistently demonstrated this appeal to their audiences' collective consciousness by fighting against staggering odds and aligning themselves as relevant heroes of this generation, and to stay engaged with their efforts, audiences have developed multiliteracy skills particular to the MCU.

Multimodal Multiliteracies

The creators of the MCU films merged the dominant concepts of continued serialization and American superheroes together to create a world of networked story arcs and suspended narratives, and this merging requires a specific form of comprehension and analysis which can be termed *continuity literacy*. In his study of literacy as ecological metaphors, David Barton clarifies that "Literacies do not exist on some scale starting with basic or simple forms and going on to complex or higher forms. So-called simple and complex forms of literacy are in fact different literacies serving different purposes."[22] Most institutions, especially educational foundations, tend to limit literacy to its most basic function: the ability to read alphabetic text and construe meaning from it. However, that simplistic view gives literacy too narrow a definition and too shallow a concept of texts. Throughout the academic study of literacy over the last half-century, definitions of literacies have differed, depending on the scholar's intentions in research and study.[23] First coined by Shirley Brice Heath in *Ways with Words*, "literacy events" refers to situations in which people engage with reading or writing for any usage at any level.[24]

While literacy events are individual uses of literacy, the term "literacy practices" refers to the larger systems that these events create within communities. An established scholar of the New Literacy Studies, Brian Street stresses that "The concept of literacy practices attempts both to handle the events and the patterns around literacy and to link them to something broader of a social kind."[25] In *Multimodality*, Gunther Kress expands the concept of events and practices to even larger frameworks of understanding literacy, not just of print or digital texts but to a wide spectrum of multimodal multiliteracies. In these broad literacies, information flows freely through alphabetic, visual, spoken, and physical signs and messages, existing "at the level of media and the dissemination of messages—most markedly in the shift from the book and the page to the screen; at the level of semiotic production in the shift from older technologies of print to digital."[26] To put it in simpler terms, new literacies develop to comprehend new and emerging texts of new media.[27]

From this wide definition of multiliteracies, where meanings take different forms and contexts under multimodalities and messages become convoluted and complicated, continuity literacy involves reading texts as a continuation of storylines and meetings rather than a singular force of comprehension or understanding. The concept of continuity literacy is not original as it represents the concept of sustained reading of serialized texts, and in particular the term refers to comic readers who first displayed this literacy. As José Alaniz reflects about Spider-Man comics of the 1960s to 1980s, readers develop their own continuity for the character so that, even when the narrative is not explicit in its storytelling to create strong moments of reader concern, "a Marvel reader's 'continuity literacy' fills in the emotional blanks."[28] Even traditional views of literacy that limit literacy to print-privilege, alphabetic texts operate under an understanding of continuity as the reader continues to read texts and sustain comprehension of the art through continuous narratives in novel series such as *Harry Potter* or *The Dresden Files*. In much the same way that an understanding of human life and human intelligence links knowledge together—people apply their understanding of the world to texts that they read, watch, or/and listen to—so continuity literacy involves comprehension of texts and complex meanings into a framework or network of patterns that spirals outward collecting more and more information.[29] What the MCU has done by supporting this type of literacy is that viewers of the films have become more involved in their stories because they are creating their own literacies to comprehend the broad range of narratives.[30]

Gaines offers a definition of continuity in *Media Literacy and Semiotics*: "The notion that meanings are produced through a logic that relies on past knowledge and experience to interpret new phenomena."[31] With most media, continuity literacy is the ability of readers/viewers to connect one medium to another or through another. The viewer sees the texts as separate and related, able to appreciate each text as a coherent story/artwork and able to understand that the texts relate to other texts in a larger network of connectivity. While intertextuality also connects texts to each other through allusion or specific reference, continuity literacy goes deeper into analysis and character development to tell a story or stories that require more space than a single visual text allows. Usually, this feat is achieved because films made from books follow the arc of the books themselves such as the *Harry Potter* films or the *Lord of the Rings/Hobbit* films that draw on the development of the books to create a story. Because the books have established readers who have witnessed the story through alphabetic, print literacy, the step to visual literacy does not impose too hard a challenge.

Viewing films requires a certain level of continuity skills, depending on the complexity of the story and the shifts between scenes that indicate a change in time or place. As W. James Potter states, "The media frequently depend on our continuity bias. Filmmakers will not present all details about what happens to each character; they leave out scenes knowing that audiences will fill in the gaps and create a continuity of the story for themselves."[32] For instance, early in *Avengers*, Black Widow has allowed herself to be captured by corrupt Russian arms dealers and must escape. In the next scene, she appears as part of the mission to secure Bruce Banner, pretending to be helpless and alone while she is actually armed and surrounded by heavy backup.

Continuity literacy is required here to understand that she has moved into action from one S.H.I.E.L.D. mission to another and that some amount of time has lapsed between the two scenes. That instance of continuity does not require any extensive linking skills beyond an average understanding of how film works to tell stories. What challenges the audiences' literacy continuity is tracing her character through multiple films of the MCU. Each film reveals a little more about her past and abilities: she displays formidable fighting skills and combat prowess in *Iron Man 2*, she used to work for the KGB and killed many targets as Loki reveals in *Avengers*, and she has the digital and technical skills to hack various military organizations in *The Winter Soldier*. Her story is not finished as she is a prominent part of *Age of Ultron*, which reveals, via fear-induced flashbacks, her early days of training with a brutal section of the KGB, a training that results in her clinical sterilization. In small segments, each film develops enough of her character that she becomes relatable and sympathetic: viewers care about her in respect to the knowledge that they learn and assimilate into their continuity of her character and storylines.

Entering into a new world of connective story telling, the onus of work rests on the shoulders of the viewer to read and connect characters, plots, histories, and worlds. Rather than participating as passive viewers, the audience must read the films of the MCU carefully, constantly searching for symbols, signs, meanings, and continuity. Terrence Wandtke explains that "The multiple worlds of superheroes simply [exist] and another one will always be added to the mix. Literate culture often understands postmodern culture as something profoundly threatening in that it seems to lack the depth of thought that leads to certainty."[33] He goes on to argue that we often see traditional strains of mythology in superheroes because despite new modern ways of storytelling, myth prevails as strident markers of human narration. As David Cole and Darren Pullen demonstrate in *Multiliteracies in Motion*, complexities appear in texts that challenge our perceptions of meaning, especially when we are moving from one text to another becoming "a platform for the multiple elements that converge."[34] Sustained knowledge gathering coupled with close reading results in a singular experience in which multimodal multiliteracies involve two paradoxical experiences: satisfaction of having derived understanding from the text at hand and its meaning, and suspended desire to engage with future texts that continue the characters, plot lines, and established world. In explaining the MCU crafting its films for repeated consumption, Derek Johnson states that

The narrative links constituting the Marvel Cinematic Universe thus encourage careful, repeated, often frame-by-frame viewing. Although these moments of interconnectivity constitute only a handful of scenes in otherwise self-contained films, when
subjected to close visual scrutiny, those scenes offer excisable seriality.[35]

This continuity implies just as much significance to understanding the readers
and their perceptions as it does about the intertextual, serialized media.

Not every viewer has the same background in his/her approach to the
MCU. Those who have engaged with Marvel comic books, especially the runs
through the 1970s to the 1990s, have more extensive continuity formed
through their earlier readings. Those familiar with action movies or other
superhero films also bring specialized knowledge in terms of expectations of
action genre conventions and story arcs. Yet, the MCU demands even more
of its readers/viewers by elevating movie-watching passivity into movie-
reading activity. In their criticism of representations of literacy and films,
Bronwyn Williams and Amy Zenger observe that

As we think about literacy as a set of culturally situated practices, rather than a set of
contextual skills, we realize that such practices are going to be an important part of
the culture's representations of itself. Movies, like all forms of cultural representation,
may not be real life but they draw on the recognizable elements of cultural and daily
life to construct narratives that are appealing and meaningful to their audiences.[36]

The MCU films have both literacy events and literacy practices, terms
coined by literacy scholar Brian Street: the main characters all read and use
alphabetical texts.[37] A few have technical and multimodal literacies such as
Tony Stark who designs his computerized suits, Bruce Banner who uses a
tracking algorithm through spectrometers to locate the Tesseract, and
Natasha Romanoff who hacks government databases. The literacy that the
MCU films require, a continuity that viewers develop to engage with the films
not as individual texts but as continued texts that build upon and reference
each other, offers great possibilities for scholarship because this type of literacy requires readers/viewers to create individualistic methods of reading,
interpreting, and remembering. Though they appeal to large audience bases,
the MCU films do not offer mindless entertainment, but the opposite—dense,
interconnected story-telling which requires careful reading and structured
patterns from the audience.

When most novels are made into film, readers often complain that the
film will fail to do justice to the novel. This is not because readers of books
lack the ability to create and find pleasure in visual literacies; it is because
the literacy of print, alphabetic texts allows the reader to form mental images
of the text in their minds that speaks to their particular imagining of the story.
However, when films attempt to create a visual rendering of these imaginings,
the visual depiction rarely matches the mental reader-response conception

that the reader has formed. In his research on superhero comics books and their various modalities, Terrence Wandkte extrapolates on the connections between the ideals of the reader and their portrayal on the screen as having multiple layers due to the technology and possibilities of the new media which affect how they were read and interpreted; he clarifies that "as new mediums were developed in the first half of the 20th century, the ideals of literacy pervaded American culture and the degree to which these new mediums would incorporate those ideals had much to do with the design and production of the various mediums."[38]

Films made from novels then become interpretations of print texts, but together the book/film correlation acts as almost a hybrid representation of a story. MCU films are able to particularly avoid this pitfall of failing to live up to previous textual depictions for three reasons. Comic books and graphic novels have a steady readership, but that audience is not nearly as big as the audiences of novels, especially young adult novels. Also, most Marvel superheroes have appeared in multiple comic book runs, assorted collected volumes, and standalone graphic novels. Captain America alone has appeared in at least eleven primary series, three spinoff series, and twenty-one notable graphic novels. Lastly, when transitioning to film, the visual interpretation must choose which stories to tell, which to admit or ignore, which to change, and which to conflate. Without the risk of offending its base audience or of trying to be too inclusive of a single demographic group, the MCU has had the space to create its framework and tease out fine minutia of details, a creative license to expand upon original ideas into a larger framework of intersecting stories.

Continuity Literacy and MCU Readers/Viewers

Most films of the superhero genre tend to patronize viewers by watering superhero complexities down.[39] References to previous comics or graphic novels often exist in these films as Easter eggs such as LexCorp and Wayne Enterprises logos in *Man of Steel* (2013) that the viewers notice but do not matter in the story. The MCU takes the opposite approach by having the continuity elements as the primary focus—each visual text fits into the framework of this universe and affects other interacting texts directly and indirectly. Directly, *The Winter Soldier's* revelation of the existence of HYDRA and official closing of S.H.I.E.L.D. results in chaos and an extended story arc change in *Agents of S.H.I.E.L.D.* as Phil Coulson must take his organization underground and Grant Ward's involvement as a sleeper HYDRA agent results in him being ostracized from the core team. In her work on fragmented and sustained stories, *Contemporary Narratives,* Fiona Doloughan explains, "as intertextuality may be understood as the absorption and transformation of one text by another, it too posits a view of creation and creativity which sees it as independent on prior production."[40]

This concept of interconnection and intertextuality goes beyond mere references from one movie to another or instances that only a scrutinizing viewer would notice (the World Tree in the opening scene of *Captain America* that is the same as the one Thor drew of the universe to show Jane Foster in *Thor*), but even these small details work to establish this universe where characters continue to exist and influence even from off screen (Natasha's arrow necklace as a signifier of her relationship with the non-present Hawkeye in *The Winter Soldier*). Most of the time noticing these details and making connections that require sophisticated criticism and close reading of the visual text do not feel like extenuating efforts for the reader/viewer but rather a reward for paying such close attention. Like many comic book readers turned superhero film viewers, this audience feels on the inside of the story rather than alienated; those who miss such small details do not necessarily feel on the outside but rather dismiss the details as particular minutia to the world of the narration they are viewing. Nevertheless, the MCU films do insist that a reader/viewer pay some attention to the expanded story lines and character development because the narration of the films do not always clarify the particular time and place that the action is occurring or the details that have led up to the current action.

The beginning of *Iron Man 3* demonstrates this as the film begins with Tony Stark having panic attacks from the Avengers' battle in New York; that battle is left unspecified so a viewer who had not seen *Avengers* would be left confused about earlier events. Also, established characters in Stark's specific story arc—Pepper Potts, Rhodey Rhodes, J.A.R.V.I.S., and Happy Hogan—appear without any explanation of their characters' development or relationship with him thus far. The viewer must use continuity literacy to link together the actions and narrative arcs of *Iron Man, Iron Man 2,* and *Avengers* to appropriately place Stark in his story so that any subsequent changes of *Iron Man 3* work into the literacies of both intertextuality and continuation.

Iron Man's story-arc(s) demonstrates the convolutions of continuity literacy as this complex character's development begins the first film of the MCU and the brief appearances of Nick Fury and Phil Coulson herald the start of S.H.I.E.L.D.'s involvement. Beginning in the first film as a genius playboy, Stark is captured in the Middle East and escapes by building a crude Iron Man suit from pieces of his own stolen weaponry. Once back in America, he creates and tests a digital/computerized suit that allows him to emerge as a superhero through his own technology. In the second film, he builds a series of suits that the U.S. government wants to commandeer, a demand led by

Senator Stern (who actually works for HYDRA as *The Winter Soldier* reveals). In *Avengers*, Stark has advanced his equipment and computers to near-impossible technical levels and has matured to the point that he is in a committed relationship with Pepper Potts.

At the beginning of *Iron Man 3*, Stark suffers from panic attacks from his heroic feats fighting aliens in *Avengers*, and while the characters and the narration make references to his history, the knowledge of past events rests on the part of the viewers having seen the previous films. Stark's story does not allow for laziness or spoon-feeding information to the viewer; the viewer must read the entirety of the films and reference them for additional information to experience a completion of the story lines and a literacy of Stark's continuity. At the beginning of *Age of Ultron*, the events of the New York battle still hound him to such an extent that he sets out to create new technology in order to combat the next threat to planet Earth. This continuity literacy might be less remarkable if the films were all centered on Stark and his narratives, but because MCU films jump from portrayals of certain characters and their indicative worlds (*Thor, Captain America*) to collective depictions of many characters (*Avengers, Agents of S.H.I.E.L.D.*), the continuity literacy of the MCU has multiple layers of meaning and connection for the reader/viewer to tease out and link.

While *Avengers* brings characters together as a group and *Age of Ultron* continues the adventures of this growing collective of heroes, *The Winter Soldier* demonstrates a wider and more effective understanding of the depth and complexity of continuity literacy. In order to grasp the intricacies of the film and its reliance on other MCU films as well as historical and political elements, the audience needs to read the films through several different lenses of critical thinking and knowledge gathering. First, they need to have seen *Captain America, Avengers*, some of *Agents of S.H.I.E.L.D.*, and possibly *Iron Man 1* and *2* to establish the previous changes and development to the characters of Rogers, Romanoff, Fury, and Bucky Barnes. Second, the audience needs to remember the politics of S.H.I.E.L.D. and its relationship with branches of the American government: S.H.I.E.L.D. has elements of the FBI, the CIA, the military, and the political atmosphere of DC rife throughout its organization. Third, they need to have some historical knowledge of America in the 20th-century, namely World War II and the Cold War, as the film references military strategy and conflicts. HYDRA, while a fictional organization, reflects World War II Nazi and Cold War Soviet organizations, and military force and ideological power structures. These three necessities complicate the reading of the films and lead to greater continuity literacy from the readers/viewers.[41]

As an illustration of these multiple levels of necessary reading, at a screening of *Captain America: The Winter Soldier* a couple voiced questions at the end of the film about what they had seen, especially regarding the end credits scene of Quicksilver and Scarlet Witch. It was explained to them that Quicksilver and Scarlet Witch were originally Magneto's children, an element not present in the MCU, who had special powers and would be featured in the next Avengers film. The couple listened, interested in hearing an explanation that provided context to what they had just seen. This incident, while seemingly insignificant, provides a microcosm understanding of the continuity literacy of the MCU. Viewing the films is not enough, regardless of how closely the viewer reads and connects characters, elements, plot points, or story arcs. Derek Johnson observes the connections that the MCU creates point "to new creative and economic relationships between film and comics. Convergence is not a uniquely digital or technological phenomenon but a reworking of media new and old, and thus the cinema of convergence must be understood in terms of collisions with extracinematic sectors of all types."[42] Because of this convergence, the resulting continuity literacy of the audience gives more to its audience by prompting them to read and research further information to go with the knowledge that they already have: to engage with the work of previous decades, to search popular culture media such as online forums, news sites, and magazines, and to discourse with others in order to reach a stage of collective knowledge that allows for greater literacy expansion and usage.

DC has made an impressive impact on both the small screen and the silver screen, but their interpretations do not necessarily occupy the same universe in terms of history and world building. *Gotham* (2014–) tells the story of the early years of Batman characters in the infamous city, but the setting is closer to that of the *Arkham* video games than Nolan's *Dark Knight Trilogy*. *Arrow* and *Flash* are from the same storytelling world, but *Batman versus Superman: Dawn of Justice* (2016) does not share this world as its setting and background. Therefore, commonalities between their visual texts act as allusions and interpretations rather than segments of continuity literacy that create a complex framework. The X-Men films have developed some continuity literacy in their accumulated movies, but *Days of Future Past* (2014) features time-travel that negates the storylines of *X-Men 2* (2003) and *3* (2006). This change may invoke better story-development, but it lessens the importance of continuity by centering the viewer's attention on the present story rather than the past history of the characters and their development/ decisions. The longer the texts sustain narration, as the MCU films do, the stronger continuity literacy becomes on the audience's part.

The implications of the MCU's success suggest that continuity literacy will continue to be a part of their approach to storytelling as they have outlined plans for future films over the next six to eight years. In trying to capitalize on Marvel's success, DC has announced similar plans for its main characters—Superman, Batman, and Wonder Woman—and will try to replicate such interlinking films that require audiences to actively participate. Many other visual texts require some type of continuity literacy as they are sequels or prequels to earlier texts and necessitate audiences to participate continuously by engaging in not only the original texts but subsequent ones.[43] Some of this phenomenon results from Hollywood's attempt to capitalize on the success of previous media and retell the story through reboots, extend the story through sequels, or re-contextualize the story through prequels: all three choices involve capitalizing on an already existing audience and using previous narratives without having to invent original stories or characters. All of this, though, makes Hollywood and especially their writers seem lazy and repetitive, but then the challenge becomes to recreate the old as fresh and new. That challenge has driven the MCU films to not only expand an existing audience base but to perpetually increase the intertextuality of continued stories and creative narratives that please a range of audience reader/viewers through a multiplicity of satisfied and suspended elements.

Conclusion

It is important that continuity literacy is recognized and researched because it speaks to the ways by which current popular media is developing throughout not only multiple texts but multiple modes as well. Continuity literacy enables the reader, as an active participant and a critical thinker, to navigate through viewing and engaging with visual text and sometimes print or traditional alphabetic text in order to comprehend deeper, more intricate stories. Because these continued narratives have broadened storytelling abilities in terms of character development and intersecting plot lines, the entirety of the MCU has brought all types of narrative display, narrative comprehension, and narrative achievement to new levels of complexity and intricacy. This is not to say that before the MCU films creators, directors, and writers thought too little of film viewers (though some of the hyper-physical, low-story level action movies produced in the last two decades might suggest otherwise), but financial restrictions, technological advances, and actor contracts prohibited the grand scale creation of intersecting and referencing films of this magnitude. The success of the Marvel films suggests that other productions may come to replicate the artistic and financial steps towards the MCU's grandiose achievements. Marinus Van Den Anker and Piet Verhoeven argue that

> Superheroes such as Captain America, Superman and Spider-Man are not only part of multiple storylines, but are part of the strategic multi-media communication policy of the companies as well [...] we can state that a strategic corporate multimedia

superhero communication flow exists for superhero media entertainment companies, which is focused on superhero comic books and all types of superhero merchandise and media platforms.[44]

The creators of the MCU films have taken an approach to turning comic books into films as one of gradualness, a slow interpretation of characters and dominant plot lines without overwhelming the viewer. In his discussion of the importance of changing and realizing texts from one medium to another, especially a bigger, more epic visual text, William Rogers states, "the relation between the interpretative system and its content is reciprocal. When one explicates the interpretative system that underwrites some particular interpretive statement, one finds out something not only about the interpreted content, but about the interpretative system itself."[45] However, the interpretative system is just the edge of possible knowledge gathering because the goal should be to discover what interpretation says about the interpreter, meaning those that are reading and understanding media and deriving meaning from the process. The longer serialized texts such as the MCU and its resulting continuity literacy are examined, the better possibility exists to understand human beings as readers and viewers. Humans grow and develop, change and adjust through these literate endeavors. When people connect with fictional characters who act and respond similarly (though granted their struggles are much more adverse than normal day-to-day challenges), they establish themselves as both readers and interpreters of extended narratives and develop new ways of reading multiple texts.

NOTES

1. This includes all MCU films which have premiered as of 2015, from *Iron Man* (2008) to *Avengers: Age of Ultron* (2015) and television's *Agents of S.H.I.E.L.D.* and *Agent Carter*.
2. Aaron Taylor, "Avengers Dissemble! Transmedia Superhero Franchises and Cultic Management," *Journal of Adaptation in Film & Performance* 7, no. 2 (2014): 186.
3. The term "superhero media" is used in this essay to describe all types of superhero narratives that include, but are not limited to, comics, films, TV shows, animation, novels, web series, and dramas. As concepts about superheroes and their literacies (both in representations of literacies in their stories and literacies of the viewers/readers) span genres and individual mediums of story-telling, the importance of not narrowing ideas about superheroes to one mode of texts must be stressed.
4. Elliot Gaines, *Media Literacy and Semiotics* (New York: Palgrave Macmillan, 2010), 126.
5. The disposability of early comics led to their high value in the latter half of the 20th-Century; their rarity has driven the cost to astronomical highs as collectors seek the few remaining original-print issues.
6. Jason Dittmer, *Captain America and the Nationalist Superhero: Metaphors, Narratives, and Geopolitics* (Philadelphia: Temple University Press, 2013), 84.
7. Josh Lambert, "'Wait for the Next Pictures': Intertextuality and Cliffhanger Continuity in Early Cinema and Comic Strips," *Cinema Journal* 48, no. 2 (2009): 19.
8. *Ibid.*
9. Henry H. Perritt Jr., "Technologies of Storytelling: New Models for Movies," *Virginia Sports & Entertainment Law Journal* 10, no. 1 (2010): 117.

10. *Ibid.*

11. Mila Bongco, *Reading Comics: Language, Culture, and the Concept of the Superhero in Comic Books* (New York: Garland Publishing, 2000), 87–88.

12. Popular entertainment has ebbs and flows in its enthusiasm for particular sub-genres. Superhero films diminished in the 1990s only to return with gusto in the mid–2000s. Conversely, cowboy stories wildly popular in the decades of the '40s, '50s, and '60s have had little success in recent years, as *The Lone Ranger* (2013) film exemplified.

13. Marco Arnaudo and Jamie Richards, *The Myth of the Superhero* (Baltimore: Johns Hopkins University Press, 2013), 11.

14. Joseph Campbell, *The Hero with a Thousand Faces,* 3rd ed. (Princeton: Princeton University Press, 1973), 321.

15. Arnaudo and Richards, *The Myth of the Superhero,* 11.

16. The heroic journey is especially prominent in *Avengers: Age of Ultron* in the fact that Tony and Bruce decide to play creator/god and create AI robots to protect earth, but their hubris sets off a change of events in which they must fight a monster of their own making.

17. Will Brooker, "We Could Be Heroes," in *What Is a Superhero?*, ed. Robin Rosenberg and Peter M. Coogan (New York: Oxford University Press, 2013), 12.

18. Richard Reynolds, "Heroes of the Superculture," in *What Is a Superhero?*, ed. Robin Rosenberg and Peter M. Coogan (New York: Oxford University Press, 2013), 51.

19. *Ibid.*

20. The definition of heroism has change in the last century of American narratives. Much like the heroes of tragedies, recent depictions of heroes (and the superhero especially) have moved from a portrayal of a perfected ideal to more realistic, gritty representation of actual people with flaws and imperfections. In *Do the Gods Wear Capes?* Ben Saunders notes the changes in Tony Stark's character from his comic book conception to his more recent film appearances by stating that Iron Man is "An almost 50 years long pop-culture exploration of the complex moral and intellectual issues that arise out of the movement from late modernity to post-modernity, from progress to process, and from humanism to post-humanism." Ben Saunders, *Do the Gods Wear Capes? Spirituality, Fantasy, and Superheroes* (New York: Continuum, 2011), 119.

21. Alex S. Romagnoli and Gian Pagnucci, *Enter the Superheroes: American Values, Culture, and the Canon of Superhero Literature* (Lanham, MD: Scarecrow, 2013), 185.

22. David Barton, *Literacy: An Introduction to the Ecology of Written Language* (Malden: Blackwell, 1994), 38–39.

23. In particular, research on literacy has taken divergent perspectives of literacy including historical (Harvey Graff), social (James Paul Gee), and ethnographic (Shirley Brice Heath, Deborah Brandt, and Brian Street); these diverse studies of literacy have emerged as the collective discipline of New Literacy Studies.

24. Heath's early work helped to broaden the NLS's view of literacy because she discussed the range of possibilities for literacy events such as writing a grocery list or reading billboards, events that are part of literacy activities but have been mostly unnoticed or ignored by early literacy scholars.

25. Brian Street, *Literacy and Development: Ethnographic Perspectives* (London: Routledge, 2001), 11.

26. Gunther Kress, *Multimodality: A Social Semiotic Approach to Contemporary Communication* (London: Routledge, 2010), 31.

27. New media, as a concept, is often designated to online texts, including written words, images, or a blend of both. However, new media can also be used in describing texts that require different interpretation, comprehension, or analysis from the reader/viewer. The series *Daredevil* on Netflix would fit this criteria: it's a TV-like drama of a superhero that never premiered on TV so it offers new opportunities of comprehension while still feeling familiar enough to not alienate large audience bases who enjoy TV-depictions of superheroes such as *Arrow, Gotham,* or *Flash.*

28. José Alaniz, *Death, Disability, and the Superhero: The Silver Age and Beyond* (Jackson: University Press of Mississippi, 2014), 211.

29. James Paul Gee explains the connection between humans' perception of ideas as needing some kind of real world founding. He argues that "humans understand content, whether in a comic book or a physics text, much better than their understanding is embodied: that is, when they can relate that content to possible activities, decisions, talk, and dialogue." James Paul Gee, *Situated Language and Learning: A Critique of Traditional Schooling* (New York: Routledge, 2004), 39.

30. Participation in fandom often extend a reader/viewer's interest in a story or stories into their own interpretations which include fanfiction, fanart, conference panels, and online discussions, all of which have particular literacies. These literacies often are ignored or belittled by mainstream and even academic communities. Abigail De Kosnik explains that "The notion of fandom has become a more accepted and privileged term in marketing and consumer circles [...] but even when considered a worthwhile use of time and money, fandom is regarded as a marginal, recreational, just-for-fun activity." Abigail De Kosnik, "Fandom as Free Labor," in *Digital Labor: The Internet as Playground and Factory*, ed. Trebor Scholz (New York: Routledge, 2013), 108.

31. Gaines, *Media Literacy and Semiotics*, 156.

32. W. James Potter, *Theory of Media Literacy: A Cognitive Approach* (Thousand Oaks: SAGE, 2004), 215.

33. Terrence R. Wandtke, *The Meaning of Superhero Comic Books* (Jefferson, NC: McFarland, 2012), 160.

34. David R. Cole and Darren L. Pullen, *Multiliteracies in Motion: Current Theory and Practice* (New York: Routledge, 2010), 2.

35. Derek Johnson, "Cinematic Destiny: Marvel Studios and the Trade Stories of Industrial Convergence," *Cinema Journal* 52, no. 1 (2012): 7.

36. Bronwyn T. Williams and Amy A. Zenger, *Popular Culture and Representations of Literacy* (New York: Routledge, 2007), 167.

37. In *Cross-Cultural Approaches to Literacy*, Street argues that "the conceptualization of literacy as ideological practice opens up a potentially rich field of inquiry into the nature of culture and power, and the relationship of institutions and ideologies of communication in the contemporary world." This critique of literacy as ideological practice directs the theoretical approach in most of this essay because those practices become reflections of American ideals regarding literacy and larger educational contexts. Brian V. Street, *Cross-Cultural Approaches to Literacy* (Cambridge: Cambridge University Press, 1993), 12.

38. Wandkte, *The Meaning of Superhero Comic Books*, 133.

39. While Nolan's *Dark Knight* trilogy gave dark, Gothic, but realistic depictions of Batman, they did not include the complexities of his character from the comics: his many Robins, his involvement with the Justice League, his history with the Leagues of Assassins, or his constant surveillance of Arkham Asylum.

40. Fiona Doloughan, *Contemporary Narrative: Textual Production, Multimodality and Multiliteracies* (New York: Continuum, 2011), 89.

41. Other knowledge bases are helpful but immediately necessary to read/understand *Captain America: The Winter Soldier*. Some of the audiences have seen other action or sci-fi movies that use technology and machinery to possibility of enhancing human capability. The espionage and plot twists of the film resemble spy thrillers of the 1970s.

42. Johnson, "Cinematic Destiny," 2–3.

43. Examples of this are *Bates Motel* and Hitchcock's *Psycho*, *Better Call Saul* and *Breaking Bad*, and *Hannibal* and *Silence of the Lambs* where the continued narrative builds on the original narrative.

44. Marinus Van Den Anker and Piet Verhoeven, "Corporate Communication: Analysing Marvel and DC," *Studies in Comics* 5, no.1 (2014): 126.

45. William Rogers, *Interpreting Interpretation: Textual Hermeneutics as an Ascetic Discipline* (University Park: Pennsylvania State University Press, 1994), 195.

"A bigger universe"

Marvel Studios
and Transmedia Storytelling

Liam Burke

"Mr. Stark, you've become part of a bigger universe. You just don't know it yet." In the brief post-credit scene that followed *Iron Man* (2008), Nick Fury announces to Tony Stark (and the audience) the arrival of the Marvel Cinematic Universe (MCU)—an ambitious attempt to bring comic book continuity to the big screen. Soon after, the franchise went transmedia with comic books such as *The Avengers Prelude: Fury's Big Week*, television shows like *Marvel's Agents of S.H.I.E.L.D.* (2013–), DVD "one-shots" including *The Consultant*, and the video game *Iron Man 2*. Thus, the term "Marvel *Cinematic* Universe" is no longer adequate to describe a narrative that has been extended across a number of media platforms. Today, the MCU might be more accurately described as one of the first successful examples of transmedia storytelling.

Transmedia storytelling is facilitated by media convergence, and since the 1990s a number of franchises such as *The Matrix*, *Doctor Who*, and *Lost* have sought to continue their narratives across multiple platforms, but none have achieved the success or scale of the MCU. Marvel Entertainment succeeded where other studios failed by applying the practices of its publishing arm to its transmedia endeavors. This essay will chart the key criteria of a transmedia franchise that Marvel was ideally positioned to meet. In doing so it will identify the industry standard model for transmedia franchises that Marvel refined for a host of current and future imitators.

When Is a Story Transmedia?

Writing in 2011, Elizabeth Evans identified a "number of phrases and models" that "have emerged that attempt to grasp" this era of media convergence, including "360 degree commissioning," "overflow," and "media matrix," but the "most pervasive is Henry Jenkins' concept of 'transmedia story-telling.'"[1] In his book, *Convergence Culture,* Jenkins defines a transmedia story as one that "unfolds across multiple media platforms, with each new text making a distinctive and valuable contribution to the whole."[2] However, the subsequent use of the term by media scholars has found Jenkins frequently reasserting his original definition. In a blog entry, Jenkins challenged David Bordwell's application of "transmedia storytelling" to The Bible, Homeric epics, and the Bhagavad Gita, noting that these examples "are simply adaptations of works produced in one medium for performance in another platform. And for many of us, a simple adaptation may be 'transmedia' but it is not 'transmedia storytelling' because it is simply re-presenting an existing story rather than expanding and annotating the fictional world."[3]

Similarly, Ivan Askwith and Jonathan Gray asserted that "Taken by itself, the term 'transmedia' simply describes the process of content moving or expanding from one medium into another ... transmedia storytelling is more specific, and is used to describe the process of further developing a coherent narrative (or elaborating a narrative universe) by distributing related story components across multiple media platforms."[4] More recently, Jeff Gomez, CEO of Starlight Runner, which describes itself as "the world's leading creator and producer of highly successful transmedia franchises," defined transmedia storytelling as, "the process of conveying messages, themes or story lines to a mass audience through the artful and well planned use of multiple-media platforms."[5]

Thus, while characters from earlier franchises like the Universal Horror cycle interacted in crossover movies such as *Frankenstein Meets the Wolf Man* (1943), this narrative was not extended beyond cinema, and therefore could not be considered "transmedia." Similarly, Derek Johnson notes how early Marvel animated series such as *Spider-Man and His Amazing Friends* (1981–1983), "leveraged interactions among different characters in a shared Marvel Universe to multiply audience appeals,"[6] yet the content was not distributed to the "three or more media platforms" that Gomez considers a "defining principle" of transmedia storytelling.[7]

Although transmedia franchises are marked by a horizontal distribution of content, they tend to rely on a "driving platform ... the medium that will reach the greatest audience and furnish the core storyline."[8] The key texts produced within this driving platform are often described as the "mother ship."[9] The mother ship will then include "flow tags" that direct consumers to other narrative units.[10] Cinema often serves as the driving platform, as can been seen in *The Matrix* franchise. The *Matrix* universe was the first high-profile transmedia story by a U.S. conglomerate, and was one of Jenkins' chief case studies in *Convergence Culture.* The franchise's creators, Lana and Lilly

Wachowski, together with conglomerate Time Warner, developed a larger story that extended the film trilogy's core narrative across an anthology of animated shorts, *The Animatrix* (2003), two video games, *Enter The Matrix* (2003) and *The Matrix Online* (2005–2009), and *The Matrix Comics* (1999–2003). Freedom fighter Niobe's reference to the "last transmission of the Osiris" during the opening of *The Matrix Reloaded* (2003) is an example of a flow tag inserted by the filmmakers.[11] This carefully placed dialogue directed consumers to the Animatrix short film "The Final Flight of the Osiris," as well as the first level of the video game *Enter the Matrix*.

Askwith and Gray later observed, "if 'the Year of the Matrix' worked to demonstrate the possibilities for transmedia storytelling, it also illustrated the inherent challenges of these possibilities."[12] The final *Matrix* film, *The Matrix Revolutions* (2003), grossed less than the first sequel *The Matrix Reloaded* and even the original film *The Matrix* (1999).[13] This quick drop in interest was partly attributed to the dense, arguably impenetrable, narrative of the expanding franchise, which made it difficult for all but the most avid consumers to follow the story.

Concluding a masterclass on transmedia storytelling, Gomez described how the Marvel Cinematic Universe "epitomizes state of the art transmedia." Indeed, unlike *The Matrix*, the franchise shows little evidence of audience attrition with subsequent installments often grossing more than earlier films.[14] Similarly, following a mixed start in television that found *Marvel's Agents of S.H.I.E.L.D* shedding viewers and *Marvel's Agent Carter* (2015–2016) cancelled after two seasons, Netflix series *Marvel's Daredevil* (2015–) welcomed sister shows *Marvel's Jessica Jones* (2015–), *Marvel's Luke Cage* (2016–), and *Marvel's Iron Fist* (2017–).[15] Factoring in the prequel comics that accompany most theatrical releases as well as the video games that often fill in the gaps in big screen narratives, Marvel Studios is the first production company to fully realize the potential hinted at in earlier transmedia efforts. Yet, what are the criteria for transmedia storytelling that the Marvel Cinematic Universe, drawing on comic book traditions, was ideally situated to meet?

Flexible Continuity

Fans and rights holders have often sought to extend cult texts into other media. For instance, long after the Universal Horror Monsters slipped back into their crypts enthusiasts continued the stories in novels such as Jeff Rovin's 1998 *Return of the Wolf Man*. However, as production of these films was fixed at a specific time these later texts are rarely viewed as canonical. Conversely, mainstream comic book publishers Marvel and DC Comics have maintained decades of monthly publication by allowing titles such as *Superman* and

X-Men to incorporate story additions, including those developed in other media.[16] For instance, Phil Coulson, as portrayed by actor Clark Gregg, was first introduced as a S.H.I.E.L.D. agent in *Iron Man*. The character's popularity saw him appearing in subsequent MCU movies, DVD "one-shots," and the *Agents of S.H.I.E.L.D.* television series. Not long after Coulson's MCU debut, a counterpart was introduced to the original comic book continuity (designated Earth-616), making Coulson "canon" in both the comic book and cinematic universes.

Such flexible continuity is commonplace in comics with Martyn Pedler noting that "Continuity isn't bulletproof; it functions more like, say, a mutant healing factor. New details are absorbed into the official storyline, and older, outdated ideas are left to fade until they eventually barely leave a scar."[17] Mainstream comics have long relied on these malleable character histories, while readers, eschewing traditional hierarchies between source and secondary text, are not averse to new creations being introduced to the comics. Such flexible continuity is valuable if a studio hopes to expand a story across other media, yet not every franchise shares this quality. Johnson points to *The Lord of the Rings* film adaptations as an example of convergence, and indeed there was much coordination between the film producers, merchandisers, and video game publishers.[18] Nonetheless, the book's inert position as a trilogy that concluded publication in 1955, as well as J.R.R. Tolkien's unquestioned status as the novel's author, limits the creative reverse engineering that serialized sources like comics allow. Consequently, an invention of the filmmakers, such as the elf warrior Tauriel in *The Lord of the Rings* prequel *The Desolation of Smaug* (2013) can never become "canon," but, through the enthusiasm of fans and Marvel's careful deployment, a character such as Coulson can become every bit as integral to a narrative universe as a hero with a seventy year publication history.

Coulson's status as a comic book hero was reaffirmed in promotional materials for 2015's "All-New, All-Different" Marvel comic book universe, where teaser images saw the mild-mannered agent standing shoulder-to-shoulder with Captain America and Thor. The "All-New, All-Different" universe was in fact a refined version of existing continuities. Following the crossover event *Secret Wars*, the long-standing comic book continuity (Earth-616) was collapsed with the more recent Ultimate Comics universe (Earth-1610) resulting in a new status quo that not only simplified character histories, but also ensured that many comic characters tallied more neatly with their audio-visual adaptations. As one example, Daredevil's costume shifted from his familiar red spandex to a black suit with red highlights that more greatly resembled the Netflix series. In a 2007 analysis Derek Johnson noted that Marvel's transmedia ambitions "first required the elimination of difference between the comic and audiovisual versions of its character properties."[19]

Indeed, the reorganization of the Marvel comic book universe since the emergence of the MCU has seen characters that appear in Marvel Studios productions emphasized over established comic heroes. After years of languishing without a monthly title, *Guardians of the Galaxy* were given a dedicated comic book in March 2013 in anticipation of the 2014 film. The subsequent popularity of the film saw the number of titles featuring the previously little known heroes rapidly expand with comics such as *Guardians 3000*, *Guardians Team-Up*, and *Marvel Universe Guardians of the Galaxy*, while *The Legendary Star-Lord*, *Rocket Raccoon*, and *Groot* all received solo titles. Conversely, Marvel's first family, the Fantastic Four, whose adaptations are still licensed to 20th Century–Fox, found themselves in 2015 without a dedicated title for the first time in more than five decades. The success of the MCU has served as the big bang for this latest permutation of the Marvel comic book universe, with titles cohering around widely seen adaptations. Thus, with transmedia paradigms demanding nimble intellectual property, it is unsurprising that Marvel's fluid continuity has trumped franchises built on more rigid texts.

Platform Neutral Storytelling

Citing Jenkins, Elizabeth Evans notes how successful transmedia stories are built on a "simultaneous sense of difference and continuity."[20] This is the underlying tension of all transmedia stories, in that the narrative units must fit together cohesively while still taking advantage of each medium in which the story is being told. Gomez also identifies these twin imperatives, noting how content should adhere "to platform specific strengths," while also advising that intellectual property should be developed on a "platform neutral basis."[21] Thus, a transmedia story needs to be malleable enough that it can extend into any form while also stressing the strengths of each medium. Many earlier franchises have failed to achieve this balance. The video game *Enter the Matrix* required that the "gamer" sit through an hour of cinematic cut sequences, a passive experience at odds with the interactivity that one associates with gaming.

As discussed above, the comics industry is well practiced at maintaining continuity amongst its characters. From the outset of the MCU the producers sought a coherent style, with Derek Johnson noting how Marvel "recast the production of comic book films and video games not in terms of specific media platforms, but instead in terms of the iconic characters Marvel had on offer."[22] This strategy has seen the semiotic gap between comics and their audio-visual adaptations narrow.

For example, when developing *Iron Man*, director Jon Favreau explicitly cited the more "mechanical" and "tech-based" suit designed by digital comic creator Adi Granov as the basis for the film's hero."[23] Granov even provided the film's concept art and first promotional materials. Conversely, as digital filmmaking techniques have afforded filmmakers greater control of the film artifact, the form could now be considered, like comics, as one of the plastic arts.[24] *Iron Man* Animation Director Hal Hickel described how his team digitally modified the live action hero to get "a Marvel moment."[25]

Other examples of the boundaries between media becoming more diffuse include: scenes from the feature film *Captain America: The First Avenger* (2011) being used as flashbacks in the television series *Agent Carter*, the inclusion of Avengers action figures and other commercially available merchandise within the diegesis of *Agents of S.H.I.E.L.D.*, movie images serving as variant covers for comics such as *The Mighty Thor* #1, and a downloadable app for iOS devices based on Tony Stark's artificial intelligence J.A.R.V.I.S. voiced by actor Paul Bettany, who also plays the character in the movies. Thus, the representational overlap between comics and other media has been systematically widened creating the platform neutral storytelling central to transmedia efforts.

Yet, while these strategies are dependent on a certain amount of platform neutrality, Marvel has also been successful at accentuating difference. As Jeffrey Sconce notes, "What television lacks in spectacle and narrative constraints, it makes up for in depth and duration of character relations, diegetic expansion, and audience investment."[26] *Agents of S.H.I.E.L.D.* actor Brett Dalton made a similar observation during a promo that linked the series with feature film *Captain America: The Winter Soldier* (2014), "The thing that *Captain America* can do is that [the filmmakers] can show all that stuff on a big scale. What we can show is how it affects people on a very personal and very intimate level."[27] As Dalton suggests, the film's plot twist—terrorist group Hydra's successful infiltration of S.H.I.E.L.D.—may have provided *Captain America: The Winter Soldier* with a bombastic third act, but the television series devoted the latter half of season one and much of season two to this status quo changing shift—a level of depth and detail a feature film could not attain.

While Marvel has taken advantage of increased television production values in shows like *Agents of S.H.I.E.L.D.*, *Daredevil* and *Jessica Jones*, they have also shrewdly focused on characters whose heroics could be realized on a more modest budget such as government agents and urban vigilantes. Other franchises have been less successful at continuing their cinematic stories across other media. The necessary costs of realizing a "galaxy far, far away" were readily apparent in one of the first attempts to extend Star Wars beyond cinema: the *Star Wars Holiday Special* (1978). The Star Wars spin-off featured the stars of the successful film reprising their roles in a two-hour broadcast that mixed variety performances, musical numbers, and guest stars with a storyline about Chewbacca needing to reach his home planet to celebrate "Life Day."

While the tone and story of the *Star Wars Holiday Special* was wildly inconsistent with the feature film released one year earlier, the production values were also jarring as the sitcom-style sets for Chewbacca's family home contrasted awkwardly with footage reused from the feature film. Robert C. Ring describes an animated introduction to bounty hunter Boba Fett as the special's "one redeeming quality."[28] Two further live action installments based on the Ewoks also failed to evoke the grandeur of the Star Wars universe and resonate with fans. Thus, it is unsurprising that following these efforts other attempts to extend the Star Wars universe to television have been animated series such as *Droids* (1985–6), *Star Wars: The Clone Wars* (2008–14), and *Star Wars Rebels* (2014–), which were better able to match the spectacle of the films.

While the Star Wars universe may match the scale of the MCU it does not share its variety. The Marvel universe runs from the squalor of New York's Hell's Kitchen (*Daredevil* and *Jessica Jones*) to the otherworldly majesty of Asgard (*Thor*). This depth allows producers working in different forms a variety of medium-appropriate entry points, while still enabling each element to fit together as a cohesive transmedia story. Nonetheless, even a model as successful as Marvel's cannot achieve complete platform neutrality. This is evident in Phil Coulson's varying appearance within different comics. While the comics that feature Coulson attempt to match actor Clark Gregg's appearance, it would often be difficult for a reader to spot the unassuming agent without some further textual clues. In the MCU comic *Fury's Big Week*, Coulson, as drawn by artist Daniel HDR, has brown hair and a strong jawline, while in *Iron Man 2: Public Enemy*, with pencils by Barry Kitson, the S.H.I.E.L.D. agent has a light frame and jet-black hair.

As Pascal Lefèvre points out in "Incompatible Visual Ontologies: The Problematic Adaptation of Drawn Images," a "drawn image offers a specific view on reality and the creator's subjectivity of this reality is built into the work."[29] Thus, medium specific differences will hinder characters, and the wider MCU narrative, from spreading seamlessly from one medium to the next. Nonetheless, as a production company well practiced in maintaining continuity across a variety of formats and creators, Marvel has walked the line between continuity and difference better than most other franchises striving for transmedia success.

Collaborative Authorship

Commenting on the high volume of material comic book companies such as Marvel produce, Bart Beaty argued that these publishers have "a great deal to teach us about collaborative authorship, audience knowledge, and editorial oversight in the culture industries."[30] Indeed, as the competing versions of Coulson from the above section suggest, publishers have extensive experience in keeping their many characters and creators in check—strategies that Marvel is now applying to a wider spectrum of media.

In his 2000 book *Batman Unmasked*, Will Brooker notes that authorship in comics "is especially hard to pin down, and comics fandom, unlike film scholarship, rarely takes the easier option of singling out a single individual from the creative team for sole praise or blame."[31] Indeed, writer Stan Lee and artist Jack Kirby may have created the first issue of *The Avengers* in September 1963, but since then hundreds of writers, artists, inkers, colorists, and editors have worked on the title, which has remained remarkably consistent given its lengthy publication history. Thus, one might argue that in mainstream comics authorship rests on an industrial level, a perception Marvel was eager to perpetuate through fan clubs such as the Merry Marvel Marching Society and art guides like *How to Draw Comics the Marvel Way*.

Evans notes of transmedia storytelling, "when texts are created across multiple media platforms, then the question of who the author is becomes even more complex."[32] Replicating its dominance of publishing, Marvel Studios has stepped into the authorship vacuum created by transmedia models, with the company's logo opening each movie, television series, comic, and video game. Furthermore, the familiar white-on-red text also appears in promotional pieces, merchandise, and, in case there was any doubt, television shows such as *Agents of S.H.I.E.L.D.* and *Daredevil* have had the "Marvel" name awkwardly affixed to their title. Thus, as in Thomas Schatz's rebuttal to the auteur theory, Marvel would have audiences believe that genius resides not in any one talented individual, but rather a system of creators working together with a shared goal and under a single banner: Marvel.[33]

In comics, fans, eager to know more about the individuals behind their favorite books, pierced the united front that Marvel presented, elevating creators such as Jack Kirby, Steve Ditko, and Frank Miller. Similarly, fans, critics, and journalists, spurred on by Romantic conceptions of authorship, sought to identify the wizard behind the curtain of Marvel Studios. However, highlighting shifting notions of authorship in a transmedia era, commentators have not located authorship with a writer-director such as fan favorite Joss Whedon (*The Avengers* and *Agents of S.H.I.E.L.D.*), but rather Marvel Studios President Kevin Feige. Feige's first screen credit was as an associate producer on *X-Men* (2000), and he has been a producer on many Marvel adaptations including all MCU films. Feige has engendered the goodwill of fans by regularly flaunting his fanboy credentials during interviews and at gatherings like San Diego Comic-Con.[34] Thus, Feige is perceived as a "supra-auteur" in that his authorship supersedes any one production or even any one medium.[35]

As Johnson noted, "By narrowing authorial agency to single companies like Marvel and single managers like Feige [...] This trade narrative thus rationalized the creative and economic restructuring pursued by Marvel, casting the effective convergence of film and comics in terms of the company's own centralized corporate management."[36]

Feige's elevation not only makes for easy copy, but transmedia producers like Jeff Gomez also subscribe to it. First among Gomez's "8 Defining Principles" of transmedia storytelling, is that "content is originated by one or a very few visionaries."[37] Comic book publishers have long practiced this model. While many comic book writers and artists were responsible for Marvel Comics' renaissance in the 1960s, as Scott Bukatman notes, writer and editor Stan Lee served as "the babbling disk jockey whose alliterative patter bound the whole *megillah* together and cajoled the willing reader into a sense of participation."[38] Thus, much like "Smiling" Stan Lee during the silver age of comics, today Kevin Feige is the public face of Marvel Studios.

While Feige's role evokes comic book editors, it also shares many parallels with the television show runner. Michael Newman and Elana Levine chart how on many modern television shows, "in addition to being the storyteller-in-chief, the showrunner has many management responsibilities, including staffing the show with writers, negotiating with network executives, and budgeting."[39] The MCU's shift to a showrunner model is exemplified by its move away from idiosyncratic directors such as Kenneth Branagh, Edgar Wright, and Patty Jenkins to directors with a background in television such as the Russo brothers and Alan Taylor.[40] These filmmakers might be described, in Francois Truffaut's unflattering terms, as "metteurs-en-scène"—filmmakers with technical competence, but no distinguishable style.[41] However, Gomez, who prefers the term "I.P. steward," suggests it is this workmanlike sensibility that collaborative authorship demands—the pieces and style are already in place, the directors that succeed are the ones who vary least from Marvel and Feige's vision.[42]

The film industry has taken note of this collaborative authorship with Paramount Pictures setting up a "writers room" to plan the future of the Transformers franchise following four lucrative feature films. The Transformers writers' room includes *The Walking Dead* comic book creator Robert Kirkman, *Daredevil* showrunner Steven DeKnight, and *X-Men: The Last Stand* (2006) screenwriter Zak Penn, *Batman Forever* writer (1995) Akiva Goldsman leading the team. When interviewed, Goldsman was open about the team's goals and inspiration:

> The whole process of the story room was really delightful, and we are seeing it more in movies as this moves toward serialized storytelling. There are good rooms around town, including the Monsters Room at Universal, the Star Wars room, and of course,

at Marvel. We're trying to beg, borrow and steal from the best of them, and gathered a group of folks interested in developing and broadening this franchise."[43]

In a 2014 roundtable conversation with *The Hollywood Reporter* film studio heads discussed their plans to replicate Marvel's success, with Universal Pictures Chairperson Donna Langley explaining that they were designing a shared universe for their Monsters franchise. After the heads of Warner Bros, 20th Century–Fox, and Paramount explained similar ambitions, the panel chair, Kim Masters, asked, "are you guys cloning Kevin Feige?"[44] Indeed, various studios have tried to replicate Marvel's franchise-runner model, with 21st Century Fox appointing *Marvel Comics: Civil War* writer Mark Millar as a "creative consultant" on their Marvel Comics properties while DC Comics Chief Content Officer Geoff Johns was promoted to co-runner of the DC Extended Universe following the critical and commercial disappointment of *Batman V Superman.*[45] While the demands of cross-platform storytelling and the success of Marvel are pushing Hollywood to adopt franchise-runner models, it was Marvel Studios that first applied the collaborative authorship and editorial supervision commonplace in comics to a blossoming transmedia franchise.

Fan/Non-Fan Balance

Among the "criteria for Successful Transmedia Franchises" producer Jeff Gomez includes, "cultivation, validation and celebration of fan base," later adding, "True *interactivity* is more than about choice. It is about *dialogue.*"[46] Such dialogue has been a fixture of Marvel comics since the 1960s when Stan Lee as writer and editor used playful captions, letters pages, and "Bullpen Bulletins" to establish a "rapport with readers" that prompted "intense loyalty."[47] Marvel recognized the importance of a dedicated fan base before its rival DC Comics and was much more successful at narrowing the boundaries between creator and consumer, with Matthew Pustz noting how Marvel adopted inclusive terms such as "we" and "us" as opposed to DC Comics' "them."[48]

Pop culture enthusiasts such as comic book fans were among the earliest adopters of the web, which amplified their reach beyond the boundaries of fandom. As Jenkins notes, "None of this is new. What has shifted is the visibility of fan culture."[49] Consequently, media producers, many of whom initially adopted a protectionist stance, have facilitated a semblance of collaboration. Unsurprisingly, Marvel, a company steeped in fan interaction, became an industry leader in engendering the goodwill of fans. In October 2014 both Warner Bros. and Marvel announced their comic book movies for the next five years. Warner Bros. made their presentation first, revealing their planned productions at an investor's meeting. Marvel, demonstrating the same shrewd manipulation of the fan base that enabled the company to trump its comic book competition, unveiled its slate at Disney's El Capitan Theatre in front of 600 screaming fans with stars Chris Evans, Robert Downey, Jr., and Chadwick Boseman making the announcement alongside the ever-present Kevin Feige. Where once the enthusiasm of those fans would not have escaped the soundproof theatre, attendee footage from the event was shared around the world via the Internet thereby amplifying interest and excitement for the MCU.

Matt Hills notes how attempts to re-inscribe "producer/fan binaries" will often see "official media producers use their control over media texts to depict and discipline fan practices."[50] For example, the antagonist of the *Batman: The Animated Series* episode "Beware the Gray Ghost" (1992) was a fan whose obsessive tendencies led him to villainous extremes. However, Marvel not only acknowledges fans at public events, but also celebrates enthusiasts within the diegesis of the MCU. Whether carrying vintage Captain America trading cards in *The Avengers*, or naming all the X-Men as a way to maintain his sanity during torture in the opening panels of *S.H.I.E.L.D.* #1, Coulson went from a deadpan man-in-black in *Iron Man* to the embodiment of a fan who turned his "avocation into their vocation."[51] In fact, bereft of any super-powers, Coulson's fanboy knowledge became his special ability, with the S.H.I.E.L.D. agent regularly depicted in movies, DVD "one-shots," comics, and TV shows skillfully manipulating Marvel heroes like pieces in a tabletop game.

Yet, Marvel has been careful to balance this avid fan base with the mass audience, recognizing that much of the larger audience has little interest in pursuing a transmedia story. As Johnson notes, unlike the dense narratives of *The Matrix* films which demanded consumption of related texts, in the MCU "moments of interconnectivity constitute only a handful of scenes in otherwise self-contained films, when subjected to close visual scrutiny, those scenes offer excisable seriality."[52] For instance, in *The Incredible Hulk* (2008) a World War II era "super-soldier" serum is partly responsible for turning villain Emil Blonsky into the Abomination. While comic readers would have recognized this serum as the same one that gave Captain America his height-ened abilities, such knowledge was not necessary for a naïve audience member. In fact, most moments of continuity in Marvel movies are corralled into mid and post-credit teasers (e.g., Nick Fury's appearance in *Iron Man*), which do not disrupt the flow of the feature film. Thus, Marvel allows the franchise's mother ship to have enough autonomy to engage a mass audience, while still including the flow tags that direct consumers to the wider transmedia story. This careful balance of fan and non-fan interests is imperative for any franchise striving for transmedia success.

Story World Depth

In *Iron Man*'s coda Fury mocks Stark for his arrogance in assuming that the Marvel Cinematic Universe began when he first slipped on his armor. Indeed, like all good universes, the MCU is vast, with each new entrant revealing a new corner. *Iron Man 2* (2010) went back to the 1960s and identified Stark's father, Howard, as one of the founders of S.H.I.E.L.D., a development further explored in the World War II-set *Captain America: The First Avenger* as well as the *Agent Carter* (2013) "one-shot" and subsequent television series. The opening of *Thor* (2011), to borrow a phrase from another popular franchise, began a long time ago in a galaxy far, far away, as the heroes of Asgard defended the Nine Realms from Frost Giants, while *Guardians of the Galaxy* (2014) reaffirmed that in the MCU, the sky is not the limit—it is simply the beginning. Transmedia producer Jeff Gomez identified a "deep rich story world with a past, present and future" as essential for successful transmedia franchises.[53] Much of this story world will go unexplored, at least in early installments, but casual references, such as allusions to the Time and Clone Wars in *Doctor Who* and *Star Wars* respectively, hint at a larger universe that can be explored years, even decades later.

Despite the newfound enthusiasm for co-creation among media producers, Jenkins cautions that not every text can support such transmedia storytelling. Citing Pierre Lévy's *Collective Intelligence*, he describes *The Matrix* franchise as a good "cultural attractor" as it has "enough depth that they can justify such large-scale efforts."[54] Not every franchise shares this depth. As a notable example, following the success of the sequel *Terminator 2: Judgment Day* (1991) further efforts to extend the Terminator franchise were met with mixed results. Although the *T2 3-D: Battle Across Time* attraction, which first debuted in 1996, still plays at many Universal Studios Parks, none of the subsequent films matched the commercial or critical success of *Terminator 2*, while the television series *Terminator: The Sarah Connor Chronicles* was cancelled after two seasons in 2009. Despite the number of Terminator texts produced, much like the movie's characters, the franchise seems to be stuck in a time loop. Rather than investigate new territory, the latest franchise entrant *Terminator Genisys* (2015) is a further reworking of James Cameron's 1984 original. Thus, rather than extend the story, with each new entrant the Terminator universe seems to contract, a fate the MCU has avoided through the judicious development of a rich story world.

While Marvel Studios might be celebrated for its carefully constructed story world, it must be acknowledged that this universe came with a road map. Few sources can match the scope for transmedia storytelling inherent in the ready-made worlds of comic book mythology. Marvel boasts in media releases that it is "one of the world's most prominent character-based entertainment companies, built on a library of over 5,000 characters featured in a variety of media over seventy years."[55] Thus, unlike James Cameron's 107-minute film, Marvel had the story world depth to sustain the creative mining of even the most ardent transmedia activities.

Brand Recognition

Today comics featuring Marvel heroes rarely sell more than 100,000 copies through North American stores.[56] Nonetheless, the characters have a position in popular culture that exceeds their finite readership. Many scholars have noted that heavily adapted characters transcend their original form and circulate more freely in the popular culture as myths or archetypes.[57] Thus, a character like Captain America who first saw print in 1941 has remained evergreen through repeated adaptation to a variety of forms, including a World War II film serial, a weekly segment in the animated series *The Marvel Super Heroes* (1966), and the 1990 direct-to-video movie *Captain America*. As Henry Jenkins suggests "Often, characters in transmedia stories do not need to be introduced so much as reintroduced, because they are known from other sources."[58]

Few planned franchises, even those based on well-known texts, share the brand recognition of Marvel heroes. In *A Theory of Adaptation* Linda Hutcheon argues "expensive collaborative art forms like operas, musicals, and films are going to look for safe bets with a ready audience—and that usually means adaptations."[59] This economic rationale might have guided Marvel's corporate partner, Walt Disney Pictures, to adapt Edgar Rice Burroughs' influential Barsoom series as the feature film *John Carter* in 2012. The Barsoom series began in 1917 with *A Princess of Mars*. Throughout his life Burroughs added many more novels and short stories to the series, which centered on Earthman John Carter's adventures on the planet Mars. However, the planned franchise-starter, *John Carter*, did not find a large audience and was ultimately deemed a box office disappointment. Commentators were quick to point to the film's diffuse marketing campaign for its failure.[60] Nonetheless, the Barsoom series had rarely been adapted to other media. Thus, unlike its hero, the film could not escape the gravitational pull of its source material—novels that had little resonance with a contemporary audience.

A further difficulty faced by *John Carter* was its lack of readily identifiable iconography. Bukatman describes how the "Mask, costume, and logo are marks that guarantee the superhero body passage into the field of the symbolic."[61] Thus, comic book characters are particularly well equipped to thrive in a transmedia landscape that places an emphasis on spreadable imagery.

For instance, Captain America's familiar shield motif can be found on T-shirts, lunch boxes, and (appropriately) flying discs. While Burroughs' descriptions of Mars in his Barsoom series are evocative, the source lacked the distinct iconography important to any fledgling franchise with multiplatform ambitions.

Beyond individual characters, the critical and commercial success of the MCU has seen Marvel develop a cultural cachet that rivals any of its heroes. For instance, following the record-breaking gross of *Guardians of the Galaxy*, a film based on characters little known outside the comic book community (or even within), *Variety* reported, "as Marvel consistently produced meticulously crafted, well-reviewed popular entertainments, crowds began to see the brand itself as synonymous with quality. They might be unfamiliar with the heroes in one film or another, as was the case with 'Guardians,' but they knew and respected the Marvel name."[62] This goodwill has extended to a variety of other releases, with the company liberally affixing its logo to its increasingly diverse offerings. Thus, from individual heroes to the company's name, Marvel has the brand recognition necessary to develop successful offerings in the many platforms that make up a transmedia story.

Conglomerate Structure

Marvel's transmedia ambitions did not begin with the MCU. The company has long sought to coordinate its content across a variety of media. First introduced in 1980, the superhero Dazzler was "an ambitious cross-pollination experiment" between Casablanca Records and Marvel Comics.[63] The goal was to create a disco-themed hero that would not only appear in comics, but would also be performed by a musician who would record an album and tour as the character. Casablanca Records also hoped to develop a feature film based on Dazzler and when actress Bo Derek expressed an interest the comic book character was designed to mirror her appearance. Ultimately, with the disco trend declining, Casablanca Records pulled out of the Dazzler project. Although Marvel still introduced the character in their comics (first appearance *Uncanny X-Men* #130) they were unable to find a record label or film studio to realize their wider goals. While DC Comics had been a subsidiary of Warner Communications, Inc. since 1972, much of Marvel's transmedia strategies had been thwarted by the publisher's independent status.[64] Ian Gordon summarized in 1998, "in the long term Marvel's weakness, compared with DC, has been their inability to invigorate their characters through Hollywood blockbuster movies."[65]

When the comic book movie trend gathered pace with *Batman Begins* (2005) and the successful Spider-Man and X-Men sequels, the Marvel Studios division of Marvel Entertainment sought once more to develop its own audio-visual content. Securing capital from the Merrill Lynch Commercial Finance Corp and a distribution deal through Paramount Pictures, Johnson notes how Marvel Studios initially tried to position itself as a Hollywood "outsider."[66] Ultimately, the success of *Iron Man* would prompt the interest of larger conglomerates with the Walt Disney Company acquiring Marvel Entertainment in 2009. While this move might have diminished the company's renegade status, it ensured that Marvel finally had the infrastructure it needed to develop a transmedia story.

Through the Walt Disney Company's diverse media and entertainment holdings the Marvel Cinematic Universe extended beyond comics and films. The Walt Disney Company subsidiary ABC produced and broadcast *Agents of S.H.I.E.L.D.* and *Agent Carter*, with many commentators suggesting that the season two renewal of *Agent Carter*, after its modest first season ratings, was due to the broadcaster's relationship with its corporate partner Marvel.[67] Thus, the structure of a media conglomerate allowed for the coordination and support necessary to sustain the MCU. This formula saw other studios also aspire to such synergistic relationships with Universal Pictures Chairperson Donna Langley suggesting of their Monsters franchise in 2014 that "it's not just about looking at movies ... we are also looking at—taking a leaf out of the Marvel book—putting them across different platforms across the company, and we are uniquely primed to do that with the theme park and Comcast."[68] Of course, Universal is not "uniquely" primed to take advantage of industrial convergence, with conglomerates such as Time Warner, 21st Century Fox, and Viacom all looking to spread intellectual property across their many subsidiaries. However, as Langley concedes, through the development of the MCU, Marvel was the first company to fully utilize a conglomerate structure to develop a sustainable transmedia story.

The Future of the Marvel Cinematic Universe and Transmedia Storytelling

The commercial success of the Marvel Cinematic Universe in video games, comics, television, and, in particular, cinema has seen Hollywood studios lining up to give their intellectual property the transmedia treatment, including: Star Wars (Walt Disney Company), Universal Monsters (Universal Studios), Transformers (Paramount Pictures), Ghostbusters (Sony Pictures Entertainment) and, of course, DC Comics (Time Warner). Nonetheless, early attempts to establish a similar shared universe have faltered. Sony Pictures Entertainment, which still holds the film rights to Spider-Man, developed plans for an integrated Spider-Man franchise that would include films focusing on villains such as the Sinister Six and Venom. However, when *The Amazing Spider-Man 2* (2014) became the lowest grossing of the Spider-Man films these plans were abandoned with the studio instead forming a partnership with Marvel Studios that allowed Spider-Man to join the Marvel Cinematic Universe. As Sony's chairman Michael Lynton explained at the time "This is the right decision for the franchise, for our business, for Marvel, and for the fans."[69] Sony's decision to align with Marvel testifies to the difficulties of establishing a successful transmedia story, as well as Hollywood's recognition of Marvel's success. So what is the formula that has proven so difficult to replicate?

Drawing on its publishing traditions, Marvel embraced the flexible continuity for which comics are known and allied it to a platform neutral form of storytelling that allowed their characters to move easily across a variety of forms. To organize these multiple iterations, the studio adopted the same style of collaborative authorship that has enabled countless comic book creators to work on their characters for more than seventy-five years. The studio also reapplied their fan appeasing strategies for a group of enthusiasts emboldened by digital technologies. Returning the favor, these fans used the Internet to amplify interest in these once niche characters. The mainstream audience was not forgotten, with Marvel tapping into the depths of comic book mythology, while producing texts with enough autonomy to engage a non-fan audience. Although few in this wider audience had ever read a comic many were familiar with the characters as they had already been the subjects of several adaptations. Marvel leveraged that brand recognition, and its own growing credibility, to reintroduce these heroes as part of a shared universe. These strategies borrowed heavily from Marvel Comics' long-standing publishing practices, but the company had never been able to implement them on a transmedia level until it became part of a media conglomerate. Once acquired by the Walt Disney Company, Marvel realized its ambitions, setting a template for transmedia storytelling.

Phase Two of the Marvel Cinematic Universe concluded with *Avengers: Age of Ultron* (2015). In the sequel's third act the villain, Ultron, raises an Eastern European city into the atmosphere with the Avengers on board. Before enacting his plan to bring the city crashing back down to Earth, he pauses to mock the assembled heroes, "Do you see the beauty of it? The inevitability? You rise, only to fall." Outside the diegesis of the film a similar trajectory was being played out in trade papers, with critics and commentators questioning whether the MCU had reached a critical mass and would soon be snuffed out under the weight of its own dense continuity.[70] When *Avengers: Age of Ultron* became the first Marvel sequel not to out-gross its predecessor these doom-laden narratives were given further weight. Not long after this "disappointment," the season two finale of *Agents of S.H.I.E.L.D.*

was beaten in the ratings by the DC Comics-based *The Flash* (2014–), which is broadcast on the youth-skewing, and traditionally lower-rated, CW network.[71]

However, to suggest that the success or failure of individual MCU entrants is indicative of the larger franchise's health is to overlook one of the great benefits of a transmedia franchise. Comics were once the most visible example of Marvel heroes; today it is cinema. As the success of Netflix's *Daredevil, Jessica Jones,* and *Luke Cage* series suggest, in the future the driving platform of the Marvel "Cinematic" Universe might be television, video games, or even stage shows. In a transmedia story like the Marvel Cinematic Universe the mother ship is free to move media, as the heroes will remain constant.

NOTES

1. Elizabeth Evans, *Transmedia Television: Audiences, New Media and Daily Life* (New York: Routledge, 2011), 1.

2. Henry Jenkins, *Convergence Culture: Where Old and New Media Collide* (New York: New York University Press, 2006), 97–98.

3. Henry Jenkins, "The Aesthetics of Transmedia: In Response to David Bordwell (Part One)," *Confessions of an Aca-Fan: The Official Weblog of Henry Jenkins* (blog), September 10, 2009, http://henryjenkins.org/2009/09/the_aesthetics_of_transmedia_i.html.

4. Ivan Askwith and Jonathan Gray, "Transmedia Storytelling and Media Franchises," in *Battleground: The Media,* ed. Robin Andersen and Jonathan Gray (Westport, CT: Greenwood, 2008), 519–520.

5. Jeff Gomez, "Transmedia Storytelling Masterclass," (presentation, Australian Centre for the Moving Image, Melbourne, Australia, October 10, 2014).

6. Derek Johnson, "Cinematic Destiny: Marvel Studios and the Trade Stories of Industrial Convergence," *Cinema Journal* 52, no. 1 (2012): 7.

7. Gomez, "Transmedia Storytelling Masterclass."

8. Gomez, "Transmedia Storytelling Masterclass."

9. Suzanne Scott, "Who's Steering the Mothership? The Role of the Fanboy Auteur in Transmedia Storytelling," in *The Participatory Cultures Handbook,* ed. Aaron Alan Delwiche and Jennifer Jacobs Henderson (New York: Routledge, 2013), 46.

10. Gomez, "Transmedia Storytelling Masterclass."

11. *The Matrix Reloaded,* directed by Lilly and Lana Wachowski (2003; Burbank, CA: Warner Home Video, 2008), DVD.

12. Askwith and Gray, "Transmedia Storytelling and Media Franchises," 524.

13. The final Matrix film, *The Matrix Revolutions* (worldwide gross of $427,343,298), grossed significantly less than the first sequel *The Matrix Reloaded* (worldwide gross of $742,128,461) and even the first film *The Matrix* (worldwide gross of $463,517,383).

14. Released after *The Avengers, Iron Man 3* became the Iron Man franchise's highest grossing film earning $1.2 billion internationally, almost twice as much as the previous installment *Iron Man 2.* Sequels *Thor: The Dark World* and *Captain America: Civil War,* also achieved franchise highs of $644 million and $1.15 billion respectively.

15. The first episode of *Agents of S.H.I.E.L.D.* achieved a total of 12 million viewers when broadcast on the U.S. ABC network, making it the highest rated debut in four years. Ratings for the series quickly declined before stabilizing for season two with an average viewership of 7 million including Digital Video Recording. Lesley Goldberg, "ABC Renews 'Agents of SHIELD,' 'Agent Carter,'" *The Hollywood Reporter,* May 7, 2015, http://www.hollywoodreporter.com/live-feed/abc-renews-agents-shield-agent-792905.

16. Superman's sidekick Jimmy Olsen and the character's Achilles heel, Kryptonite, first

appeared in *The Adventures of Superman* radio show in 1940 and 1943 respectively, before making their way to the source material in *Superman* #13 and *Superman* #61. Similarly, the X-Men comics have adopted a number of characters first introduced in animated series, such as the female clone of Wolverine, X-23, who was developed for the animated series *X-Men: Evolution* before being added to the comics.

17. Martyn Pedler, "Morrison's Muscle Mystery Versus Everyday Reality ... and Other Parallel Worlds!," in *The Contemporary Comic Book Superhero*, ed. Angela Ndalianis (New York: Routledge, 2009), 255.

18. Johnson, "Cinematic Destiny," 3.

19. Derek Johnson, "Will the Real Wolverine Please Stand Up?" in *Film and Comic Books*, ed. Ian Gordon, Mark Jancovich, and Matthew P. McAllister (Jackson: University of Mississippi, 2007) 67.

20. Evans, *Transmedia Television*, 29.

21. Gomez, "Transmedia Storytelling Masterclass."

22. Johnson, "Cinematic Destiny," 16.

23. "I Am Iron Man," *Iron Man (Ultimate Two Disc Edition)*, directed by Jon Favreau (2008; Hollywood, CA: Paramount Pictures, 2008), DVD.

24. In his 2002 book *The Language of New Media*, Lev Manovich argues that the control afforded to filmmakers in the digital age has seen cinema become "a particular case of animation that uses live action footage as one of its many elements." Lev Manovich, *The Language of New Media* (Cambridge: MIT Press, 2002), 302.

25. "Wired: The Visual Effects of Iron Man," *Iron Man (Ultimate Two Disc Edition)*, Directed by Jon Favreau (2008; Hollywood, CA: Paramount Pictures, 2008), DVD.

26. Jeffrey Sconce, "What If? Charting Television's New Textual Boundaries," in *Television after TV: Essays on a Medium in Transition*, ed. Lynn Spigel and Jan Olsson. (Durham: Duke University Press, 2004), 95.

27. Morgan Jeffery, "Marvel's Agents of SHIELD Stars Talk Captain America 2 Twist," *Digital Spy*, April 8, 2014. http://www.digitalspy.com/tv/captain-america/news/a563322/marvels-agents-of-shield-stars-talk-captain-america-2-twist-video.

28. Robert C. Ring, *Sci-fi Movie Freak* (Iola: Krause Publications, 2011), 216.

29. Pascal Lefèvre, "Incompatible Visual Ontologies: The Problematic Adaptation of Drawn Images," in *Film and Comic Books*, ed. Ian Gordon, Mark Jancovich, and Matthew P. McAllister (Jackson: University of Mississippi, 2007), 8.

30. Bart Beaty, "Comic Studies: Fifty Years After Film Studies," *Cinema Journal* 50, no. 3 (2011): 109.

31. Will Brooker, *Batman Unmasked: Analyzing a Cultural Icon* (New York: Continuum, 2000), 252.

32. Evans, *Transmedia Television*, 32.

33. In his oft-cited book, *The Genius of the System: Hollywood Filmmaking in the Studio Era*, Thomas Schatz challenges the emphasis many film scholars place on individual filmmakers, "We would do well, in fact, to recall French film critic André Bazin's admonition to the early auteurists, who were transforming film history into a cult of personality. 'The American cinema is a classical art,' wrote Bazin in 1957, 'so why not then admire in it what is most admirable—i.e., not only the talent of this or that filmmaker, but the genius of the system.'" Thomas Schatz, *The Genius of the System: Hollywood Filmmaking in the Studio Era* (Minneapolis: University of Minnesota Press, 2010), 8.

34. Brooks Barnes, "With Fan at the Helm, Marvel Safely Steers Its Heroes to the Screen," *The New York Times*, July 24, 2011, http://www.nytimes.com/2011/07/25/business/media/marvel-with-a-fan-at-the-helm-steers-its-heroes-to-the-screen.html.

35. Paul Wells, *Animation: Genre and Authorship* (London: Wallflower, 2002), 101.

36. Johnson, "Cinematic Destiny," 17–18.

37. Gomez, "Transmedia Storytelling Masterclass."

38. Scott Bukatman, "Secret Identity Politics," in *The Contemporary Comic Book Superhero*, ed. Angela Ndalianis (New York: Routledge, 2009), 111.

39. Michael Z. Newman and Elana Levine, *Legitimating Television: Media Convergence and Cultural Status* (Oxon: Routledge, 2012), 39–40.

40. Marc Graser, "Edgar Wright Exits Marvel's 'Ant-Man' as Director," *Variety*, May 23, 2014, http://variety.com/2014/film/news/edgar-wright-exits-marvels-ant-man-as-director-1201190458. When Marvel first announced its own film productions in 2006, *Shaun of the Dead* writer/director Edgar Wright was attached to *Ant-Man*. Wright stayed with the film through its lengthy pre-production even shooting test footage that screened at the 2012 San Diego Comic-Con. However, shortly before production was due to begin Wright left the film with Marvel explaining that the company and filmmaker had parted ways "due to differences in their vision of the film." *Yes Man* director Peyton Reed ultimately replaced Wright, with *Ant-Man* released in 2015. Similarly, Alan Taylor who had previously directed episodes of *Game of Thrones*, *Mad Men*, and *Boardwalk Empire* replaced *Monster* director Patty Jenkins at the helm of *Thor: The Dark World*.

41. François Truffaut, "A Certain Tendency of The French Cinema," *Movies and Methods: An Anthology Vol. 1.*, ed. Bill Nichols (Berkeley: University of California, 1976), 233.

42. Gomez, "Transmedia Storytelling Masterclass."

43. Mike Fleming, Jr. "Akiva Goldsman Explains 'Transformers' Writers Room as Paramount Adds Scribe Pair," *Deadline*, June 4, 2015, http://deadline.com/2015/06/transformers-akiva-goldsman-writers-room-michael-bay-paramount-1201438017.

44. Pamela McClintock and Kim Masters, "Executive Roundtable," *The Hollywood Reporter*, Nov. 12, 2014. http://www.hollywoodreporter.com/news/executive-roundtable-6-studio-heads-748102.

45. Rob Keyes, "Mark Millar to Oversee Fox's Marvel Cinematic Universe," *Screen Rant*. Sept. 27, 2012. http://screenrant.com/x-men-fantastic-four-movies-fox-mark-millar.

46. Gomez, "Transmedia Storytelling Masterclass."

47. Pierre Comtois, *Marvel Comics in the 1960s: An Issue-by-issue Field Guide to a Pop Culture Phenomenon* (Raleigh: TwoMorrows, 2009), 96.

48. Matthew Pustz, *Comic Book Culture: Fanboys and True Believers* (Jackson: University of Mississippi, 1999), 167.

49. Jenkins, *Convergence Culture*, 135.

50. Matt Hills, "Fiske's 'Textual Productivity' and Digital Fandom: Web 2.0 Democratization versus Fan Distinction," *Participations: Journal of Audience and Reception Studies*, 10, no. 1 (2013): 146.

51. Randy Duncan and Matthew J. Smith. *The Power of Comics: History, Form and Culture* (New York: Continuum, 2009), 171.

52. Johnson, "Cinematic Destiny," 7.

53. Gomez, "Transmedia Storytelling Masterclass."

54. Pierre Lévy, *Collective Intelligence: Mankind's Emerging World in Cyberspace* (Cambridge: Perseus Books, 1997), 97.

55. "Disney to Acquire Marvel Entertainment," Marvel.com, Aug. 31, 2009. http://marvel.com/news/ comics/9360/disney_to_acquire_marvel_entertainment.

56. In April 2015 comic books featuring Avengers, *Thor*, *All New Captain America*, and *Superior Iron Man* sold 71,372, 38,199, and 34,446 copies respectively through North American stores. "April 2015 Comic Book Sales Figures," *Comichron*, accessed January 25, 2017, http://www.comichron.com/ monthlycomicssales/2015/2015-04.html.

57. Dudley Andrew, *Concepts in Film Theory* (Oxford: Oxford University Press, 1984), 98; André Bazin, "Adaptation, or the Cinema as Digest," in *Film Adaptation*, ed. James Naremore (New Brunswick: Rutgers University Press, 2000), 23; Brooker, *Batman Unmasked*, 11.

58. Jenkins, *Convergence Culture*, 123.

59. Linda Hutcheon, *A Theory of Adaptation* (New York: Routledge, 2006), 87.

60. Dawn C. Chmielewski and Rebecca Keegan, "Why Did Disney's 'John Carter' Flop?," *Los Angeles Times*, Mar. 13, 2012, http://articles.latimes.com/2012/mar/13/entertainment/la-et-john-carter-flop-20120313.

61. Scott Bukatman, *Matters of Gravity: Special Effects and Supermen in the 20th Century* (Durham: Duke University Press, 2003), 54.

62. Brent Lang, "Why 'Guardians of the Galaxy' May Be Marvel's Most Important Movie," *Variety*, Aug. 3, 2014, http://variety.com/2014/film/news/guardians-of-the-galaxy-marvel-analysis-1201274603.

63. Sean Howe, *Marvel Comics: The Untold Story* (New York: Harper, 2012), 221.

64. Eileen Meehan, "Holy Commodity Fetish, Batman!: The Political Economy of a Commercial Intertext," in *The Many Lives of the Batman: Critical Approaches to a Superhero and His Media*, ed. Roberta E. Pearson and William Uricchio (New York: Routledge, 1991), 52.

65. Ian Gordon, *Comic Strips and Consumer Culture, 1890–1945* (Washington, D.C.: Smithsonian Institution, 1998), 156.

66. Johnson, "Cinematic Destiny," 5.

67. Goldberg, "ABC Renews 'Agents of SHIELD.'"

68. McClintock and Masters, "Executive Roundtable."

69. Stuart Oldham, "Spider-Man Returns to Marvel; New Movie Coming in 2017," *Variety*, Feb. 9, 2015, http://variety.com/2015/film/news/spider-man-marvel-sony-movies-12014 29508.

70. Graeme McMillan, "The Flaws of Marvel's "It's All Connected" Cinematic Universe," *The Hollywood Reporter,* May 3, 2015, http://www.hollywoodreporter.com/heat-vision/flaws-marvels-all-connected-cinematic-792904.

71. James Hibberd, "'The Flash' Beats 'SHIELD' for First Time Since Premiere," *Entertainment Weekly's EW.com*, April 29, 2015, http://www.ew.com/article/2015/04/29/flash-beats-shield.

#ITSALLCONNECTED
Assembling the Marvel Universe

LISA K. PERDIGAO

Focused on the supporting cast behind the Marvel superheroes, ABC's *Agents of S.H.I.E.L.D.* (2013–) offers a unique portrayal of the foundations of the Marvel Cinematic Universe on the small screen. As the pilot episode of *S.H.I.E.L.D.* begins, we learn that Agent Phil Coulson survived his big-screen death in *The Avengers* (2012), written and directed by Joss Whedon, who, along with Jed Whedon and Maurissa Tancharoen, created *Agents of S.H.I.E.L.D.* Rewriting Coulson's cinematic last act, *S.H.I.E.L.D.* gives new life to the Marvel Universe, suggesting new possibilities for adaptation between mediums. Derek Johnson writes that with its 2008 film *Iron Man*, Marvel Studios "launched a unique model for cinema production in the age of convergence."[1] Johnson's description of the individual films as "mere episodes in a larger, cohesive work" anticipates *S.H.I.E.L.D.*'s experiments with blurring the boundaries between film and television screens.[2] *S.H.I.E.L.D.* is Marvel's convergence strategy writ large; its episodic formula drives and is driven by developments in the Marvel Cinematic Universe.

The aptly titled season one episode "Turn, Turn, Turn" represents a turning point for experimentation with convergence. Featuring a crossover with Anthony and Joe Russo's *Captain America: The Winter Soldier* (2014), "Turn, Turn, Turn" demonstrates S.H.I.E.L.D. Agent Maria Hill's statement that "Everything's changing," specifically in the ways that television and film are reconceived in the 21st century.[3] After *The Winter Soldier* dismantles S.H.I.E.L.D. in its narrative, the television series rebuilds the organization and itself. The release of Whedon's *Avengers: Age of Ultron* (2015) introduces another opportunity to reestablish *S.H.I.E.L.D.*'s position within the Marvel Cinematic Universe. Although Ultron threatens the Avengers' extinction, the Avengers and S.H.I.E.L.D. are revitalized on the big screen. When *S.H.I.E.L.D.*

returns after *Age of Ultron*'s opening weekend with the episode "Scars," Coulson reveals that his organization's mysterious "Theta Protocol" was responsible for the restored helicarrier that saved the citizens of Sokovia.[4] In "Scars," *S.H.I.E.L.D.* suggests its redefined role in the Marvel Cinematic Universe: rather than being affected by developments in the Marvel films as it had with *The Winter Soldier*, the television series "lead[s] the way" for Marvel when it names the Inhumans, the subject and title of the series released on both the big and small screen two years later in 2017.[5] Answering Ultron's challenge to "evolve," *S.H.I.E.L.D.* reconfigures Marvel's model of convergence as an open circuit, creating new paths to and for the future.[6]

On March 18, 2014, ABC aired a special titled "Assembling a Universe" in the *S.H.I.E.L.D.* timeslot to demonstrate how "it's all connected." The airing of the episode "Turn, Turn, Turn," featuring the phrase #ITSALLCONNECTED in the bottom corner of the screen, was timed to coincide with the release of *The Winter Soldier*, and its narrative is structured on the film's plot. In a way, the "destiny" of *S.H.I.E.L.D.* was always already decided by *Captain America*. It is appropriate, as Agent Coulson is nostalgically connected to the hero, a "touchstone to the past."[7] As "Turn, Turn, Turn" relies on the viewers' knowledge of the film (and, conversely, presenting "spoilers" for those who had missed it on opening weekend), the series expands on the self-referentiality that is a marker of the Marvel Universe, a heightened self-consciousness about its own source material that is extended to—and expected of—its viewers. Demonstrating how "it's all connected," speaking to viewers through the language of social media, and introducing how television reflects real time, *S.H.I.E.L.D.* is poised between Marvel's past and future. Its narrative is informed—and even directed—by its source material, yet it is an innovative series that suggests new ways of conceiving adaptation across mediums.

The introduction of Phase One of the Marvel Cinematic Universe with the releases of Jon Favreau's *Iron Man* (2008) and Louis Leterrier's *The Incredible Hulk* (2008) follows the publication of Henry Jenkins' study of convergence culture in 2006. The films produced in this era of convergence evidence how theory meets practice. James N. Gilmore and Matthias Stork write that Marvel Studios' *Avengers* films reflect Jenkins' theory of a "convergence aesthetics found in certain films, television shows, video games, web comics, and other forms of media" that "reflect an overarching industrial model of media consolidation and synergy."[8] Jenkins' description of transmedia storytelling as a "process where integral elements of a fiction get dispersed systematically across multiple delivery channels for the purpose of creating a unified and coordinated entertainment experience" so that "each medium makes its own unique contribution to the unfolding of the story" is suggestive for what is at work within the Marvel Cinematic Universe, particularly in the relationship between the Marvel films and television series.[9]

While Marvel's strategies of convergence and synergy have been identified in the *Avengers* films, television presents a new medium for analyzing how convergence works between big and small screens.[10] According to Jason Mittell, a "new paradigm of storytelling" involving a "reconceptualization of the boundary between episodic and serial forms, a heightened degree of self-consciousness in storytelling mechanics, and demands for intensified viewer engagement focused on both diegetic pleasures and formal awareness" emerged in the past two decades of television narrative.[11] While Mittell identifies Whedon's *Buffy the Vampire Slayer* (1997–2003), *Angel* (1999–2004), and *Firefly* (2002–2003) as representing this "new paradigm in storytelling" in his 2006 study, the description equally applies to *Agents of S.H.I.E.L.D.*, a series that he cites in *Complex TV* (2015).[12] Mittell writes, "Most prime time television programs serve as the core text of their transmedia franchises, with the unusual example of *Marvel's Agents of S.H.I.E.L.D.* as a rare exception pointed toward a more balanced approach in which comics and films are seemingly more central to the narrative."[13] *Agents of S.H.I.E.L.D.* can be seen as challenging the basic definition and understanding of transmedia storytelling, demonstrating Whedon's evolution in television production.[14]

S.H.I.E.L.D. creator/writer/executive producer and writer/director of *The Avengers* and *Age of Ultron* Whedon is no stranger to adaptation. His first television series *Buffy the Vampire Slayer* began as a film and was given new life after the end of its run on the small screen in canonical comic books. The television series *Firefly* reverses Buffy's teleology with a big screen reboot in *Serenity* (2005). According to Stacey Abbott, the film adaptation of *Firefly* marks "the point where Whedon's television and cinema career came full circle."[15] For Rhonda V. Wilcox, the 2012 releases of *The Avengers* and Whedon's film adaptation of Shakespeare's *Much Ado About Nothing* are significant: she writes that although "the step from Marvel Comics movie to Shakespeare may seem incongruous," "to many it seems a natural move, part of a unified body of work."[16] While the term Whedonverse is itself expansive, representing a world of productions in film, television, comic books, and webcasts, the individual texts that populate the Whedonverse have an extensive reach; they are self-referential and richly allusive. Intertextuality is at the center of the Marvel Cinematic Universe and Whedon's return to the small screen with *S.H.I.E.L.D.*

With *The Avengers* and *S.H.I.E.L.D.*, Whedon comes full circle yet again. Coulson's resurrection on the small screen recalls *Buffy the Vampire Slayer*'s origins and the character's literal return from the grave in season six when the series moved from The WB to UPN in 2001. Abbott's statement that *Serenity* is "more regeneration than resurrection" highlights what is at work in *S.H.I.E.L.D.*'s experiments with convergence.[17] In "End of the Beginning," John Garrett, Grant Ward's superior officer (s.o.), tells Skye, "I guess it all comes full circle…. Turn, turn, turn."[18] While Garrett is referring to Ward's role as Skye's s.o., his line recalls Abbott's statement about Whedon's work coming full circle and her comment that "Whedon's circle thus continues to turn."[19] But perhaps a more representative shape for Whedon's work is a Moëbius strip, without beginning and end, which is fitting, given the title of this episode and the season one finale "Beginning of the End."

Reflecting the self-consciousness that is a marker of the Whedonverse and the Marvel Cinematic Universe, *S.H.I.E.L.D.* depicts its characters struggling to figure out the organization's role within the Marvel Universe. "End of the Beginning" signals the changes that will come for the series in the wake of *The Winter Soldier*'s release, and "Turn, Turn, Turn" demonstrates how the series redirects its course to offer a distinct model of transmedia storytelling. In its first season, *S.H.I.E.L.D.* is directed by events in the Marvel Cinematic Universe; however, the attempts to rebuild S.H.I.E.L.D. after the fallout from *The Winter Soldier* are more generally suggestive of what is at work in the series.

The *S.H.I.E.L.D.* plot coinciding with the release of *The Winter Soldier* introduces questions about who is directing the narrative. The team works to locate the Clairvoyant that has infiltrated S.H.I.E.L.D. In "End of the Beginning," the Clairvoyant is identified as Thomas Nash, a psychic who, due to paralysis, speaks to the team through a computer that generates his words. His greeting to Coulson, "You're here because we are destined to meet," reflects the story-world of the Marvel Universe and its concept of destiny.[20] It is also suggestive of the origins of a television series that is bound by developments in the *Captain America* franchise. The plan for the second *Captain America* film was shared with *S.H.I.E.L.D.*'s executive producers when the series was greenlighted; it had to be worked into the series from the very beginning. Nash—as the Clairvoyant—says, "You fear what's about to happen…. It is the inevitable. A force beyond your comprehension is coming for you."[21] Nash's reference to destiny can be applied to the emplotted nature of the text, the constraints felt by producers, writers, and showrunners. This metafictionality extends beyond production to include interpretation. Nash is positioned in front of numerous computer screens, offering a visual representation of the omniscience that he is believed to possess.

By the episode's end, the team learns that Nash is not the Clairvoyant; however, the significance of the computer screens is affirmed with the revelation of who the Clairvoyant might actually be. Coulson concludes that the Clairvoyant "…doesn't have abilities. He has security clearance. He's an agent of S.H.I.E.L.D."[22] The Clairvoyant has power in the story-world of *S.H.I.E.L.D.* because he has access to information. Here *S.H.I.E.L.D.* self-consciously examines the nature of programming; the viewer, like the Clairvoyant, is able to see the complete picture. The "Clairvoyant" (later revealed as Garrett) was especially insightful to set the stage with Nash as he did: Nash presents a picture of control over the screens, over the story-world. He bears some similarities to *Serenity*'s Mr. Universe who is positioned in front of a wall of screens and whose motto "Can't Stop the Signal" comes to define the Browncoats' mission within the film and in fan communities, a call to sustain the narrative. In contrast, in *S.H.I.E.L.D.*, the signal is jammed, and the team—like the viewers—must attempt to decode it. When the message is translated to reveal HYDRA's call—and a connection to *The Winter Soldier*—it appears on a computer screen. *S.H.I.E.L.D.* reflects the new model of television narrative that Frank Rose describes as "nonlinear," "participatory," and "immersive."[23] Information—and access to it—goes both ways, particularly in a convergence culture.

Viewers positioned in front of screens playing *Agents of S.H.I.E.L.D.* and *The Winter Soldier* are given a unique vantage point on the Marvel Cinematic Universe, a certain kind of "clairvoyance." In addition to the intersection of the narratives in real time, the plots of *S.H.I.E.L.D.* and *The Winter Soldier* are centrally concerned with time. While Coulson argues for the relative "timelessness" of Captain America and the values that he represents, Rogers struggles to retain his identity in a new unfamiliar world and after experiencing extensive reconditioning. In *The Winter Soldier*, the past is forever present, preserved like the Captain America Smithsonian exhibit that Rogers visits. He is both in time and outside of time—seemingly impervious to time but insistent on reminding himself of it. *The Winter Soldier* forces the series to similarly confront time in a radical way. The work of *S.H.I.E.L.D.* is to create a foundation that can support an expansive Marvel Cinematic Universe, developing a sense of continuity while creating new characters, storylines, and narrative techniques.

In a model of reciprocity, *Captain America*'s narrative impacts the television series, and it is also informed by *S.H.I.E.L.D.* In *The Winter Soldier*, Rogers is introduced to a plot that begins in *S.H.I.E.L.D.* Agent Jasper Sitwell leaves the S.H.I.E.L.D. mobile command aircraft (the Bus) in "End of the Beginning," walking offscreen, and reappears in the *Captain America* film as the representation of S.H.I.E.L.D.'s politics ("S.H.I.E.L.D. doesn't negotiate") and its deconstruction ("Hail HYDRA").[24] Yet the television series *S.H.I.E.L.D. must* negotiate with the film's narrative, navigating the space between the distinct texts in its frames. *The Winter Soldier*'s Agent Peggy Carter, Rogers' former love interest, tells the hero, "The world has changed. None of us can go back," lines reminiscent of Agent Hill's assessment that "Everything's changing" in *S.H.I.E.L.D.*'s "Pilot."[25] In *The Winter Soldier*, *S.H.I.E.L.D.* is compromised and, ironically, without agency, providing a crisis and an opportunity for the series.

When *S.H.I.E.L.D.* returned on Tuesday, April 8, 2014, with the episode

"Turn, Turn, Turn," just four days after the April 4 premiere of *The Winter Soldier*, the series began a new course. In this episode, Agent Victoria Hand's statement that "Once that encoded transmission went out, everything changed" is indicative of *S.H.I.E.L.D.* post–*Winter Soldier*.[26] With everything changed, the television series uses the episode to direct and redirect its narrative's course. The episode is rich with allusions to the series' future, the possible paths it can follow. After an initial sequence featuring a drone attack on Garrett, Melinda May and Coulson are in a standoff, trying to figure out what is happening and whom they can trust. May defends herself against Coulson's accusations that she is the informant, saying, "I didn't set this new course" as she identifies an override of the aircraft's program.[27] Coulson says, "We don't even know where our plane is headed," and, later in the episode, "You know what this means? We can't change course and we have no idea what's waiting for us at the Hub."[28] In *S.H.I.E.L.D.*, the team's struggle to decode the signal is indicative of its position in relation to *The Winter Soldier*'s story-world. The characters are virtually left in the dark, on autopilot to some unknown location. In contrast, viewers who saw *The Winter Soldier* during its opening weekend are more aware of the plot than the characters are; here again Whedon returns to the Bard and some good old-fashioned dramatic irony.

But perhaps the most significant turn in the episode is when the characters are brought "Out of the Shadows and Into the Light," following HYDRA's message, as they learn what unfolded in *The Winter Soldier*. Here is where the episode's experiment is most radical. While news of the fall of S.H.I.E.L.D. is a blow to the agents and viewers in the dark about the film's plot, it is the revelation of a central character's death that is most jarring, particularly in how the news is delivered. Coulson forces May to place a call on the encrypted line to S.H.I.E.L.D. Director Nick Fury. When someone finally answers, May realizes that it's not Fury; the man on the other end of the phone then blurts out, "Director Fury is dead."[29] Yet that's only part of the story. In *The Winter Soldier*, HYDRA is not the only thing brought back from the dead. The film's regeneration plot includes the "destiny" of Nick Fury when the Director apparently dies on the operating table after being shot by the Winter Soldier. Reversing or rejecting the big-screen death that Coulson performs in *The Avengers*, Fury is restored and reintroduced into the narrative of *The Winter Soldier*. A crisis for the franchise is averted. However, in "Turn, Turn, Turn," Fury's death is delivered as a blow to the team and many viewers.

Both Coulson and Fury can be seen as convergence characters: the two characters are regenerated (if not resurrected) in the narratives and cross over between big and small screens. They represent a story coming full circle. *S.H.I.E.L.D.* gives Coulson new life on the small screen while it negates that possibility for Fury who is initially only regenerated on the big screen. Conversely, Coulson does not appear in *Avengers: Age of Ultron*.[30] *S.H.I.E.L.D.* is framed by Coulson's regeneration through Project T.A.H.I.T.I. and questions about it drive the narrative, notably in "Turn, Turn, Turn." Jemma Simmons studies Skye's blood, searching for clues about the regenerative properties of the serum that saved Skye and Coulson, something that the Clairvoyant is also trying to discover. Regeneration is key to a S.H.I.E.L.D. organization that is dismantled after HYDRA's attack and to a series trying to chart its own course.

The end of "Turn, Turn, Turn" presents a self-conscious meditation on where the series will go in the future. As the episode approaches its conclusion, Hand and Coulson study the aftermath of the events of *The Winter Soldier* on computer monitors. Hand announces that Captain America successfully defeated the HYDRA-controlled helicarriers, but "his status is unknown."[31] This statement is suggestive of the series as it begins its second season. As season two begins, S.H.I.E.L.D. is in crisis. The episode "Shadows" begins in Austria, in 1945, with Agent Carter. In the present day, S.H.I.E.L.D. is operating in the "shadows" after the resurgence of HYDRA led to the apparent collapse of the two organizations. In "Shadows," a television screen reads "S.H.I.E.L.D. and HYDRA are no more."[32] Despite their attempts to keep S.H.I.E.L.D. alive, Bobbi Morse admits, "S.H.I.E.L.D. isn't S.H.I.E.L.D. anymore."[33] This point is underscored by the revelation of the "real" S.H.I.E.L.D. that challenges Coulson's organization and role as director. However, instead of beginning season two with a present-day S.H.I.E.L.D., the series returns to the past to reclaim what S.H.I.E.L.D. was meant to be and can be again.

This framing device serves an additional purpose: highlighting the convergence strategies that define the series. Promotions for the ABC series *Agent Carter*, which premiered on January 6, 2015, ran during episodes of *S.H.I.E.L.D.* In "Shadows," Carter defines S.H.I.E.L.D.'s purpose after collecting and containing a HYDRA "artifact": "Someone needs to establish a permanent unit during peacetime … and watch over people like Stark who are toying with it. Until then, all we can do is box it up, lock it up, and dedicate ourselves to making sure it never sees the light of day."[34] As S.H.I.E.L.D. struggles to rebuild itself in season two, its past, present, and future are reconciled on the small screen. At the end of "Turn, Turn, Turn," when May asks Coulson, "What are we planning to do next?," Coulson's response is "Survive."[35] At the beginning of season two, after the team secures a Quinjet, Coulson says, "Now we have a chance to survive."[36] Agent Carter's S.H.I.E.L.D. is redefined by Coulson who says that they must "disappear, become ghosts. That's how we have to live now, in the shadows to save people, even when they don't know it, don't want it."[37] *S.H.I.E.L.D.* demonstrates how the organization conceived after World War II is made meaningful in the 21st century.

While the second season is driven by the past, it also leads to the future of a new S.H.I.E.L.D. organization and series. Similar to the Clairvoyant that was a central character in season one, directing and guiding the plot, the Diviner becomes a central prop and plot device in season two. "Shadows" introduces the object when Carter boxes it for safekeeping, and the episode's plot involves S.H.I.E.L.D.'s attempts to regain possession of it from HYDRA. Daniel Whitehall, revealed to be regenerated HYDRA agent Dr. Werner Reinhardt, seeks the "obelisk" for its power as a weapon. However, Skye's father Calvin Zabo (Cal) corrects him by saying that the Diviner is "not a weapon" but a "key."[38] He says, "It can kill you, sure, but only to protect itself from those it doesn't divine … hence the catchy name … to be worthy."[39] Season two reveals the power of the Diviner for "special people" "worthy of unlocking its true power."[40]

Where *S.H.I.E.L.D.* self-consciously examines its course in season one, it explores the possibilities of evolution and transformation in season two. In the episode "Heavy is the Head," Raina tells Coulson that Garrett, season one's Clairvoyant, was "enlightened"; she says, "He witnessed our fate, what we've become. Have you?"[41] Raina continually asserts that she was destined for something greater, and, in the season two finale, she realizes that her role is not to lead but to "illuminate."[42] Season two is focused on illumination, and answers to the mysteries of Coulson's "Writing on the Wall," the Diviner, the alien city, and Skye's "true" identity are given. Raina asks Skye, "Haven't you ever felt lost? Or have that feeling that you were part of something bigger, like you were special?"[43] After Skye asks if Raina means "alien," Raina replies, "We're human, Skye. We just have the potential to be more. But the Diviner, now that is most definitely alien."[44] The midseason finale, "What They Become," enlightens the viewers who witness the characters' "fate." After Skye "emerge[s] from the chrysalis," transformed by Terrigenesis, she reveals what she was "always meant to be": Daisy Johnson/Quake from the Marvel comics.[45]

After the transformations of key characters, including Raina who is given the "gift" of prophecy, *S.H.I.E.L.D.* offers a vision of a Marvel world still in cinematic making. In "Aftershocks," Leo Fitz first uses the term "inhuman" to describe Skye's heartbeat, measured at 300 beats per minute at the time of the temple's collapse.[46] However, the term is imbued with new meaning in the episode "Scars." After Coulson says, "From our perspective, we don't even know what to call them," Skye says, "Inhumans. Our ancient ancestors called themselves Inhumans, and we just want to be left alone."[47] After revealing the location of the Inhumans, "Scars" takes S.H.I.E.L.D. to "Afterlife," a liminal space between film and television screens. Where Abbott distinguishes resurrection and regeneration in the case of *Serenity*, *S.H.I.E.L.D.* symbolically finds new life with the introduction of the Inhumans. By mapping the world of the Inhumans, a transformed *S.H.I.E.L.D.* enters its own "Afterlife." Skye emerges from the mist as a convergence character like Coulson and Fury, crossing between big and small screens. Raina does not survive to become part of the "bigger picture," but the other Inhumans are destined for important roles in the Marvel Cinematic Universe.

Fittingly, "Scars" bears the traces of what the television series has always been, intricately connected to the Marvel films; however, it also evolves into something else. When Ultron is created, he comes to life through a network of connections. His "birth" from darkness takes him through flashes of consciousness represented by shots from the Marvel films. A model of convergence—the proliferation of screens that constitute the Marvel Cinematic Universe—produces the "age of Ultron." Similarly, when *S.H.I.E.L.D.* returns after *The Winter Soldier* and *Age of Ultron*, the agents watch the film scenes on their own screens. Their actions, similar to Ultron's, are influenced by those images. However, after *Age of Ultron*, "Once that encoded transmission went out, everything changed" again.[48]

Age of Ultron introduces a new era for *S.H.I.E.L.D.* and for television narrative. Ultron considers the Avengers outdated and calls for their extinction. As Johnson writes, "Convergence is not a uniquely digital or technological phenomenon but a reworking of media new and old."[49] *Age of Ultron* introduces a revitalized S.H.I.E.L.D. that appears at exactly the right time to save thousands—if not millions—of people. As Rogers says, "This is what S.H.I.E.L.D. was meant to be."[50] The restored helicarrier is a visual metaphor for what *S.H.I.E.L.D.* attempts to do in its second season by introducing Agent Carter's vision for S.H.I.E.L.D. alongside Coulson's repurposed one. Michael Curtin and Jane Shattuc describe the transition from "centralised production and transmission to an undifferentiated mass audience" in the classical network era to "interactive exchanges, multiple sites of productivity and diverse modes of interpretation and use" in the matrix era.[51] *S.H.I.E.L.D.* capitalizes on this new model, becoming an example of "complex TV" that is ever-evolving.

At the end of "Turn, Turn, Turn," Coulson says that *S.H.I.E.L.D.*'s plan is to "survive." After its renewal for a second season, *S.H.I.E.L.D.*'s directive is to "evolve." Where afterlife in the Whedonverse had meant sustaining television series in comic books and films, with *S.H.I.E.L.D.*, the concept of afterlife takes new meaning. *S.H.I.E.L.D.*, like its characters, is transformed into something new, what it was "meant to be." However, reflecting the Inhumans' prophecy, season two also reveals what the series always was. In a network era where series exist "on the bubble," in a space between life and death, between renewal and cancellation, *S.H.I.E.L.D.*'s meditations on its future with, despite, and because of convergence come at just the right time.

Notes

1. Derek Johnson, "Cinematic Destiny: Marvel Studios and the Trade Stories of Industrial Convergence," *Cinema Journal* 52, no. 1 (2012): 1.
2. *Ibid.*, 6.
3. "Pilot," *Agents of S.H.I.E.L.D.*, Season 1, Episode 1, written by Joss Whedon, Jed Whedon, and Maurissa Tancharoen, directed by Joss Whedon, ABC, September 24, 2013.
4. "Scars," *Agents of S.H.I.E.L.D.*, Season 2, Episode 20, written by Rafe Judkins and Lauren LeFranc, directed by Bobby Roth, ABC, May 5, 2015.
5. Alex Zalben, "This Week's 'Agents of S.H.I.E.L.D.' Is the Real 'Age of Ultron' Tie-In," *MTV News*, May 5, 2015, http://www.mtv.com/news/2151760/agents-of-shield-scars-preview. An *Inhumans* film was initially given a release date of 2018 before being delayed to 2019, and, in April 2016, Marvel Studios president Kevin Feige reported that the film was being pulled off of the release schedule. Will Robinson, "It's Official: Marvel's *Inhumans* Pulled from Release Schedule," *Entertainment Weekly*, April 22, 2016. In November 2016, Marvel and ABC announced that an *Inhumans* television series was slated to appear on big and small screens, with the first two episodes playing in IMAX theaters for two weeks starting on September 1, 2017, before the series' run on ABC. Brooks Barnes, "Marvel's 'Inhumans' TV Series Will Arrive via Imax Theaters," *The New York Times*, November 14, 2016, https://www.nytimes.com/2016/11/15/business/media/marvels-inhumans-tv-series-will-arrive-via-theaters.html.
6. *Avengers: Age of Ultron*, directed by Joss Whedon (2015; Burbank, CA: Buena Vista Home Entertainment, 2015), DVD.
7. "0-8-4," *Agents of S.H.I.E.L.D.*, Season 1, Episode 2, written by Maurissa Tancharoen, Jed Whedon, and Jeffrey Bell, directed by David Straiton, ABC, October 1, 2013.
8. James N. Gilmore and Matthias Stork, "Introduction: Heroes, Converge!," in *Superhero Synergies: Comic Book Characters Go Digital*, ed. James N. Gilmore and Matthias Stork (Lanham: Rowman & Littlefield, 2014), 1.
9. Henry Jenkins, "Transmedia Storytelling 101," Confessions of an Aca-Fan (blog), March 22, 2007, http://henryjenkins.org/2007/03/transmedia_storytelling_101.html. Jason Mittell draws on this definition to discuss how "transmedia storytelling problematizes the hierarchy between text and paratext," citing *S.H.I.E.L.D.* as an exception to more traditional relationships between core and peripheral texts. Jason Mittell, *Complex TV: The Poetics of Contemporary Television Storytelling* (New York: New York University Press, 2015), 294.
10. Matthias Stork, "Assembling the Avengers: Reframing the Superhero Movie through Marvel's Cinematic Universe," in *Superhero Synergies: Comic Book Characters Go Digital*, ed. James N. Gilmore and Matthias Stork (Lanham: Rowman & Littlefield, 2014), 79. Stork writes, "Marvel presented the cinematic universe as a special event of synergy and convergence within the event-driven, risk-averse sphere of franchise filmmaking. It offered a *new* type of movie cycle that incorporates and adapts the logic of comic production and is designed to update and energize the genre and its commodity value within the market sphere."
11. Jason Mittell, "Narrative Complexity in Contemporary American Television," *The Velvet Light Trap* 58 (2006): 38–39.
12. *Ibid.*, 30–31.
13. Mittell, *Complex TV*, 294–296. Mittell writes, "The rising prevalence of transmedia television alongside the increase in complex seriality has complicated this question of cumulative canon, forcing producers to make difficult choices about how transmedia serial storytelling situates its paratexts in relation to the core television canonical mothership."
14. The issue of canonicity is of particular significance with *S.H.I.E.L.D.*'s resuscitation of Coulson, particularly given Whedon's comments about Coulson's "fate." Whedon says, "A lot of people come back in *The Winter Soldier*. It's a grand Marvel tradition. Bucky was supposed to die. And the Coulson thing was, I think, a little anomalous just because that really came from the television division, which is sort of considered to be its own subsection of the Marvel universe. As far as the fiction of the movies, Coulson is dead"; however, he admits that "it's difficult because you're living in franchise world—not just Marvel, but in most big films—where you can't kill anyone, or anybody significant.... So

my feeling in these situations with Marvel is that if somebody has to be placed on the altar and sacrificed, I'll let you guys decide if they stay there." Dana Schwartz, "Q&A: Joss Whedon on Super Heroes, Killing Characters, and Existing Outside the Pop Culture Mainstream," *Mental Floss*, April 15, 2015, http://mentalfloss.com/article/63120/qa-joss-whedon-super-heroes-killing-characters-and-existing-outside-pop-culture.

While media outlets ran the story that *S.H.I.E.L.D.* is not canon, Whedon's comments suggest something different by highlighting the viewers' roles in making sense of the layered simultaneity of the Marvel Universe.

15. Stacey Abbott, "'Can't Stop the Signal': The Resurrection/Regeneration of *Serenity*," in *Investigating* Firefly *and* Serenity: *Science Fiction on the Frontier*, ed. Rhonda V. Wilcox and Tanya R. Cochran (London: Tauris, 2008), 227.

16. Rhonda V. Wilcox, "Introduction: Much Ado About Whedon," in *Reading Joss Whedon*, ed. Rhonda V. Wilcox, Tanya R. Cochran, Cynthea Masson, and David Lavery (Syracuse: Syracuse University Press, 2014), 1.

17. Abbott, "'Can't Stop the Signal,'" 229.

18. "End of the Beginning," *Agents of S.H.I.E.L.D.*, Season 1, Episode 16, written by Paul Zbyszewski, directed by Bobby Roth, ABC, April 1, 2014.

19. Abbott, "'Can't Stop the Signal,'" 238.

20. "End of the Beginning," *Agents of S.H.I.E.L.D.*; Johnson, "Cinematic Destiny," 21–22. Johnson analyzes how Marvel Studio's "trade narratives" utilize the concept of destiny to legitimate their business practices. Johnson writes that their "self-reflexive appeal to 'destiny' ... suggested that their foray into film production was inevitably predisposed to success, drawing on narrative tropes central to Marvel's core brand identities."

21. "End of the Beginning," *Agents of S.H.I.E.L.D.*

22. *Ibid.*

23. Frank Rose, *The Art of Immersion: How the Digital Generation Is Remaking Hollywood, Madison Avenue, and the Way We Tell Stories* (New York: Norton, 2011), 2–3.

24. *Captain America: The Winter Soldier*, directed by Anthony Russo and Joe Russo (2014; Burbank, CA: Buena Vista Home Entertainment, *2014*), DVD.

25. *Ibid.*; "Pilot," *Agents of S.H.I.E.L.D.*

26. "Turn, Turn, Turn," *Agents of S.H.I.E.L.D.*, Season 1, Episode 17, written by Jed Whedon and Maurissa Tancharoen, directed by Vincent Misiano, ABC, April 8, 2014.

27. *Ibid.*

28. *Ibid.*

29. *Ibid.*

30. In the season one episode "Yes Men," a crossover episode with the Thor narrative, Coulson tells Lady Sif that he wants to be the one to tell Thor that he is alive. However, *Age of Ultron* reflects Whedon's statement that "As far as the fiction of the movies, Coulson is dead," at least for now. "Yes Men," *Agents of S.H.I.E.L.D.*, Season 1, Episode 15, written by Shalisha Francis, directed by John Terlesky, ABC, March 11, 2015.

31. "Turn, Turn, Turn," *Agents of S.H.I.E.L.D.*

32. "Shadows," *Agents of S.H.I.E.L.D.*, Season 2, Episode 1, written by Jed Whedon and Maurissa Tancharoen, directed by Vincent Misiano, ABC, September 23, 2014.

33. "Heavy Is the Head," *Agents of S.H.I.E.L.D.*, Season 2, Episode 2, written by Paul Zbyszewski, directed by Jesse Bochco, ABC, September 30, 2014.

34. "Shadows," *Agents of S.H.I.E.L.D.*

35. "Turn, Turn, Turn," *Agents of S.H.I.E.L.D.*

36. "Shadows," *Agents of S.H.I.E.L.D.*

37. *Ibid.*

38. "The Things We Bury," *Agents of S.H.I.E.L.D.*, Season 2, Episode 8, written by Daniel J. Doyle, directed by Milan Cheylov, ABC, November 18, 2014.

39. *Ibid.*

40. *Ibid.*

41. "Heavy Is the Head," *Agents of S.H.I.E.L.D.*

42. "S.O.S., Part One," *Agents of S.H.I.E.L.D.*, Season 2, Episode 21, written by Jeffrey Bell, directed by Vincent Misiano, ABC, May 12, 2015.

43. "...Ye Who Enter Here," *Agents of S.H.I.E.L.D.*, Season 2, Episode 9, written by Paul Zbyszewski, directed by Bill Gierhart, ABC, December 2, 2014.

44. *Ibid.*

45. "Aftershocks," *Agents of S.H.I.E.L.D.*, Season 2, Episode 11, written by Jed Whedon and Maurissa Tancharoen, directed by Bill Gierhart, ABC, March 3, 2015; "One Door Closes," *Agents of S.H.I.E.L.D.*, Season 2, Episode 15, written by Lauren LeFranc and Rafe Judkins, directed by David Solomon, ABC, March 31, 2015.

46. "Aftershocks," *Agents of S.H.I.E.L.D.*

47. "Scars," *Agents of S.H.I.E.L.D.*

48. "Turn, Turn, Turn," *Agents of S.H.I.E.L.D.*

49. Johnson, "Cinematic Destiny," 3.

50. *Avengers: Age of Ultron.*

51. Michael Curtin and Jane Shattuc, *The American Television Industry* (London: Palgrave Macmillan, 2009), 176.

America Assemble

The Avengers *as* Therapeutic Public Memory

DEREK R. SWEET

In his May 11, 2012, article for *The Guardian* entitled "*The Avengers*: Why Hollywood Is No Longer Afraid to Tackle 9/11," J. Hoberman suggests the horrific events of 9/11 have "finally been superseded by another catastrophe, namely the financial meltdown of September 2008." Hoberman notes the paucity of reviews making a connection between Joss Whedon's *The Avengers*' (2012) climactic battle, a sprawling conflict resulting in spectacular damage for much of Manhattan, and the disturbing real life images replayed relentlessly in the aftermath of the traumatic terrorist attacks. Initially, post–9/11 Hollywood tread lightly through the cultural rubble and avoided any reference to the terrorist attacks: visuals were edited, releases delayed. Over the course of the ensuing months and years however, the Hollywood machine churned out a variety of treatments pertaining to war in a general sense (e.g., *Black Hawk Down* [2001] and *War of the Worlds* [2005]) and 9/11 in a specific sense (*United 93* [2006], *World Trade Center* [2006]). Released ten plus years after the attacks, Hoberman dismisses *The Avengers* as fun, but politically irrelevant. As Martin Fradley observed of Hoberman's remarks, "*The Avengers* invokes the geopolitical primal scene of 9/11 with a wholesale absence of ethical, social, or political resonance."[1] In other words, visions of 9/11 no longer haunt the collective mind of the cultural imaginary. Instead, more recent disasters command the attention of the American psyche. Although he characterizes it as "a bit of a stretch," Hoberman suggests one might read the heroic actions of the assembled Avengers as an economic allegory for President Obama's (Nick Fury's) efforts to stop the Great Recession from inflicting long-term damage on the global economy.

Despite Hoberman's inability to track down writers connecting 9/11 and

The Avengers, there are those who do exactly that. In his May 4, 2012, *New Yorker* blog post, Richard Brody describes *The Avengers* as a "mythopolitical" superhero spectacle that manages to present a coherent "post–9/11 fantasy … against the backdrop of unpopular foreign wars." Building on Brody's brief observation, my reading of the film positions *The Avengers* as a kind of therapeutic public memory that not only conjures the perceived social and political failures surrounding 9/11 but also offers an opportunity to rehabilitate those failures. In essence, *The Avengers* criticizes the American intelligence apparatus, armed forces, and national fortitude as ill equipped to conduct contemporary counterterrorism efforts. At the same time, Whedon's allegorical retelling of the 9/11 attacks offers a cultural restorative revolving around the familiar theme of redemptive violence.

Popular Texts, Cultural Trauma and Therapeutic Rhetoric

Sixteen years after the 9/11 terrorist attacks, few question the long-lived cultural trauma experienced by Americans. After a decade of color-coded Homeland Security Advisory System alerts, governmental calls to maintain a terrorism preparedness kit, sustained anti-terrorism combat operations, and public service announcements asking people to report suspicious activities—constant reminders of both the horrific events of 9/11 proper and the likelihood of additional terrorist attacks—it should come as no surprise that the trauma experienced by Americans continues to reverberate throughout the national consciousness. Not unlike the individual trauma experienced by the victim of a rape, mugging, or accident, national or cultural trauma involves psychological distress at a broader, community level. As Arthur Neal explains, "national trauma involves sufficient damage to the social system that discourse throughout the nation is directed toward the repair work that needs to be done."[2] Frequently deemed "The Day Everything Changed," a day the American public will "Never Forget," 9/11 left an entire national community wounded and shaken, never quite capable of moving beyond the traumatic event. The emotional impact of 9/11 ripples through the national consciousness and, as evidenced by diminished privacy rights, extraordinary rendition, enhanced interrogations, increased security measures, tighter immigration-screening, and debates over the construction of Muslim community centers, continues to influence public policy and private lives. The public discourses addressing these matters of public consequence shift an understanding of cultural trauma and public memory into the realm of rhetoric.

If rhetoric is, as Kendall Phillips attests, "an art of crafting public sentiment" by way of any number of communicative texts—e.g., spoken and written word, art, film, television—mediated texts emerge as important voices in the cultural process of making sense of, and responding to, traumatic public memories.[3] Highlighting rhetoric as an important means of negotiating public memory suggests memories of culturally significant events are sites of deliberative struggle and community dialogues. Important for this project is the way in which popular culture functions as a legitimate voice in such public negotiations. As Ron Eyerman explains in his exploration of slavery and the long lasting impact of cultural trauma, popular culture representations—films, television, and comic books—contribute to the way a community makes sense of a traumatic event. He writes, "a national trauma must be understood, explained, and made coherent through public reflection and discourse."[4]

Eyerman is not the only author who argues media representations play a part in public discourses concerning national trauma. In his article examining Joss Whedon's *Firefly* (2002) as a response to the significant cultural trauma stemming from September 11, Matthew Hill suggests Americans experienced a "loss of faith when confronting the monumental failures in security, intelligence, and preparedness that caused, failed to prevent, or exacerbated the cultural traumas of this decade: the September 11 attacks, the ill-starred and ill-planned aftermath of the war in Iraq, and Hurricane Katrina."[5] Rather than relying on the well-worn depiction of redemptive violence, a cultural myth Whedon embraces in *The Avengers*, *Firefly* depicts a cast of characters more concerned with survival than revenge. Similarly, J.M. Tyree identifies *Batman Begins* (2005) and *The Dark Knight* (2008) as "fairly transparent fables of counter-terrorism."[6] Replete with terrorist attacks, enhanced interrogation, and unlawful wireless phone tapping, Christopher Nolan's superheroic portrayal of the Caped Crusader offers a moral to the story reverberating with the War on Terror justifications of the Bush administration. In an effort to ensure public safety and bring villains to justice, there are times when a hero may be required to take villainous actions.

In reading these texts in ways that uncover mediated solutions to perceived socio-political problems (e.g., terrorism and the war on terror) that result in communal anxiety, authors like Hill and Tyree illuminate the therapeutic potential thereof. Making the allegorical references less ambiguous, such texts engage the public imaginary by simultaneously recalling past traumatic events while also offering ways to reconceptualize these traumatic memories. This representation is therapeutic in that characters, even superheroes, work through problems similar to those of the viewing audience. Given this mediated dialogue between film and viewer, "The text involves the audience in a psychological situation where there is a problem, and through the characters formulates psychological responses and resolutions to the problem."[7] Put simply, onscreen therapeutic rhetorics provide audience members an ameliorative invitation to reconstitute a public memory in way that assuages cultural anxieties.

The Avengers *and Cultural Trauma*

The similarities between 9/11 and Whedon's superhero narrative are too obvious to ignore. Early in the film Loki reveals his plan to recraft the earth as a world free from the burdens of "freedom." "Freedom is life's great lie," he explains. Loki's denouncement of freedom situates him within public conversations attempting to make sense of 9/11 and the rise of al-Qaeda and similar terrorist groups. For instance, when President Bush addressed a joint session of Congress on September 20, 2001, he argued terrorists targeted the United States because, "They hate our freedoms: our freedom of religion, our freedom of speech, our freedom to vote and assemble and disagree with each other." *The Avengers* conjures 9/11 visually as well. From repeated long shots of smoke rising from the Manhattan skyline, to first responders making their way through devastated metropolitan canyons, to chaotic images of panicked bystanders fleeing the destruction, Whedon's film references the images made so familiar during the almost non-stop 9/11 media coverage. As if these general references might not be powerful enough, Whedon also incorporates several other moments referencing 9/11 directly. Shots of Stark Tower emanating an energy beam used to open a portal for the invading alien horde bear a striking resemblance to the Towers of Light used to commemorate the Twin Towers annually. More disturbing is Whedon's reconceptualization of the terrifying "Falling Man" photograph as Tony Stark plummets from his hubristic monument to American exceptionalism.[8] And one can hardly fail to notice a central plot point of the film revolves around the attempted skyjacking of the S.H.I.E.L.D. Helicarrier, an obvious nod to the hijacked 9/11 airliners.

As suggested earlier, anxieties associated with 9/11 continue to reverberate throughout the cultural imaginary. While the collective sense of fury, shock, and loss fades with the passing of time, the nation still winces from reports of terror attacks around the globe and national rage has been replaced by a slow, simmering anger that reminds citizens to "Never Forget." As the United States enters its sixteenth year of the never-ending war on terror, the idea that "everything changed" on September 11, 2001, appears to hold true. *The Avengers* portrays the nation's continuing discomfort and uneasiness deftly. Captain America, who the film reminds us is literally a man out of time, struggles to reconcile his memories of a previous life with the radically changed world in which he is forced to live. No matter how much he might long for the good old days, Steve Rogers must negotiate the sometimes harsh realities of his present moment.

Similarly, Nick Fury represents the intense feelings of powerlessness experienced by the everyperson in the wake of 9/11. Not unlike the citizens of the U.S. and their lack of agency in facing global terror—short of military service, most citizens find themselves in the oft frustrating place of relying on the government for protection—Nick Fury must rely on others to ensure the nation's safety. Black Widow, on the other hand, manifests the insecurities experienced when one discovers a friend is now an enemy. Hawkeye's "brainwashing" at the hands of a radical religious extremist (Loki) and Black Widow's distress over this fact depicts a nation coming to the uncomfortable realization that a citizen might turn against her or his own people (e.g., John Walker Lindh, aka the American Taliban). Black Widow also demonstrates, particularly in her confrontation with the Hulk, how irrational fear and rage might cause significant harm to the nation. Like the Muslim American or peace protestor, Black Widow witnesses the damage resulting from misplaced anger and unfocused rage.

While representations of cultural anxieties evoke powerful emotional memories, and arrest contemporary states of mind, the film also identifies several material failures contributing to 9/11. The two most prominent failures pertain to the inadequacies of the U.S. intelligence apparatus and the U.S. military's lack of preparedness to fight an evasive, highly mobile enemy. In the opening minutes of the film, the audience's attention is directed toward Hawkeye. As a S.H.I.E.L.D. operative and director of security for the mysterious Tesseract project, Hawkeye functions as an allegorical representation for the inability of intelligence agencies to see or hear unfolding terrorist plots from afar, typically from the distance of an orbiting satellite or digital database. As Rand Lewis makes clear in his analysis of U.S. intelligence practices, the vast majority of intelligence data comes from signal intelligence (e.g., intercepted email or phone calls) and image intelligence (photographs and films from surveillance aircraft and satellites). With the advent and continued development of sophisticated surveillance technologies, human intelligence—traditional spy work conducted by covert operatives—assumed a lesser priority. In the late 70s and early 80s, suggests Lewis, the Central Intelligence Agency turned to "Science and technology ... in the effort to gather information and clandestine activities decreased...."[9]

Hawkeye, a loner who presumably doesn't play well with others (he doesn't appear to interact with the people he's watching and protecting), remains in his perch and fails to take note of the signal intelligence pointing toward a pending attack. His failure to recognize developing danger makes an allegorical nod toward pre 9/11 intelligence agencies' inability to work together and coordinate preemptive action. Rather than a collaborative approach to gathering data, *The Avengers* points out the failures arising from a lack of interagency cooperation. Without proper warning from those monitoring the Tesseract project, S.H.I.E.L.D. forces—not unlike those of the FBI, CIA, NSA, and local law enforcement—find themselves woefully unprepared to thwart Loki's opening salvo.

Caught flat footed and unable to marshal its considerable forces, the U.S. military responded slowly to 9/11 attacks. Built more to fight massive land wars on the Cold War battlefields of Eastern Europe and the Korean peninsula, the U.S. military took several weeks to move troops into Afghanistan, a country that would become synonymous with the War on Terror's operational codename: Enduring Freedom. After an extended air campaign and ground invasion, operations that did result in the expulsion of the Taliban regime, U.S. forces were unable to capture Osama Bin Laden and other members of al-Qaeda as they slipped into the rugged, mountainous borderlands between Afghanistan and Pakistan. While U.S. military boots on the ground operations kept the Taliban from regaining governmental control, they could not stop Taliban and al-Qaeda fighters from continuing to harass various tribal regions and villages. Not unlike Captain America, a character who finds himself physically out of time and mentally handcuffed by World War II black and white idealism, the U.S. military found itself fighting an enemy who did not follow the same rules of engagement. Nowhere is this more apparent than in Captain America's initial encounter with Loki. Facing a foe for whom he isn't prepared, an outclassed Captain America represents the U.S. military's lack of "strategic mobility," or the ability to deploy "the right forces to the proper place in space and time to allow combatant commanders to deter, de-escalate, or decisively defeat an adversary."[10] Only when Iron Man streaks into the skirmish, a moment that calls to mind the nighttime Tomahawk cruise missile launches so often broadcast by news media, does the tide of the battle turn.

The Avengers also offers a critique of American fortitude: the nation's physical, emotional, and spiritual ability to face adversity courageously and justly. The Hulk's immense rage and penchant for mass destruction stands as an analog for the misdirected anger of the post–9/11 American citizenry. Volatile, unstoppable, and undisciplined, the Hulk takes out his anger on the nearest target. As the scene in the Helicarrier illustrates, the point of a terrorist attack is to use the citizenry's own emotions against themselves. Just as the Hulk lays waste to the interior of the Helicarrier and attempts to destroy two allies in the process, the American people's zest for vengeance impacted the nation's social structure. The recurring animosity between Hulk and Thor, for example, emphasizes the post–9/11 tensions between a desire for violent, unrestrained retribution and a spiritual ethos grounded in decency and brotherly love as evidenced by Thor and his attempt to bring Loki, his brother, back to Asgard peacefully. In his editorial appearing in the July 30, 2010, issue of *The Christian Science Monitor*, Thomas W. Young—a flight engineer for the West Virginia Air National Guard—writes of his positive experiences with Bangladeshis and cautions Americans to avoid "sloppy thinking."[11] He explains, "In the post–9/11 world, it's way too easy to get sloppy in our thinking and extend our anger over terrorism to Muslims in general."[12] Such uncritical discernment extended beyond the distrust and mistreatment of Muslims and manifested in other forms. In the name of righteous indignation, citizens channeled their fear, rage, helplessness, and desire for vengeance into a number of questionable behaviors and practices. As Morgan, Wisneski, and Skitka detail, 9/11's deep psychological resonance manifested in a variety of ways: curtailed civil liberties, political, ethnic and religious intolerance, and overwhelming support for violent retribution. The increase in these attitudes, argue the three authors, contributed to a national atmosphere conducive to a rise in profiling, reduced privacy, increased hate crimes, and support for the misguided Iraq war.[13]

The Avengers *and Therapeutic Public Memory*

After a decade of war, intelligence operations, and targeted killings via drone strikes, it has become apparent that a "war on terror" is unwinnable. Rather than trying to stomp out an ideology embraced by extremists, containment and protection has emerged as the favored political policy. *The Avengers'* articulation of anxieties and failures arising post–9/11 reinforces a new counterterrorism status quo: "the inability to rely upon traditional definitions of order, safety, and protection has become ever more apparent."[14] With the selfless death of S.H.I.E.L.D. agent Phil Coulson, a non-superheroic character who represents the readiness, conviction, and sacrifice necessary to confront extremism, the film turns away from reiterating the failures associated with post–9/11 policy and shifts to the work of rehabilitating the public consciousness. Coulson's death at the hands of Loki calls the Avengers, as well as the average viewer, to recognize the need to move beyond business-as-usual responses to radical extremism. Coulson makes this clear during his deathbed conversation with Nick Fury. Lamenting the inability of the Avengers to come together and face the threat posed by Loki, Coulson positions his own death as a necessary catalyst when he states, "It's okay, boss. This was never gonna work if they didn't have something ..." Although Coulson dies before completing his final sentence the implication is clear: the Avengers, the American people, need a banner around which to rally.

Responding to the clarion sounded by Coulson's sacrifice, the disparate individuals who comprise the Avengers—each with her or his unique skill set—come together to offer a reconceptualized public memory, a symbolic coming together of U.S. intelligence, armed forces, and fortitude. At this point in the film, the Avengers begin the work of reconfiguring public consciousness and reworking painful public memories into a hopeful vision wherein the intelligence community, military, and national fortitude work toward singular purpose. Hawkeye's redemptive story arc provides an excellent example of this transformation. At the beginning of the film, Hawkeye symbolized the inability of the intelligence community to work collaboratively, coordinate extensive intelligence gathering assets, and analyze potential threats. During the climactic battle for New York, Hawkeye engages in all of these activities simultaneously providing substantive guidance and support for his colleagues. He uses his unique vantage point (on top of a building rather than monitoring cell phone signals and satellite imagery) to analyze enemy movements and direct resources, both air and ground, to conflict hot spots. He provides Iron Man with valuable intelligence about enemy weaknesses and brings two different groups of endangered civilians to the attention of Captain America and Black Widow. Rather than staying aloof or confronting threats directly, Hawkeye utilizes a skill set that plays to his strengths: observation, analysis, and surgical strikes. His actions parallel what an August 30, 2013, *Voice of America* article titled "US CIA Role Escalates Since 2001 Terrorist Attacks," describes as a post–9/11 CIA focused on "providing direct support to military operations and carrying out operations of its own, including drone strikes...." As a metaphor for CIA capabilities, Hawkeye disrupts Chitauri transportation by using an arrow to shoot a vehicle out from under one attacker and attempts to eliminate enemy leadership by targeting Loki.

This reading of *The Avengers* would be remiss if it did not also acknowledge the Black Widow as representative of the intelligence community's resurgent human intelligence apparatus.[15] To some degree, Natasha Romanoff represents Vice President Dick Cheney's call to "spend time in the shadows of the intelligence world."[16] Black Widow admits to a shadowy past with "red in my ledger," acknowledges a "very specific skill set," and doesn't object when Loki describes her as someone willing to "lie and kill in the service of liars and killers." She traverses the shadows, utilizing strategic skullduggery to extract valuable intelligence from her targets and performing targeted killings—assassination—when elimination proves more advantageous than information. Displaying the ability to coax information from a hostile prisoner or captor alike—an ability she displays while working undercover early in the film—she dupes Loki into revealing his plan to unleash the Hulk against the Avengers. Near the conclusion of the film, her ability to gather information in the field provides the means to seal the interdimensional portal and disable the invading army.

In addition to the redemption of the intelligence community, *The Avengers* also grants the U.S. military with a much needed overhaul. Echoing real world shifts in military combat operations, Iron Man and Captain America (loose metaphors for the Air Force and Army) coordinate their efforts with the intelligence community. Selecting targets through minute-by-minute communication with S.H.I.E.L.D. and Hawkeye, Iron Man represents the rapid deployment of high tech weapons systems and high yield payloads. Much like a drone or laser guided smart bomb, Iron Man attempts to soften the enemies' defenses and draw attention away from the efforts of ground troops. The epitome of the military's 21st century commitment to adaptation, innovation, and ingenuity, Iron Man adjusts his technological tactics to fit a rapidly evolving battlefield situation. While Iron Man represents the technological versatility of counterterrorism efforts, Captain America calls to mind the tactical and operational adaptability required of both military leadership and rank and file soldiers. All branches of the U.S. military, asserts Fred Kaplan in his September 2, 2011, piece for Slate.com titled "The Post-9/11 Military," emphasize a fighting force in "which soldiers are trained and equipped to pivot on a dime from head-on combat to stability operations to counterinsurgency." Just as a Marine in Afghanistan might find herself or himself engaging Taliban insurgents one moment and working with local tribal leaders the next, Captain America and the Avengers also find themselves required to display a heightened degree of flexibility. Captain America fights insurgents on the street, organizes noncombatant evacuations with local law enforcement, and extracts civilians from a hostage situation. The lesson presented in *The Avengers* is clear: an effective counterterrorism operation benefits from coordinated action between the intelligence community and a flexible, mobile fighting force.

Just as *The Avengers* offers a refashioned intelligence community and military, the film also reenvisions American fortitude. In the weeks and months following 9/11, the Bush administration let the global community know "an active, changed America ... would unleash the full might of its military" in an effort to eliminate the al-Qaeda threat.[17] In a similar sense, Tony Stark's penthouse discussion with Loki warns the demigod that the Avengers intend to unleash an army of their own: the Hulk. Traditionally, the Hulk has been interpreted as a contemporary Jekyll and Hyde representation of societal tensions between the rapid, awe-inspiring scientific discoveries of the 20th century and the fear that humanity might not possess the ethical maturity to use such advances wisely. While such a tension permeates any portrayal of the Hulk, *The Avengers* depiction resonates more with the "primal rage, pent-up fury, egotism, and potential for destructive mayhem" of the everyperson than with a critique of the relationship between the scientific community and the military industrial complex.[18]

In the moments before the Battle for Manhattan commences in earnest, Banner turns to his teammates and apologizes for the destruction he caused during a loss of control. A repentant and focused Banner channels his anger and unleashes the Hulk's fury on the approaching invaders. Rather than lashing out wildly and indiscriminately, the Hulk focuses his smashing on legitimate threats. The Hulk's focus on enemy combatants and eventual thrashing of fanatical religious leadership in the form of Loki, a Norse god, signifies the public's efforts to reign in unrestrained rage and focus their righteous indignation toward Islamic extremists rather than Islam in general. According to the Federal Bureau of Investigation's *Uniform Crime Reports*, hate crimes against Muslims spiked by 1600 percent immediately following 9/11. Within weeks, however, crimes against Muslims began a steep corrective trend downward.[19] Reinforcing this theme, Thor—by virtue of his identity as a demigod—represents the strength of a dignified, deeply spiritual community and the need to employ violence justly. He also connotes religious freedom and equality, particularly in his confrontational conversation with Loki. When Loki shares he intends to rule the human race as their superior, Thor chastises his brother for missing the "truth of ruling." Thor's verbal rebuke, as well as his actions throughout the film, posits leadership founded on principles of self-lessness, egalitarianism, and service to others.

America Assemble!

From the outset of his article on the film, Ensley Guffey positions *The Avengers* as a war movie. He writes, "*The Avengers* is not only a war film but a deliberately old-fashioned war film."[20] As this reading of the film advances, Whedon's film is envisioned as a war on terror movie. This particular war, however, is something of an alternative history. With its clear visual parallels, coupled with the resonant on screen anxieties, *The Avengers* transports viewers back to 9/11 and offers a historical revisioning wherein the heroes overcome their respective deficits, deficits contributing to the inability to prevent the terrorist attacks as well as complicating the subsequent national response, and win the day. The film encourages viewers to revisit the cultural trauma inflicted on September 11, 2001, to meditate on the way the actions of the Avengers "reflect and influence the hopes and fears of the average American during a given historical era," and calls to mind the failures of the intelligence community, armed forces, and national fortitude.[21] The failures of the individuals who eventually come together and form the Avengers compel audience members to relive the anxieties frequently experienced post–9/11. Unable to rely on a government to keep them safe and secure, painfully aware of their own inability to direct anger and rage constructively, audiences see the shortcomings of the nation laid bare.

The painful reexamination of past lapses, however, is a necessary narrative move setting up the redemptive arc presented during the film's latter half. In order to dispel the anxieties present in the cultural imaginary, the film must first call forth the still lurking emotional demons. Richard Slotkin describes this privation, conversion, and reclamation narrative as the core of the American revenge fantasy, a fantasy he establishes as essential to the nation's mythology. He asserts, "the Myth represented the redemption of American spirit or fortune as something to be achieved by playing through a scenario of separation, temporary regression to a more primitive or 'natural' state, and regeneration through violence."[22] Through the various depictions of a rehabilitated intelligence apparatus, a retooled military, and a redirected sense of national fortitude, *The Avengers* emerges as a therapeutic text offering a psychological curative for 9/11. The heroes needed to repel another terrorist attack—the well trained intelligence gatherer and analyst, the mobile and adaptable soldier, the purposeful citizen—stand tall in the Battle of Manhattan and the cultural consciousness.

NOTES

1. Martin Fradley, "What Do You Believe In? Film Scholarship and the Cultural Politics of the Dark Knight Franchise," *Film Quarterly* 66, no. 3 (Spring 2013): 15–16.

2. Arthur G. Neal, *National Trauma and Collective Memory: Major Events in the American Century* (New York: M.E. Sharpe, Inc., 1998), 5.

3. Kendall Phillips, "The Failure of Memory: Reflections on Rhetoric and Public Remembrance," *Western Journal of Communication* 74, no. 2 (2010): 218.

4. Ron Eyerman, *Cultural Trauma* (New York: Cambridge University Press, 2002), 2.

5. Matthew B. Hill, "'I Am a Leaf on the Wind': Cultural Trauma and Mobility in Joss Whedon's Firefly," *Extrapolation* 50, no. 3 (2009): 490–491.

6. J.M. Tyree, "American Heroes," *Film Quarterly* 62, no. 3 (Spring 2009): 32.

7. David Payne, "The Wizard of Oz: Therapeutic Rhetoric in a Contemporary Media Ritual," *Quarterly Journal of Speech* 75, no. 1 (1989): 28.

8. The picture dubbed "The Falling Man" depicts a man plunging to his death from the upper floors of the World Trade Center. Associated Press photographer Richard Drew is credited with capturing the disturbing image.

9. Rand C. Lewis, "Espionage and the War on Terrorism: Investigating U.S. Efforts," *Brown Journal of World Affairs* 11, no. 1 (Fall 2004): 178.

10. Kenneth E. Hickens, "Strategic Mobility," *Army Sustainment* 42, no. 2 (March-April 2010), accessed June 7, 2015, http://www.alu.army.mil/alog/issues/MarApr10/spectrum_strategy_mobility.html.

11. Thomas W. Young, "War on terror's other cost: undeserved anger at all Muslims," *The Christian Science Monitor*, July 30, 2010, accessed January 30, 2017, http://www.csmonitor.com/Commentary/Opinion/2010/0730/War-on-terror-s-other-cost-undeserved-anger-at-all-Muslims.

12. *Ibid.*

13. G. Scott Morgan, Daniel C. Wisneski, and Linda J. Skitka, "The Expulsion from Disneyland: The Social Psychological Impact of 9/11," *American Psychologist* 66, no. 6 (September 2011): 447–454.

14. Mathias Nilges, "The Aesthetics of Destruction: Contemporary U.S. Cinema and TV Culture," in *Reframing 9/11: Film, Popular Culture and the War on Terror*, ed. Jeff Birkenstein, Anna Froula, and Karen Randell (New York: Continuum International Publishing, 2010): 26.

15. As Brian Bennet writes in a November 17, 2014, article for the *Los Angeles Times* titled "CIA Intelligence Gap Hinders Counter-terrorism efforts in Syria, Iraq," the CIA and Pentagon expanded their spying capabilities significantly after the invasions of Afghanistan and Iraq. Most of these intelligence operations were mothballed when U.S. combat troops exited the respective countries.

16. Dick Cheney, "The Vice President Appears on *Meet the Press* with Tim Russert," President George W. Bush White House Archives, September 16, 2001, accessed August 20, 2013, http://georgewbush-whitehouse. archives.gov/vicepresident/news-speeches/speeches/vp20010916.html.

17. Joshua A. Geltzer, *U.S. Counter-Terrorism Strategy and al-Qaeda: Signaling and the Terrorist World-view* (London: Routledge, 2010), 110.

18. Robin J. Dugall, "Running From or Embracing the Truth Inside You? Bruce Banner and the Hulk as a Paradigm for the Inner Self," in *The Gospel According to Superheroes: Religion and Popular Culture*, ed. B.J. Oropeza (New York, Peter Lang Publishing, Inc., 2005): 147.

19. According to FBI annual hate crime statistics, hate crime incidents against Muslims peaked in 2001 (481 reported incidents); 2013, the last year for which data is available, registered 135 reported incidents. Statistics available at the FBI: Federal Bureau of Investigation Hate Crime statistics site, accessed June 5, 2015, http://www.fbi.gov/about-us/cjis/ucr/hate-crime.

20. Ensley F. Guffey, "Joss Whedon Throws His Mighty Shield: *Marvel's The Avengers* as a War Movie," in *Reading Joss Whedon*, ed. Rhonda V. Wilcox, Tanya R. Cochran, Cynthea Masson, and David Lavery (New York, Syracuse University Press, 2014): 292.

21. Marc DiPaolo, *War, Politics, and Superheroes: Ethics and Propaganda in Comics and Film* (Jefferson, NC: McFarland, 2011), 3.

22. Richard Slotkin, *Gunfighter Nation: The Myth of the Frontier in Twentieth Century America* (New York: Macmillan, 1992), 12.

"Your ancestors called it magic"

Building Coherence in the MCU Through Continuity with the Past

WILLIAM L. SVITAVSKY

In the pilot episode of *Agents of S.H.I.E.L.D.* (2013–), Deputy Director Maria Hill (making a guest appearance after being established in the Marvel movies) discusses the agency's important role:

> Everything's changing. A little while ago, most people went to bed thinking that the craziest thing in the world was a billionaire in a flying metal suit. Then aliens invade New York then were beaten back by, among others, a giant green monster, a costumed hero from the 40's, and a god…. The battle of New York was the end of the world. This—now—is the new world. People are different. They have access to tech, to formula, secrets they're not ready for.

The Marvel Cinematic Universe demands of viewers something they have rarely encountered with other movies—to accept not just one fantastic premise, but rather a number of seemingly unconnected premises that range from military hardware fantasies to Norse myth. Film scholars, filmmakers, and audiences often discuss the "willing suspension of disbelief," holding that "realism" is not necessary so long as a fiction is internally consistent.[1] In the shared universe of the Marvel films, where problems might be solved with brilliant engineering, with a magic hammer, or with the assistance of a galactic police force, consistency seems rather low, and yet the coherence of the universe is one of the major selling points of each movie. The feeling of consistency is achieved in large part through coherence with the past. It is a revised past, resembling real-world history but fictionalized and made fantastic, and altered even from the history of the Marvel Comics universe, itself prone to

76

"retcon" but studied and loved by comics fans. It is an imperfect past, but it holds meaning and promises perfectibility.

Early screen adaptations of superhero stories paid relatively little attention to internal logic within the individual work, let alone consistency with other works. Serials such as *The Adventures of Captain Marvel* (1941) and *Batman* (1943), live action TV shows such as *The Adventures of Superman* (1952–58) and *The Amazing Spider-Man* (1977–79), and numerous animated series freely mixed super-science and magic, took liberties with character premises, abilities, and motivations, and generally targeted young or unsophisticated audiences. The *Batman* television series (1966–1968) appealed to older, hipper viewers by highlighting the absurdities of the superhero genre with the exaggerated theatricality of camp. It was in this context that the modern superhero movie emerged.

Richard Donner's *Superman: The Movie* (1978) was the first film to play a hero relatively straight for a general audience. Its science fictional approach, emphasizing Superman's extraterrestrial origin and Lex Luthor's science (mostly restrained to the level of stolen atomic weapons), fit easily into the post–*Star Wars* era. The producers, less daring than Donner, insisted on a campy presentation of Luthor; but with lead actor Christopher Reeve, Donner made Superman a dignified, sympathetic, contemporary hero. The emphasis on science fiction persisted through the film's sequels, which featured more Kryptonians, a super-computer, and an evil clone of Superman even as the tone of the series regressed to campiness. Tim Burton's *Batman* (1989) and its sequels followed a similar pattern, starting with an initial tight premise of well-equipped vigilantism and a relatively plausible villain, with threats becoming more fantastic (mind control and freeze rays) as the series grew campier.

These patterns continued in the movie adaptations of Marvel characters that preceded the Marvel Cinematic Universe. Marvel characters first got the big-budget movie treatment starting in Bryan Singer's *X-Men* (2000). This film and its sequels stuck tightly to the central premise of superpowered mutants, avoiding the aliens, robots, magic, and other wide-ranging superhero trappings that figured significantly into the X-Men's comic book adventures. Even the robotic Sentinels and the complications of altered timelines—prominent recurring challenges in the comics—don't appear until *X-Men: Days of Future Past* (2014), well after the Marvel Studios movies had changed expectations of what superhero movie audiences would accept. Arguably, the tightly defined premise contributed to the poor reception of the third X-Men movie, *The Last Stand* (2006); the much revered "Dark Phoenix Saga"—which played out in the comics as an interstellar conflict with cosmic consequences—was drastically reduced in scope and drama in this film, leaving it virtually a subplot in yet another conflict with Magneto.

As the series has continued through the *Wolverine* movies and the 2011, 2014 and 2016 prequels, the films have lost consistency with contradictory depictions of characters and irreconcilable timelines. *Spider-Man* (2002) likewise started with a relatively tight premise of super-science and radiation-based transformation (going so far as to have Spider-Man's webs be a part of his mutation rather than a gadget he invented, creating controversy among comics fans), but *Spider-Man 3* (2007) lost coherence when it introduced an alien costume with minimal explanation while cramming in too many new characters and subplots.

In short, prior to the MCU movies, superhero films had difficulty expanding the scope of the setting beyond the initial story. Internet commenters have remarked upon this as a "third movie syndrome" where series creators, in attempting to raise the stakes while repeating the preceding films' premises, inevitably ended up with a third film that was "totally excessive and incoherent."[2] *The Avengers* (2012), which united the preceding MCU series before any of them had reached a third installment, succeeded dramatically and commercially because the MCU had built a universe big enough to grow the story. The Marvel Cinematic Universe has followed the pattern laid by Marvel Comics in the 1960s, where characters from one series frequently showed up in another. This simultaneously promoted sales, as readers of one Marvel series were introduced to others which might capture their interest, and built a rich setting where heroes could interact, face off against villains who'd been introduced in other series, or otherwise face situations established in a growing, elaborate setting: the Marvel Universe.

The success of the Marvel Studios movies has clearly interested other studios in the commercial advantages of a shared universe; Warner Bros. has launched interconnecting movies featuring the DC Comics characters; Sony considered a Robin Hood cinematic universe and aspired to build a universe of *Spider-Man* characters; Universal is attempting to build a cinematic universe featuring their classic horror monsters (whose original films were arguably the first cinematic universe); a host of *Star Wars* films is on the way. The commercial success of a shared universe may depend upon the successful use of its narrative possibilities. In interviews about Marvel Comics, Stan Lee has made little distinction between continuity as marketing strategy and continuity as storytelling: "I felt that having the characters meet each other and get involved in each other's stories made the whole thing realistic."[3]

The perception of realism is also valued by filmmakers and audiences, perhaps especially so in a genre which centers on extraordinary phenomena and unlikely human behavior. In discussion of fantastic stories, Samuel Taylor Coleridge's notion of the "willing suspension of disbelief" is frequently invoked.[4] The phrase is from his *Biographia Literaria*: "In this idea originated the plan of the 'Lyrical Ballads'; in which it was agreed, that my endeavours should be directed to persons and characters supernatural, or at least romantic, yet so as to transfer from our inward nature a human interest and a semblance of truth sufficient to procure for these shadows of imagination that willing suspension of disbelief for the moment, which constitutes poetic faith."[5] He elaborates the concept further in another chapter: "That illusion, contra-distinguished from delusion, that negative faith, which simply permits the images presented to work by their own force, without either denial or affirmation of their real existence by the judgment."[6]

The method most frequently discussed for attaining this suspension is internal consistency, an idea popularized by J.R.R. Tolkien who described art as "giving to ideal creations the inner consistency of reality."[7] Richard J. Gerrig argues that believing stories comes effortlessly to human beings, so that the willing suspension of disbelief is better described as absence of the "willing construction of disbelief"; he views the experience of narrative as both a sense of transportation to another place and a performance of the reader resembling that of an actor.[8] Andrew McGonigal and Ben Caplan debate the theory of fictional truth in serial fiction, McGonigal takes a relativist stance that the truth value of an assertion in a serial depends on which other episodes are salient.[9] Caplan contends that truth can be determined by context, but that context changes over time.[10] Anthony J. Ferri reviews application of willing suspension of disbelief in films in relation to a wide range of audience reception theory from psychology and literary scholarship as well as film theory, including (among other concepts) imaginative involvement shaped by framing, the audience experience of transportation to another place, audiences' development of identity and ego, narrative as a process of anticipating what might happen, and states of mindlessness and mindfulness.[11]

Rick Busselle and Helena Bilandzic offer a complex model of narrative engagement that seems particularly useful in considering the Marvel Cinematic Universe.[12] They distinguish external realism, which is rooted in similarity to the actual world, from narrative realism, which requires plausibility and coherence within the narrative. Readers' first approximation of the story world assumes that it works like the actual world, but as the story world deviates from real life, the audience must modify its understanding of the world's logic.[13] Experience of a narrative is engaging when the reader (or viewer) can assemble coherent mental models of setting, events, characters and their relationships, and can hypothesize explanations and anticipate incoming information. In some respects, the shared universe of the MCU would seem destined to fail in this engagement; the logic of the first two Iron Man films could neither explain nor anticipate the alien invasion in *The Avengers;* the Norse epic of *Thor* (2011) is literally a world removed from the gritty noir of *Daredevil* (2015–). But the "situation model" which Busselle and Bilandzic posit as the primary mental model in story comprehension "refers back-wards."[14]

A coherent past is assembled in the present, but that past allows us to anticipate the future. In the MCU, a coherent past is vitally important. Howard Stark, the father of Tony (Iron Man) Stark, first appeared posthumously in newspaper clippings in *Iron Man* (2008), then in old film footage in *Iron Man 2* (2010), and has since reappeared in *Captain America* (2011) (set primarily during World War II), in the *Agent Carter* (2013) "one-shot" short feature and the *Agent Carter* (2015–2016) television series (both in a post-war setting), in a 1980s sequence in *Ant-Man* (2016), and in a flashback to his death in 1991 in *Captain America: Civil War* (2016); he has been played by two different actors, each repeatedly, depending on his age at the time. Peggy Carter, Captain America's romantic interest in his first film, has been the central heroine in the *Agent Carter* one-shot and television series, appeared as an elderly woman in *Captain America: The Winter Soldier* (2014) (a similar scene was filmed but cut from *The Avengers*), in flashbacks in *Agents of S.H.I.E.L.D.* (2013–), in a dream sequence in *Avengers: Age of Ultron* (2015), again with Howard Stark in *Ant-Man's* 1980s sequence, and her funeral was shown in *Captain America: Civil War*.

These characters have been central to an increasingly detailed history preceding the present-day MCU movies, detailing the establishment of S.H.I.E.L.D. and the growing awareness of super-humans; additional characters including the "Howling Commandos" and Arnim Zola have also recurred in storylines spanning decades. *Ant-Man* even established the entire career of Hank Pym as the first hero by that name taking place in the MCU's past. Busselle and Bilandzic assert, "Whether a lack of external realism leads to a disruption of narrative processing should depend in part on how much the story explains deviations from the real world."[15] The MCU deviates a great deal from the real world, and individual MCU films seemingly deviate from one another, but this elaborately established history goes to great lengths to explain these deviations. The Hulk's creation was an unintended consequence of the Super Soldier experiments that created Captain America. Howard Stark participated in those experiments; his son would inherit his genius and create the Iron Man armor. Captain America fought against technologies created with the Tesseract, which was brought to Earth by Thor's father Odin, and is in fact one the Infinity Stones sought by Thanos, and so on. Each fantastic story is justified by the others.

In most of the films of the MCU so far, the rhetoric of this justification has been primarily scientific in feel. Sam Moskowitz famously defined the science fiction genre by this sort of justification: "Science fiction is a branch of fantasy identifiable by the fact that it eases the 'willing suspension of disbelief' on the part of its readers by utilizing an atmosphere of scientific credibility for its imaginative speculations in physical science, space, time, social science, and philosophy."[16] Marvel comic books from the 1960s onward have used scientific sounding jargon and loosely applied scientific principles to explain fantastic phenomena; where creators have failed to do so, fans have stepped in, offering in letter pages and discussion elsewhere scientific explanations as to how the Human Torch flies or how Spider-Man sticks to walls.[17] The Marvel Cinematic Universe has relied on this comic book science, laying its foundation with one of the most blatantly technological superheroes. *Iron Man* might have passed for a science fiction movie, centering on Tony Stark's powered armor and culminating in a battle with a similarly armored enemy. *The Incredible Hulk* (2008) continued in this vein, premised on the radiation-induced monstrous mutations of the Hulk and the Abomination, and *Iron Man 2* continued to center on gadgetry. This adherence to a tight premise may have eased the audience's suspension of disbelief, but it has also frustrated some viewers who prefer a broader scope of superheroic action; author and comics fan George R.R. Martin has complained,

> I am tired of this Marvel movie trope where the bad guy has the same powers as the hero. The Hulk fought the Abomination, who is just a bad Hulk. Spider-Man fights Venom, who is just a bad Spider-Man. Iron Man fights Ironmonger, a bad Iron Man. Yawn. I want more films where the hero and the villain have wildly different powers. That makes the action much more interesting.[18]

As the cinematic universe has grown, however, the comic book science has been pushed farther and farther into the magical. In *Iron Man 2*, Agent Phil Coulson tells Tony Stark he's been reassigned to New Mexico; Stark remarks, drolly, "Fantastic. Land of enchantment."[19] Coulson's assignment is revealed in the fourth MCU movie, *Thor*, where audiences are asked to accept Norse gods in this shared setting, with suspension of disbelief aided only by a generous application of "Clarke's Third Law" that "any sufficiently developed technology is indistinguishable from magic."[20] Richard Reynolds examines the *Thor* comic book—where, unlike the film version, Thor and his people are overtly supernatural—as representative of a wider tendency of the superhero genre to treat science as magic: "Science is treated as a special form of magic, capable of both good and evil. Scientific concepts and terms are introduced freely into plots and used to create atmosphere and add background detail to artwork—but the science itself is at most only superficially plausible, often less so, and the prevailing mood is mystical rather than rational."[21] Reynolds argues that Thor's success in comics is rooted in Jack Kirby's artwork portraying the figures of Norse myth in a science fiction/fantasy style consistent with other superhero comics, in an existing complexity of superhero mythologies that could accommodate the grafting on of the whole of Norse myth, and in Marvel writers Stan Lee and Roy Thomas treating the Asgardian characters "as superheroes from a ready-made, legendary background—not as an excuse for reanimating the Eddas."[22]

In the superhero genre, magic is not a contradiction of the science fictional setting but rather an expansion of it; this is what the creators of the Marvel Cinematic Universe had to establish for a movie audience relatively unfamiliar with decades of comic book storytelling. Thus, *Thor* begins with scientists—astrophysicist Jane Foster and her team observing an astronomical phenomenon which leads to an accidental collision with the mysterious figure who will eventually be revealed as Thor; only then does the film flash back to Thor's past, introduced by Odin's narration which frames Asgard as more otherworldly than supernatural:

> Once, mankind accepted a simple truth: that they were not alone in this universe. Some worlds man believed home to their Gods. Others they knew to fear. From around the cold and darkness came the Frost Giants, threatening to plunge the mortal world into a new ice age. But humanity would not face this threat alone.... And though we have fallen into man's myths and legends, it was Asgard and its warriors that brought peace to the universe.

This scientific framing of magic persists prominently throughout *Thor*. When The Destroyer, a magical champion controlled by Loki, appears on Earth, a S.H.I.E.L.D. agent asks, "Is that one of Stark's?" Robots or animated battlesuits are not out of place in the MCU, even when they come from a newly introduced world. When Eric Selvig dismisses a children's book of Norse mythology as an explanation for the strange events he and his colleagues have become entangled in, exclaiming "I'm talking about science, not magic," Jane Foster replies "Well, magic's just science we don't understand yet," citing Arthur C. Clarke. Later in the film, Thor himself furthers this idea, explaining to Jane that "Your ancestors called it magic … but you call it science. Well, I come from a place where they are one and the same thing." Ultimately, the introduction of Asgardians into the MCU not only rationalizes magic with science, but it waves away any distinction between them. Loki's tricks may be enabled by advanced technology, but they're virtually indistinguishable from the charms and illusions one might see in a high fantasy story.

In the MCU's "Phase Two" (taking place in the aftermath of *The Avengers*, comprising the films from *Iron Man 3* through *Ant-Man*), the introduction of these elements has a profound impact on the heroes and on the world they live in. Disruption runs strongly as a theme in these movies. In *Iron Man 3* (2013), Tony Stark must cope with post–traumatic stress disorder after fighting among Asgardians and aliens. In *Thor: The Dark World* (2013), Jane Foster ponders the effects of a cosmic Convergence: "The walls between worlds will be almost non-existent. Physics is gonna go ballistic. Increases and decreases in gravity, spatial extrusions. The very fabric of reality is gonna be torn apart." *Guardians of the Galaxy* (2014) expands the scope of the MCU through the far reaches of space. On television, the *Agents of S.H.I.E.L.D.* deal with a world where "Everything's changing." In the Netflix *Daredevil* series, Matt Murdock lives in a Hell's Kitchen devastated by the Battle of New York in *The Avengers*. While the denizens of the MCU are traumatized by this expansive experience, MCU audiences have proven willing to accept more and more fantastic premises, even as the stories have offered less and less rationalization. A popular web meme critiqued the Warner/DC reluctance to offer a female-led superhero movie by comparison with Marvel's narrative boldness in *Guardians of the Galaxy*:

DC: "The world isn't ready for a Wonder Woman movie."
Marvel: "Here's a talking raccoon."

In *Ant-Man*, scientist Hank Pym warns the hero of another threat disruptive to previous rational experience: "If that regulator is compromised, you would go subatomic.... It means that you would enter a quantum realm... . It means that you would enter a reality where all concepts of time and space become irrelevant as you shrink for all eternity." Pym sees his works as qualitatively different from what we've seen previously: "This is not some cute technology like the Iron Man suit. This could change the texture of everything." The MCU is moving beyond rational comprehensibility and even rationalization. The first season of *Daredevil* hints at a supernatural origin of the character Madame Gao with no attempt to offer a scientific explanation; in the second season, the reanimated dead ninjas of the Hand seem unapologetically mystical. As of this writing, *Doctor Strange* is still a few months away, but the trailers are clearly presenting a magical hero.

When the physical rules of the setting are in question, even to the characters within that setting, Busselle and Bilandzic's backward-referring situation model becomes all the more important. The first *Iron Man* included relatively little history of the fictional setting, but rooted itself with a good deal of verisimilitude: Tony Stark becomes Iron Man in the context of the war in Afghanistan and the current era of international terrorism. Stark's witty banter is an ongoing barrage of contemporary cultural references. This hip credibility echoes the appeal of Marvel comics from the 1960s onward. As Pustz observes, Marvel "claimed that its comic books were traditionally realistic by reflecting the world in which the creators and readers lived."[23] While DC Comics of the 1960s offered escapist fantasies in fictional cities like Metropolis and Gotham City, Marvel stories were set primarily in New York and other real-world locations and were far more likely to incorporate current events and trends.

Yet the second MCU film, *The Incredible Hulk*, began to draw more heavily on history within the fiction. Notably, this movie does not retell the Hulk's origin; instead, it assumes that the audience is familiar with Bruce

Banner's transformation and his relationships with Betty Ross and her father while deftly dodging any questions of consistency with the relatively recent *Hulk* (2003) directed by Ang Lee. It evokes the character's history with winking references to the television series starring Bill Bixby and Lou Ferrigno; Banner watches a few moments of Bill Bixby in another role while flipping television channels, while Ferrigno appears in the movie alongside Stan Lee as a pair of security guards. Most importantly, Robert Downey, Jr., reprises his role as Tony Stark in a post-credit discussion of the Avengers Initiative with General Ross. With the incorporation of the Avengers Initiative, the narrative has gone beyond evoking the familiarity of a character; it is now picking up a plot thread from *Iron Man* that will continue through the Marvel movies to come.

As of this point, there is a Marvel Cinematic Universe wider than any one character's milieu. *Iron Man 2* Is centered on a theme of legacy, developing the story of Howard Stark, while exploring the implications of the proliferation of superheroes. *Thor* establishes a distant past in the MCU, but that past is soon tied to the 1940s and then to the present day in *Captain America: The First Avenger*, setting up a major convergence of characters and plot threads in *The Avengers*. In the various MCU productions, we have seen significant moments set in ancient history, during World War II, and through Howard Stark, Peggy Carter, and Hank Pym, a surprising number of incidents in the years between Captain America's World War II career and the emergence of Iron Man. When Steve Rogers is sent into action with the Avengers, he questions the relevance of his uniform: "Aren't the stars and stripes a little … old-fashioned?" Agent Coulson responds, "With everything that's happening, the things that are about to come to light, people might just need a little old-fashioned."

A little old-fashioned reassures the MCU audience as much as it does the fictional inhabitants of that universe. The past provides realism by referencing known events and situations, but also by establishing fictional foundations for ongoing plot threads. This fictionalized past even revises past fictions; audiences are gratified by acknowledgment of the Bixby/Ferrigno Hulk, while comics fans might appreciate Hank Pym being re-inserted into Marvel history after being written out of his place as a founding Avenger. One of the pleasures of watching an MCU movie is the validation of the viewer's experience in watching what has come before.

The MCU's emphasis on this continuity has deep roots in Marvel's comic books. Pustz observes, "Marvel realism also involved the company's reliance on continuity, on how the stories about the Fantastic Four, Spider-Man, and all the rest fit into a single narrative that had a past, present, and future. By the 1970s Marvel was publishing comics set in all three of these periods, requiring fans have knowledge of hundreds of years of events to completely appreciate the Marvel universe and its continuity-based realism."[24] The first intertwining of superhero stories occurred in 1940 when the Human Torch and the Sub-Mariner met in *Marvel Mystery Comics* #8. These heroes would continue to interact, as would many other characters in superhero comics. A few months later, *All-Star Comics* #3 introduced the Justice Society of America, a team that included multiple heroes published by All-American Comics and National Periodical Publications (the companies that would form the core of DC Comics). Superhero teams became a sub-genre, and superhero team-ups a common narrative trope. But in the 1960s, Stan Lee began interconnecting superhero stories on a greater scale; Marvel characters interacted frequently and significantly, and events occurring in one Marvel series were likely to have effects in other series. By the end of that decade, storylines could start in one series and continue in another. Characters changed over time, with references to past stories often footnoted. In the 1970s, Lee's successor as editor-in-chief, Roy Thomas, kept index cards recording characters' abilities and where they had last appeared; by the 1980s, that information was kept in a database.[25]

Clearly, comic book continuity has served publishers as a form of cross promotion; readers of one series are compelled to buy another if they want to get "the whole story." But for those readers, continuity doesn't just extend the narrative; it adds depth to it. Reynolds comments, "The continuity of an individual character, and the relationship of that character to the entire 'universe' which they inhabit, provides a guarantee of the authenticity of each individual story."[26] Lincoln Geraghty builds on Reynolds: "Therefore, the integrity of the characters depends on the existence of a 'universe' in which all the characters owned by a particular company inhabit the same fictional world."[27]

The interconnectedness of the Marvel Cinematic Universe allows movie audiences to share in this comic book fan notion of realism, founded on an understanding of canon. A knowledgeable MCU fan knows the texts of the universe—the movies, the "One Shots," the television and Netflix series—and knows which texts are non-canonical: movies about Marvel characters produced by other studios like Fox and Sony (though the upcoming Sony co-production of *Spider-Man: Homecoming* will in fact be canonical), older movies based on Marvel characters, and movies based on non–Marvel heroes like *Batman v Superman: Dawn of Justice* (2016).

Fans of both comics and the MCU will have other layers of understanding, noticing the differences between the cinematic and printed characters and storylines and catching subtle references to comic book creators and other Marvel lore. Jeffrey Brown describes this fannish knowledge among comic book fans in terms of Pierre Bourdieu's concept of cultural capital: "The cultural economy of comic fandom is based on the ability to acquire canonical texts, as determined by either plot or creator significance. By possessing these comics, the reader substantiates his or her participation in fandom, building a knowledge of creators, characters, and storylines."[28] Brown further observes, "For a *real* fan the comic can't just be bought. It must be understood and enjoyed. The economic aspects of collecting are false. Simply acquiring the books is the act of a heartless villain: an investor. The fan collects because he or she loves the medium and the stories it tells."[29] MCU fans command similar knowledge in ways that Brown, writing in 1997, did not anticipate. For Brown, the cultural capital of comic book fandom was unique in revolving around distinctly possessable objects, where other forms of culture might be either impossible to physically possess or readily available in a variety of formats and editions.

Since that time, movies have passed through the DVD era, when the medium became not just easily possessable but conveniently searchable and frequently appended with commentary and explanation, and into the still more accessible form of streaming video. In addition, the Web has made available countless online scripts, images, and video clips. In short, movies have become as open to reference as comic books, to an audience far larger than comic book fans who build their collections with considerable effort and expense. Derek Johnson describes how Marvel Studios' greater adherence to the comics than past adaptations gained the trust of "fanboys" who read comics and are a major target for summer blockbuster films.[30] But the emulation of comics continuity has advantages for movies beyond appeal to the relatively small audience of comics readers. Chuck Tryon suggests that the widespread availability of commentary, deleted scenes, and other supplemental texts in DVDs fed into the fragmentation of the original text of a film, giving rise to a sense of textual incompleteness that fostered film franchises where detail after detail can be filled in.[31] Bart Beaty observes that seriality began to increase in superhero movies even before the Marvel Studios movies—notably in the X-Men movies, in the Sam Raimi Spider-Man films, and in *Superman Returns*—positing that the films that are more successful with critics and audiences are those that "take seriously the visual and narrative complexity of the genre."[32]

In *Thor*, Odin seemingly enchants the hammer Mjölnir with the incantation "Whosoever holds this hammer, if he be worthy, shall possess the power of Thor"; Thor's heroism and ultimate ascension to the throne require his attaining worthiness. In *Avengers 2: Age of Ultron*, the superheroes ponder the nature of how that "enchantment" restricts the use of Mjölnir:

> TONY STARK: It's biometrics, right? Like a security code? "Whoever is carrying Thor's fingerprints" is, I think, the literal translation.
> THOR: Yes, well that's a very, very interesting theory. I have a simpler one: You are not worthy.

The Marvel Cinematic Universe doesn't simply gloss over the contradictions between its heroes' milieu; it revels in them. But it also unites them in a complex history in which divergent backstories intertwine, with a recurring narrative pattern in which power is linked with worthiness; a hero, whatever his or her past failings, can justify power by attaining moral authority. Thor can learn humility. Tony Stark can move beyond arms manufacturing and narcissism. Bruce Banner can use his inner monster to help people. S.H.I.E.L.D. can be rebuilt and redeemed. Ex-con Scott Lang can turn his life around. In the MCU, heroism is a quality that arises from an imperfect and complicated past. Perhaps this narrative has particular appeal for audiences of the early 21st century. Today's world is one of information overload; science has reached specialized complexity beyond even basic understanding to many, while consensus has been lost regarding basic facts of political and social existence as politicized media shape increasingly polarized worldviews. The MCU promises hope, whatever the failings of the past and the conflicts of the present. Compared to a "realistic" drama, the fantastic world of the MCU seems extravagant in its details and rationales, but ultimately it is a microcosm which a dedicated fan will more easily make sense of than the infinite complexities of the real world. These films offer the escapist pleasures of a rich fictional world, but they also offer reassurance that it is possible to thrive amidst complexity.

NOTES

1. See "Consistency," *TV Tropes*, accessed May 28, 2015, http://tvtropes.org/pmwiki/pmwiki.php/Main/Consistency.
2. Lightninglouie, "Did Marvel Beat The 'Third Movie' Syndrome?" *Observation Deck*, accessed May 29, 2015, http://observationdeck.kinja.com/did-marvel-beat-the-third-movie-syndrome-1568386602.
3. Les Daniels, *Marvel: Five Fabulous Decades of the World's Greatest Comics* (New York: Harry N. Abrams, 1991), 100.
4. See, for example, "Willing Suspension of Disbelief," *TV Tropes*, http://tvtropes.org/pmwiki/pmwiki.php/ Main/WillingSuspensionOfDisbelief.
5. Samuel Taylor Coleridge, *The Collected Works of Samuel Taylor Coleridge* (Princeton: Routledge & Kegan Paul, 1983), 6.
6. *Ibid.*, 134.
7. J.R.R. Tolkien, "On Fairy Stories," in *The Tolkien Reader* (New York: Ballantine, 1966), 46.
8. Richard Gerrig, 1–19, 239–40.
9. Andrew McGonigal, "Truth, Relativism, and Serial Fiction," *British Journal of Aesthetics* 53, no. 2 (2013): 165–179.
10. Ben Caplan, "Serial Fiction, Continued," *British Journal of Aesthetics* 54, no. 1 (2014): 65–76.
11. Anthony J. Ferri, *Willing Suspension of Disbelief: Poetic Faith in Film* (New York: Lexington Books, 2007), 13–33.
12. Rick Busselle and Helena Bilandzic, "Fictionality and Perceived Realism in Experiencing Stories: A Model of Narrative Comprehension and Engagement," *Communication Theory* 18, no. 2 (2008): 255–80.
13. *Ibid.*, 259.

14. *Ibid.*, 258.

15. *Ibid.*, 269.

16. Sam Moskowitz, *Explorers of the Infinite: Shapers of Science Fiction* (Cleveland: Meridian Books, 1963), 11.

17. Matthew Pustz, *Comic Book Culture: Fanboys and True Believers* (Jackson: University Press of Mississippi, 1999), 52.

18. Dustin Rowles, "George R.R. Martin Sounds Off On 'Ant-Man' And Marvel's Villain Problem," *Uproxx: The Culture of What's Buzzing*, July 23, 2015, http://uproxx.com/tv/george-r-r-martin-on-antman-marvels-villain-problem.

19. Thanks to Paul Gindlesperger for reminding me of this exchange.

20. Arthur C. Clarke, "Hazards of Prophecy: The Failure of Imagination," in *Profiles of the Future: An Enquiry into the Limits of the Possible* (New York: Harper and Row, 1973), 36.

21. Richard Reynolds, *Superheroes: A Modern Mythology* (Jackson: University Press of Mississippi, 1994), 16.

22. *Ibid.*, 53–4.

23. Pustz, *Comic Book Culture*, 52.

24. Pustz, *Comic Book Culture*, 52.

25. Sean Howe, *Marvel Comics: The Untold Story* (New York: HarperCollins, 2012), 156.

26. Reynolds, *Superheroes: A Modern Mythology*, 45.

27. Lincoln Geraghty, "'Realities ... blending as one!': Film Texts and Intertexts in the Star Trek/X-Men Crossover Comics," *Extrapolation* 48, no. 1 (Spring 2007): 112.

28. Jeffrey A. Brown, "Comic Book Fandom and Cultural Capital," *Journal of Popular Culture* 30, no 4. (Spring 1997): 26.

29. *Ibid.*, 27.

30. Derek Johnson, "Cinematic Destiny: Marvel Studios and the Trade Stories of Industrial Convergence," *Cinema Journal* 52, no. 1 (Fall 2012): 19.

31. Chuck Tryon, *Reinventing Cinema: Movies in the Age of Media Convergence* (New Brunswick: Rutgers Univ. Press, 2009), 19.

32. Bart Beaty, "The Blockbuster Superhero," in *The Wiley-Blackwell History of American Film*, ed. Cynthia Lucia, Roy Grundmann, and Art Simon (Chichester: Blackwell Publishing, 2012), 236–240.

Section II
"Establish justice":
The Social Context
of the Cinematic Universe

Since the early days of the genre, superheroes have been defenders of the American Way, regardless of their company of origin. Creators have traditionally associated this phrase with ideal abstractions such as "truth" and "justice," believing it to embody the positive five virtues of U.S. culture. As the growing scholarship on comics points out, creators have made choices over the genre's history that have privileged particular races, ethnicities, classes, and genders over others. In doing so, creators have codified the status quo on the basis of social difference, and made superheroes defend this vision of the American way in order to perpetuate social inequality.

Filmmakers on the Marvel Cinematic Universe have, whether they realize it or not, inherited this subtextual aspect of the genre from their print predecessors. While they have created parallels to some of the existing tropes which evolved in print adventures of Marvel superheroes, filmmakers have also created their own distinctive vision of how the United States is and how it should be with regard to the relationship between social distinction and status difference.

Stark Contrasts

Reinventing Iron Man for 21st Century Cinema

SARAH ZAIDAN

Iron Man has been at the center of the Marvel Cinematic Universe (MCU) from the moment he rocketed onto the silver screen in 2008. A mainstay of Marvel Comics' stable of superheroes since the 1960s, Iron Man has always attracted a loyal fan following, but the place he occupied in popular culture was significantly smaller than that of such stalwarts as Superman and Batman.[1] No longer. Whether clad in his trademark red and gold armor or in a tailored suit as his alter ego Tony Stark, Iron Man's popularity in the 21st century is uncontested. Marvel Creative Director Bill Rosemann reveals that "once the Iron Man movie hit, once all three hit, we now realized that he's our most popular character worldwide,"[2] and box office figures certainly agree: at the time of writing, Marvel's *The Avengers* is the third highest grossing film of all time, and *Iron Man 3* is number seven on that same list.[3]

Was his meteoric rise to mainstream fame caused by the medium of cinema and its ability to reach a wider audience than his comic book incarnation ever could? Is it the character himself, described in his own words (and with his trademark lack of modesty) as a "genius, billionaire, playboy, philanthropist," whom audiences worldwide have found so appealing? Was it the timing of his first cinematic appearance in a world still reeling from the financial crisis of 2007 and still healing from the devastating attacks of September 11, 2001? Or is it the choice of casting Robert Downey, Jr., an actor whose triumph over his personal and professional struggles parallels Stark's in many ways?

The critical success factors behind Iron Man's international acclaim can be found through answering these questions, as well as in the character's representation of humanity's hopes and fears surrounding technology. An in depth analysis of Stark's character that places him within the sociopolitical context of the 21st century, combined with material drawn from Iron Man's appearances in Marvel's comic universe over the past four decades, brings to light the character's relationships with his friends, enemies, and the United States Armed Forces, reverse-engineering this uniquely 21st century super-hero.

Forged in the Fires of War

To understand how Iron Man has become the icon he is today, it is necessary to explore his origins. Although this essay focuses on the character as he appears on film, Iron Man's comic book beginnings and the political landscape of the world he entered into provide context for his present-day popularity. It was March of 1963, the height of the Cold War. Marvel Comics was riding high on the success of its flawed, relatable heroes like Thor and the Hulk, when Issue 39 of *Tales of Suspense* debuted "the newest, most breathtaking, most sensational super-hero of all." A full-body illustration of the character in question appeared below rivet-studded letterforms proclaiming "Iron Man!" Don Heck's art presents readers with a blocky metal behemoth who might be easily mistaken for a robot if not for a sequence of three vertical panels where visibly human hands are shown picking up boots, helmet and gauntlets in turn as their owner dons the armor hidden from his audience's eyes. A caption assures readers that "the talented bull-pen where the Fantastic Four, Spider-Man, Thor and your other favorite super-heroes were born!" is behind this unconventional hero, and this was perhaps the greatest pull of all on a cover whose text and images work hard to spark interest in this new character.

Following the post-war slump in superhero comic sales, and the devastating effects the Comics Code had on the industry's fortunes in 1955,[4] Marvel Comics rose to prominence in the early 1960s. Responsibility for this shift rested largely on the shoulders of writer-editor Stan Lee and artist Jack Kirby, whose fresh combination of snappy dialogue and dynamic art took readers' imaginations by storm. Marvel superheroes were different. They lived and operated in a recognizable New York City. The Fantastic Four had personalities as individual as their powers, and bickered like a family. Spider-Man might save the day, but his powers did not keep him from experiencing a teenager's worries like breaking curfew or getting a date.[5]

Iron Man's origin story begins in a South Vietnamese jungle, where Tony Stark demonstrates transistor-driven magnets to a collection of Army brass who start off skeptical but are subsequently awe-struck by the tiny yet powerful devices. A pair of flashback panels establishes Stark's playboy reputation and his ease at navigating both intellectual and social spheres. Larry Lieber's script ominously reveals that "this man who seems so fortunate, who's envied by millions—is soon destined to become the most tragic figure on Earth!" but it is Stark's role within the military industrial complex that is first cemented in the reader's mind. President Kennedy's announcement on October 22, 1962, that American reconnaissance planes had discovered Soviet surface-to-air missile sites in Cuba and the tense weeks that followed would certainly have been fresh in the minds of Iron Man's audience. Although the Cuban Missile Crisis was averted by late November, fears of nuclear war "overhung the lifetime of the generation that lived through those days of October 1962."[6] Iron Man's origin story assumes audience familiarity with, as Stark puts it, the "problem in Vietnam" and with the "Red hordes" his weapons are to be used against.[7] Marvel superheroes had been pitted against Communist villains as early as 1954,[8] but the escalation of America's involvement with the Vietnam War coincides with Iron Man's debut.

Soon after his introduction, Stark steps on a land mine and is captured by the tyrannical Communist warlord Wong-Chu. The explosion leaves him with a deadly piece of shrapnel lodged in his heart and Stark immediately sees through Wong-Chu's bargain to design a super-weapon for him in exchange for life-saving surgery. With the help of fellow prisoner and physicist Yinsen, the aforementioned transistor technology and a pile of scrap metal, Stark creates a suit of armor that provides him with both the means to escape and a pacemaker for his heart, keeping the shrapnel at bay through magnetic repulsion. Upon his return to the USA, Stark maintains his playboy image while he secretly fights Communist threats as Iron Man. But not all Stark's wounds are of the body. As the 1960s gave way to the 1970s and beyond, he evolved from war profiteer to philanthropist, lost and regained his fortune on several occasions, and faced his inner demons in a battle with alcoholism.[9]

It is no coincidence this narrative will seem familiar to fans of Iron Man's films. A superhero's origin story provides a reference point for their personality, their friends and foes, their powers, conflicts and world. Key narrative elements transcend time and media formats as these serial stories are retold and reinvented. Tony Stark does not set out to be a superhero, but his triumph over seemingly impossible odds provides the catalyst for the personal growth that leads him down that path. He may be imprisoned by a Communist tyrant or by a terrorist ring. The shrapnel killing him by inches may come from a land mine or, in an intensely symbolic scene from *Iron Man*,[10] a missile stamped with Stark's own name. A world away from his life of privilege and wealth, Stark is always the engineer of his own survival, whether the events play out in Vietnam, Afghanistan, or somewhere else entirely.

In examining Iron Man's origin story, several reasons for the character's popularity become evident. Tony Stark was created in a time of conflict and pervasive cultural anxiety. His audience would have been aware that the ingenuity and inventiveness that won Stark his freedom and saved his life was the selfsame trait that established his fortune and career as an arms dealer. American innovation carried a dark undercurrent ever since August 1945, when atomic bombs were dropped on Hiroshima and Nagasaki. Unable to stop the advance of Iron Man, Wong-Chu flees with the intent of executing all of his remaining prisoners. In an act of desperation, Iron Man uses the last of his armor's energy to destroy his enemy by setting fire to a cache of weapons, causing an explosion presented as a zoomed-out image of a violet cloud. Whether intentional or subconscious on the part of Heck and Lieber, this visual evokes a far more destructive cloud, and brings to mind the message that conflict cannot always be ended bloodlessly. Technology had changed postwar America for both good and ill, and Iron Man represents this duality. As Stark and as Iron Man, he embodies his audience's fears of what technology can lead to when used in the service of warfare, the cultural guilt over what these weapons are capable of, and the desire for redemption he literally embodies through becoming an instrument of peace. These themes have become no less relevant with the passage of time; on the contrary, the ubiquity of technology in the present day and its intersection with the military industrial complex has heightened their importance.

Rosemann asserts, "we were just waiting for a worldwide audience to discover [Iron Man]. He hasn't changed at all from his origins in the 60s. We just had to *bring* him to the audience."[11] The medium of cinema has certainly accomplished this aim, and the outward trappings of Iron Man's first film appearance diverge from the comics only in ways that add contemporary relevance to Stark and his story in a post financial crisis, post–September 11 world. The fateful weapon test is transplanted from the Vietnamese jungles to the deserts of Afghanistan, and once again Stark's first appearance links him to the U.S. Armed Forces as he rides with soldiers in a Humvee away from the testing site. The flashback panels make their way into the narrative, although this incarnation of Stark is less the Silver Age sophisticate and more a combination of arrogance, irresponsibility and charisma that frustrates those nearest to him, such as friend Colonel James Rhodes and long-suffering personal assistant Pepper Potts. The Ten Rings terrorist group that captures him is international in scope, with no explicit political or religious affiliation. Yinsen, Chinese in his comic book incarnation, now hails from the fictional Afghani village of Gulmira, and it is his words of encouragement in addition to his heroic sacrifice that spur Stark into creating the Mark I armor. Transistors and magnets are replaced by the arc reactor, a fusion device and source of clean energy. Although Stark still sets fire to the weapons cache, the Ten Rings' commander Raza, who serves an analogous role to Wong-Chu, survives the experience, and his death comes later at the hands of antagonist Obadiah Stane. None of these changes alter what Iron Man represents fundamentally, and his narrative remains one steeped in American cultural context. In the globalized world of 2008 it was unlikely an international audience would have been alienated by the images of American culture and military as presented in *Iron Man,* but I argue that Tony Stark's worldwide popularity largely stems from who he is as a person.

I Am Iron Man

A wealth of character information is communicated in Tony Stark's first appearance in *Iron Man.*[12] The first part of him viewers see is in fact his hand, a spiritual echo of the cover to *Tales of Suspense #39.* The context, however, could not be more different. A comic book engages the eyes, the mind and the imagination. A film engages all these in addition to the sense of hearing, and it is AC/DC's 1980 rock anthem *Back in Black* that accompanies the image of Stark's hand, holding a tumbler of Scotch rather than a piece of the Iron Man armor. He puts the soldiers guarding him at ease with witty quips and a sense of humor that veers into the inappropriate. This is Stark the playboy, Stark the party animal, Stark the celebrity. Although this scene chronologically takes place minutes after the weapons demonstration that introduces viewers to Stark the genius inventor, this facet of his character is shown via a flashback that also introduces Stark the showman and a missile called the Jericho that foreshadows the repulsor technology the Iron Man armor will later incorporate. Biblical references aside, Stark's speech hearkens back to his character's Cold War roots and references the concept of American national identity being tied to its punching power on the world stage:

> *They* say the best weapon is one you don't have to fire. I respectfully disagree. I prefer the weapon you only have to fire *once.* That's how Dad did it, that's how America does it … and it's worked out pretty well so far.

Stark's audience onscreen is captivated by the potential that lies in owning such a destructive weapon. His audience offscreen is captivated by the notion that this man will somehow overcome his lack of self-awareness and accountability to become a hero by the time the credits roll; they want to come along for the ride. The time may be different, the medium may be different, but the narrative techniques that breathed new life into the superhero genre four decades ago are in full force here. Tony Stark is not yet a hero when he escapes his captors and destroys their stockpile of what he believes to have been illegally acquired Stark Industries weapons. His heroism awakens when, following his traumatic experience in Afghanistan, he begins applying the skills that make him a creative genius—a sharp and curious mind, the determination to learn from a project's mistakes and improve upon them for the next iteration—to himself. He reflects on whether or not his late father ever questioned his company's role in funding conflict. He shuts down the weapons manufacturing arm of his company. He continues to develop his armor in secret, acknowledging that it must not fall into the wrong hands.

This is where the first of Stark's defining traits as a hero emerges: assuming responsibility for his actions, inventions, and politics. As fellow Marvel superhero Spider-Man can attest to, with great power comes great responsibility. This will reappear as a motif throughout the MCU, and it carries a powerful resonance with audiences worldwide. Personal responsibility does not require billions of dollars or access to the latest technology. It requires strength of character and emotional intelligence, qualities any viewer can aspire to. Witnessing Stark making this change, watching him fly to Afghanistan and defend the villagers of Gulmira from the Ten Rings in his perfected suit of red and gold armor is an inspirational moment that transcends the character's race, politics and wealth. However, the inverse of this motif is also repeated throughout his films: Iron Man's villains are by and large the product of his own actions. They also share superficial aspects of Stark's character, albeit lacking that all-important sense of personal responsibility. *Iron Man* is no exception: Stark's business partner Obadiah Stane is a savvy corporate shark who projects a jocular façade. He is also filled with jealousy and resentment for the self-indulgent young man he has cleaned up after for years and believes himself entitled to Stark Industries. Stane is revealed to have been selling weapons to the Ten Rings, whom he subsequently betrays. He paid the terrorists to carry out the attack on Stark while he was overseas demonstrating the Jericho, which introduces what will become a another recurring theme with Stark's antagonists: the true nature of their motivations is never what it seems on the surface. Stane ultimately faces off against Stark in a modified Mark I armor as the Iron Monger.

It is fortunate, then, that Stark has more than just his considerable intelligence and engineering skill behind him: he is also capable of forming strong friendships based on mutual trust. This trust, along with moments of genuine emotional honesty, forms the cornerstone of his relationship with Potts, with whom Stark eventually enters into a business and romantic partnership. It is Potts's intervention that allows Stark to successfully defeat the Iron Monger. This is the beginning of a pattern: Stark's enemies form allegiances based in power, money or fear, characterized by double-dealing and betrayal. They treat technology as a means to an end, with a distinct lack of respect or responsibility. Their efforts inevitably collapse when faced by Stark, who is aided each time by friends and the technology he has humanized such as JARVIS and DUM-E, to say nothing of the Iron Man armor that casts him as a modern-day knight. In the closing moments of *Iron Man*, Stark continues the theme of personal responsibility and eschews the convention of a superhero's secret identity by announcing, "I am Iron Man" at a press conference. He has committed to his new role; there's no going back now.

After all of this positive character development, Stark's apparent return to his hedonistic myopia makes for difficult viewing in *Iron Man 2*.[13] However, this narrative direction affirms Stark's humanity and relatability. Faced once again with his mortality, this time via blood poisoning from the very device that is keeping him alive, Stark's fear and anxiety causes his worst traits to come to the fore. He takes refuge in alcohol and masks his insecurity with arrogance. He fixates on honoring his father's legacy, and alienates the people closest to him as he grows increasingly desperate. Time is running out for this man just as he has found his true calling and his acts of self-destruction are as much acts of penance.

Stark is his own worst enemy in *Iron Man 2*, but the patterns Stane established hold true in villains Justin Hammer and Ivan Vanko. Hammer, desperate to discredit Stark and position himself as the wunderkind of the arms race, is an ugly exaggeration of Stark's previous entitled behavior. Vanko, armed with an arc reactor and seeking to avenge his father (Howard Stark's former creative partner), further highlights the complicated relationship between Stark and his own father. Stark's salvation comes in the form of S.H.I.E.L.D director Nick Fury, who takes him to task for his behavior and provides him with a posthumous message from Howard Stark that holds the key to curing the poison and asserts that his son was his greatest creation. Stark rebuilds his life and repairs his relationships with Rhodes and Potts in time to defeat both villains, who thematically play upon real-world fears surrounding the use of drones in the military.

The character of Howard Stark made his comic book debut seven years after *Tales of Suspense* #39 was published.[14] It also takes seven years for the MCU to showcase him in his prime. In the 2015 television series *Agent Carter,* Howard demonstrates a fascinating divide between in-universe chronology and production chronology in both forms of media he appears in. While his influence on his son is undeniable, the opposite is true from a writing standpoint: father was created after son, and any similarities are purely intentional. When Howard is under Senate investigation for allegedly selling weapons to enemies of the United States and responds to questioning with arrogance and humor, it is impossible not to draw comparisons with a similar scene in *Iron Man 2*.[15] Howard's lack of humility and womanizing ways are the subjects of running jokes throughout the first season, until he admits to that being a self-made man with working-class origins has made him adept at telling lies.[16] His tendency to underestimate women alienates ally Peggy Carter and turns out to be the reason his weapons were stolen in the first place by a female sleeper agent working with Soviet psychiatrist Johann Fennhoff, as part of a plot to take revenge on Howard for inventing a chemical weapon that killed his brother.

In the season one finale, Fennhoff confronts Howard, laying bare the core differences between father and son. Howard is not immune to guilt; but even as he is given over to self-recrimination, he deflects responsibility for this particular weapon's misuse.[17] Tony Stark makes no such excuses. When faced with his misdeeds, he does not backpedal or justify, he pours his energy—more often than not obsessively—into making things right. Despite his playboy past, he views the women in his life, like Potts and Avenger teammate Natasha Romanoff, as equals and he treats them with respect. In fact, it is Tony's interactions with the man who Howard Stark once called "the one thing I've done that brought good into this world," that are fraught with tension in *The Avengers*.[18]

The external threats posed by villain Loki and the impending Chitauri alien invasion of New York City form the backdrop to an ideological clash between Stark and Steve Rogers' Captain America. When the two men argue over what could very well turn out to be a suicide mission, Rogers accuses Stark of fighting only for himself and demands that he stop pretending to be a hero. Stark retorts "everything special about you came out of a bottle," indicating the pride he takes in being the engineer of his own destiny. He contradicts Rogers' assumption of him by flying a nuclear missile into the Chitauri mother ship, almost sacrificing his life in the process. He is revived by the intervention of the Hulk, thanks to the friendship Stark formed earlier with his alter ego Bruce Banner, and proving once again that Stark's victories are tied to his human connections.

Of all of Iron Man's cinematic outings, it is *Iron Man 3*[19] that gets to the heart of Stark's unconventional brand of heroism as its narrative repeatedly asks the question posed to him by Captain America in *The Avengers*: "take [the armor] off, what are you?" It is also the first of Stark's appearances where he explicitly admits to the creation of his own demons. At New Year's Eve party in 1999, painfully awkward, disabled Aldrich Killian is desperate for validation from his hero Stark, who promises him a meeting that he never shows up to. Killian is shown alone and shivering on the hotel roof, contemplating suicide as Stark engages in a one-night stand with botanist Maya Hansen. "I just created demons. And I didn't even know it," declares Stark's voiceover as he looks back on his younger self.

Stark in the present day is experiencing the grip of another set of demons altogether: post–traumatic stress from his near-death experience in *The Avengers*. Unable to sleep, he spends night after night in his laboratory, developing suit after suit in an attempt to create the perfect defense. He experiences debilitating panic attacks at the mention of New York and the film never stigmatizes Stark for his panic disorder; he is never presented as less of a person or hero for what he is going through.

When Killian makes his next appearance, he is suave, charismatic, patterned after Stark by his own design. Although he flirts unsuccessfully with Potts and shows no respect for her personal space as he pitches the EXTREMIS project that promises to upgrade humanity's DNA, his reemergence in the narrative is an afterthought when compared to the Mandarin. Presented as a Middle Eastern warlord whose televised broadcasts issue such chilling proclamations as, "you know who I am. You don't know where I am. And you will never see me coming," the Mandarin is educated, theatrical, and unstoppable. When he claims responsibility for an explosion at Mann's Chinese Theater that critically injures Stark's close friend Happy Hogan, Stark responds with a televised announcement where he threatens the Mandarin's life, declaring "there's no politics here, it's just good old-fashioned revenge. There's no Pentagon, it's just you and me."

He concludes by providing his home address, and in no time at all the missiles arrive. Stark and Potts escape with their lives intact but their home destroyed. This storyline engages directly and viscerally with this age of War on Terror; the bearded Mandarin in his flowing robes is the embodiment of the narrative that has pervaded in Western media since the tragedy of September 11, but *Iron Man 3* is no exception to the rule governing the villains of this series: all is not what it seems. Stark's mission to prevent the Mandarin from carrying out his next attack sees him flying to the backwoods of Tennessee in the sole suit of armor to survive the assault, which rapidly loses power, leaving him to rely upon his own ingenuity and the aid of a young boy. Once again Stark is a world away from his considerable resources and suffering from wounds—this time psychological—that he must overcome if he is to save not only himself but his country. When JARVIS traces the Mandarin's broadcasts to a compound in Miami, Stark's incredulity is mirrored in his audience.

When he infiltrates the compound equipped with a hoodie and home-made weapons, and comes face-to-face with the Mandarin, the narrative that has been building until this moment is elegantly subverted. Trevor Slattery is a washed-up British actor hired by Killian, the film's true antagonist, as a scapegoat for the human bombs his EXTREMIS project creates. Maya Hansen turns out to have been Killian's accomplice, although he shoots her in cold blood when she makes a stand against him. To further communicate the message that evil transcends race or religion, Killian's operation is revealed to go all the way up to the Vice President of the United States. Through the teamwork of Stark and Rhodes, along with the plethora of suits he has dubbed the Iron Legion, Killian is defeated, although it an EXTREMIS-powered Potts who lands the final blow. The events of *Iron Man 3* give Stark permission to finally remove the shrapnel from heart. In his powerful concluding speech, he recognizes that he no longer needs to carry a physical reminder of the man he once was within himself:

I guess I'd say my armor, it was never a distraction, or a hobby. It was a cocoon. And now, I'm a changed man. You can take away my house, all my tricks and toys. One thing you can't take away? I *am* Iron Man.

By the time *Avengers: Age of Ultron*[20] takes place, Stark has overcome his panic disorder, but he remains haunted by New York, driven by an obsessive need to prepare for what he is certain will be a return of the Chitauri. The film quickly establishes that Stark has refined his suit's remote capabilities; stepping out of it to explore a Hydra base, he calls it to him when needed like an extension of his body. Contrary to Stark's assertions at the end of *Iron Man 3*, the Iron Legion is still active, albeit commanded by JARVIS. And once again, his warmongering days continue to impede him in the present: Eastern European twins Wanda and Pietro Maximoff were orphaned when a bomb destroyed their home—a bomb with Stark Industries emblazoned on its side. Now grown, the twins ally themselves with Ultron to destroy Stark from the inside out. Wanda's powers of mental manipulation cause Stark to experience his greatest fear: The Avengers lie dead as aliens circle in the sky below an enormous wormhole. Captain America lives just long enough to give voice to Stark's innermost anxieties, "you could've saved us. Why didn't you do more?" This galvanizes Stark to use Loki's scepter and the Mind Stone within it as a power source to build Ultron, an AI system that will act as a suit of armor around the world. The man who once flippantly declared he'd be out of a job with peace is now actively working toward his own obsolescence in the name of peace.

On paper, Ultron is a pedestrian villain representing humanity's anxieties surrounding artificial intelligence, and the concept of a robot with the goal of exterminating humanity has been seen before in James Cameron's *Terminator* films. In practice, however, Ultron is easily the most disturbing villain to come out of the MCU. He ticks all the boxes for an *Iron Man* antagonist: here is the lack of personal responsibility; here is the dark reflection of Stark's knowledge and charisma, here is the persistent belief that his actions are justified. He creates a false sense of empathy with his accomplices as Hammer and Killian have done before him. Like Stane, his urbanity masks a violent temper. Like Vanko, he references morality and religion. But Ultron utterly lacks humanity and his superficial simulations of it unsettle. He may identify with Pinocchio and actively work toward becoming a "real boy," but he and his legions are the hollow men, the stuffed men.[21] He is the inverse of his creator even as he apes him, and when Wanda is finally able to glimpse into his mind, what she finds there horrifies her so thoroughly that she and Pietro abandon their crusade against Stark, standing alongside the Avengers in the battle against Ultron and his army of hollow men.

The timing of *Agent Carter*'s introduction of Edwin Jarvis could not have been more appropriate, given the Vision's role in Ultron's defeat. Here in the flesh is the man who inspired Stark's faithful AI system and it soon becomes clear why Stark sought to immortalize him. Jarvis is astute and resourceful, a staunch ally to Howard Stark who is not afraid to challenge his decisions.[22] He is a devoted and loving husband to his wife Anna, and he extended that same care and compassion to his employer's son[23] JARVIS is of course not a recreation of Jarvis; he is an operating system based on Stark's perception of the man. Nor is the Vision precisely JARVIS, by his own admission. However, the Vision could not have existed in his present form without the JARVIS AI, and perhaps this being who is worthy of lifting Thor's hammer, who finds grace in humanity's failings and considers it a privilege to exist among them, is informed not only by the Mind Stone, but in some small part by the father figure Stark could not let go of.[24]

The Man Behind the Mask

In the closing scenes of *Avengers: Age of Ultron*, Stark takes his leave of The Avengers and will return in *Captain America: Civil War*.[25] His personal growth and achievements in and out of the Iron Man armor are undeniable, but he remains a danger to himself when motivated by fear. *Iron Man* director John Favreau has explicitly stated Robert Downey, Jr., was cast in this role because of how his own life mirrored that of the character, stating, "the best and worst moments of Robert's life have been in the public eye. He had to find an inner balance to overcome obstacles that went far beyond his career. That's Tony Stark."[26]

Rosemann expands upon the effect this casting had on the way Iron Man is marketed:

> In focus groups, kids thought [Iron Man] was a robot. That's why the casting of Robert was so important. Because they needed someone so communicate how flawed and fascinating and sexy Tony Stark is as a character. There are many, many movie posters of Iron Man with his mask off to show hey, there's a man in there and he's Robert Downey Jr. There's a man in there and he's cool and he's crazy and you're gonna love him.[27]

The complexity and believability of Tony Stark has not been realized on film through skillful writing and clever direction alone. Robert Downey Junior's portrayal of Stark, whether taken alongside or separately from his own heroic rebuilding of his life and career cannot be underestimated when examining why Iron Man is such an international phenomenon, and in the minds of many fans, he *is* Iron Man.[28]

Conclusion

Iron Man is a hero with something for everyone. His hero's journey shows that it is possible to overcome past mistakes, personal demons and panic attacks. In his respect for technology, he demonstrates what it can achieve when unencumbered by fear or hubris. Each of Stark's appearances in the MCU between 2008 and 2015 build upon one another to construct a portrait of a man who is at once flawed, relatable, complicated, inspirational and just plain fun to spend time with. He may have come to life during the 1960s, but the Iron Man of film proves that Cold War anxieties surrounding mechanized warfare and the ubiquity of technology are even more relevant in the 21st century. In an age of increased political awareness and reliance upon technology that has the power to change lives for both good and ill, Iron Man's international cinematic success demonstrates the character's resonance and relevance to viewers on a worldwide scale.[29]

NOTES

1. Bill Rosemann (Marvel Creative Director) in discussion with the author, 4 April 2015.
2. *Ibid.*
3. Box Office Mojo, *"All Time Box Office."* Last modified July 30, 2015, http://www.box officemojo.com/alltime/world/
4. Amy K. Nyberg, *Seal of Approval: The History of the Comics Code.* (Kindle Edition, University Press of Mississippi, 1998), Kindle location 1123.
5. Les Daniels, *Marvel: Five Fabulous Decades of the World's Greatest Comics.* (New York, Harry N. Abrams, Inc. 1991) 95.
6. Walter LaFeber, *America Russia and the Cold War 1945–1992 7th Edition.* (New York: McGraw-Hill, 1993) 226–228, 195–254.
7. Stan Lee, Larry Lieber, and Don Heck. *Tales of Suspense* #39, March 1963. (New York: Marvel Comics).
8. John Romita, *Captain America* #76. (New York: Atlas Comics, 1954).
9. David Michelinie and Bob Layton, *The Invincible Iron Man* #120–128. (New York, Marvel Comics, 1979).
10. *Iron Man,* directed by John Favreau (2008; Los Angeles: Paramount, 2008), DVD.
11. Bill Rosemann (Marvel Creative Director) in discussion with the author, 4 April 2015.
12. *Iron Man.*
13. *Iron Man 2,* directed by John Favreau (2010; Burbank, CA: Marvel Studios, 2010), DVD.
14. Archie Goodwin, *Iron Man* #28. (New York: Marvel Comics, 1970).
15. *Iron Man 2,* directed by John Favreau (2010; Burbank, CA: Marvel Studios, 2010), DVD.
16. Brandt Englestein, *Agent Carter* Episode 4 "The Blitzkrieg Button." Original airdate January 27, 2015.
17. Michelle Fazekas and Tara Butters, *Agent Carter* Episode 8 "Valediction." Original airdate February 24, 2015.
18. *Marvel's The Avengers,* directed by Joss Whedon (2012; Burbank, CA: Marvel Studios, 2012), DVD.
19. *Iron Man 3,* directed by Shane Black (2013; Burbank, CA: Marvel Studios, 2013), DVD.

20. *Avengers: Age of Ultron*, directed by Joss Whedon (2015; Burbank, CA: Marvel Studios, 2015), DVD.

21. T.S. Eliot, "The Hollow Men." *Poems 1909–1925*. 1925.

22. Brandt Englestein, *Agent Carter* Episode 4 "The Blitzkrieg Button." Original airdate January 27, 2015.

23. Joe Casey and Justin Theroux, *Iron Man 2: Public Identity Vol. 2*. (Marvel Digital Comics, 2010).

24. *Avengers: Age of Ultron*, directed by Joss Whedon (2015; Burbank, CA: Marvel Studios, 2015), DVD.

25. Captain America: Civil War, directed by Anthony Russo and Joe Russo. (2016; Burbank, CA: Marvel Studios).

26. Scott Bowles, "First Look: Downey Forges a Bond with 'Iron Man' role." Last April 26, 2007. http://usatoday30.usatoday.com/life/movies/news/2007-04-26-iron-man_N.htm.

27. Bill Rosemann (Marvel Creative Director) in discussion with the author, 4 April 2015.

28. Trevor D. Richardson, "Futurists: The Parallels of Robert Downey, Jr., and Tony Stark." Last modified 2008. http://www.subtopian.com/futurists-the-parallels-of-robert-downey-jr-and-tony-stark/

29. Further reading:

Bernard A. Weisberger, *Cold War, Cold Peace: The United States and Russia Since 1945* (New York: American Heritage Publishing, 1984) 201–278.

Comics Continuum, "Questions-and-Answer: Iron Man Director John Favreau." Last modified March 3rd, 2008. http://www.comicscontinuum.com/stories/0803/03/jonfavreau.htm.

John Donovan, "Cold War in Comics: Clobberin' Commies and Promoting Nationalism in American Comics." *Ages of Heroes, Eras of Men*. (Newcastle upon Tyne, Cambridge Scholars Publishing, 2013).

Robert Genter, "With Great Power Comes Great Responsibility: Cold War Culture and the Birth of Marvel Comics." *The Journal of Popular Culture* vol. 40. Issue 6 (2007): 953–978.

Roger Stahl, *Militainment, Inc.: War, Media and Popular Culture*. (New York, Routledge, 2010) 46.

Roth Cornet, "Captain America: Civil War-Robert Downey, Jr., and Chris Evans on What Drives Captain America and Iron Man Apart." Last modified April 15, 2015. http://www.ign.com/articles/2015/04/15/captain-america-civil-war-robert-downey-jr-and-chris-evans-on-what-drives-cap-and-iron-man-apart?watch.

Stanley Karnow, "Ho Chi Minh: He Married Nationalism to Communism and Perfected the Deadly Art of Guerilla Warfare." Last modified April 13, 1998. http://content.time.com/time/magazine/article/0,9171,988162,00.html.

Stephen Hess and Marvin Kalb, *The Media and the War on Terrorism*. (Washington D.C., Brookings Institution Press, 2003).

Silly Love Songs, Gender, *Guardians of the Galaxy* and *Avengers: Age of Ultron*

JAMES ROVIRA

"Without contraries there is no progression"
—William Blake

Marvel's *Guardians of the Galaxy* was without question the premier summer blockbuster of 2014, grossing over $774 million at the box office. As such, it takes a significant place in the history of Marvel's contribution to 20th and 21st century youth culture, a history that began its current incarnation in 1961 with the release of the first *Fantastic Four* comic book. Arising during a period of a burgeoning countercultural awareness while still being directed, at least initially, toward adolescent and pre-adolescent male audiences, Marvel comics have vacillated between stereotypical views of women portrayed with unrealistic, hypersexualized presentations of the female body and an impulse to develop strong, leading women who break cultural stereotypes that serve as inspiring female role models. Marvel's film version of *Guardians of the Galaxy* begins to resolve this tension, serving as a culmination, so far, in Marvel's development of female characters and in its presentation of gender. Read in the context of the history of androgyny in Western discourse from Plato to Cixous, *Guardians'* treatment of male and female roles ultimately dissociates gender and biological sex, establishing a new pattern of gender roles in the Marvel Cinematic Universe that extends into *Avengers: Age of Ultron.*

The plot of *Guardians* is a fairly straightforward end-of-world scenario that positions the film as a (to date) tangential contribution to the Infinity Wars plot currently being developed within the Marvel Cinematic Universe.

Peter Quill (Chris Pratt), an Earth native, was abducted from Earth in 1988 at the age of 10 by Yondu Udonta (Michael Rooker), the alien leader of the mercenary Ravagers. This abduction took place the day that Quill's mother died. Since being abducted, Quill has been a member of the Ravagers, but the title sequence introducing the adult Peter Quill shows him acting independently of Yondu to retrieve an orb so that he can sell it for his own profit and live independently.

The orb contains one of six infinity stones that grant their bearers immense power, including the power to destroy all organic life on a planet. This orb is also sought by Ronan (Lee Pace), a Kree radical who seeks to destroy the Nova Empire, and who has agreed to retrieve the orb (ignorant of what it contains) for Thanos (Josh Brolin, uncredited) in exchange for the destruction of Xandar, the central planet in the Nova Empire. Thanos loans to Ronan his technologically enhanced adopted "daughters" Gamora (Zoe Saldana) and Nebula (Karen Gillan) to carry out this task. Ronan sends Gamora to retrieve the orb, but Gamora, like Quill, desires to steal it for herself and sell it at a very high price to the Collector (Benicio del Toro). In the meantime, Yondu has put a bounty on Quill's head, and bounty hunters Rocket (Bradley Cooper) and Groot (Vin Diesel) find Quill on Xandar where he is attempting to sell the orb. Quill, Gamora, Rocket, and Groot all converge and fight on Xandar, where they are captured by Xandarian police and imprisoned.

While in the prison Kyln, they meet Drax (Dave Bautista), who is seeking revenge on Ronan for killing his family, and as a group they agree to work together to escape, sell the orb to the Collector, and split the bounty. When they meet the Collector at the space station Knowhere, which is built within the giant severed head of an alien being, they learn what the orb is and how dangerous it is, but before the sale is complete, the group is subject to separate attacks by both the Ravagers and Ronan's army. Ronan captures the orb, learns what it is, gains control over it, and then resolves to go to Xandar to destroy all life on the planet using the orb. Once Quill makes peace with Yondu, he and Gamora convince him to help them recapture the orb, promising him the orb in exchange for his help, but Gamora and Quill intend only to capture and keep the orb in order to hand it over to Nova Prime (Glenn Close), leader of the Nova Empire, so that she can keep it safely locked up. The prisoners have now become a team; working with the Ravagers, they recapture the orb, use it to defeat and kill Ronan, and then hand it over to Nova Prime, who does as expected with it. Yondu is fooled into thinking he has been given the orb until it is too late.

As a creative work representing an androgynous ideal, *Guardians of the Galaxy* is only one recent development within a long history of androgyny in western literature and philosophy. The first important source for western androgyny is Plato's *Symposium*, a dialog in which participants argue in support of different theories of love. One of the participants, Aristophanes, asserts that humanity was originally and naturally three-sexed: male, female, and androgynous, and that all human beings were essentially double in form, having two heads, four arms, four legs, and two sets of genitals. Males and females had two sets of same-sexed genitals while androgynous humans had one male and one female set of genitals. These original humans were so powerful that they posed a threat to the Olympian gods, leading Zeus to split them in half in order to reduce their threat without destroying humanity. The immediate result was that all human beings sought to bond again with their original counterparts: males derived from fully male or fully female humans desired reunion with members of the same sex, while originally androgynous human beings sought reunion with opposite-sexed partners. Besides presenting a very early theory that normalizes sexual desire in terms of both heterosexual and homosexual *identity*, Aristophanes' narrative supports a normative view of androgyny, one in which heterosexual desire itself is a pursuit of an androgynous ideal in which male and female are not de-sexed but combined in one person.[1]

The androgynic ideal resurfaces in the late eighteenth-century poetry of William Blake, specifically *The [First] Book of Urizen* and *The Four Zoas*. In Blake's mythological works of the 1790s and later, all of which written during a time of widespread European war, the ideal human is presented as a fourfold being, so that Blake's mythology narrates a primal unity followed by a fall into division that culminates in a reintegration into a single whole. Within this narrative, division into sexes represents an extension of the fall from primal unity rather than an ideally created state, similar to Aristophanes. While sexual difference as a fall may be implied in Genesis in the form of Eve being created from Adam's rib, Blake's *The [First] Book of Urizen* makes explicit its presentation of sexual division as a fall: "9. All Eternity shudderd at sight / Of the first female now separate / Pale as a cloud of snow / Waving before the face of Los / 10. Wonder, awe, fear, astonishment, / Petrify the eternal myriads; / At the first female form now separate / They call'd her Pity, and fled."[2] The female in this account embodies the phenomenology of pity (Enitharmon) found in the human imagination (Los) as it views fallen reason (Urizen), so that redemption or reintegration begins as female emanations bond once again with their male counterparts.

Over 100 years later, Virginia Woolf and Hélène Cixous employ the concept of androgyny to define human creativity and to recover the significance of both genders. Woolf's *A Room of One's Own* (1929), itself written during a period between two world wars, follows Blake's contemporary, Coleridge, in her suggestion that the best writers have androgynous minds. Woolf was addressing a hypermasculine era in which male authors had to be demonstrably and vociferously anti-feminine while female writers could reap the benefits of androgyny, so she sees a deficiency in male authors who lack an androgynous mind. Similarly, Hélène Cixous in "The Laugh of the Medusa" (1976) celebrates the union of the two sexes in one person: "Besides, isn't it evident that the penis gets around in my texts, that I give it a place and appeal? Of course I do. I want all. I want all of me with all of him."[3] Cixous's androgyny, like Woolf's, sees the feminine loss of the masculine as a loss for the feminine and, similarly, the masculine loss of the feminine as a loss for the masculine.

Blake's, Cixous's, Woolf's and the *Symposium*'s presentations of androgyny pose two questions that bear upon the profile of androgyny in *Guardians of the Galaxy*. The first question has to do with androgyny's seeming reliance upon stereotypically masculine and feminine characteristics. Doesn't androgynic discourse perpetuate the gender divisions that it seeks to eradicate? The next question regards the definition of androgyny: Is it a union of, or balance between, the masculine and feminine or a fusion of the two?[4] Does androgyny as an ideal seek a psychological hermaphroditism or an asexual humanity? In the way that it addresses these questions, *Guardians of the Galaxy* advances the representation of gender in Marvel's Cinematic Universe. While *Guardians* relies upon traditional conceptions of gender characteristics to do so, it undermines the association of gender and sex by inverting and mixing traditional gender characteristics as they are applied to biological sex.

Peter Quill is a nexus of converging forces, embodying a contradiction between biological sex and gender. He is simultaneously human and alien, having a human mother and an alien father. In relationship to the Nova Empire, he is a criminal and an outsider but also its greatest protector, and in relationship to the Guardians themselves, he is a mercenary, a pirate, a selfish opportunist, a loner, and an inspiring team leader. Most important, however, is his association of the earth with his mother, an association extended and maintained by the mixtape she made for him that is his only remaining tie to earth. Director James Gunn calls Quill's Walkman[5] an "umbilical cord" connecting him to earth, which ties it very closely to his lost mother, with the maternal, and with nurturing in general.[6] Alternatively, the cosmos is almost exclusively hypermasculine. This film tells readers nothing about Quill's father except that he was an alien and that the closest thing Quill has to a father figure, Yondu Udonta, believes that Quill's father is a "jackass." Apart from Quill's absent father, the film's villains embody masculine stereotypes such as physical strength and physical and psychological aggression: Thanos, Ronan, the prison guards, and Drax—who winds up as a supporting character for the protagonist Quill—spend almost the entire film attempting to out-man one another through murder, serving as the masculine counterpart to the feminine forces in the film.

The sole alien exception to this hypermasculine cosmos is Nova Prime, the female leader of the Nova Empire who is first seen taking a protective stance for families living on the outskirts of her territory as they are suffering from Ronan's attacks. Like Quill's mother, she occupies primarily a protective role and represents on a planetary scale the "damsel in distress." Her planet, Xandar, is in danger of being destroyed by Ronan and must be saved by Peter Quill, the Guardians, and Yondu's mercenary forces while she passively watches and waits. So there is no question that the film begins with a very stereotypical baseline conception of the masculine and the feminine, and that the cosmos as a whole is caught in a conflict between masculine and feminine forces. In *Guardians of the Galaxy*, the feminine is represented primarily by a beloved, absent woman who has died of cancer who stands in for the Earth, so that a feminized Earth is being juxtaposed against a hypermasculine cosmos. The film's teleology, then, if it seeks to affirm an androgynous ideal, is toward the preservation and rejuvenation of the feminine.

This rejuvenation begins with the masculine becoming feminized. "Feminization" within *Guardians* should be usually understood in terms of the acquisition of some traditionally feminine characteristics in an otherwise (and otherwise still remaining) hypermasculine male. The alien Drax experiences the most significant character development in this way. Having witnessed his wife and children being murdered by Ronan, Drax is filled with rage and bent on revenge, so that the loss of feminine characteristics is driven by the loss of significant women in this male's life. The loss of the wife and/or mother is a common motivator for male rage in Marvel films and in film in general. See, for example, *The Hulk* (2003): "The film represents the emotional and physical destruction of the family by the loss of the mother. [...] Only the restoration of the female—in this case Betty Ross (perf. Jennifer Connelly)—can calm the Hulk's rage and, presumably, bring emotional healing as well."[7] Both in the 2003 version of *The Hulk* and in the character of Drax, the loss of the female and, by extension for these characters, either the physical or emotional loss of the father's children (who in Drax's case is a daughter) is the focal point for male rage. These losses are both the immediate and extended effects of the severing of primal androgynous humans, recalling the axe of Zeus, which severed the female from the male. In this case, it does so by murdering the female.

Drax, however, abandons his rage after nearly causing the deaths of his fellow Guardians (although they had not yet identified themselves as a team), causing the capture of Quill and Gamora by Yondu and his team, and after nearly being killed himself in his long-desired confrontation with Ronan. He soon sees that he has rebuilt a family of sorts as a member of a team: while he does not abandon his quest for vengeance, he realizes he is no longer motivated by blinding rage and that he has reestablished emotional bonds with friends who are becoming family to him. His archetypal masculine characteristics—

he acts alone, he is driven by rage, and he provokes confrontation without thought for consequences—have now given way to a sense of belonging to a group and a feeling of connection with, and responsibility to, others. He begins to acquire feminine characteristics.

Gamora, as Drax's female equivalent and as the one character within the team most at odds with him, is a hypermasculine female. Trained and technologically modified by Thanos to be an assassin after having seen her parents killed, Gamora is a killing machine bent on gaining her freedom from Thanos by capturing the orb herself and selling it for her own profit. She, like Drax, is violent, driven by anger, and committed to acting alone. Unlike her comic book equivalent, who has a predatory sexual appetite strong enough to leave Tony Stark traumatized after lovemaking, the film's Gamora is almost completely both masculinized and desexualized when she first appears in the film. However, her interactions with Quill, who is attracted to her as a woman and who attempts to interact with her romantically, move her toward traditionally feminine characteristics. Quill's music has the strongest effect on her. While they are waiting on Knowhere to meet the Collector, Gamora asks Quill about his Walkman. He demonstrates it for her by putting his headphones on her and starting the tape, which is queued to Elvin Bishop's "Fooled Around and Fell in Love," a romantic, 1970's soft rock love song. She enjoys the music, begins to let Quill dance slowly with her, but then pushes him down and holds a knife to his throat, telling him that she refuses to succumb to his "pelvic sorcery." At this stage in Gamora's character development, she is uncomfortable with her identity as a woman, with her reproductive potential, and with the vulnerability that would attend a romantic relationship with Quill.

Perhaps the best illustration of Gamora's character is in the contrast between her actions and Quill's when the Guardians are escaping Kyln. Rocket has a list of items that he needs in order to execute his escape plan that includes a mechanical prosthetic leg and a control panel mounted to the arms of the prison guards. As Quill retrieves the leg and Gamora the control panel, camera shots alternate between Peter politely asking the prisoner for his leg (he winds up transferring him 30,000 credits in exchange for his leg) and Gamora defeating several guards in hand-to-hand combat, breaking one's arm and ripping the control panel off of it. At that moment, she is a hypermasculine female starkly contrasted with a male who achieves his ends nonviolently, by talking. While Quill also fights and shoots when necessary, what distinguishes him from the non–Earth characters is that he does not do so when unnecessary. He is the off-earth extension of his mother's consideration and care while Gamora embodies rage and aggression.

Despite her hypermasculinity, however, Gamora is still moved by the music on Quill's Walkman. Gamora is not the only character in the film so affected by that music, however. The prison guard impounding the Guardians' clothing and personal effects is particularly drawn to Quill's Walkman, confiscating it for himself. He adopts a relaxed, peaceful pose while listening to it. In a scene cut from the film, the same guard dances through the prison while listening to "Magic" by Pilot.[8] At the end of the film, when the Guardians are confronting Ronan on the surface of Xandar, Quill dances to "Ooh Child" by The Five Stairsteps, which is playing in the background from his destroyed ship. He distracts Ronan long enough for Rocket to fire an improvised weapon at the hammer in which Ronan has lodged the Infinity Stone, affording Quill the opportunity to retrieve the stone and defeat Ronan. Quill's music, as the extension of his mother's love and care through time and space, contributed to the ultimate defeat of the film's hypermasculine villain.

One song in particular, "Cherry Bomb," is a focal point for the convergence of feminine elements as resistance to a masculine cosmos. "Cherry Bomb" was written and performed by the Runaways, an all-female band, and in this song "cherry" is being used as both a sign and a celebration of the singer's womanhood, "cherry bomb" referring to both the singer's own powerful femininity, to the all-female band itself and its music, and to a large firecracker popular in the 1970s that used up to a ¼ stick of dynamite, signifying the power of the feminine.[9] This song plays while the Guardians and the Ravagers prepare to attack Ronan's ship, which identifies their resistance to the hypermasculine Ronan as the "cherry bomb" itself, the return of femininity and its resistance to destructive hypermasculinity extended through time and space from Quill's mother to the present.

The film's music consistently serves in this way as commentary on the film's action. "I'm Not in Love" by 10CC plays while a young Peter Quill sits outside his mother's hospital room while she is dying, indicating his management of grief by denial. "Come and Get Your Love" by Redbone plays while Quill is retrieving the orb, associating the orb with his desire for freedom and perhaps anticipating how it will lead him to Gamora. That song is followed up by the Raspberries' "Go All the Way," which plays as Quill is rocketing off the planet with the orb. Blue Swede's version of "Hooked on a Feeling" plays while Quill is being processed in the prison Kyln, which includes him being beaten and subject to electric shock. While the director described the relationship of this song to the action as "ironic" in that it is an upbeat song playing during horrifying action, he also suggests that the song represents Meredith Quill's "positivity" helping her son Peter get through these hard times.[10] The song could also signify that Quill's life has been a prison, and that his escape from Kyln may also be an escape from past self-defeating patterns.

As the team is leaving Xandar, Quill finally gains the courage to open the gift his mother gave him on the day of her death. It is another mixtape,

"Awesome Mix Vol. 2," and the first song on the tape is "Ain't No Mountain High Enough" by Marvin Gaye and Tammy Terrell, projecting Meredith Quill's future hopes for her son. The film ends with "I Want You Back" by the Jackson 5, a song about lost love, and very likely a mother helping her son express his grief while she shares her own. The song is again ironic: the relational context is painful grief while the song itself is very upbeat, which may be the very way that Meredith Quill's music infused Peter with strength in his most difficult circumstances.

Nineteen seventies' mixtapes were predecessors of iTunes playlists and could be simple collections of favorite songs. Some people still burn them on CDs. They could be themed. Arrangements of playlists can now be automated by genre, grouping, performer, or songwriter, but someone putting together a mixtape on cassette had to select the songs and record them onto the cassette one song at a time, so that they were very intentional products. When mixtapes were given as gifts, the sequence of songs could be a subtle (or not so subtle) message to the recipient: it was a low-risk way of sharing your feelings with a possible girlfriend or boyfriend, who could pretend to just enjoy the music but not get the message if your feelings weren't shared. Since Peter Quill is listening to the film's music on a mixtape, then, this music isn't just a soundtrack artificially laid over action taking place independently of it. The music exists in the world of the film. In addition, the film was scored in part before it was shot, so that the film was timed to match the music and not the other way around.[11] When the music is not part of the film itself (as it is in any sequence in which a character is listening to Quill's Walkman), it is part of Quill's mental soundtrack. It is the music he has listened to over and over again as the last remnant of his time on Earth and of the mother whom he carries with him everywhere. It is also a collection of messages sent to him by his mother that is then carried by him beyond Earth. Because all of the songs included in the film have romantic love as its object, the soundtrack in Quill's head both emphasizes the androgynic ideal and extends the power of the feminine through the cosmos.

The scene in which Ronan is finally defeated deserves further attention as both the climax of the action and the final and most powerful imagine of the union of masculine and feminine forces. Once Rocket successfully shatters Ronan's hammer with a projectile, Quill grabs the loose Infinity Stone. That act should have destroyed him, as happened to the Collector's slave, Yarina (Ophelia Lovibond), in Knowhere when she attempted to grab the stone to use it to gain her freedom. Quill being only half human, with an alien side that is something "quite ancient," undoubtedly helps him hold the stone. However, when he first seizes the stone, he begins to be ripped apart, and as that was happening, Gamora reaches out to him so that some of the stone's destructive effects can be transferred to her as well. Once all of the Guardians are joined, Quill is not only able to hold the stone, but to control it long enough to use it to destroy Ronan.

This scene does more than reinforce the film's emphasis on community, however; it explicitly equates Gamora with Quill's mother, effectively unifying the masculine and feminine. When Gamora reaches out to Quill, she yells to him, "Take my hand." At that moment Quill's vision was transferred to his mother, who on her deathbed also asked Quill to take her hand. As a child, Quill was afraid; as an adult, he reached out to his mother/Gamora, uniting with her (the feminine), and in so doing he gained the strength that enabled him to hold the stone. The film could not more explicitly represent the girlfriend as a substitute mother, or the union of the masculine and feminine as the means of defeating destructive hypermasculinity. But the film is not simply joining a male representative of masculinity with a female representative of femininity: Quill is more feminized than Gamora, as Gamora had been almost completely masculinized when she first met Quill. Masculinity and femininity, then, are detached from biological sex, each being possessed in varying degrees by both sexes. The association of these characteristics with biological sex in the film is merely incidental or conventional. The film therefore idealizes an androgyny that dissociates gender from sex and allows for a variety of gender constructions. Its androgyny is not artificially asexual, nor does it confine or restrict gender to sex.

As mentioned above, many of these elements are present in other Marvel films, but *Guardians* represents a significant departure from previous films and establishes a pattern replicated in *Avengers: Age of Ultron.* I have already illustrated how the pattern is followed in the 2003 version of *The Hulk:* the dead/absent mother is the cause of the hero's rage, which is only calmed through a girlfriend who fills the void left by an absent wife/mother. *The Incredible Hulk* (2008) shares similar plot devices, but more importantly, in *Thor: The Dark World* (2013), Loki (Tom Hiddleston) follows this pattern. Loki's support for Asgard was finally galvanized only by the murder of his mother, a murder that took place in the presence of Thor's (Chris Hemsworth) girlfriend, Jane Foster (Natalie Portman). Again, the son passes from mother to girlfriend. Most important in all of these films is that, unlike in *Guardians,* biological sex is always closely aligned with traditional gender expectations, so that the female is always the damsel in distress, never the fighter, and the male is the focal point of rage and violence who can only be calmed by female compassion. Thor's character in *Thor* (2011) was one characterized by impatience, anger, a little bit of stupidity, and a quickness to rush into battles in which he reveled, a character depiction consistent with the Thor of the *Eddas* and carried forward to some degree in *The Avengers* (2012).

The most controversial development of this pattern by far, however, is found in *Avengers: Age of Ultron* (2015). Both the film and its self-professed feminist director, Joss Whedon, have been taken to task in the media and on Twitter for its conflicted representation of the most important woman in the Marvel Cinematic Universe, Natasha Romanoff, who is also known as Black Widow (Scarlett Johansson). Those critical of the film attack its presentation of Romanoff because of the "lullaby" scene and because her backstory. The lullaby scene occurs early in the film, which opens with an intense action sequence. Once the Hulk is no longer needed, Black Widow calls him to herself, and as the Hulk allows it, she gently strokes his fingers and wrist, calming him down enough to transform back into Bruce Banner. As the Hulk shrinks in size, the camera focuses on Black Widow, who smiles to herself at the power she has over the Hulk.

This power, however, is a traditionally feminine power: it is calming and gentle in the face of rage. *Age of Ultron* reveals a now feminized Black Widow who finds herself attracted to a man because he doesn't want to fight. Her intentions are for a serious, long-term relationship with Banner, who is more completely divided between hypermasculine and traditionally feminine characteristics than any other Marvel character. Bruce Banner regrets all of the Hulk's killing and destructiveness, regardless of context. He is unable to fight until he has transformed into the Hulk, but as the Hulk, he is a "big green rage monster" whose destructive capability is almost unstoppable. She lives in a world of fighters, as she says in her conversation with Banner, and the Hulk is the strongest and most frightening—especially to her personally—fighter that she knows. Romanoff is deeply attracted to Banner precisely because he does not want to fight, and she is also attracted to him as the Hulk because she can exercise non-violent, feminine power over him.

Black Widow's character, developed over the course of four films—*Iron Man 2*, *The Avengers*, *Captain America: The Winter Soldier*, and *Avengers: Age of Ultron*—parallels Gamora's character development. She is first seen in *Iron Man 2* in a boxing ring. In her job as a spy, she is a masculinized, deadly fighter who has killed or immobilized dozens of male or masculinized opponents. She wears her feminine sexuality as a mask, using it as a tool to bring down male defenses for information, but her closest relationships are all with men as a fellow team member. She is therefore largely asexual, and she only begins to acquire a sexual identity capable of intimacy with a male as she develops feelings for Bruce Banner.

Banner fears having a relationship with her, however, primarily fearing for Romanoff's safety. In the scene that became the focal point of controversy about the film's presentation of Black Widow's character, Banner is still coping with the destruction the Hulk caused to a city after coming under the influence of Wanda Maximoff's (Elizabeth Olsen) psychic manipulation. Banner has every reason to fear for Romanoff's life if they were in a romantic relationship and concludes his list of reasons for not getting involved in a romantic relationship with the fact that he can never have a family: he cannot conceive a child. Romanoff responded in kind, with a list of her own faults:

> BANNER: I can't ever.... I can't have this [points around to the child's bedroom in which the conversation is being held]. I can't ever ... do the math. I physically can't.
>
> ROMANOFF: Neither can I. In the red room, where I was ... trained ... where I was raised ... um ... they have a "graduation" ceremony. They sterilize you. It's efficient. One less thing to worry about. The one thing that might matter more than the mission. It makes everything easier. Even killing. You still think you're the only monster on the team?

Some pro-feminist responses to this dialog on Twitter and in other media have read this scene as Romanoff calling herself a "monster" only because she cannot have children, and they see the "lullaby" scene as a means of returning to her a child in the form of the Hulk. These respondents are understandably frustrated with the loss of childbearing potential as the source of the Black Widow's monstrosity because doing so defines womanhood only by reproductive capacity.[12] Pro-feminist responses more sympathetic to Whedon[13] read the line in the context of the two prior flashback scenes in which Romanoff was being trained to fight and required to shoot and kill a bound and hooded man. Her self-professed monstrosity is, in this reading, found in the ease with which she can now kill, not her sterility, which is merely one means of ensuring that Black Widow becomes the most effective trained killer possible.

The latter reading of these lines is well-supported by previous dialog in the first Avengers film in which Black Widow says that she has "red in her ledger" because of a conversation with Loki in which he recounted some of her worst killings. Furthermore, the idea that motherhood is so much more powerful than killing that a female assassin who became a mother would give up her life as an assassin isn't unusual in action films. Quentin Tarantino's *Kill Bill* films are based on this premise. Besides being a life-affirming moment in an otherwise violent action film, however, femininity being defined by motherhood is not the most important issue at stake at this moment in the film. *Avengers: Age of Ultron* is another creation anxiety film modeled on *Frankenstein* in which a "mad scientist" creates via technology a new form of life which then turns on its human creator in an apocalyptic rage. The "mad scientist" was a trope used by Tony Stark (Robert Downey, Jr.) in the film itself, invoking this literary tradition. *Blake and Kierkegaard: Creation and Anxiety* (2010) observes that this plotline originates in English literature in Blake's *The [First] Book of Urizen*, finds its most famous formulation in Mary Shelley's *Frankenstein*, and then continues throughout the nineteenth and twentieth centuries in novels, plays, and films from *R.U.R.* to *Ex Machina* and any number of direct adaptations of Shelley's *Frankenstein* itself.[14] *Blake and Kierkegaard* argues that this intrinsic fear of one's creation originates as a response to Enlightenment models of the self, so that the human race fears what it creates because it no longer understands itself as a created, organic product, but rather something more like a machine. But since the most significant text articulating this myth, *Frankenstein*, was written by Mary Shelley, the creation anxiety myth may also project female fears of independently male procreation, so that the monstrous is that which is created by the male apart from female agency. Romanoff and Banner's union, then, as one between a masculinized female and a feminized male, affirms the principle of androgyny in ways that Stark did not. Stark, motivated by fear and denying the principle of androgyny, initially created a monster that reflected his fears.

In *Guardians of the Galaxy*'s reconfiguration of gender in the Marvel Cinematic Universe, asexuality does not seem to be a viable option, not only because it is inconsistent with the everyday lives of most people, but also because "asexual" usually means either "male" or "a sexually unavailable female" in much current film. MCU films, then, seem to be moving in the direction of a principle of androgyny that exists independently of biological sex, perhaps one that might require us to find alternative terms for abstract qualities such as "masculinity" and "femininity," as these are too closely associated with biological sex. Taking a broader view, identifying the Earth and, by extension, the entire human race with the feminine is a projection of the physical weakness and vulnerability that human beings feel in the face of an immeasurable, mysterious cosmos: it is not a coincidence that both Blake's and Woolf's formulations of anxiety arose in times of widespread European war. If there is life out there that can reach us, it is stronger than we are, because we cannot reach it; thus, we are vulnerable, and so Earth is assigned the position of the feminine as a sign of our feelings of vulnerability. *Guardians of the Galaxy* explores the power of the feminine to resist this threatening cosmos in order to empower humanity against the unknown, accepting Earth's feminine identity and viewing it as an asset, while *Avengers: Age of Ultron* explores what may happen if we simply react to our worst fears and attempt to beat power with a hypermasculine, greater power. What the MCU idealizes instead is the union of opposites, not only in its presentation of gender and sex, but in its emphasis upon teams such as the Avengers and the Guardians of the Galaxy that are characterized by internal conflict. Like William Blake, the creators of the MCU seem to believe that "without contraries there is no progression," which perhaps is the most hopeful sign possible. The conflicts that seem to be splitting us apart—even the arguments over how gender is represented in film—may be the very means by which we progress in all of the best ways. Not all who fight are enemies.

Notes

1. Diane Hoeveler's *Romantic Androgyny: the Women Within.* University Park: Penn State University Press, 1990, influenced my consideration of androgyny within this essay.

2. William Blake, *The Complete Poetry and Prose of William Blake,* revised ed., ed. David Erdman (New York: Anchor Books, 1982), 78.

3. Hélène Cixous, Keith Cohen, and Paula Cohen, "The Laugh of the Medusa," *Signs* 1, no. 4 (Summer, 1976): 892.

4. Marilyn R. Farwell, "Virginia Woolf and Androgyny," *Contemporary Literature,* 16, no. 4 (Autumn, 1975): 433–451.

5. The Walkman shown in the film has been identified as a 1979 Sony TPS-L2 that at the time of this writing is selling on eBay for $2995.00 because of the film's popularity.

6. Sam Ashurst, "*Guardians of the Galaxy:* James Gunn's Trailer Breakdown," *Games Radar+,* last modified April 24, 2015, http://www.gamesradar.com/guardians-of-the-galaxy-james-gunn-s-trailer-breakdown.

7. James Rovira, "Finding Hulko: Secondary Colors," *Metaphilm,* July 22, 2003, http://metaphilm.com/index.php/detail/finding_hulko.

8. Eric Eisenberg, "The 15 Songs *Guardians of the Galaxy* Was Originally Planning to Use," *CinemaBlend,* December 18, 2014, http://www.cinemablend.com/new/15-Songs-Guardians-Galaxy-Was-Originally-Planning-Use-68750.html.

9. I know this from my own childhood growing up in 1970's Cerritos, California, which was in Los Angeles County on the border of Orange County. Neighborhood friends detonated firecrackers called "cherry bombs" in the middle of the street, typically suspended three or four feet from the ground using a ladder to keep from blowing a hole in the pavement. The Runaways were a 1970's L.A.–based band.

10. Alex Suskind, "Director James Gunn on How He Chose the Music for *Guardians of the Galaxy,*" *Vulture,* August 4, 2014, http://www.vulture.com/2014/08/how-guardians-of-the-galaxy-music-soundtrack-was-chosen.html.

11. Sandy Schaefer, "James Gunn on *Guardians of the Galaxy* Composer Tyler Bates' Approach," *ScreenRant,* April, 2013, http://screenrant.com/guardians-galaxy-movie-2014-composer-tyler-bates-score.

12. Meredith Woerner and Katharine Trendacosta, "Black Widow: This Is Why We Can't Have Nice Things," *iO9,* May 5, 2015, http://io9.com/black-widow-this-is-why-we-can-t-have-nice-things-1702333037.

13. Adam B. Vary, "Joss Whedon Calls 'Horsesh*t' on Reports He Left Twitter Because of Militant Feminists," *Buzzfeed,* May 6, 2015, http://www.buzzfeed.com/adambvary/joss-whedon-on-leaving-twitter#.dqbOKwJeJ. Joss Whedon mentions Feminist Frequency founder Anita Sarkeesian as a sympathetic and supportive viewer in this interview.

14. James Rovira, *Blake and Kierkegaard: Creation and Anxiety* (New York: Continuum, 2010).

Hooked on the Wrong Kind of Feeling

Popular Music and Nostalgia in the Marvel Cinematic Universe

MASANI MCGEE

Many contemporary films make the choice to incorporate popular music into their diegesis, but in most cases this is incidental to the narrative itself—a way to highlight a particular emotion or theme, or even as a comedic touch. Within most cinematic genres, music is largely a promotional tool to sell film soundtracks. The recent batch of superhero films released in the past 15 years has primarily used this approach to music in film, usually including popular songs from the rock and pop genres. Films like the *Iron Man* franchise have capitalized on such a relationship by using the soundtrack to emphasize the film's brand, with the second soundtrack featuring songs solely by Australian band AC/DC. And while there are some references within the franchise that point towards its music—Stark is shown blasting the aforementioned band during a fight in *The Avengers*—occurrences of intra diegetic music, or music that directly affects the narrative itself, have been rare. This tactic changed somewhat with the introduction of two recent films within the Marvel Cinematic Universe. *Captain America: The Winter Soldier* and *Guardians of the Galaxy* both feature instances where intra diegetic music has a very significant bearing on the narrative in each film. While in the former case only one song is relevant to the story, the latter features an entire soundtrack that has a distinct impact on its characters.

Using intra diegetic music to make these deep connections with both characters and narrative is a deliberate attempt to invoke a sense of nostalgia within its viewers. According to Christine Sprengler, "[N]ostalgia is, and has always been, a concept shaped by the cultural and political contexts in which

116

it circulates, by its uses and theorizations as well as by prevailing views on history and memory."[1] Sprengler's emphasis here is on the way in which nostalgia is as much a product of a given cultural moment as it is of the past. Utilizing nostalgia as a cinematic technique could be flawed in this case however, given the primary audience for both films. The millennial generation, both the largest generation currently living and a valuable source of revenue for the film industry, was not alive for the cultural references these films attempt to make. Due to their age, many within this group do not have direct knowledge of the context for the themes and concepts that each narrative tries to invoke by the inclusion of this music. It is necessary to question then, how millennials will engage with these cultural references. I contend that *Captain America: The Winter Soldier* and *Guardians of the Galaxy* attempt to invoke a false sense of nostalgia in millennial viewers through the use of musical and cultural artifacts from the 20th century. Yet due to this disconnect, millennial spectators have the opportunity to critique both the time periods being represented in these films in addition to examining how these texts interpret specific historical moments.

Functions of Music and Nostalgia in Film

The significance of intra diegetic music in invoking nostalgia in these films is dependent on the use of popular music. In his essay addressing popular music within the cinema, Rick Altman relates the following about how audiences respond to scores versus popular songs:

> "[C]lassical" music involves audiences mentally more than bodily, inviting them to internalize rather than externalize their reactions.... In contrast, popular song depends on language, and is predictable, singable, rememberable, and physically involving in ways that "classical" music usually is not.[2]

The physical reaction that Altman describes here is an imperative factor in gauging nostalgic reactions. As an audience hums or sings along with songs familiar to them, they connect back to familiar and perhaps happier memories that in turn encourage them to have a more positive response to a film than they would otherwise. While I would not completely assert that film scores cannot accomplish the same, popular soundtracks have an ability to more consistently encourage this type of response.

Captain America: The Winter Soldier and *Guardians of the Galaxy* are notable for using not only music to evoke nostalgia, but also genre; the films are homages to 70s political thrillers and space operas respectively. More specifically, the songs used in these films can connect with those genres by way of lyrical or musical elements within a given track. David Bowie's "Moonage Daydream," found on the *Guardians* soundtrack, not only contains space-themed lyrics, but a psychedelic sensibility that coincides well with the general eccentricity of the film. Reflecting on these elements serves as a bridge to remembering the space operas of the '70s and '80s, such as the original *Battlestar Galactica* television series or 1984 film *The Last Starfighter*.

The aesthetics of genre from both a musical and cinematic standpoint can say a great deal about the specific time period a production is made in. Music from different eras can often be identified by specific types of instrumentation or techniques; for example, one might easily identify dance music from the '70s or '80s (or at least music inspired by said time periods) through the use of a Moog synthesizer. Robert M. MacCallum et al. insist that what allows the popularity of music to persist over time has as much to do with individual tastes of an audience as it does with artistic innovation (12085).[3] The same can equally be said of film genres, as shifts in culture and history help to determine what stories are told on screen. In his discussion of the genre, James Naremore mentions that film noir "film noir functions rather like big words such as romantic or classic. An ideological concept with a history all its own, it can be used to describe a period, a movement, and a recurrent style."[4] Given the myriad ways genres have been stretched, reinterpreted, or even deconstructed in the new millennium, perhaps the same could be said of all genres. Keeping the concept of genre within the forefront of their minds allows viewers to more thoroughly critique musical choices within these films.

Music, Narrative and Political Memory in *Captain America: The Winter Soldier*

While critical engagement with popular culture can be useful, that doesn't necessarily mean it will be encouraged by filmmakers. Case in point is Anthony and Joe Russo's *Captain America: The Winter Soldier*. While there are some useful points of critique supported by the narrative, the film also misses a very large chance to examine the role of race within the film and the MCU as a whole. Many of the cultural issues to be explored within the film are focused around Marvin Gaye's "Trouble Man," which effectively frames the narrative in *The Winter Soldier*. We are first introduced to the song when Sam Wilson, also known as The Falcon, insists to Steve Rogers that the soundtrack from which the song hails is "everything you missed, jammed into one album."[5] This reference is a nod, like so much in the film, to cultural and political events of the 1970s, as well as how Gaye's output during this time commented on this time period. Wilson excitedly conceives of the song as being a compendium of late 20th century American history, yet the knowledge to be gained from the soundtrack and its title song is far from something to celebrate. In his discussion of the cultural impact of Gaye's work in the '70s, Mark Anthony Neal asserts that the "memorable title track … effectively summarizes black urban life for a displaced working class and burgeoning underclass."[6] While the film alters the focus of the song, the song's concern with hardship and adversity remains.

The ending montage, the first place in which the song is actually heard, depicts life continuing on for the characters in the aftermath of S.H.I.E.L.D.'s demise. While some of the film's antagonists are apprehended for their crimes, not all are, and the heroes must find ways to continue to do good in their new jobs throughout the public and private sectors. It is significant that there is a distinct emphasis on work in the montage; instead of focusing on the characters' emotional reactions to the events of the film, we are instead presented with the very pragmatic concern that many of these people now find themselves out of a job. This reflects a subtle theme within the film, specifically how a person is defined through the work they do. The identities of the characters, particularly Natasha Romanoff and Nick Fury, are deeply connected to their work, so much so that they are somewhat lost when their professions are taken from them. Rather than reveal himself to be alive to the public after faking his death earlier in the film, Fury decides to completely disappear from society, becoming a kind of ghost. Romanoff mentions to Rogers that "I blew all my covers; I gotta go figure out a new one."[7] The relationship between employment and selfhood equally applies for other characters; Sharon Carter, Maria Hill, and—more direly—villains Brock Rumlow and Senator Stern, also have to deal with the very practical concern of being out of a job. While as spies these characters are both used to conceiving new identities for themselves, the fact that they must do so without the safety net provided by gainful employment means venturing into uncertain territory. For the first time, it appears that Fury and Romanoff must decide for themselves what an identity really means, separately from the work that defined them.

The correlation between work and identity points to larger concerns regarding how characters define themselves within the film, particularly in the face of national ideals. It is notable that a song as bleak as "Trouble Man" was chosen for *The Winter Soldier*, given that the title character is so associated with the hope and ideals of a nation. The song emphasizes a sense of inevitability that "trouble" will always come. Yet Captain America, the "star-spangled man," as he is described within the franchise, is supposed to be a shield against that trouble, the one that triumphs over the problems of his country. The concept of the "star-spangled man" also creates a significant musical juxtaposition; the title is taken from another intra diegetic song found in *Captain America: The First Avenger*. "Star-Spangled Man" is unapologetically jingoistic, and if we consider the lyrics of this piece in comparison to "Trouble Man," there is a tension between the idyllic notions that the former relates and the bleakness of the latter. Including Gaye's song within the narrative is perhaps saying that the problems of America and the world are too much to place on the shoulders of one person, or even a group of super-powered individuals like the Avengers.

The ending montage of the film once again highlights this sense of disillusion, with most of the characters attempting to find ways of continuing on in the aftermath of S.H.I.E.L.D.'s destruction. Despite the resolution of the characters, a sense of loss is inescapable in their demeanors, from the scars present on Rogers' face as he lies in a hospital bed, to the cynical and long-suffering smirk on Agent Hill's face when she is forced to find work at Stark Industries, a position far beneath her former station. Heroic as they are, the Captain and his allies contend with mundane issues as much as anyone else.

While *The Winter Soldier* is able to appropriate "Trouble Man" in a manner that is relevant to both the film's narrative and a more contemporary mindset, there is danger in removing the song from its original context, specifically on a racial level. Like much of Gaye's output during the '70s, the song makes a distinct political argument framed by the Civil Rights movement. The trouble that is referred to in the song is the result of oppression, both economic and racial. The singer states that the only way to survive in life as a black man is to step outside of the law.[8] While both Rogers and Wilson do have to tear down the established authority of S.H.I.E.L.D. in order to save the day, they can do so from a position of privilege and agency; as super-heroes, they each have advantages that an average citizen would not in addressing injustice. Wilson specifically is completely detached from the context of "Trouble Man," which is especially aggravating given the fact that he is African American. It seems rather galling (and more than a bit like tokenism) to have one of the primary characters of color suggest the song, given its distinct cultural context. To simply suggest to Rogers that the song is "everything you missed" while not giving his newfound friend any kind of knowledge about its cultural relevance renders Wilson's character as ignorant of his own history, in addition to highlighting the film's racial myopia as a whole. Because it has such a distinct relationship with African American history and experience, "Trouble Man" cannot be displaced from its original context to serve the needs of this film. To do so without any authentic appreciation of the past prevents the kind of critical engagement that could make the use of Gaye's song have a contemporary relevance for Millennial audiences. In contrast, James Gunn's *Guardians of the Galaxy* is hyper-aware of its audience, and encourages viewers to think not only about their relationships with both popular culture and history.

Musical and Cultural Artifacts in Guardians of the Galaxy

Much like Steve Rogers, the characters within *Guardians* must come to terms with personal and cultural histories. This is once again accomplished with the use of intra diegetic music, as well as through a discussion of how nostalgia can be fetishized. In contrast to *The Winter Soldier* however, there is little in the way of political commentary; instead, the film critiques how we engage with and often romanticize popular culture. Protagonist Peter Quill is depicted as being obsessed with late 20th century music, primarily due to his abduction from earth in the late '80s. The film makes extensive use of its soundtrack to explore what it means to be divorced from one's culture, and how that culture gets interpreted and distorted as a result.

The songs of *Guardians* create deep feelings of immersion within the film's universe and connection with its characters. From the narrative's very beginning, viewers are captivated by the rich and textured melody of 10cc's "I'm Not in Love." As the image quickly reveals to us, the music we are hearing is the same as what a young Peter Quill is listening to through the headphones of his Walkman. This connection with the character is so complete that when his headphones are removed—eliminating the audience's ability to hear the music as well—it is jarring. Yet the bond between audience and character remains, and it is in those instances where Quill listens to music that his experience as a displaced human in an unfamiliar environment becomes more distinct. Though not all of the songs within the soundtrack are thematically linked on a lyrical or musical level, they inevitably begin to function as a narrative through the way Quill, and inherently the audience, experiences them. When each song plays, Quill is experiencing a particular emotion or conflict. Often these instances have a humorous slant to them, such as when he listens to "Escape (The Pina Colada Song)" while literally escaping from jail. Even in these cases however, it is apparent that these songs act as narrative signposts, in addition to advancing character development. By the time the film arrives at Marvin Gaye and Tammi Terrell's "Ain't No Mountain High Enough," there is the sense that the story being told here has reached a resolution. This is significant as the song is the first point in the musical narrative that looks towards the future and comes to term with the past. For the majority of the film however, being stuck in the past is what drives much of the conflict for each character.

It is equally relevant to consider the objects that Quill holds onto as much as the music he seems obsessed with. The contents of his backpack that were with him when he was abducted remain even more significant in his adult years than they did as a child. Not only is there a strong sense that he takes the utmost care of these objects, it is explicitly shown that he has found ways to reproduce these items. In addition to the Sony Walkman Quill carries with him, he has built a tape deck into his ship, unironically named the "Milano" after popular '80s actress Alyssa Milano. The protagonist's obsessive attachment to these objects—and particularly how he attempts to impress the significance behind those objects on those around him—can be related to Pierre Bourdieu theory of cultural reproduction, which contends that cultural ideology is passed down from generation to generation, in addition to being reinforced by social institutions such as education.[9]

Cultural reproduction and its consequences are at the center of Quill's character development, as well as his relationships with his alien friends. Quill's fixation on American popular culture can almost certainly be seen as a way to advocate American exceptionalism. In almost every interaction he has with his fellow Guardians, he uses his knowledge of popular culture to present his knowledge of "proper" behavior as superior to that of the various alien cultures he encounters; a particularly relevant scene is his first real conversation with future teammates Rocket and Groot as they are processed by prison guards at the Kyln:

> QUILL: I had a lot of folks try to kill me over the years. I ain't about to be brought down by a tree and a talking raccoon.
> ROCKET: What's a raccoon?
> QUILL: What's a raccoon? It's what you are, stupid.
> ROCKET: Ain't no thing like me, 'cept me.[10]

Already Quill is attempting to enforce his worldview on Rocket, defining his identity despite Rocket's insistence otherwise. He continues to use popular culture references to define both Rocket and Groot, snarkily calling them "Giving Tree" and "Ranger Rick." This occurs despite the fact that Quill has at least a working understanding that alien species have their own distinct cultures, arguably with far more history and diversity than that of Earth. But given how the character was instilled with a strong appreciation of human culture from a young age, it is not surprising that he continues to value that culture above all others.

Quill's relationship with his mother does a great deal to explain his xenocentrism. Before her death, she often made mixtapes for him containing songs from her own childhood. As a result, the value she placed on music gets passed down to Quill, shaping his later passion for it. Additionally, there are temporal concerns at work; when Quill is abducted from Earth in 1988, it effectively stops time for him from a cultural standpoint. When he imparts the cultural values of his home world onto the people he encounters then, it is not only the values of a particular place, but also a specific time. This overly narrow focus may contribute to the frequent misunderstandings that occur when he attempts to promote his culture to others, resulting in instances where Kevin Bacon is assumed to be a great hero of Earth.

While it is clear that Quill's ideas about his culture are in part derived from a fear of leaving the past behind, it is still necessary to question the authenticity of those ideas. His nostalgia may be authentic on a very personal level, but realistically it is suspect. His ideas regarding American popular culture are filtered through a rather distorted experience given his abduction from Earth and his age at the time of departure. Quill presents himself as an authority on the culture of his planet, but this is somewhat impossible as he was only a child when he left. For example, he explains to his teammates that "I come from a planet of outlaws—Billy the Kid, Bonnie and Clyde, John Stamos...."[11] For viewers this statement is immediately called into question; few would regard actor John Stamos in the same fashion as actual outlaws. Though the scene can be viewed as Quill's attempt at comedy, Sprengler's discussion of how we utilize nostalgia rings true here. Quill has constructed his own particular mythology about American popular culture in a way that supports the identity that he has formed for himself.

While all of the songs used in the film evoke a sense of nostalgia in various ways, none directly address this concept in the way that Blue Swede's "Hooked on a Feeling" does. In a frequently promoted scene, Quill proclaims his ownership over the song. Enraged that a prison guard is listening to his beloved mixtape, he screams that "Hooked on a Feeling.... Blue Swede ... 1973 ... That song belongs to me!"[12] Quill is almost hysterical in his desire to claim possession over his Walkman and the song itself, and does so in a way that clearly illustrates his deep, personal connection to these objects. Sprengler asserts that the type of nostalgic feeling evoked in this scene "tells us something about our own historical consciousness, about the myths we construct and circulate and about our desire to make history meaningful on a personal and collective level."[13] In a practical sense, Quill's habit of creating his own interpretations of popular culture is not only a way to maintain his memories and identity; he uses it on a strategic level as well.

In perhaps the most strangely hilarious moment of the film, he distracts villain Ronan the Accuser by singing and dancing to The Five Stairsteps' "O-O-H Child." Here it is precisely because he takes the song out of its original context that he is able to successfully divert Ronan's attention. More significantly, he is employing a variety of pop culture references to act against the antagonist, such as the dance battles popularized by breakdancers, and specific choreography originated by Michael Jackson. In their text examining the millennial generations' impact on American culture, Morley Winograd and Michael D. Hais maintain that the group as a whole employs a variety of sources when creating their own pop culture texts, including works from different ethnicities or subcultures.[14] Unlike earlier points in the film where he uses American culture to seem superior, Quill deliberately uses his knowledge to make a fool out of himself. And while this does have a practical purpose, it also functions as a sign that the character has begun to understand the importance of cultural relativism. Accepting that each of his team members has something to contribute to their goal of defeating Ronan allows Quill to relinquish his hold on nostalgia and the xenocentrism that came with it. His over-the-top performance reflects a need to embrace diverse ways of seeing culture, perhaps even as a way to navigate entrenched ideologies regarding historical eras.

The protagonist's strategy for understanding his culture in the face of contrasting worldviews could easily be seen as a metaphor for the millennial generation and how they are navigating contemporary popular culture. Sprengler asserts that "[i]n order to recuperate this nostalgia and show that it is not inevitably regressive or reactionary, we must consider the relationship between the nostalgic experience (e.g., the longing for an irretrievable ideal) and the nostalgic object (i.e., what one is nostalgic for)."[15] Quill's story is a strong case for Sprengler's argument. Much like he picks and chooses which aspects of his native culture are useful and define him as a person, millennials must decide which aspects of American culture are most relevant to their lives. Millennials are increasingly faced with not only various interpretations of past and present American culture, but also various global cultures that cannot be ignored as they were by prior generations. This requires them to constantly analyze the concepts and objects being produced by mainstream and niche sources.

The aspects of music that allow the medium to create nostalgia equally allow it to be a useful marketing tool, a factor that Marvel Studios was quick to hone in on. The strong emotions evoked by the music used in both films easily made consumers more likely purchase a ticket. What is worth considering is how successfully the production company was able to bridge the divide between generations marketing-wise. According to *Guardians* director James Gunn, not everyone at the company was sold on the idea:

> "One of the Marvel folks who gave notes on the script kept saying we were crazy to put Seventies songs in the movie, that it was going to be alienating to kids," the director says. "I guess he thought Quill should have learned how to download Beyoncé and Ke$ha off iTunes. Now I see little kids all over the world singing me "'Hooked on a Feeling.'" Nothing could make me happier than to have folks take a second look at these songs.[16]

If this is the case, then it appears that contemporary music lacks the ability to connect listeners in the same manner that classic songs do. It could be argued that Gunn's hopefulness about reconnecting with these songs is misplaced if—much like musically-oriented television shows such as *Glee* and *American Idol*—the engagement with the *Guardians* soundtrack is largely superficial. This really isn't the case however. Unlike in the example of *Captain America: The Winter Soldier*, there is a level of metafictional awareness that is built into watching *Guardians of the Galaxy*, and that awareness extends to the soundtrack. This is a film that encourages viewers to think about what they are consuming, whether it is contemporary or classic.

Conclusion

The various films within the Marvel Cinematic Universe have vastly different approaches to how they choose to engage their fans. Encouraging audiences to view Marvel films with a critical eye seems to be a far more successful gambit than encouraging passive consumption, yet the company seems to struggle with this notion. This in part can be traced back to genre; the more comedic films tend to allow for more self-aware viewing than action heavy films, the *Iron Man* trilogy and *Guardians* being the primary examples. Yet it seems counter-productive to encourage critical viewing in one group of films, while largely negating that comprehension in their non-comedic properties. While repeating the formula of using intra diegetic music may or may not be a strategy for future films, their success with audiences, particularly Millennial ones, will likely depend on Marvel's ability to treat viewers as critical thinkers capable of reflecting on their roles within popular culture.

NOTES

1. Christine Sprengler, *Screening Nostalgia: Populuxe Props and Technicolor Aesthetics in Contemporary American Film.* (Oxford: Berghahn Books, 2009), 1–2.

2. Rick Altman, "Cinema and Popular Song: The Lost Tradition," in *Soundtrack Available: Essays on Film and Popular Music,* edited by Pamela Robertson Wojcik and Arthur Knight. (Durham: Duke University Press, 2001), 24.

3. Robert M. MacCallum, et. al. "Evolution of Music by Public Choice," *Proceedings of the National Academy of Sciences of the United States of America* 109, No. 30 (July 24, 2012): 12081–12086.

4. James Naremore, *More Than Night: Film Noir in Its Contexts.* (Berkeley: University of California Press, 2008), 6.

5. *Captain America: The Winter Soldier,* directed by Anthony and Joe Russo. (Burbank, CA: Walt Disney Studios Motion Pictures, 2014), Blu-Ray.

6. Mark Anthony Neal, "Trouble Man: The Art and Politics of Marvin Gaye," *Western Journal of Black Studies* 22, no. 4 (Winter 1998): 252–259.

7. *Captain America: The Winter Soldier.*

8. Marvin Gaye, "Trouble Man," by Marvin Gaye, in *Trouble Man: Motion Picture Soundtrack,* Tamla, 1972, MP3.

9. Pierre Bourdieu. "Cultural Reproduction and Social Reproduction," in *Knowledge, Education, and Cultural Change,* edited by Richard Brown. (London: Tavistock Publications, 1973), 56.

10. *Guardians of the Galaxy,* directed by James Gunn. (Burbank, CA: Walt Disney Studios Motion Pictures, 2014), Blu-Ray.

11. *Guardians.*

12. *Ibid.*

13. Sprengler, *Screening Nostalgia*, 3.

14. Morley Winograd and Michael D. Hais. *Millennial Momentum: How a New Generation Is Remaking America*. (New Brunswick, NJ: Rutgers University Press, 2011), 212.

15. Sprengler, 2.

16. Kory Grow, "Hooked on a Feeling: Inside the Hit Guardians of the Galaxy Soundtrack," *Rolling Stone*, last modified September 3, 2014, http://www.rollingstone.com/music/features/inside-guardians-of-the-galaxy-soundtrack-20140903.

Tracing Views of Nature in the Marvel Cinematic Universe

Elizabeth D. Blum

Introduction

In the March 1963 issue of *Tales of Suspense*, Marvel introduced "the invincible Iron Man." Wealthy businessman, scientist, and playboy Tony Stark, while assisting the American military in South Vietnam, falls over a hidden tripwire, is badly injured, and captured by brutal communists. Recognizing Stark from newspaper stories, the evil leader Wong-Chu forces Tony to build a weapon for him. Tony feigns agreement, but secretly works on his means of escape: an iron suit of armor designed not only to keep the shrapnel from his heart, but also to destroy the communists.[1] Marvel followed the same basic outline 45 years later. In the 2008 film version, brilliant, sarcastic, and superior Tony Stark travels to Afghanistan to demonstrate a newly minted missile. Terrorists hit Tony's convoy, wounding him in the process and delivering him to the terrorists deep within a cave. Again, his capture serves as a vehicle to create a gadget-filled suit of armor, after developing a power source to keep the shrapnel away from his heart.[2]

Fans knowledgeable about the earlier comic content noticed the update of the movie from fighting jungle-dwelling communists in South Vietnam to fighting terrorism in dusty Afghanistan. Yet moving along with that update was another change involving the outcome of Stark's imprisonment. In the 1960s comic, Stark's commitment to technology as a solution to the world's problems, particularly against communists, grows as a result of his kidnapping. The 2000s version of Stark, however, goes through a profound shift in attitude, closing his profitable arms production division and choosing to

127

focus instead on the issue of clean, sustainable energy. Both shifts reflected the ideals and concerns of the period—from concerns about communism to terrorism, and from seeing technology as the solution to global problems to an awareness of global warming and the complications of the effects of technology.

Marvel's movies of the early 2000s reveal views of nature and the environment reflective of changes in public perceptions over 40 years. Although Marvel prided itself on relevancy in its comics, early 1960s origin stories lacked engagement with progressive environmental ideas, sticking to entrenched ideas and concepts. Certainly, popular culture can lag significantly behind popular environmental attitudes of the time: the *Star Trek* series and movies trailed prevalent environmental attitudes by as much as a generation.[3] In addition, ideas may change but leave behind remnants of old views. Although the Marvel cinematic universe reflects significantly increased awareness of the dangers of technology, the importance of clean energy, and views of nature as relaxing and calming, earlier conflicting attitudes linger.

Context: Environmentalism from the Mid–1960s to the Early 2000s

Rachel Carson opened a Pandora's box with her presentation of the dangers of pesticides in *Silent Spring*. Her 1962 book described the health and environmental effects of chemicals on nature, and led many Americans to change how they thought about the environment. More and more, highly publicized events of the 1960s aptly demonstrated additional consequences of unfettered technological and business development. In 1969, a huge oil spill flooded the pristine Santa Barbara coastline, causing many wealthy, white residents to become active in environmental causes. Lake Erie became so polluted in the late 1960s that it lost oxygen content, a process known as eutrophication. Because of this, lake life saw massive die offs. The Cuyahoga River, polluted by the discharge of innumerable industries, spontaneously caught fire several times during the 1960s. Los Angeles suffered from numerous bouts of smog so potent authorities advised residents to stay inside. Each of these events caused Americans to think about the issue of pollution in different ways.[4]

Post–World War II, the chemical industry produced not just pesticides, but a cornucopia of other highly toxic products with even more toxic by-products. Companies like DuPont and Monsanto often exhibited little care with disposal of these products, an issue which came to light in a Niagara Falls neighborhood known as "Love Canal" in 1978. Local women's activism forced the government to remove the residents and later pass Superfund legislation to provide a means for cleanup of other toxic sites. Superfund often proved problematic or inadequate, and failed to solve other issues that came to light. Activists soon correlated increased environmental hazards with lower class and neighborhoods of color, a phenomenon known as "environmental injustice." These neighborhoods followed the Love Canal example, either working to get out of their polluted areas or prevent the siting of landfills or hazardous waste facilities. Chemicals, as a product of modern technology and science, came to be more commonly linked with health and environmental problems in the late 20th century.[5]

Other post–World War II trends fed into an enlightenment about the natural world. In 1956, President Dwight Eisenhower oversaw the passage of the Interstate Highway Act, one of the largest public works project in history. The interconnected highways spurred suburbanization, which altered views of the environment. Bulldozers leveled areas for construction, leaving no trees and sparse landscaping. Residents, missing the amenities of open space, began to see nature as a necessary part of their lives. In addition to suburbanization, the highways allowed for easier and quicker travel by car. For millions of Americans looking for inexpensive family vacations in the prosperous 1950s and 1960s, this meant trips to national parks.[6]

Other ideas shifted as well. Earlier views reinforced ideas of "wilderness" as dangerous, but in the 1950s, groups like the Sierra Club promoted trips to nature as restorative, restful, and spiritual. Several highly publicized battles over protected areas illustrate the increased importance of this attitude. Following the ideas of their founder John Muir, the Sierra Club and Wilderness Society joined forces to successfully battle against the construction of a dam in Dinosaur National Monument. In addition, ecology developed as a science and became a household word. Children learned from the earliest years in school that the nature linked and integrated life from top to bottom, and that eliminating one part of the "chain of life" damaged the entire chain. The federal government also became an agent of change. Environmental legislation and new bureaucracies proliferated during the 1960s and early 1970s, including the Wilderness Act, the Clean Air Act, the Clean Water Act, the Toxic Substances Control Act, and the National Environmental Policy Act, along with the creation of the Environmental Protection Agency.[7]

As the 20th century ended, pollution took on a global significance as scientists made the public aware of global warming or climate change. Massive use of fossil fuels had dumped large amounts of carbon dioxide into the Earth's atmosphere. This carbon dioxide upset the balance of the Earth's delicate heat exchange system. With more carbon dioxide, daytime heat remained trapped in the Earth's atmosphere and ground, causing polar and mountain ice to melt and raising ocean levels. The 2006 documentary *An Inconvenient Truth* brought the issue to a wide public and received significant international attention. Both Gore (the star of the film) and the Intergovernmental Panel on Climate Change shared the Nobel Peace Prize for their efforts in 2007. Although the energy industry hotly contested the science of global warming, man's overreliance on fossil fuels and the need for cleaner sources of energy became key issues in the early 21st century.

Environmental Views in the Early 2000s Marvel Movies

The late 20th century saw environmental ideas morph into a national movement, with widely known (if superficially held) values. Americans no longer saw technology with an uncritical eye, realizing that it often has detrimental consequences, particularly regarding effects on the natural world. The health and environmental effects of industrial pollution and toxics of various types became better known and protested against. Importantly, as well, many Americans accepted humans as a part of the natural world, with a concurrent limit on certain activities. The idea that life is connected and interrelated became more prevalent. In addition, parks and wild areas have been lauded as positive spaces, with peaceful, restful, restorative qualities. Dramatic changes have taken place in environmental views in the 40 years since the comic origin stories, and creators cautiously reflect these alterations in the 2000s Marvel Universe films.

Environmentalism and Technology

Much like the focus on fighting communists in the 1960s Marvel comic book stories, the focus of clean, reliable energy and the responsible control of energy sources weaves through the films. For example, in the first of the Marvel Universe series, *Iron Man* (2008), Stark returns to the United States after his Afghan imprisonment and surprises business partners and the military by speaking directly about his and his company's part in a "bad system," believing now that he has more to offer than just new ways to blow things up. He commits to shutting down the weapons division of Stark Industries to focus on the development of clean energy, primarily through arc reactor technology. Friends try to talk him out of his new focus: business partner Obadiah argues against the "cost effectiveness" of such work, and even close friend Col. Rhodes thinks Stark needs time to "get his mind right." Tony ignores such advice and sticks vehemently to his course, developing a more advanced Iron Man in the process.[8]

The arc reactor and Iron Man link to Tony's ideas of societal justice. He eschews corporate profit and increased militarism for environmental benefits. He sees the development of clean energy as atoning for past wrongs and being more responsible to the planet and uses Iron Man as a way to seek and promote justice as well. Further, he carries this idea in other ways, donating to other environmental causes, including wind farms and plastic treatment facilities.[9] By the time of the first Avengers movie, Tony has made considerable progress on his research. Using his office building as a test case for the arc reactor, Stark Towers becomes "a beacon of self-sustaining energy."[10]

When a culture adopts a new value, old ones rarely disappear completely. Sometimes the previous ideas continue to exist alongside the new ones in a conflicting array. In this instance, the Marvel Universe ideas about technology reflect a balance shift from a dominant attitude of technology as a cure all in the 1960s to a dominant attitude of technology as a prime cause of problems, particularly with nature in the 2000s. Storylines accepted that technological innovations sometimes have effects and consequences on nature. At the same time, however, the films paradoxically present technology as a simplistic solution to problems.

Numerous examples demonstrate the filmmakers' skepticism about the nature and uses of technology. In the first Avengers movie, Nick Fury assembles the Avengers to locate the glowing cube called the Tesseract, an immense power source stolen by Loki. Fury describes the Tesseract to Steve Rogers as the "key to unlimited sustainable energy," and "something the world sorely needs." Loki wants the Tesseract for other reasons, however. It also has the power to open portals between worlds. The heroes congregate, but soon develop reservations about the S.H.I.E.L.D.'s intentions. Even super-patriot Rogers is skeptical, remarking that Fury should have left it in the ocean. Both Stark and Bruce Banner also question Fury's motives in locating the Tesseract. Rogers soon discovers that S.H.I.E.L.D. hopes to use the Tesseract in a campaign to make new weapons of mass destruction. The Avengers generally react negatively, with Thor stating that humans lack the ability to deal with the power of the Tesseract.[11] This resistance by the heroes to accept S.H.I.E.L.D.'s military use of power reflects doubts about technology and its effects.

The Marvel Universe films depict both chemicals and radiation as having severe consequences on the human body, even for superheroes. Stark, Banner, and Rogers all suffer from their interactions with chemicals and radiation.[12] In *Iron Man 2* (2010), for example, Tony hides the fact that his "palladium core" arc reactor that keeps the shrapnel from his heart is slowly poisoning him. In effect, the arc reactor pollutes his blood, indicating the possibility that his technological achievement is not the poster child for clean energy as initially thought.[13]

Bruce Banner also suffers from blood polluted by technology and science gone awry. In *The Incredible Hulk* (2008), General Ross persuades Banner that his research holds the key to radiation resistance, when it actually links to the super soldier program that produced Captain America. Banner's transformation into the Hulk occurs after he tests the gamma rays on himself. His blood is then so dangerous to other humans that Banner panics when he cuts himself and a drop falls into the bottle production line at a soft drink plant. He misses a drop, however, which gets into a drink and surprises an unsuspecting consumer some time later. When he discovers later in the film that Mr. Blue, a scientist helping him find a cure, has been storing and reproducing his blood for research, Banner immediately asserts that the blood "cannot be controlled," and demands its destruction because it is "too dangerous."[14]

Steve Rogers, in contrast to his early 1960s comic-book counterpart, also suffers after his chemical and radiation-induced transformation to Captain America. First, although his physical prowess improves to superhuman standards, military leaders use him as a propaganda tool in a song-and-dance show. Derided by active soldiers, he leaps into service and sacrifices himself in an attempt to retrieve the Tesseract from fleeing Nazis.[15] Thawed from the ice 50 years later, Rogers suffers from a continual sense of dislocation. He has problems sleeping and doubts his purpose in life. Peggy Carter, now aged and suffering from Alzheimer's, laments that Rogers "didn't get to live his life." The fact that the serum allowed him to live through the freezing has actually robbed him of life, rather than giving him more.[16]

Most importantly, attempts to mimic the experiment that produced Rogers or the Hulk through chemical and radiation experiments on the human body lead to significant problems, and indicate concern about the effects of chemicals on the human body. The Winter Soldier, the result of Dr. Zola's experiment on captured Bucky Barnes, has superior strength and agility, but no memory, conscience, or human friendships, and suffers great pain when his memory is erased. Gung-ho soldier Emil Blonski gains physical prowess from his Hulk-derived chemical injections (also a spin-off of the super soldier program), but becomes much more aggressive and less controlled, eventually morphing into an even more animal-like Hulk.[17]

Technology and science also has dire effects on mental health both in *Iron Man 3* (2013) and *Guardians of the Galaxy* (2014). Aldrich Killian developed a project called "Extremis," a serum that alters DNA and regrows limbs. Unfortunately, for many of the test subjects, Extremis also leads to bodies overheating and causing tremendous explosions. Killian tests Extremis on himself, causing heightened physical ability, but also dangerous psychopathic behavior.[18] Rocket, a genetically altered raccoon, regularly suffers from humiliation and degrading comments. Drunk and furious over an insult, Rocket notes that he "didn't ask to get made ... [or] to be torn apart and put back together over and over."[19] For both Killian and Rocket, attempts to control and enhance nature leads to instability: Chemical, biological, and radiation induced changes come at a high price in the 2000s Marvel stories.

Nature also appears as a foil or contrast to technology, often serving to reflect the gap between what technology has become and harmony with the natural world. One of the clearest examples of this occurs in *Iron Man 2* (2011). Rhodey and Stark, as Iron Patriot and Iron Man respectively, on the run from the onslaught of Ivan Vanko-developed Iron Men prototypes, land in a parklike setting in the Stark Expo pavilion. Shortly thereafter, Vanko's minions arrive and a huge battle ensues, which completely wreaks havoc with the surroundings of the park. Tony slices trees in half, lasers blow the glass out of the dome, scattering it over the surface, and power beams cause huge explosions.[20] The power and violence of technology in the scene serve as a jarring juxtaposition against the idyllic setting of the park. Filmmakers assume audiences will see the park as relaxing, calming, and restorative and therefore enhance the effect of the battle. Certainly, as well, filmmakers may have been pointing to the potential for technology to pollute and damage the natural world, a theme reinforced with the pollution of Stark's and Banner's blood.

Despite the prominent recognition of negative effects of technology, moviemakers still adopt conventions of technology as easy solutions to problems. For example, although the Avengers and particularly Stark decry the militarization of technology, only a nuclear weapon launched at the Chitauri mother ship defeats Earth's invaders and closes Loki's portal. Earthlings never have to grapple with the destructive power source again, as Thor whisks both it and Loki to Asgard for justice. Delving into his father's research provides Tony with the knowledge to make a new atom to replace the problematic palladium. Predictably, the new element, placed in his arc reactor, solves all of Tony's problems, restoring him to health and clearing his blood of the polluting elements.[21] Finally, Stark shifts his company's focus to clean energy, but the way Marvel decides to do this demonstrates huge limitations in popular culture's way of dealing with difficult issues. As Tony develops the arc reactor further and presents a test case of its usefulness by using it as Stark Tower's the sole power source, moviemakers completely skirt the difficult issues surrounding energy use in the early 21st century. Tony presents an easy fix—a new technology to deal with energy issues that automatically solves all problems. The arc reactor is clean, limitless, and workable. Consumers and businesses are not asked to make any tough decisions or changes in their energy consumption patterns, wasteful lifestyles, or production of polluting products, issues that haunt the search for solutions in the 21st century.

Views of Wilderness and Urban Spaces

In the mid– to late 20th century, views of wilderness shifted from a place of danger to a place of restoration, relaxation, and spirituality that needed to be protected rather than dominated and developed.[22] Although views of wild spaces changed in many ways across the late 20th century, the 2000s Marvel movies portray a conflicted view of wilderness, just as they portray a conflicted view of technology.

Generally, wilderness receives a positive interpretation. The films prominently feature the idea of wilderness and nature as having a calming effect, particularly seen in *The Incredible Hulk* (2008). As in the comics, the film-version Hulk represents man's bestial, animalistic, primitive side. Film Banner consistently changes to the Hulk in stressful situations, but he has found ways to influence his change back to human—primarily through contact with wild nature. When he changes early in the film, the Hulk escapes to the forested environment of Guatemala, where Banner begins his long trek home. After an early encounter with the military, where Elizabeth is wounded, Hulk takes her and escapes to the wilderness again—Smoky Mountain National Forest this time—where he is calmed, relaxed, and returns to his human form. At the end of the film, Hulk again returns to the wilderness as he ventures to Bella Coola, British Columbia, to escape stressful and angering situations.[23] In the films, the calm, peaceful, transformational power of wilderness aids the transition from the violent, single-minded beast into the rational, thoughtful Banner.

Urban areas offer opportunities for escape through anonymity. Banner flees to Rocinha Favela, Brazil, a densely populated, poverty-stricken city of box-like buildings crowded into every conceivable space. He lives for almost six months there, "incident" free, before General Ross finds him. At the beginning of *Marvel's The Avengers* (2012), Black Widow finds Banner in an impoverished, crowded Indian city, where he provides medical care to locals.[24] Urban spaces provide Banner with a place to hide and escape not only the military, but his alter ego as well.

Wilderness also causes a transformation of a positive kind with other characters. Stark emerges from the wilderness of the Afghan desert a man transformed; his wilderness experience makes Tony Stark a more civilized, responsible member of society. A wilderness of a different type provides another transformational space for Tony suffering from PTSD after the incident in New York City. After a violent, destructive attack by the terrorist Mandarin, Tony loses consciousness in an Iron Man suit. He revives after crash landing in the small, rural town of Rose Hill, Tennessee, the site of a previous Mandarin-like explosion. For Tony, Rose Hill is a virtual wilderness. In the freezing night, his Iron Man suit inoperable, Jarvis uncommunicative, and no dream lab in sight, Tony must work with a young boy to restore the suit and save the country from the Mandarin.[25] Rose Hill ably forces him back to his roots as a "mechanic" and restores his faith in himself. He transforms back to himself in this wilderness.

In the films, landscape and locations can also be reflective of the characteristics of a people in general and indicate older conceptions of wilderness as well. "Wilderness" areas in these instances serve as reflections of a corrupt, dead, evil, or morally bankrupt civilization. In *Thor* (2011), for example, the Frost Giant world is frozen, desolate, dark, craggy and rocky with no visible life. The Frost Giants have lost power in the universe, and seek it again through evil means of theft and violence.[26] In *Thor: The Dark World* (2013), the elves of Malekith have a similar lifeless, craggy world, albeit more dusty and desert-like, and they also seek to turn everything to darkness and destroy all life.[27] *Guardians of the Galaxy* (2014) echoes these themes as well. Knowhere, the "severed head of an ancient celestial being" serves as the Wild West. Under extremely dangerous conditions, and "no regulations whatsoever," workers mine highly valuable organic material for the black market. The location's environment matches its purpose: Knowhere is dark, dirty, crowded, and lacking any green space.[28]

The idea that evil cultures live in desolate wilderness environments contrasts with the depiction of other worlds—notably, Asgard, Xandar, and Vanaheim. A model of enlightened civilization, Asgard, a highly urbanized, glittering, clean, and wealthy city, has well-fed, well-behaved, neatly clothed citizens led by a benevolent, wise monarchy.[29] In *Guardians of the Galaxy* (2014), Xandar, another highly advanced, cultured planet, contains gleaming buildings of curved glass and open park spaces under blue skies. The Guardians find this planet so valuable they agree to risk their lives to protect it from the evil Ronan.[30] While urban areas are seen as positive developments in a civilization, rural, green areas are seen as stepping stones to civilization. *Thor: The Dark World* (2013), for example, finds Asgard engaged in a series of battles to bring peace to the universe. Thor and his friends lead the fight on Vanaheim, a very green, rural, low technology planet. They quickly defeat the natives, who just as quickly bow to the peace and goals imposed by Asgard.[31] Urban areas seem the height of civilization, to contrast with lifeless worlds, and bring civilized ideas and peace to green, life-filled worlds through war.

Marvel presents cracks in this façade of beauty and order: In many ways, Asgard takes the role of the United States—a civilized, wealthy place that brings peace and prosperity through "necessary" wars to bring evil to justice. Thor notes perceptively the irony in Asgard's role during the first *Avengers* film. He notes that Asgard pretends to be "more advanced, but we come here battling like bilgesnipe," creatures he describes as "huge, scaly, [with] big antlers…. They are repulsive."[32] Thor sees the price paid for arrogance and a peacekeeper role, linking that to his world, and, by extension, the United States.[33]

Control of Nature

Major differences in Thor's character reveal shifts in perception about nature. The 1960s comic book Thor constantly used his control of nature as a way to dominate enemies and show his power.[34] The film version of Thor offers different messages. Early in the first *Thor* movie, the impetuous, arrogant Thor ventures to the Frost Giant planet to punish them for invading Asgard. He liberally uses his hammer during the ensuing battle, but only as a show of strength and power, not as a way to control natural forces. Punished by his father for his transgression, Thor spends most of the rest of the movie actually stripped of his powers, and must learn humility and self-sacrifice on his way to leadership. In the first film, he only uses his ability to control weather when he creates a tornado to destroy Loki's giant robot and save his friends. In the other movies featuring Thor, his ability to control nature and his use of that power is greatly downplayed.[35] Thor uses his hammer to fly, arguably controlling the natural force of gravity, but in general Mjolnir only destroys objects or tests others' characters as in the second Avenger movie.

Other aspects of the Thor story reflect changes in attitudes about nature. The screen version of Thor generally demonstrates a different worldview than that of Don Blake's 1960s alter-ego. In the *Thor* (2011), he draws a picture of the universe for Jane Foster as he knows it. He describes the different worlds as part of a tree, indicating that everything is connected and tied together in the universe—like branches of a tree. His views demonstrate a much more holistic, ecological-type view of worlds. In addition, Thor argues vehemently against the destruction of an entire race when Loki commits to wiping out the Frost Giants. In fact, he even destroys the rainbow bridge, jeopardizing his contact with Jane, to keep Loki from carrying out his threat.[36] Gamora severs her ties to Thanos and risks her life to protect Xandar from complete destruction as threatened by Ronan. She tells Quill that she could not simply stand by and see another planet destroyed as her homeworld had been.[37] Jane Foster's character (a nurse in the original comics) also represents a change. Marvel comic-character scientists of the early 1960s, exclusively male, sought to use their knowledge and skills to manipulate nature. Foster's astrophysical research seeks merely to explain and understand it. Overall, a more ecologically-based argument about the universe emerges, stressing the value of all life as well as the connectedness of worlds in the *Thor* movies.

This theme of nature as valuable in its own right receives its greatest personification in the character of Groot. Described as a "humanoid plant," Groot appears as a giant walking tree with an extremely limited vocabulary.[38] Groot exhibits great physical strength and moral courage and frequently sacrifices himself to protect his friends. At one point, he loses both his arms protecting Rocket. At the climax of the movie, Groot envelops the entire team within a sphere of his branches, saving everyone but himself when Ronan's ship, the *Dark Aster*, explodes on Xandar. Yet he also demonstrates powerful regenerative capabilities—a twig planted by Rocket begins to grow back into Groot as the film ends.[39] Where the Hulk represents nature's wild, untamed side, Groot reflects a contrasting view of nature, existing to serve and sacrifice himself for other characters. Although certainly depicted as a strong hero, Groot's regenerative capacity certainly indicates an attitude of nature being able to "return to normal" on its own, despite damage from man.

Along with the theme of control of nature, control of the Hulk changes in the 21st century Marvel Universe. In the 1960s comics, teenage boy Rick Jones often controlled the Hulk, reflecting the comic theme of male-dominated mastery of wild nature. Banner himself in the comics could control his transformation for a time.[40] In the recent movies, the Hulk's character remains more consistently wild and uncontrollable. Hulk's wildness causes him to lash out at enemy and friend alike, making him a danger even to his fellow Avengers. While Banner can control his heartrate to some extent, the Hulk appears regularly in stressful, anger-inducing situations.

However, uncontrollable nature still must be controlled. As noted earlier, Banner uses the calming effect of wilderness to influence the change. In the modern versions, women, especially those important to Banner, have strong wilderness-like influences over the Hulk. Elizabeth Ross, for example, can communicate with and soothe the Hulk where others cannot. She tells Banner that she thinks Hulk knew her and recognized her at the college campus, and even brings out Hulk's sense of mercy, preventing him from killing Blonski's raging creature.[41] In *Avengers: Age of Ultron* (2015), the Avengers use Black Widow as a calming influence on Hulk. She approaches him and speaks calmly to him, stroking his hand to induce the switch back to Banner.[42] Interestingly, this move echoes the long-standing stereotype of women as closer than men to nature.[43]

Conclusion

Environmental messages have permeated many aspects of American popular culture in the late 20th and early 21st centuries. Movies in particular have flooded children and adults with the message that the environment is in crisis and needs "saving." Critiques of technology and its role in society have played a strong role in these films, as they have in the Marvel Universe. *The China Syndrome* (1979) presciently warned of the meltdown of a nuclear plant shortly before the real Three Mile Island accident. In 1992, *Ferngully: The Last Rainforest* aptly described conditions in the rapidly disappearing Amazon rainforest. *Erin Brockovich* (2000) brought modernized Love Canal–type activism to the movie screen. *Wall-E* (2008) decried the wasteful, throw-away culture prominent in the United States. *Happy Feet* (2006) provided a venue for concerns about overfishing. Even the James Bond franchise focused on the issue of control of water resources in *Quantum of Solace* (2008). Box office smash *Avatar* (2009) combined many of these issues into a visually stunning film condemning commodification of nature and modern humans' lack of connection with and concern about the natural world.

Americans in the late 20th century saw dramatic changes in perceptions of their roles in the natural world. These changes revealed struggles with solutions to the problems presented. Environmental values often seemed to require a trade-off. Urbanites wanted to visit natural parks, but more visitors made the area less "wild." They wanted a cleaner environment and less reliance on foreign energy sources, yet often proved unwilling to make changes in living styles or consumer habits to reflect those values. The 21st century, therefore, has often revealed conflicted environmental values as seen in the Marvel movies of the time. 21st century Marvel Universe films decry the effect of technology and rely on it for easy solutions; see wilderness as relaxing and yielding positive transformations, and also as a location for evil cultures; portray nature both as existing to serve man and as valuable in its own right; and deemphasize male control of nature while promoting stereo-typical views of women as closer to nature. Overall, the environmental movement's influence has proven dramatic but incomplete in the Marvel series.

NOTES

1. Stan Lee and Don Heck, "Iron Man Is Born," in *Marvel Masterworks: The Invincible Iron Man Volume 1* (New York: Marvel Worldwide, 2010), 2–9. (Originally published in *Tales of Suspense* #39, March 1963).

2. *Iron Man*, directed by Jon Favreau (2008; Paramount Pictures and Marvel Entertainment, 2008.), DVD.

3. Elizabeth Blum, "Save the Whales and Beware Wilderness: Star Trek and Reflections of the Modern Environmental Movement," in *The Influence of Star Trek on Television, Film and Culture (Critical Explorations in Science Fiction and Fantasy)*, edited by Lincoln Geraghty (Jefferson, NC: McFarland, 2007), 82–99.

4. Linda Lear's *Rachel Carson: Witness for Nature* (New York: Henry Holt, 1997) stands as the best biography of Carson and presentation of her work. For good overviews of the development of the environmental movement, see, Hal Rothman, *The Greening of a Nation? Environmentalism in the United States Since 1945* (Fort Worth: Harcourt Brace, 1998); and Robert Gottlieb, *Forcing the Spring: The Transformation of the American Environmental Movement* (Washington, D.C.: Island Press, 1993).

5. Elizabeth D. Blum, *Love Canal Revisited: Race, Class, and Gender in Environmental Activism* (Lawrence: University Press of Kansas, 2008); Ellen Griffith Spears, *Baptized in*

PCBs: Race, Pollution, and Justice in an All-American Town (Chapel Hill: University of North Carolina Press, 2014).

6. Adam Rome, *Bulldozer in the Countryside: Suburban Sprawl and the Rise of American Environmentalism* (New York: Cambridge University Press, 2001); Ronald A. Foresta, *The Land Between the Lakes: A Geography of A Forgotten Future* (Knoxville: University of Tennessee Press, 2013).

7. The classic work on the development of the idea of wilderness is Roderick Nash, *Wilderness and the American Mind*, 3rd ed. (New Haven: Yale University Press, 1982).

8. *Iron Man.*

9. *Iron Man 2*, directed by Jon Favreau (2010; Paramount Pictures and Marvel Entertainment, 2010), DVD.

10. *The Avengers*, directed by Joss Whedon (2012; Marvel Studios and Paramount Pictures, 2012), DVD.

11. *The Avengers.*

12. This contrasts deeply with the messages in the early 1960s comics, where human interaction with chemicals and radiation have few downsides.

13. *Iron Man 2.*

14. *The Incredible Hulk*, directed by Louis Leterrier (2008; Universal Pictures and Marvel Enterprises, 2008), DVD.

15. *Captain America: The First Avenger*, directed by Joe Johnston (2011; Paramount Pictures and Marvel Entertainment, 2011), DVD.

16. *Captain America: The Winter Soldier*, directed by Anthony Russo and Joe Russo (2014; Marvel Entertainment and Marvel Studies, 2014), DVD.

17. *Captain America: The Winter Soldier; The Incredible Hulk.*

18. *Iron Man 3*, directed by Shane Black (2013; Marvel Studios and Paramount Pictures, 2013), DVD; *Guardians of the Galaxy*, directed by James Gunn (2014; Marvel Studios and Marvel Enterprises, 2014), DVD.

19. *Guardians of the Galaxy.*

20. *Iron Man 2.*

21. *Iron Man 2.*

22. See, Nash, *Wilderness and the American Mind.*

23. *The Incredible Hulk.*

24. *The Incredible Hulk; The Avengers.*

25. *Iron Man 3.*

26. *Thor*, directed by Kenneth Branagh (2011; Paramount Pictures and Marvel Entertainment, 2011), DVD.

27. *Thor: The Dark World*, directed by Alan Taylor (2013; Marvel Studios, 2013), DVD.

28. *Guardians of the Galaxy.*

29. *Thor; Thor: The Dark World.*

30. *Guardians of the Galaxy.*

31. *Thor; Thor: The Dark World.*

32. *The Avengers.*

33. *Thor: The Dark World.*

34. See, for example, Stan Lee and Jack Kirby, "Stone Men from Saturn," *Marvel Masterworks: The Mighty Thor, Volume 1* (New York: Marvel Worldwide, 2013), 5–8. (Originally published as *Journey into Mystery* #83, August 1962); Stan Lee and Jack Kirby, "The Mighty Thor vs. the Executioner," *Marvel Masterworks: The Mighty Thor, Volume 1* (New York: Marvel Worldwide, 2013), 20–24. (Originally published as *Journey into Mystery* #84, September 1962); Stan Lee and Jack Kirby, "Trapped by Loki, the God of Mischief!" *Marvel Masterworks: The Mighty Thor, Volume 1* (New York: Marvel Worldwide, 2013), 32. (Originally published as *Journey into Mystery* #85, October 1962); Stan Lee and Jack Kirby, "On the Trail of the Tomorrow Man!" *Marvel Masterworks: The Mighty Thor, Volume 1* (New York: Marvel Worldwide, 2013), 51, 55. (Originally published as *Journey into Mystery* #86, November 1962); Stan Lee and Jack Kirby, "Prisoner of the Reds!" *Marvel Masterworks: The Mighty Thor, Volume 1* (New York: Marvel Worldwide, 2013), 64. (Originally published as *Journey into Mystery* #87, December 1962).

35. *Thor.*
36. *Thor.*
37. *Guardians of the Galaxy.*
38. At one point, Quill refers to Groot as "the giving tree," a reference to Shel Silverstein's children's book of the same name, and a rather accurate description of his character.
39. *Guardians of the Galaxy.*
40. Stan Lee and Jack Kirby, "Banished to Outer Space," *Marvel Masterworks: The Incredible Hulk, Volume 1* (New York: Marvel Publishing, 2009), 55–61. (Originally published as *The Incredible Hulk* #3, September 1962).
41. *The Incredible Hulk.*
42. *Avengers: Age of Ultron*, directed by Joss Whedon (Marvel Studios, 2015).
43. For the classic discussion of the historic links and origins of the stereotypical connections between women and nature, see, Carolyn Merchant, *The Death of Nature: Women, Ecology and the Scientific Revolution* (New York: HarperCollins, 1980).

Bodies That Shatter
Violence and Spectacle in The Avengers

ANTONY MULLEN

Marvel's *The Avengers* (2012) brings together a range of human, non-human and post-human characters from earlier Marvel films.[1] The skilled-in-combat human agents Nick Fury, Hawkeye and Black Widow are joined by Tony Stark, whose human body becomes cyborgic when merged with the Iron Man suit. The genetically enhanced Captain America, the humanoid god Thor, and Dr. Bruce Banner, whose human body mutates into the monstrous Hulk, are also members of the group. While Thor, who is from another planet, is markedly non-human, and Fury, Hawkeye and Black Widow are all human, the others occupy a place between these two categories that might be understood as posthuman. The concept of the posthuman emerges from science fiction and philosophical thought and identifies a state of existence that has overcome the perceived limitations of the human body. N. Katherine Hayles has argued that "the posthuman offers resources for rethinking the articulation of humans with intelligent machines" rather than replacing the human altogether, or representing something that is anti-human.[2] Iron Man, Captain America and the Hulk all in different ways exemplify the description Hayles offers: while Stark's Iron Man suit makes explicit his engagement with intelligent machinery, Captain America and the Hulk's biological make-up has been permanently altered by science and technology, resulting in their posthuman attributes.

In addition to the Avengers, the film also exhibits other non-human characters. The Avengers must defend America from Loki—Thor's shape-shifting brother and anti-human god—and his army of cyborgs, some of which are humanoid, while others resemble giant mechanical leviathans: unlike Iron Man, for example, the base forms of these machines are not human. Despite Loki's shape-shifting ability and his remarks that humans

142 Section II: "Establish justice"

are an inferior race, his decision to adopt an Anglophone human guise is suggestive of the superiority that such a body has over other bodies in the film. Indeed, the elite worth of specifically American human bodies—or the bodies of those whose nations are allied with America—is something that emerges from the film's representation of killing. By considering *The Avengers* in relation to Giorgio Agamben's theory of *homo sacer* in order to expose the value placed upon different lives in the film, it becomes possible to view the narrative as one in which the loss of a single American life is represented as a pivotal and traumatic narrative event while the killing of a non-human is a spectacle to which attention is drawn. Furthermore, the significance of the film's post–9/11 context, and specifically how the act of border crossing and its perceived threat can be used to justify imposing a "state of exception" upon those at the heart of the nation's anxieties, is made clear in the representation of these spectacular killings.

Agamben defines *homo sacer* as a person that "may be killed and yet not sacrificed," and as being "included in the juridical order [...] solely in the form of its exclusion (that is, of its capacity to be killed)."[3] The sovereign, to "whom the juridical order grants the power of proclaiming a state of exception" upon others, excludes *homo sacer* from the legal system's recognition and its protection.[4] Agamben's analysis of the sovereign is underpinned by similar principles to those of Nick Fury: Fury commands S.H.I.E.L.D.—an extra-governmental espionage division—and extends to the Avengers, on the sovereign's behalf, the right to declare a state of exception and eliminate enemies at will in order to save Americans. Agamben asserts that human life is founded "on a community not simply of the pleasant and the painful but of the good and the evil and of the just and the unjust."[5] A similar good/evil dichotomy is integral to *The Avengers'* narrative, and is also integral to America's vision of itself in historical conflicts. Dan Hassler-Forest notes that by echoing the "themes and images associated with the [September 2001] terrorist attacks," the film draws upon recent history to cast America in "the role of victim in history rather than its violent oppressor" and reinforces the distinction between the good and just America and its evil and unjust enemies.[67] These simplistic "us" versus "them" politics are evidently at work in the film, with the "them" category referring to those who are not culturally or politically allied with America. This divide does not emerge in this film, but rather it continues on from the political principles established in several previous films, and so it is necessary to return to an earlier film to analyze it.

Anthony R. Mills reads the Marvel films as a critique of capitalism, and cites Tony Stark's speech in *Iron Man* (2008) in which Stark says "I saw young Americans killed by the very weapons I created to defend and protect them" as such a critique.[8] What Mills overlooks is that Stark is a capitalist billionaire arms dealer who considers his business ventures ethical until his weapons are used against Americans. As the *Iron Man* films do not feature non-human enemies, Stark's allusion to the "Other" from whom he aimed to "defend and protect" America underlines his complacency with his weapons being used against non–Americans. The value placed upon American lives is emphasized by the film's treatment of death, and the emphasis on protecting Americans continues into in *The Avengers*. The nationality of those who threaten the American metropolis and its civilians in Marvel works depends upon the political context of production: for the post–9/11 interpretation of Stark, the threat is an Afghan terrorist group and not, as in the original Vietnam War–like comic, a Vietnamese tribe; the threat to Captain America is Nazi Germany, which he is created to defeat. Significantly, by the modern-day world of *The Avengers*, a German is killed by having his eye ripped out, but no American is subjected to an equivalent act of violence. Evidently *The Avengers* bares anxieties about those who have threatened America in the past, as well as those who do so in the present.

The array of killing methods that *homines sacri* are subjected to reveals their state of exception. The Avengers' post/non-human enhancements and skills provide many spectacular ways to kill their enemies. The violence to which the Avengers subject the cyborgs includes Hawkeye firing an explosive arrow into an enemy's head, Thor electrocuting a hostile group, the Hulk crushing a cyborg's skull, and Captain America using his shield to dismember another. The use of the shield—a symbol of defense after which Fury's division is named—to kill an enemy underlines most effectively the extent to which the violence displayed in these scenes is justified on the grounds of defending American life from a foreign enemy, even if that means subjecting the enemy to the forms of violence from which Americans are being protected. That these methods are visually spectacular draws attention to the act of killing, and represents the non-human, cyborgic body as part of a homogenous mass which only exists within the film to allow the Avengers to exhibit their fantasy powers: this is emphasized by the lyrics of AC/DC's "Shoot to Thrill" which Stark introduces into the diegetic soundtrack during his initial conflict with Loki. This is most fully articulated in the 36-second-long take during the battle sequence where the Avengers improvise collaborative ways to kill: these include Captain America using his shield to reflect Iron Man's repulsor beams into a crowd of enemies, and Thor running an electrical current through a metal shard that the Hulk has lodged into a cyborgic leviathan's back. These acts are accentuated by the fact that this single take is almost five times as long as the sequence's average shot length (see Table 1.1).

Non-human lives are not mourned and their murder is without consequence for the perpetrator, as prominently outlined in the battle sequence. The sequence is 1,415 seconds long, and the average shot length is 2.29 seconds:

in this time the entire alien arsenal is killed, either on Earth or when their home planet is destroyed, and yet there are no suggestions that humans are physically harmed during this scene. While Hayles has posited that the posthuman body "need not be apocalyptic," the film presents it as having the capacity to be such and, what is more, that it can be created with the intention such but only for particular forms of life.[9] From an Agambian perspective of the film, Hayles' comment holds true in that posthumanism does not threaten human existence, but the Avengers' posthuman capabilities primarily serve to bring about the destruction of a significant proportion of a non-human race. Hayles' position is underpinned by the notion that posthumanism could in theory threaten to end human existence should these technologies of the body be used against humans, but what *The Avengers* posits is that posthumanism can also serve to protect and prolong humanity by acting in its defense. That the non-human body's function is merely present to be subjected to the Avengers' posthuman capabilities is foregrounded by the speed of the editing. The editing quickly moves from one kill to the next, allowing no time to reflect upon the implications of a non-human's death.

By contrast though, the death of S.H.I.E.L.D. agent Phil Coulson is represented as a sacrifice—something that, in Agamben's terms, cannot be true of *homines sacri*—followed by a traumatic period of mourning. Coulson appears as a supporting character of little importance in the previous films and serves in an adjunct role to Fury: prior to this he had only served as the protagonist of *A Funny Thing Happened on the Way to Thor's Hammer*, a Marvel one-shot included on the Blu-Ray for *Captain America: The First Avenger* and not shown during the cinematic release. However, in *The Avengers* Coulson is given a greater on-screen presence and the film gestures for the first time in a cinematic release towards elements of his private life, as seen in his conversation with Stark's girlfriend Pepper Potts where they are, to Stark's bemusement, on first-name terms. Coulson also reveals his Captain America fandom, and his awkward attempts to have his vintage playing cards signed provide recurring comic relief, a function with which Coulson has not previously been associated. The reworking of Coulson into a significant character that has, for the first time in the Marvel films, established personal relationships with other characters adds to the poignancy of their mourning following his death. Unlike when the non-humans are killed, Coulson's stabbing is not explicitly represented but rather implied by the soundtrack and his pained appearance: a stark contrast to the numerous scenes of cyborgic bodies being destroyed elsewhere in the film. He is immediately grieved by Thor against a slow, morose non-diegetic soundtrack, but his death is not instant: first he confronts Loki with a speech about human perseverance and conviction before using an experimental weapon against him. When Coulson dies, Nick Fury is present and the impact of his loss is suggested by the reintroduction of the mournful soundtrack and the slow-motion long takes, suggestive of Fury's trauma at the loss of Coulson. This scene's pace of editing is also a particularly notable contrast to the fast-paced editing during the spectacular battle sequence. The slow motion continues as the film cuts to each Avenger's saddened face when receiving the news from Fury that Coulson, euphemistically, "is down."

From an Agambian perspective, when Fury discusses the necessity to avenge Coulson for the sacrifice that he made to further the Avengers' cause, the film again posits a significant difference between the worth of a single human life and numerous non-human lives. Taking the lives of *homines sacri* is, in Agamben's terms, unworthy of being considered a sacrificial act; the distinction between human and non-human life posited by the film similarly uses the notion of sacrifice to foreground the worth of Coulson's life. Thus, Henry Jenkins' view that the film creates a "space that [...] denies death and mortality" might be reconsidered in this context.[10] Non-human lives are taken throughout the film without consequence, and the loss of a single American life is the traumatic pivotal point in the narrative that encourages the disillusioned Avengers to reunite to protect Manhattan.

Table 1.1
Statistical Analysis of Shot Length
(calculations are by the author)

Length of Sequence	23 minutes and 35 seconds
Number of Shots	618
Length (seconds) ÷ Shots	1415 ÷ 618 = 2.28964401294
Average Length (2dp)	2.29 seconds

As previously noted, the media images of 9/11 and the destruction of the metropolis caused by enemies breaching American borders is of metaphorical significance. While it is not the case that the film's plot is a consciously written reflection of the events of 9/11, it is clear to see that the ways in which threat and destruction are expressed in this post–9/11 context stem from the media images associated with it, and particularly influenced by a 21st-century understanding of what mediated images of the metropolis looks like when it is subjected to acts of terror. A prime example of this is when the cyborg army invades through an illicitly-opened border and conducts an aerial assault on New York: a porthole opens in the sky through which the enemies enter American airspace in a way which echoes the "out of the blue" neoconservative rhetoric of accounts of the September 2001 terrorist attacks. Not dissimilar to the 2001 terrorist attacks, the nature of the invasion shows a likeness to the events that allowed America to declare itself a victim of history, but is also clearly not a direct response to these events. Indeed, the collateral damage gestures to the aforementioned 9/11 media images to establish the consequences that enemy invasions pose, and metaphorically alludes to the loss of human life in lieu of actually depicting any human causalities. This reinforces the film's "us" and "them" politics: Loki and his army are merely avatars for a range of potential threats to America and, indeed, 9/11 is just one historical conflict that Marvel films gesture towards to evoke memories of such threats (past *and* present).

However, while the Avengers largely signify a force for good, they do also come to momentarily occupy a problematic space which is common across superhero films, one in which they are "simultaneously an asset and a liability" to the nation.[11] Though Jason Bainbridge is talking about the *Spider-Man* films, this description can be aptly extended to the Avengers: while they defend America, they do so in illegal ways and thus cast doubt upon the nation's victimhood, particularly as no civilians are killed but the invaders are. What is more, not only are the invaders killed, but the Avengers take pride in killing them. While this contradictory position temporarily complicates the simple good/evil dichotomy that the narrative had hitherto established and supported, the battle sequence's climax reinstates it.

As the Avengers become outnumbered and are near defeat, the World Security Council orders Nick Fury to command a nuclear strike on Manhattan. What the World Security Council's proposed action suggests is that there is an ethical justification to ending a number of American lives, writing them off as collateral damage, if this is the only way to also save an even greater number of Americans. Fury, however, does not share this position and his view continues to support the notion that each individual American life bears an intrinsic value that is worth protecting from extremes of violence and suffering, in this case a nuclear strike, but that to inflict this violence on other bodies is justifiable in the name of defense. Fury elects to ignore this and "will not order a nuclear strike against a civilian population": he is overruled on the grounds that "if we don't hold them here we lose everything." The anxiety that the attack could spread beyond Manhattan is used by the World Security Council to justify using the nuclear missile. Following its launch, Fury informs the Avengers of the bomb and Tony Stark intercepts it and flies across the border between Earth and the invaders' fleet. Stark, though he acknowledges that this is a suicide mission, nonetheless survives while the cyborg fleet is destroyed. The scene posits that using nuclear weapons against a non-human (or, indeed, non–American) race is ethical but to do so against an American population is not: it is, as Fury puts it, "a stupid-ass decision." Evidently the non–American cyborg holds the position of *homo sacer*, as revealed by the scene's nuclear politics and more so by the fact that Stark survives against the odds.

What is more, when the alien mother ship is destroyed there are three different shots of the cyborgs on Earth collapsing to their death, no longer posing a threat, and reinforcing the positive implications for America that come from the bombing of a foreign world. The revelation that destroying the enemy fleet was the solution to prevent further attacks on the metropolis reaffirms the already established notion that killing American humans is unjust, but killing non–Americans in the name of protecting America is within all legal and ethical boundaries. Furthermore, in the context of this scene, the film threatens that failing to destroy a significant proportion of the enemy race would only allow for the danger that they pose to spread, quashing any moral ambiguities that may arise from the Avengers' actions.

Ultimately, then, the representations of killing in the film exposes the different values attributed to American and non–American lives. While the fast-paced editing and the Avengers' powers make a spectacle of a non-human onslaught, the death of a single American is shown to be a traumatic turning point in the narrative: the same cannot be said of the German whose death is more akin to the invading cyborgs' than Agent Coulson's. Coulson's murder is hidden from sight and, indeed, the film's 12A certificate classification in the UK and PG-13 classification in the U.S. further accentuates that it is acceptable for a young, mass audience to witness the graphic murder of non–Americans, but to witness Americans subjected to the same is inappropriate. While the idea that death is presented as a spectacle to be observed may be a general point true of a number of Hollywood blockbusters, what makes it unique in *The Avengers* and in superhero texts more generally is the extent to which the superheroes' post-human powers are foregrounded as a method of killing non-human enemies. What is more, the film can be understood in the context of post–9/11 America. The invasion of the cyborgs echoes that of the terrorists who conducted an aerial assault on New York, and the act of border crossing proves threatening. A state of exception is imposed upon those who threaten America, and the film's nuclear politics reveals that while it is unjust to use nuclear weapons against Americans, using them against a non–American race, a race of *homines sacri,* does not transgress ethical or legal boundaries.

Overall, the film represents a world in which new post- and non-human identities are integrated into the established categories of nationhood. The text's theorization of the non-human, cyborgic Other offers opportunities for the expansion of Agamben's theory to be used as a critical methodology to intervene in the reification of American anxieties: in the context of post–9/11 when the nation has declared itself a victim, it allows for an understanding of how the film proposes that America is entitled to impose a state of exception upon, and to regard as *homines sacri*, those at the heart of its anxieties.

NOTES

1. *The Avengers,* directed by *Joss Whedon* (2012; Los Angeles: Marvel Studios, 2012), DVD.

2. N. Katherine Hayles, *How We Became Posthuman: Virtual Bodies in Cybernetics, Literature, and Informatics.* (Chicago and London: University of Chicago Press, 1999), 287.

3. Giorgio Agamben, *Homo sacer: Sovereign Power and Bare Life.* (Stanford: Stanford University Press, 1998), 12.

4. Agamben, 17.

5. Agamben, 10.

6. Dan Hassler-Forest, *Capitalist Superheroes: Caped Crusaders in the Neoliberal Age.* (Croydon: Zero Books, 2012), 78.

7. Hassler-Forest, 72.

8. Anthony R. Mills, *American Theology, Superhero Comics, and Cinema: The Marvel of Stan Lee and the Revolution of a Genre.* (London: Routledge, 2014), 178.

9. Hayles, 288.

10. Henry Jenkins, *The Wow Climax: Tracing the Emotional Impact of Popular Culture.* (New York: New York University Press, 2007), 66.

11. Jason Bainbridge, "Spider-Man, the question and the meta-zone: exception, objectivism and the comics of Steve Ditko," *Law Text Culture* 16, no.1: 2012: 225.

Section III
"Provide for the common defense": The Geopolitical Context of the Cinematic Universe

Paralleling the rise of the superhero genre during World War II, the creators of the Marvel Cinematic Universe developed their works in the wake of the September 11, 2001, terrorist attacks and the global war on terror that followed.

Filmmakers have utilized this geopolitical context as a frame of reference for the audience in order to ground their tales of superheroic fantasy in a reality with which viewers can relate. In doing so, creators have articulated some major concerns of the American public about the foreign threats faced by the United States, while at the same time offering critiques about how American policy makers have gone about defending the country from its external and existential foes.

"You were the world's first superhero"

Marvel Studio's Superheroes, Law and the Pursuit of Justice

JASON BAINBRIDGE

Introduction

In Marvel Studios' *The Avengers*[1] while travelling en route to their mobile base the Helicarrier, the following exchange occurs between S.H.I.E.L.D. special agent Phil Coulson (Clark Gregg) and Steve Rogers, Captain America (Chris Evans):

> COULSON: You were the world's first superhero.... I gotta say, it's an honor to meet you officially. I've sort of met you. I mean I watched you while you were sleeping.... We made some modifications to the uniform. I had a little design input.
> ROGERS: The uniform? Aren't the stars and stripes a little old-fashioned?
> COULSON: With everything that's happening, the things that are about to come to light, people might just need a little old-fashioned.

This exchange is important for three reasons. First, it extradiegetically displaces rival company Warner Brothers/DC Comics' stable of heroes in the public imagination (commencing with Superman and Batman) by chronologically establishing Marvel's Captain America as "the world's first superhero." Whereas reimaginings and retcons of DC's characters in comics and film mean that they are constantly being updated to the present (from their creation in 1938 and 1939 respectively), Captain America consistently remains a product of his time of creation during World War II (1941 in the comics/1942 in the film *Captain America: The First Avenger*[2]).

Second, the exchange diegetically links the superhero to the state—and more specifically superheroes as military applications in the Marvel Cinematic Universe (MCU); Captain America was a "super soldier" created through the injection of Doctor Abraham Erskine's (Stanley Tucci) experimental serum; The Hulk (Edward Norton/Mark Ruffalo) is a monster created through an attempt to duplicate that super soldier serum using gamma radiation; Iron Man (Robert Downey, Jr.) uses technology developed for the military to become an armored hero powered by a self-sustaining energy source; Thor (Chris Hemsworth) is an alien soldier; Black Widow (Scarlett Johansson) and Hawkeye (Jeremy Renner) are a government spy and soldier respectively. As described in more detail below, this idea of the superhero being a normal person affected by "modernity" (weird comic-book science as filtered through that specific Cold War anxiety framing science in the 1960s, which viewed science in terms of its terrible potential to create what we would today term weapons of mass destruction) is a specific feature of the Marvel superhero as established in the comic book source material. In the Marvel Cinematic Universe (hereinafter MCU) this is almost always repositioned as scientific advancement within the military/industrial complex as a way of dealing with the direct threat of terrorism.

Finally, the exchange's concluding reference to "the things that are about to come to light, people might just need a little old-fashioned" indicates a point of demarcation in the MCU that occurs with *The Avengers.* According to the president of Marvel Studios, Kevin Feige, the MCU is broken into "phases," and Phase One comprises six films that introduce the individual heroes—*Iron Man, The Incredible Hulk, Iron Man 2* (introducing Black Widow), *Thor* (also introducing Hawkeye) and *Captain America: The First Avenger*—that then come together as the "super team" the Avengers. *The Avengers* (and more importantly the staging of the Battle of New York between the Avengers and Loki's Chitauri forces at the film's conclusion) marks the conclusion of Phase One but also gestures ahead to the concerns of Phase Two. I argue that it is at this point, during the Battle of New York, that the super soldiers largely created (and co-opted) by the state during Phase One truly become superheroes, "old fashioned" symbols of justice that often must exist in opposition to the state (or alternative authority figures) in the following Phase Two films where "the things" the state conceals are ultimately brought "to light."

This essay is an analysis of this repeated trope of superhero justice versus authorized law commencing in *The Avengers* and continuing throughout the Phase Two cycle of films, particularly *Thor: The Dark World*[3] and *Captain America: The Winter Soldier.*[4] It is my contention that the most important effect of Marvel Studios' incredible run of critical and commercial success— from *Iron Man*[5] through to *Guardians of the Galaxy*[6]—has been the confirmation of the superhero as *the exemplar of justice* in popular culture as they move from their comic book origins to mainstream media (through movies, merchandising and assorted media tie-ins). All of the Phase Two Marvel films are in some way engaged with this dichotomy between justice and law and it is therefore the argument of this essay that it is the cinematic transition of the Marvel superhero that has driven them to operate as a locus in which ideas of law and society are played out and explored, even more so than their comic book progenitors.[7]

The idea that superheroes could be central to any consideration of popular media's thinking about law should not be surprising because superheroes offer us the perfect revenge/control fantasy; power without the constraint of law. As a form of wish fulfillment superheroes therefore also necessarily become a study of the perceived deficiencies in society and what "being heroic" actually means. They represent the endpoint of conventional law precisely because they are unconventional; unlike the soldier, the policeman or the government agent they often have to work completely outside legal categories. Much of the tension in the MCU therefore arises from the co-option of the superhero by the state as a super soldier; can the Avengers trust S.H.I.E.L.D.? Will Thor disobey Odin? Can the Guardians of the Galaxy work with the Nova Corps?

Superheroes are "created" by scientific augmentation, experiment or accident that places their super nature at odds with the rationality of modernity. They are also more involved in crime control rather than due process. This means that superheroes generally have a relatively limited legal affiliation or state sanction and therefore have to be co-opted by the state (usually through a government organization, such as S.H.I.E.L.D. or the Nova Corps). Most importantly, superheroes can be proactive rather than merely reactive (i.e., they don't have to wait for a crime to happen and they're not limited by questions of jurisdiction). The superhero is therefore constructed in relation to rationality (in opposition to it), in relation to modern law (supplementing its failures) and in relation to action (they are proactive). In these ways the MCU superhero and their relationship with the state becomes another way for thinking discursively about law because of the superhero's unique perspective on both society and its perceptions of the effectiveness of law. This is particularly true within the larger context of the real-world War on Terror that continues to inform and echo throughout these films.

The MCU

The "Marvel" in the MCU is derived from the title of the first comic published by pulp publisher Martin Goodman in November 1939, *Marvel Comics* #1. It was a direct response to DC's superhero comics that Goodman saw as eroding his pulp empire and has been the name of the comics group

(Marvel Comics) on which the MCU is based since the 1960s, (after brief periods calling itself Atlas and Timely).

The idea of the MCU being a "Universe" emerged as early as 1941 with a lengthy battle between the Human Torch and the Sub-Mariner[8] beginning a long tradition of heroes meeting, fighting and reconciling (mirrored in the fight between Iron Man, Thor and Captain America following Loki's capture in *The Avengers* film). But it was with the rebirth of an interest in superheroes twenty years later (known to comics book fans as "the Silver Age"), and again as a response to DC Comics (most particularly the popularity of their super team The Justice League of America), that the Marvel Universe truly came into being with the publication of *The Fantastic Four* #1 in November 1961. Closely followed by Spider-Man, the Hulk, Iron Man and Thor, the Marvel Universe benefited from the unified vision of its architects—Stan Lee, Jack Kirby and Steve Ditko—whose crossovers and guest appearances (especially during 1963) quickly created the idea that all of this superhero action was taking place in one cohesive universe. The return of Namor in *Fantastic Four* #4 in May 1962 and Captain America in *The Avengers* #4 in March 1964 only confirmed that this was indeed the same Marvel Universe that had commenced with the Sub-Mariner and Human Torch back in 1939.

To a large extent the "Universe" of the MCU is bounded by a series of licensing decisions Marvel made in the mid–'90s, including licensing the X-Men and Fantastic Four to Fox and Spider-Man to Sony in 1999. This meant that when Marvel Studios moved from character licensing to self-financing their own films (commencing under David Maisel in 2004) they had a greatly reduced slate of characters with which to work, mostly comprised of character rights that had reverted back to them because of non-production, *Avengers* related (as with Iron Man and Captain America) or characters deep in their back catalogue who had never been optioned before (as with the Guardians of the Galaxy). For the purposes of this essay the MCU's circumscribed version of the Marvel Universe is interesting because those heroes that are left as part of the MCU are those most closely aligned with (or at the very least co-opted by) the state, the heroes that make up the Avengers. Loner heroes (like Spider-Man[9]), independent explorers (like the Fantastic Four) or outcasts (like the X-Men) are largely excluded from the MCU by Marvel's prior licensing deals. Indeed, it has only been with the release of *Guardians of the Galaxy* and the slate of Netflix television series focused on Marvel's "street level characters" (including Daredevil, Luke Cage and Jessica Jones) that the worldview of the MCU has started to shift away from governmental concerns toward a broader view of what it means to be a superhero in the Marvel Universe.

As such the interconnectedness of the MCU largely rests on two central ideas. First, the Avengers Initiative developed by Nick Fury (Samuel L. Jackson), Security Director of the clandestine government organization S.H.I.E.L.D. and threaded through the Phase One films in mid- and post-credit sequences. As Fury describes it:

> The idea was to bring together a group of remarkable people to see if they could become something more. To see if they could work together when we needed them to, to fight the battles that we never could [The Avengers].

This is where that tension between superhero and the state is played out, where the state attempts to exert its control over the superhero, when the superhero is co-opted as a soldier into the Avengers Initiative. Here the superhero becomes another weapon, another agent of the state; as an Avenger, the superhero becomes a super soldier for deployment by the state and thereby becomes a tool of the government (and thus part of the legislative arm).

Second, the Infinity Stones, powerful "relics that pre-date the universe itself" (Odin qtd. *Thor: The Dark World*) and frequently appearing in the MCU films as weapons (the Tesseract, the Scepter, the Aether and the Orb) used by the antagonists (the Red Skull, Loki, Malekith and Ronan the Accuser) to give them mastery of time, space, mind-control and other unearthly powers. As Taneleer Tivan, the Collector (Benecio del Toro) describes them:

> Before creation itself, there were six singularities. Then the universe exploded into existence, and the remnants of these systems were forged into concentrated ingots. Infinity Stones. These stones, it seems, can only be brandished by beings of extraordinary strength [*Guardians of the Galaxy*].

The twin story engines of the MCU are therefore a state-based expansion of power (through the Avengers Initiative) and weapons of mass destruction (the Infinity Stones). When thought of this way, both are clearly informed by the context in which the MCU has grown and evolved, the ongoing War on Terror (or Global War on Terrorism or Overseas Contingency Operation, as it is referred to under President Obama's administration) that started in the wake of the September 11, 2001, terrorist attacks on the United States.

Comic book superheroes were born (and enjoyed their greatest popularity) during times of transition and uncertainty, when America was moving from economic crisis into armed conflict. Superman and Captain America emerged as the nation was coming out of the Great Depression and going into World War II in the late '30s and early '40s. The bulk of Marvel's superheroes similarly emerged during another period of cultural transition in the early 60s alongside the counter culture movement, in the shadow of the space race with Russia, as the nation was debating the expansion of military intervention into Vietnam. Perhaps it is unsurprising then, that the development of the MCU (commencing with 2008's *Iron Man* in 2008) is similarly informed by the War on Terror. In addition to these twin story engines, the

MCU antagonists are frequently sleepers, extremists and/or terrorists: the Nazi science cell Hydra (headed by the Red Skull and later the sleeper agent Alexander Pierce); the terrorist group the Ten Rings (headed by the Mandarin) and AIM (a front for the Ten Rings headed by Aldrich Killian); the Frost Giant "sleeper agent" Loki; the Dark Elf extremists lead by Malekith; the Kree extremists lead by Ronan the Accuser; and the mad titan Thanos (a Bin Laden like figure, plotting devastation from a remote location in the universe).

The State

At the core of the MCU are authority figures: on Earth it is the state as represented by the government agency S.H.I.E.L.D., the army headed by General Thaddeus "Thunderbolt" Ross (William Hurt) and the World Security Council to whom S.H.I.E.L.D. reports; on Asgard it is Odin the All-Father (Anthony Hopkins); in the larger universe it is Nova Prime (Glenn Close), head of the Nova Corps, the peace-keeping authority of Xandar.

While it is risky to generalize in relation to representation across a number of popular cultural forms, overwhelmingly the most common recurring signifier of law in popular visual media is the father. This is true of the MCU whether they are literal fathers, as in the case of Odin (father to Thor) or General Thaddeus "Thunderbolt" Ross (father to Bruce Banner's lover Betty Ross) or symbolic fathers, like Nick Fury (head of S.H.I.E.L.D. and the 'father' who brings agents like Maria Hill, Hawkeye and Black Widow together) and the World Security Council (representative "fathers" of their regions, the U.S., India and Asia); exceptions to the rule are Nova Prime and the lone female member of the World Security Council, Councilwoman Hawley (Jenny Agutter).

This idea of the law being paternal has its roots in the Roman idea of the "*pater imporiosius* who himself bears both the character of the father and the capacity of the magistrate ... the magistrate's *imperium* is nothing but the father's *vitae necisque potestas* extended to all citizens."[10] As Austin Sarat notes, law has long been conceptualized as "patriarchal in its norms and methods,"[11] citing precedents from Abraham and Isaac, to *DeShaney v. Winnebago*, to Freud, to Jerome Frank's famous pronouncement that "the Law ... inevitably becomes a partial substitute for the Father-as-Infallible-Judge."[12] Though this is not unproblematic, or without its critics (including Sarat himself), Sarat admits that legal scholars continue to display a "longing for ... paternal power and the overwhelming power that fathers exercise as basic to legal authority."[13] We can therefore characterize Nick Fury, for example, as the *pater imporiosius,* simultaneously the Avengers' father figure and signifier of law providing the Avengers with a code to be followed.

Legal scholar Peter Fitzpatrick refers to Freud (and more specifically Freud's work in *Totem and Taboo*) as "an origin myth for law" because Freud saw law as central to "modern, self-sufficient" society.[14] In this formulation, law is located in the taboos and transgressions society wishes to control, signified by the totem of the father.[15] Law and society therefore become inextricably linked to the father-as-signifier of both law and the process of modernity more broadly. It is perhaps unsurprising then that popular cultural signifiers of law are so often paternal, in either a literal or figurative sense. For while popular cultural representations of the father are constantly in flux and always subject to changing "cultural, economic, political, technological, and geographical contexts"[16] rather then following any through-narrative of either improvement or decline,[17] the one common element of almost all of these representations of father is the father's continuing signification of law and authority.

Most importantly, Nick Fury, Odin and even Nova Prime all consistently signify a *modern* idea of law. By a *modern* idea of law I'm referring to "black letter law," based around the idea of the Rule of Law. I have termed this concept "modern law" because the Rule of Law is itself at the very heart of modernity, both as an important part of the public sphere and as a way of ensuring the continuing maintenance of "order" and "certainty," two of the central concerns of modernity.[18] Modernity's belief in progress through rationalism resulted in a corresponding rise in the presence of the courtroom and the idea of empirical argumentation as a locus of justice, leading Max Weber to conclude that law itself legitimated the modern state.[19]

The increasing prevalence of "the state" as signifier of law in the MCU parallels the increasing intervention of "the state" in the real world, particularly post–September 11 and particularly in the area of proactive law where there has been a notable expansion and concentration of power in the executive[20] and a move toward interventionist justice. In the United States, the *Patriot Act's*[21] expansion of the investigative powers of the Federal Bureau of Investigation lead to accusations of racial profiling and discrimination. (Both were defended as proactive measures). Similarly the ongoing War on Terror was itself designed to be interventionist, continually couched in terms of spreading freedom in the world and therefore regarded as "an urgent requirement of our nation's security."[22]

Part of the problem in legislating against terrorism seems to be in defining the term "terrorism" itself. There remains no accepted definition at international law. More particularly, the problem is in *distinguishing acts of terrorism from an armed struggle waged by national liberation movements.* The United States, for example, defined the September 11 attacks as acts of war rather than crimes outside a war context which lead to terrorism being treated as *sui generis* (of its own kind) rather than a crime under existing modern law. This encourages the use of the metaphor "war on terror," with the word "war" itself justifying the use of "emergency powers," the "suspension" of certain liberties and the demarcation of a clear beginning (an act of war, i.e., the September 11 attack), rather than politically contextualizing the attacks or responding through the modern legal system—as a number of European countries do. Aldrich Killian (Guy Pearce) plays with such stereotypical signifiers of terrorism in *Iron Man 3* when he employs a drunken English actor (Trevor Slattery/Ben Kingsley), heavily codified in speech and appearance, to represent terrorism as "The Mandarin" who acts as a distraction while Killian works on his own weapon of mass destruction, Extremis.

Such a shift in policy is also echoed in a number of real-world sources. For example, the Justice Department and the FBI blamed their intelligence failures on September 11 to their over-reliance on a criminal justice (modern) approach to counterterrorism.[23] Similarly, the policy shift is underscored by the frequent restatement of the U.S. administration's aim to "bring terrorists to justice for their crimes"[24]—with its deliberate connection to justice rather than trial, crime control rather than due process. The zenith of such an approach is realized in the MCU in Nick Fury's explanation of Project Insight to Steve Rogers, Captain America in *Captain America: The Winter Soldier*:

> FURY: This is Project Insight. Three next-generation helicarriers synced to a network of targeting satellites…. We're gonna neutralize a lot of threats before they even happen.
> ROGERS: Thought the punishment usually came after the crime.
> FURY: We can't afford to wait that long.
> ROGERS: Who's "we?"
> FURY: After New York I convinced the World Security Council we needed a quantum surge in threat analysis. For once we're way ahead of the curve.
> ROGERS: By holding a gun to everyone on Earth and calling it protection.
> FURY: You know, I read those SSR files. "Greatest Generation?" You guys did some nasty stuff.
> ROGERS: Yeah, we compromised. Sometimes in ways that made us not sleep so well. But we did it so that people could be free. This isn't freedom. This is fear.
> FURY: S.H.I.E.L.D. takes the world as it is, not as we'd like it to be. And it's getting damn near past time for you to get with that program, Cap.
> ROGERS: Don't hold your breath.

Here the law has become completely proactive, suspending rights and due process in favor of crime control at the barrel of the Helicarriers.

Perhaps the greatest irony is that, as Michael German notes, "Terrorist groups almost never refer to themselves as terrorists, but rather as soldiers, revolutionaries, holy warriors"[25]; therefore terrorists themselves are enacting a form of action they see as impliedly legal in its links back to both the sacred and the belief that justice is on their side. The main antagonist of *Guardians of the Galaxy*, Ronan (Lee Pace) for example, is described by the Broker

(Christopher Fairbank) as "a Kree fanatic, outraged by the peace treaty, who will not rest until Xandarian culture, my culture, is wiped from existence." In contrast, Ronan himself notes: "They call me a 'terrorist,' 'radical,' 'zealot,' because I obey the ancient laws of my people, the Kree, and punish those who do not. Because I do not forgive your people for taking the life of my father, and his father, and his father before him. A thousand years of war between us will not be forgotten!" Ronan therefore justifies his actions in the context of a greater struggle, reaching back to the sacred ("ancient laws") and a belief that justice is on his side (he does not forgive past infractions).

This line between terrorist and hero therefore becomes a matter of perspective with the idea of "the right enemy" becoming increasingly important for defining someone as either a super soldier or a superhero; each one is only justified in their actions because they are "in the right." Two key scenes reveal how this operates in the MCU. In *The Avengers* the superheroes confront Nick Fury to ask why he has been using the Tesseract (previously used by the Red Skull) to "build weapons of mass destruction" (Bruce Banner):

> FURY: Last year, Earth had a visitor from another planet who had a grudge match that leveled a small town. We learned that no only are we not alone but we are hopelessly, hilariously, outgunned… And you're not the only threat. The world's filling up with people who can't be matched, that can't be controlled.

Here Fury consistently uses the "right enemy" argument. Escalation is necessary to combat the new threats that are emerging.

Similarly in *Thor: The Dark World*, Thor questions Odin's approach to dealing with Malekith and the Dark Elves:

> ODIN: If and when he comes his men will fall on 10,000 Asgardian blades.
> THOR: And how many of our men shall fall on theirs?
> ODIN: As many as are needed! Ah! We will fight! Till the last Asgardian breath. Till the last drop of Asgardian blood.
> THOR: Then how are you different from Malekith?
> ODIN: [laughs] The difference, my son, is that I will win.

Here, even more than in *The Avengers*/Fury example, "the difference" between authority and terrorist seems increasingly hard to find. Odin and Malekith's strategies—and beliefs—are virtually the same.

Interestingly the order that both Odin and S.H.I.E.L.D. profess to pursue is precisely the goal of several of their antagonists. Loki describes his actions (in *The Avengers*) as being to remove freedom for the greater good. He tells his father Odin, "I went down to Midgard to rule the people of Earth as a benevolent god. Just like you" (in *Thor: The Dark World*). Thanos' servant, the Other (Alexis Denisof), also suggests that order without freedom is the end goal of Thanos himself when he suggests (at the end of *The Avengers*) that humans are "unruly and therefore cannot be ruled." Similarly Nazi scientist (now analogue artificial intelligence) Arnim Zola (Toby Jones) describes HYDRA as being

> … founded on the belief that humanity could not be trusted with its own freedom. What we did not realize was that if you try to take that freedom, they resist. The war taught us much. Humanity needed to surrender its freedom willingly. After the war, S.H.I.E.L.D. was founded and I was recruited. The new HYDRA grew. A beautiful parasite inside S.H.I.E.L.D. For 70 years HYDRA has been secretly feeding crisis, reaping war and when history did not cooperate, history was changed…. HYDRA created a world so chaotic that humanity is finally ready to sacrifice its freedom to gain its security.

The state has gone so far in its efforts to impose order that the line has blurred so much no one even notices the substitution of "the terrorist" for "the authority" in these films; HYDRA successfully infiltrates S.H.I.E.L.D. in *Captain America: The Winter Soldier* (though it is "revealed" by Captain America) and Loki successfully replaces Odin at the end of *Thor: The Dark World* (and thanks to his magicks remains undiscovered at the end of that film).

The state and their enemies have therefore become so aligned in their pursuit of "order" at any cost that the differences between them become negligible. As HYDRA leader Alexander Pierce (Robert Redford) explains to Nick Fury:

> Our enemies are your enemies, Nick. Disorder. War. It's just a matter of time before a dirty bomb goes off in Moscow, or an EMP fries Chicago. Diplomacy? A holding action, Nick. A band-aid. And you know where I learned that. Bogota. You didn't ask. You just did what had to be done. I can bring order to the lives of seven billion people by sacrificing 20 million. It's the next step, Nick. If you have the courage to take it.

Ultimately, with the failure of the state in the MCU, it falls to the superhero to offer up a potential alternative—"justice." As Mark Tushnet notes, often in legal texts "law is associated with the Dominant, usually the white male, and justice with the Other."[26] The MCU inverts this by having Fury (an African American male) represent law but the comparison otherwise holds.

Tushnet goes on to claim that the tension is derived from a clash between the two because, as has already been outlined above, "Western culture valorizes both law and justice."[27] In defining the Other, Tushnet explains,

> The Other may be an indigenous person, a woman, a man who somehow has escaped the bonds of the Dominant, an immigrant or older person as in Twelve Angry Men or, as in The Caine Mutiny, a man who would ordinarily be the Dominant.[28]

This is an idea that Tushnet traces back to *The Leatherstocking Tales* with Natty Bumpo as the Other standing for justice against Judge Temple, as Dominant, standing for law. Similarly in the MCU we can find echoes of the Other in those who have been deliberately "othered": by their intelligence, their wealth and, most importantly, their abilities (and thus "somehow escaped the bonds of the Dominant")—the superhero.

The Marvel Superhero

The name of the "first" superhero, Superman, comes from Nietzsche's term *ubermensch* coined in 1883 for an individual whose creativity transcends ordinary human limitations. As such a superhero's "super nature" can include anything from super strength (like Thor and the Hulk) through to a more subtle transcendence of human limitations such as the ability to be incredibly athletic or fire arrows consecutively hitting targets over long distances (like Black Widow and Hawkeye).

More particularly, as I have written previously,[29] the Marvel superhero has consistently been represented as a melodramatic hero, working through trauma to restore virtue. In the MCU this is evidenced in Steve Rogers (Captain America) coming to terms with being a man out of time, adjusting to a new age and dealing with the old age (and dementia) of his former girlfriend Peggy Carter; or Peter Quill (Star-Lord) filling the absence of his family (losing his mother to cancer, never knowing his father and being abducted from his planet) with casual sex and later a new family in the form of the Guardians of the Galaxy; or Bruce Banner (the Hulk) trying to control his bestial alter ego; or Tony Stark (Iron Man) trying to save/protect the world as Iron Man and develop clean energy initiatives, to work through his guilt of previously being a weapons manufacturer.

In each case the alter ego is a real person—Steve Rogers, Peter Quill, Bruce Banner, Tony Stark—and the "trauma" they are working through is the dark side of "modernity," most often "weird comic book science." Steve Rogers becomes Captain America, Peter Quill becomes Star-Lord, Bruce Banner becomes the Hulk, Tony Stark becomes Iron Man, with this act of becoming being a two-fold process. First there is the scientific experiment or accident that creates the superhuman, be it the super soldier serum, an alien abduction, the gamma bomb or the arc reactor. Second there is the assumption of the superheroic role, Steve Rogers puts on the uniform of Captain America, Peter Quill puts on the mask of Star-Lord, Bruce Banner "gets angry" and turns into the Hulk, Tony Stark puts on the armor of Iron Man. The alter ego therefore dresses up as the superhero; in only the case of Thor (and then, very briefly) does the alter ego become the disguise that the superhero wears to pass as normal. Marvel heroes must work through their heroism—a heroism based on ideas of individual advancement, of enduring trials and emerging, virtue restored, at the other end.

So many of these traumas that form the basis for this melodrama spring from what Stephen King refers to as the "Twisted Pursuit of Forbidden Science," in his study of horror, *Danse Macabre*:

> where for every superhero such as Spiderman [sic] or Captain America, there seem to be a dozen freakish aberrations: Dr Octopus…. The Sandman … and most ominous of all, Dr Doom, who has been so badly maimed in his Twisted Pursuit of Forbidden Science that he is now a great, clanking cyborg who wears a green cape, peers through eyeholes like the archers' slits in a medieval castle, and who appears to be literally sweating rivets … the undesirable side effects of modern science."[30]

While few of these characters appear in the MCU, the statement holds true—MCU heroes are most usually the product of science, augmentation or experimentation in pursuit of progress and protecting the state (the development of super soldiers or new weapons) the very essence of modernity. It is also interesting to note that when the origin stories of these heroes are revised for the MCU, the science is continually updated so these heroes are forever doomed to be "the undesirable side effects of modern science." For example, the injury that prompts Tony Stark to don his Iron Man armor changes from the weaponry of Vietnam (as in the comic books) to weaponry he helped create in Afghanistan (as in 2008's *Iron Man*). The one exception to this rule of course remains Captain America, who must necessarily remain "the world's first superhero," the super soldier created during World War II.

Even Thor, the most premodern and mythological of Marvel's characters is forced to submit to modernity, for in the MCU the premodern, the sacred, the mythological, are all in fact products of science and technology. The Norse Gods and their enemies the Frost Giants and Dark Elves are in reality alien races; their city Asgard is itself a repository of scientific advancement masquerading as magic; their rainbow bridge, the Bifrost, a teleportation device capable of transporting them all over the universe.

But the MCU superheroes take more than just the "super" prefix from Nietzsche for they challenge, as Nietzsche did, both notions of truth and the status quo.[31] This is most obvious in subversive superhero texts like Frank Miller's *The Dark Knight Returns* or Alan Moore's *V for Vendetta* where individual "superheroes" are pitted against totalitarian governments but it also recurs throughout the MCU. The Avengers must stop a nuclear missile launched by their own government on New York. Captain America must fight against a government organization that has been secretly infiltrated. Thor must go against his father's wishes to save Asgard. The subversion is also more subtly present in the way the superhero challenges the rationality of modernity by presenting a world founded on irrationality, be it the capabilities of the title character (i.e., a man who can fly, a raccoon who can speak and fire large weapons) or the locations they visit (i.e., a flying aircraft carrier, a universe of alien invaders). In so doing, the superhero presents an alternative or corollary to modernity, a process of estrangement by which to critique the present system. In this sense they follow the comic tradition (established as far back as the first appearance of the newspaper comic strip character the Yellow Kid in 1896) that comics can provide serious social critique. More precisely, in the MCU, the wish fulfillment embodied in the superhero becomes a way of interrogating the role of the state in the War on Terror.

Both *The Avengers* and *Guardians of the Galaxy* present the idea that justice may be better achieved by a superhuman individual—or team of individuals—rather than a legal system again suggests that justice is something that can exist quite apart from the legal system. Indeed, the legal system—as demonstrable from the authority that controlled S.H.I.E.L.D., the World Security Council's actions, or Nova Corps' inaction—can itself be an impediment to justice (being more concerned, as it is in both cases, with resolution—bomb the attackers or maintain the treaty respectively—rather than justice).

As presented throughout the MCU Phase Two, the relationship between justice and the legal system can therefore be best classified as postmodern. As Jacques Derrida (1992) claimed in his keynote speech at a Cardozo Law School symposium on deconstruction and law, since justice transcends the legal system it can never be wholly imminent. Following Plato,[32] Derrida views justice as something "beyond" the legal system, something quite apart from legal rights and remedies[33]—allowing for the possibility that justice can exceed or even exist in contradiction to the law.[34] Indeed, Derrida quotes Montaigne when he states: "Laws keep up their good standing not because they are just but because they are laws."[35]

Justice is therefore something inevitable as well as something that cannot be deconstructed. Such a position has traces of both natural law and legal positivism but ultimately remains neither, remains postmodern, because justice is that moment of *difference*, of aporia or indecisiveness, that forces a choice amongst a range of possibilities, the very oscillation that postmodernity demands. Legal scholar Douglas Litowitz sees Derrida, both here and again in the *Specters of Marx*[36] as "laying the groundwork for an approach to jurisprudence which insists upon an almost dialectical struggle between law and justice"[37]: or more precisely that "the call to do justice to the other is what spurs the deconstructive process into action, and hence the very process of deconstruction is a process of seeking justice"[38] where "justice and law differ *in kind*; justice is transcendent or (quasi-transcendent) and is not deconstructible, while law is imminent and deconstructible."[39] Here then the act of seeking justice itself shapes the law, a struggle that we can see played out across these Phase Two films.

Take for example the following exchanges from *Guardians of the Galaxy* where the titular characters, a rag tag group of criminals, murderers and thieves slowly come to realize that they alone must bring Ronan to justice:

ROCKET: What are you, some saint all of a sudden? What has the galaxy ever done for you? Why would you wanna save it?

STAR-LORD: Because I'm one of the idiots who lives in it!

…

STAR-LORD: And usually life takes more than it gives. But not today. Today, it's given us something. It has given us a chance.

DRAX: To do what?

STAR-LORD: To give a shit. For once. Not run away. I, for one, am not gonna stand by and watch as Ronan wipes out billions of innocent lives.

ROCKET: But Quill, stopping Ronan, it's impossible. You're asking us to die.

STAR-LORD: [sighs] Yeah I guess I am.

ROCKET: [sighs] Oh, what the hell. I don't got that long a lifespan anyway.

Here the Guardians, like all the superheroes in the MCU, become the only reliable repositories of justice in their film. This draws on most mythologies' notion of justice being *embodied,* from the blindfolded figure of Justice herself[40] to Greek ideas of the Furies and Nemesis. Whereas law often remains nebulous and abstract (secrets within secrets as the relationship between S.H.I.E.L.D., the World Security Council and HYDRA makes clear), justice is more capable of personification. The use of justice rather than law also helps maintain this division between the two terms, again suggesting—following Plato—that justice may be something quite apart from law, an unattainable ideal that exists *outside* the legal system. Superheroic justice is necessarily interventionist and comes from above. As a result legal institutions are undermined and to some extent ignored; prisons cannot hold Loki, armed forces cannot stop (or locate) the Hulk, Nick Fury has to rely on the Avengers, the Nova Corps must rely on the Guardians of the Galaxy.

It is the MCU's superheroes who clearly embody this notion of transcendent justice (through superpower) above equality and emotion over rationality (their physicality often accentuated by their form-fitting capes and costumes, or lack of costuming in the case of the Hulk or Drax), while still maintaining a sense of progress by "bringing villains to justice" and therefore making the societies of which they are a part better, safer and therefore more efficient. Even the most rational of the MCU superheroes (geniuses like Tony Stark and Bruce Banner) are ultimately seen to abandon their intellect at a certain point to put on the armor or "Hulk up." In these films it is the defeat of the villain that replaces the delivery of the verdict at trial as the moment of catharsis, providing both resolution and a sense of justice, superheroes often congratulating themselves or being congratulated afterwards for getting "results."

Just as Derrida famously pronounced, "deconstruction *is* justice"[41] the MCU superheroes deconstruct the apparatus of the state, revealing the deficiencies in their authority. The MCU superhero displays ambivalence to due process and follows the Nietzschean model of being "beyond good and evil," beyond both the legal system and its definitions of legality.[42] In the absence of law, in the zone of indeterminacy, the superhero is forced to become the justice figure. Furthermore, just as the legal system finds it difficult to keep up with change, superheroes point to the way the legal system finds it difficult to keep up with technology (through the technologically advanced Chitauri for example, or the spate of technologically advanced criminals like Iron Monger, Whiplash and the Extremis soldiers who emerge in the wake of Tony Stark's scientific advances).

The MCU's Intellectual Work About Law and Justice

If we accept the above as evidence that the MCU Phase Two can be read as being in a dialogic relationship with American society and therefore actively commenting upon notions of law and justice, then we can also understand these character's shift from super soldiers to superheroes as indicative of Derrida's notion that "deconstruction *is* justice"[43] or more precisely "the call to do justice to the other is what spurs the deconstructive process into action, and hence the very process of deconstruction is a process of seeking justice."[44]

It is the MCU superhero that makes visible the changes in government policy and the commensurate mutability of law as a term of definition as they actively promote debate about the relationship between law and justice and the balance involved in preserving human rights while protecting security interests. Cultural theorist Douglas Rushkoff has previously suggested that "popular cultural forums" (like film) offer a "conceptual interface between the order of our laws and the chaos of our world" that make them "the place for us to evaluate our rules and customs"[45]—and certainly this is what seems to be occurring here.

Talking about *Captain America: The Winter Soldier*, co-director Anthony Russo noted that

It's hard to make a political film that's not topical. That's what makes a political thriller different from just a thriller. And that's what adds to the characters' paranoia and the audience's experience of that paranoia. But we're also very pop-culture-obsessed and we love topicality, so we kept pushing to [have] scenes that, fortunately or unfortunately, played out [during the time that Edward] Snowden outed the NSA. That stuff was already in the zeitgeist. We were all reading the articles that were coming out questioning drone strikes, pre-emptive strikes, civil liberties—[Barack] Obama talking about who they would kill.... We wanted to put all of that into the film because it would be a contrast to [Captain America]'s greatest-generation [way of thinking]."[46]

This was picked up on by critics of the film who noted its "topicality" and connection to what was currently occurring in the world. Such a film thereby encourages debate around surveillance, freedom of information and suspension of individual rights in pursuit of order, calling into question the whole relationship between law and justice.

Conclusion

At the end of *The Avengers* the following exchange occurs between S.H.I.E.L.D. agent Maria Hill and Director Nick Fury:

> HILL: Sir how does it work now? They're gone their separate ways. Some, pretty extremely far. If we get into a situation like this again, what happens then?
> FURY: They'll come back.
> HILL: Are you really sure about that?
> FURY: I am.
> HILL: Why?
> FURY: Because we'll need them to.

Similarly, *Captain America: The Winter Soldier* concludes with the Black Widow warning a committee on Capitol Hill:

> You're not going to put me in a prison. You're not going to put any of us in a prison. You know why? … Because you need us. Yes, the world is a vulnerable place and yes, we help make it that way. But we're also the ones best qualified to defend it. So, if you want to arrest me, arrest me. You'll know where to find me.

In both films, the deficiencies of law are highlighted; the state comes to depend on the superhero (and it is the independent superhero rather than the authorized, co-opted super soldier, freed of their shackles to a stagnant and corrupt central authority) to locate justice. It is a confirmation of both the failures of the state in their pursuit of order at any cost and the success of the MCU superheroes as personifications of a transcendent and interventionist justice. In so doing the MCU superheroes continue to interrogate the law and push the boundaries of what law can be, beyond the relatively limited and circumscribed spaces of the S.H.I.E.L.D. boardrooms and courtrooms, towards a highly visible notion of "justice" enacted in the wider society. This is a form of intellectual work similar to the notion of "work[ing] at the limits of what the rules permit, in order to invent new moves" that Jean Francois Lyotard advances,[47] in that it not only moves the law closer to justice but also prompts debate amongst the viewers of the MCU about how law and justice can work together in the real world.

NOTES

1. *The Avengers*, directed by Joss Whedon (2012; Disney/Marvel Studios, 2012), DVD.

2. *Captain America: The First Avenger*, directed by Joe Johnston (2011; Disney/Marvel Studios, 2011), DVD.

3. *Thor: The Dark World*, directed by Alan Taylor (2013; Disney/Marvel Studios, 2014), DVD.

4. *Captain America: The Winter Soldier*, directed by Anthony Russo and Joe Russo (2014; Disney/Marvel Studios, 2014), DVD.

5. *Iron Man*, directed by John Favreau (2008; Paramount/Marvel Studios, 2008), DVD.

6. *Guardians of the Galaxy*, directed by James Gunn (2014; Disney/Marvel Studios, 2014), DVD.

7. While outside the remit of this essay it is worth noting that both of the concluding films in Phase 2, *Avengers: Age of Ultron* (2015) and *Ant-Man* (2015), continue this trend. The former, paralleling *Captain America: The Winter Soldier* (2014), similarly explores the limitations and dangers in proactive law—in this instance the Ultron global defence program that, upon achieving sentience, determines humanity itself is the problem and seeks to eliminate the species. In the latter, fears around weaponised technology (in this case a miniaturization process), leads inventor Hank Pym (Michael Douglas) to hire ex-con thief Scott Lang (Paul Rudd) to steal back his technology. The tensions between what is legal and what is just therefore continue to inform the development of the MCU.

8. In Ray Gill, and Sid Greene, "The Human Torch Battles the Sub-Mariner" Parts 1, 2 and 3, *Human Torch* # 5, Fall 1941 (New York: Timely Publications.)

9. Again, while outside the remit of this essay, it is worth noting that at the time of writing Marvel Studios and Sony (license holder of Spider-Man) have come to an agreement whereby Spider-Man (and his supporting cast of characters) will become part of the MCU. Kevin Feige has publicly stated that this MCU iteration of Spider-Man will be a teenager and that this is a purposeful decision to provide a different view of the MCU world from what we have seen before, largely supporting my analysis.

10. Giorgio Agamben, *Homo Sacer: Sovereign Power and Bare Life*. (Standford, CA: Standford University Press, 1998 [1995]), 89.

11. Peter Goodrich, "Maladies of the Legal Soul: Psychoanalysis and Interpretation in Law," *Washington & Lee Law Review*, 54 (1997): 1047.

12. Jerome Frank, *Courts on Trial: Myth and Reality in American Justice*. (Princeton, NJ: Princeton University Press, 1949), 18.

13. Austin Sarat, "Rethinking Law and Fatherhood: Male Subjectivity in the Film *A Perfect World*," *Genders*, 30 (1999). http://www.genders.org/g30/g30_sarat.html.

14. Peter Fitzpatrick, *Modernism and the Grounds of Law*. (Cambridge: Cambridge University Press, 2001), 1.

15. Sigmund Freud, *Totem and Taboo*, translated by J. Strachey. (New York: Norton, 1950), 103–104.

16. S. Coltrane and R.D. Parke, *Reinventing Fatherhood: Toward an Historical Understanding of Continuity and Change in Men's Family Lives*. (Philadelphia: National Center on Fathers and Families, December 1998), 1.

17. R. LaRossa, C. Jaret, M. Gadgil, and R.G. Wynn, "The Changing Culture of Fatherhood in Comic-Strip Families: A Six-Decade Analysis," *Journal of Marriage and Family*, 62(2) (2004): 375–387.

18. Madan Sarup, *Identity, Culture and the Postmodern World*. (Edinburgh: Edinburgh University Press, 1996), 50, citing Zygmunt Bauman.

19. Max Weber, *Protestant Ethic and the Spirit of Capitalism*, translated by Talcott Parsons (London: HarperCollins Academic, 1991).

20. Paul R. Pillar notes that this is very much a product of the times. Post Watergate and the Pike and Church committees there had been a curtailing or controlling of executive power rather than an expansion. See Paul R. Pillar, "Perceptions of Terrorism: Continuity and Change" in *Law vs. War: Competing Approaches to Fighting Terrorism Conference Report* (July 2005), 6. http://www.carlisle.army.mil/ssi.

21. Full Citation: "The Uniting and Strengthening America by Providing Appropriate Tools Required to Intercept and Obstruct Terrorism (USA PATRIOT ACT) Act of 2001" (HR 3162).

22. George W Bush, "Second Inaugural Address," 2005, http://www.whitehouse.gov/news/releases/2005/01/20050120-3.html.

23. *The 9/11 Commission Report* (July 22 2004), 423, http://www.9-11commission.gov/report/911Report.pdf.

24. U.S. Department of State, *Patterns of Global Terrorism 2002* (April 2003), ix. http://www.state.gov/documents/organization/20105.pdf.

25. Michael German, "Squaring the Error" in *Law vs. War: Competing Approaches to Fighting Terrorism. Conference Report* (July 2005), 11. http://www.carlisle.army.mil/ssi.

26. Mark Tushnet, "Class Action," in *Legal Reelism: Movies as Legal Texts*, edited by John Denvir (Chicago: University of Illinois Press, 1996), 244.

27. Tushnet, 1996, 244.

28. Tushnet, 1996, 247.

29. Jason Bainbridge, "'Worlds Within Worlds'—The Role of Superheroes in the Marvel and DC Universes," in *The Contemporary Comic Book Superhero*, edited by Angela Ndalianis (Routledge: New York), 64–85.

30. Stephen King, *Danse Macabre*. (London: Futura, 1986 [1981]), 51.

31. Friedrich Nietzsche, *The Will to Power*, translated R.J. Hollingdale and Walter Kaufman (New York: Vintage, 1968).

32. Jack Balkin, "Transcendental Deconstruction, Transcendental Justice," *Michigan Law Review,* 92 (1994): 1131.

33. Jacques Derrida, "Force of Law: The 'Mystical Foundation of Authority,'" in *Deconstruction and the Possibility of Justice*, edited by Drucilla Cornell, Michael Rosenfield and David G. Carlson (New York: Routledge, 1992), 10.

34. Derrida, 1992, 16.

35. Derrida, 1992, 12.

36. Jacques Derrida, *Specters of Marx*, translated by Peggy Kamuf (New York: Routledge, 1994).

37. Douglas E. Litowitz, *Postmodern Philosophy and Law* (Lawrence: University Press of Kansas, 1997), 97.

38. Litowitz, 1997, 102.

39. Litowitz, 1997, 97.

40. Martin Jay, "Must Justice Be Blind?," in *Law and the Image: The Authority of Art and the Aesthetics of Law*, edited by Costas Douzinas and Lynda Nead (Chicago: Chicago University Press, 1999).

41. Derrida, 1992, 15.

42. Nietzsche, 1968, 34.

43. Derrida, 1992, 15.

44. Litowitz, 1997, 102.

45. Douglas Rushkoff, *Media Virus: Hidden Agendas in Popular Culture* (New York: Random House, 1994), 51–52.

46. Quoted in Frank Lovece, "Soldier Showdown: Joe and Anthony Russo Take the Helm of 'Captain America' Franchise," *Film Journal International,* April 2 (2014).

47. Jean-Francois Lyotard, *Just Gaming*, translated by Wlad Godzich with Jean-Loup Thebaud (Minnesota: University of Minnesota Press, 1985), 100.

Enemies, Foreign and Domestic

Villainy and Terrorism in Thor

SASHA-MAE ECCLESTON

In the cold open of Marvel Studio's *Thor* (2011), an astrophysics research team investigates an aurora-like disturbance in the New Mexican desert. While marveling at the phenomenon, the team hits an object later identified as the film's titular hero, Thor. The primary researcher, Jane Foster, looks at Thor and asks, "Where did he come from?" prompting a voiceover that explains the story world's quasi-historico-scientific background.

This voiceover transports the audience far afield temporally and spatially. As the yet unnamed Odin—Thor's father and king of Asgard—begins speaking, a subtitle reads "Tønsberg, Norway 965 A.D." Odin's first word, "once," nods to Thor's distant origins in another realm, another time, and in a non–American mythological tradition. Thor is neither American, nor an Earthling, or even human. As such, Foster's simple question introduces a key facet of Marvel Studio's film adaptation of this hero's storyline by highlighting Thor's otherness in a quaint, non-problematic way.

Thor's otherness is integral to his eponymous franchise. It chronicles the adventures of an alien who allies himself to the United States and, through it, Earth. Like DC's *Superman*, Marvel's *The Mighty Thor* juxtaposes the enfeebled human existence of Dr. Donald Blake with his previously unknown identity on a distant planet as Thor. Heir to a cosmic throne with superhuman physical powers, Thor is not an average man who feels small and powerless against foreigners, women, and urban life, like Blake.[1] In fact, the Marvel Cinematic Universe (MCU) only alludes to this *alter ego*. Instead, the movies glorify Thor as an extraterrestrial with more brawn and knowledge of the cosmos than any human could ever possess. Even when shown as a child, he is receiving lessons on cosmic kingship, marking his political role as extraordinary as well. These gestures encourage viewers to consider Thor as thoroughly non-human, albeit on the desirable end of the spectrum that defines otherness. These desirable qualities help make humanity's eventual alliance with him more desirable in turn.

Because otherness is a constantly shifting identifier in the *Thor* franchise, tension on this alliance between humankind, conflated with America, and Thor repeatedly arises as the MCU's interlacing storylines rejigger the audience's understanding of the cosmos. As outer space grows more complicated, otherness will be linked to terrorism, political instability, and familial betrayal. Thor is an alien from Earth's perspective, but his "brother" Loki will be revealed to be an alien, from Asgard *and* Earth's perspective, desperate for the power birthplace and birth order have denied him. Loki's shaky alliance with his homeland and Thor's shaky faith in him will disturb any simple human trust in the Asgardians when disaster strikes.

Disaster always strikes in the MCU and, while these films seem to discuss contemporary geopolitics very little, the problems of its fantasy world cannot be untethered from problems in ours. The *Iron Man* and *Captain America* franchises deal with human responses to human created terror. *Thor* and its related narratives give terror an extraterrestrial origin and stage with cosmic scope. Even so, like other works in this decade's superhero boom, the contours of otherness dramatized in the *Thor* franchise reflect anxieties about race and ethnicity's relationship to terrorism in post–9/11 America. *Thor* (2011) and *Thor: Dark World* (2013) render humanity a monolith when compared to perilous variety of beings out "there," taking mere sideswipes at the events of that horrific September day and life afterwards. But *The Avengers* (2012) rehearses 9/11, this time with Loki as extraterrestrial catalyst. Because Loki perpetrates recognizable acts of terror on Earth, problems out "there" cannot be severed from life "here" and the dynamics of evil in the cosmos can be tracked according to more familiar identity politics.

Comic book history bears witness to this trend. Scholars have demonstrated how superhero narratives, from comic books' Golden Age of the 1930s and 40s to the present, map anxieties about contemporary society onto struggles between (super)heroes and their foes.[2] Crime, destruction, and terror are the genre's mainstays, with always-imminent violence giving the hero a reason to exist and a new storyline to emerge. Comics were likely respond to the September 11 attacks and the subsequent Global/American War on Terror because the scale of the events made them hard to ignore. This was especially true for Marvel print comics because, unlike the *DC* universe, many Marvel heroes lived in New York City. Moreover, circumstances surrounding the events and the era it ushered in were particularly akin to the genre. First, "the Bush administration's depiction of a Manichean post–9/11 world of heroes and villains sounded at times like a classic comic book scenario."[3] Secondly, the American public saw the attacks replayed often, with talking heads repeating information as vignettes of New York City, the Pentagon, and rural Pennsylvania went on loop. These events' ubiquitous representations on screens big and small gave them an inextricably immediate graphic dimension apt for this narrative medium.[4] The fodder was there and stories that dealt with terrorists, espionage, and cataclysmic violence proliferated.

In the case of Marvel Studio's *Thor, The Avengers*, and *Thor: Dark World*, in particular, the parameters of otherness reflect post–9/11 concerns about the security of the United States figured as both domestic space and the cosmos. *Thor* reinforces nativist fears about a homeland made vulnerable by an enemy within: according to this logic, danger comes from people who *look* like "us" but are not truly like "us." In the film, Loki superficially resembles an Asgardian but his Frost Giant origins drive him to betray his adopted homeland. The plot heroizes Thor, whose response to terrorism is first decried as childishly impetuous, by displacing the threat of otherness entirely on his brother. This reorientation legitimizes Thor's reactionary violence. In *The Avengers*, Loki's otherness wreaks havoc on Earth as he becomes a terrorist extraordinaire. His villainy initially evokes Nazi Germany, but echoes of 9/11 multiply as he first destroys a defense agency's headquarters and then his forces emerge from a clear blue sky to destroy New York City skyscrapers. Furthermore, Loki's methods and his underlying otherness pander to the racialization of terrorism post–9/11. The Avengers, the team forged to check his attack, recall American attempts to build international coalitions for decidedly American purposes and the jurisdictional problems that emerge from them. Finally, *Thor: Dark World* recycles the formula of foreigner as terrorist: less human looking aliens storm the palatial home of the Asgardian rulers in search of a powerful weapon. This time the danger to domestic space is played out across gendered lines, picking up on further aspects of America's image of itself as the guardian of freedom and justice worldwide.

Brother, Who Art Thou?

After the 9/11 attacks, the Bush administration attempted to shore up the boundaries between "us" and "them" to comfort Americans. The administration's efforts masked anxieties about these very boundaries. Airplanes were not the only things crossing international borders on September 11. Information, money, and ideologies had been, were being, and would continue to be exchanged fluidly across a variety of borders fixed in the ground, observed in the sky, and heeded in practice. The American public was told reducing the porosity of the United States promoted the security and well-being of those … everywhere. As revisiting a few 9/11 era documents will make clear, the Bush administration's rhetoric urged Americans to think of themselves as one unit and the nation in terms of domestic space, and to conflate that space and its interests with the preservation of universal peace. Evil and insane, an oversimplified "they" were bound to fail against an equally problematic and oversimplified "us."

In the aftermath of the attacks, President George W. Bush often expressed this totalizing viewpoint, mapping one nation (U.S.) onto the entire globe and each side of the conflict with an end of the moral spectrum. On October 8, 2001, former Pennsylvania Governor Tom Ridge was sworn in as the first director of the Office of Homeland Security, later called the Department of Homeland Security (DHS). In his introductory remarks, the President described the department as a means of combatting terrorism "without sacrific[ing] the freedoms that make [the U.S.] unique."[5] However, in the very next sentence, he asserts that terrorist acts committed on American soil could only be handled properly through a "global effort" that involved "lovers of freedom" worldwide. Binding the American people to the concept of freedom, he converts the political decision to become a wartime ally with the United States into a moral one. Abstaining from the War on Terror was to abstain from a Global War for Freedom and to resist bringing "evildoers to justice." As he continues, Bush calls 9/11 a watershed moment, historically and morally: on that day, he claims, Americans saw "that evil was real" and learned "of a mentality of people that will destroy innocent folks." Apparently, America had been in a state of prelapsarian bliss until 2001.

Whereas imagining the United States as the world inflates the American position against terrorism, imagining the United States as domestic space personalizes terrorism and reinforces limits in order to obscure difference. In this same brief speech, Bush first describes America on the offensive against terrorism. Then, pivoting towards introducing the new agency's director, he focuses on the Ridge Family. He thanks the three Ridge children for their "sacrifice," recognizing, on the one hand, that military service affects more people than the singular serviceperson and, on the other hand, militarizing the family unit. He then describes America's reaction to the loss of "innocent folks" on 9/11 thusly: "A compassionate land will rise united to not only protect ourselves, not only make our homeland as secure as possible, but to bring the evildoers to justice so that our children might live in freedom." Shifting from a mere physical descriptor, "land," to a metaphorically laden one, "homeland," Bush underscores the term's association with domesticity by focusing on the image of children. It isn't merely land that lies vulnerable to attack but the defenseless members of the household, instead. As

Amy Kaplan has explained, synonyms for "homeland" include fatherland and motherland, terms with more obvious nativist undertones because they connote kinship and fixity.[6] "A recent term in the American lexicon," "homeland" had not been used in such a concerted effort to refer to American soil before the Bush administration and spatial metaphors that had been used referred to mobility instead of fixity.[7] The president's down-home word choice ("folks") also shares a valence with the term, since homeland's rustic quality distracts from the urban target of the World Trade Center attack.[8] That target, New York City, is a city profoundly connected to the history of immigration in the United States, to the openness of its borders and the mobility that populated the country. The term "homeland" distracts the public's attention from New York City's specific past and so plays to efforts to unite the American polity by erasing difference within it. "Homeland" occludes the multiplicity and diversity that makes the United States what it is by linking the national identity to a space of intergenerational continuity instead of a porous membrane associated with intergenerational disruption.

Nevertheless, the Bush administration responded strongly to the reality that the "homeland" was not only populated by kinsmen who shared a fixed "way of life." Because one of the assailants of the September 11 attacks had entered the United States on a student visa, "immigration and counterterrorism policy became far more closely intertwined" afterwards.[9] Programs that limited entry to the nation on a limited (vacation entry, visas) or protracted basis (naturalization) and that monitored the activities of those on American soil in a more thorough and clandestine manner multiplied post–9/11. On October 26, 2001, Congress signed into law the "Uniting and Strengthening America by Providing Appropriate Tools Required to Intercept and Obstruct Terrorism Act of 2001." Better known by its acronym, the USA PATRIOT Act legalized monitoring previously protected parts of private life, including emending the Bank Secrecy Act and making it easier to gather information without a previously issued warrant, because it was these very parts of American life that abetted acts against American interests. Furthermore, the Homeland Security Act of 2002 upgraded the Office of Homeland Security into the DHS to execute the PATRIOT Act's goals. The attainment and assessment of large tracts of data, including emails, medical records, and travel histories that could by all rights fall under the protection of the Fourth Amendment, was tied to the development of Total Information Awareness program, started later in 2002 under the aegis of the Information Awareness Office. Bipartisan criticism of this program renamed it the Terrorism Information Awareness program, seemingly confined it to mining data on suspected terrorists instead of American citizens, and subsequently abolished it.[10]

These programs, when combined with hate crimes against Arab Americans and Muslim Americans after 9/11 (oddly addressed in a "Sense of Congress condemning discrimination against Arab and Muslim Americans" in Title I. Sec. 102 of the PATRIOT Act), paint a different picture of the homeland. It is not merely a harmonious space whose moral unity, kinship, and homogeneity point suspicious glances ever outwards, over "there." Suspicion over the domestic space's inhabitants turned those outwards glances into x-rays, surveillance videos, and data mining algorithms used "here." In his 2002 State of the Union Address, the President called on America's allies to come to action against an "axis of evil," but, after describing the DHS, he says America "will continue to depend on the eyes and ears of alert citizens" to "secure our homeland." One should recall that things within earshot and eyeshot are never that far away.

Bush's vision of the "homeland" reworked Reagan-era images of American exceptionalism. President Reagan's America was a "shining city upon a hill" as opposed to the U.S.S.R., America's Cold War foe. America was "God-blessed" for "people from every corner of the Earth who had a special love for freedom" to inhabit and to spread the moral value of free-markets and democracy worldwide.[11] Outfitted with "ports that hummed with commerce and creativity," Reagan saw America as a "a beacon ... for all who must have freedom, for all the pilgrims from all the lost places who are hurtling through the darkness, toward home."[12] Coincidentally, in his remarks at the Spirit of America Rally in 1984, President Reagan used the term "homeland" to refer to places those who would settle the United States left behind and associates the term with loss. The Bush Administration's "homeland" does not conjure loss, but it still recycles the same vision of America's place on the global stage that would make emigrating worthwhile, the United States as the bastion of freedom leading the rest of the world to democracy from darkness. The irony of policies enacted for the sake of the United States "homeland" that heavily monitored the freedoms of citizens and legal residents did not escape notice. As many observed, the U.S. government seemed to be making itself the true exception: it no longer had to do what everyone else had to do, i.e., be bound by the law and preserve individual freedoms above all else.

Like Reagan's exceptionalist rhetoric, the Bush Administration's use of the term "homeland" was racially simplistic and problematic. Reagan often referred to the variety of "pilgrims"/"Pilgrims" who colonized North America. But he homogenized that diversity by erasing the devastation of indigenous peoples necessary to colonization, associating non–American space with oppression and primitivism, and binding America's ideological colonization of non–American space with moral rectitude. In fact, Reagan began elucidating what it means to be a "shining city upon a hill" in his farewell address by damning the ethos of the 1960s. This ethos had stifled "the feeling that America was special" by "teaching history based on what is in fashion [and not] "what's important."[13] Of course, this "fashion" addressed the histories of those oppressed within and for the sake of the United States as well as those oppressed by Communist regimes. It included the contemporary struggle for civil rights for those who most likely did not resemble Reagan's imagined Pilgrims. Likewise, Bush's homeland did not include all Americans comfortably, especially those from the "East." After 9/11, Americans confused a religious identity (Islam) with terrorist groups (Al-Qaeda), entire nations (Iraq, Afghanistan), language traditions (Arabic), and geographic regions (the Middle East). As legal scholar Leti Volpp summarized:

> September 11 facilitated the consolidation of a new identity category that groups together persons who appear "Middle Eastern, Arab, or Muslim." This consolidation reflects a racialization wherein members of this group are identified as terrorists, and are disidentified as citizens.[14]

Security officials, citizens, and corporations racially profiled individuals who could be *interpreted* as Muslim, Middle Eastern, or of Arabic descent, even if they did not *actually* belong to any of those groups. Even practicing Sikhs and those of South Asian origin were targeted and reported as threats to American safety.[15] Encouraging citizen vigilance and tip-offs while demonizing ethnic, linguistic, and religious difference removes neutrality from the term "homeland." This imaginary space had been and would continue to be selective, its advantages benefitting a few subsets of America's population.

Thor *(2011)*

Like Bush's exceptionalizing rhetoric conceptualizes the U.S., *Thor* conceptualizes its hero's physical home and homeland, Asgard, as the sole hope for universal peace. Its villain, Loki, embodies nativist post–9/11 fears: he threatens cosmic peace because his unnoticed difference gave his inborn, foreign wickedness unrestricted access to Asgard's domestic space and political power. Moreover, as in Bush's exceptionalist imaginary, world peace depends on the fate of one community of white-skinned extraterrestrials with a penchant for surveillance and seizing weapons of mass destruction. Through these similarities, the logic of the *Thor* franchise legitimates the fears underlying the term "homeland," the institutionalization of emergency state powers, and the conflation of American interests with world security, subordinating the differences that hinder such totalizing and the infringement of civic liberties.

Thor's otherworldly origins are first couched in terms of humankind's ignorance of its ongoing need for protection against aliens intent on destroying it. During his voiceover, Odin discards his family's alien identity under the rubric of "simple," as the idea of life on other planets becomes secondary to other concerns. These other concerns revolve around humanity's understanding of their *relationship* to non-human inhabitants of other planets and cosmic entities instead of their mere existence. He reports that humankind's ancestors "believed" that their gods inhabited some worlds and "knew" to fear other worlds. Odin thus associates certainty (i.e., knowing) with fear and uncertainty (i.e., mere believing) with the need for protection. In this cosmology, humanity should always be on high alert.

The Frost Giants epitomize why that is the case as the danger of otherness lies squarely with them. Odin describes their land as a place of "cold and darkness." The audience then sees the Frost Giants, swathed in the dark of night, destroying boats, outing fires with streams of ice, and provoking womanly screams. Odin, on the other hand, arrives via a stream of rainbow-hued light, wielding a scepter and dressed in gold. A golden armored legion at his back and his white, human-like skin gleaming, Odin opposes Laufey and the Frost Giants. This juxtaposition is telling. The Frost Giants' eyes are red. Their bluish skin seems impervious to the cold and wounds, thus requiring less protection: they wear loincloths instead of armor. Their skin is thus marked both as non-human (armor-less) and non–European (remember the human community pictured lived in Norway and Odin's forces resemble then); their land looks nothing like Earth, lacking the sunlight necessary to sustain human life and any signs of development; and their desire to bring darkness to the universe signals a malevolence that the audience surely would reject. Characterizing the Frost Giants in this way legitimizes a curious plot point: only Laufey's "weapon of mass destruction" is confiscated for the good of the cosmos at the end of the "Great War" although both groups possess weapons with otherworldly power. The film's logic puts us on high alert about the Frost Giants in order to valorize Asgard.

Indeed, like Reagan's America, Asgard is a beacon of hope for cosmic peace and quite literally a "shining city upon a hill." As Odin narrates the return to his home planet, the screen's color palette changes from a blue-black to a white cloud filled sky until the camera settles on an Earth-like swirl of greenish-blues and golds. Monumental statues, crystal clear bodies of water, and verdant hillsides appear. On one stands the palace, Asgard. It is a fit home for someone who claims to have "defended ... the lives of innocents across the nine realms" as America would do in the War on Terror on behalf of worldwide freedom against an "axis of evil."

Whereas the first half of Odin's voiceover establishes this relationship between Earth and extraterrestrial realms, the film's real drama will take place within Odin's household, with Earth experiencing its aftershocks. Odin's commentary transforms into a history lesson when he appears, aged, in conversation with two boys. Odin must explain why the Asgardians possess this foreign, destructive weapon, the labor that produces peace and, most germane to the unfolding story, how *one* of the boys will have to defend this peace. Terrorism has political ramifications for Asgard since its ruler must double as a cosmic protector against evil and politics here are dynastic, i.e., within the physical and metaphorical house of Odin. The brunette son, Loki, asks whether Frost Giants still exist: having grown up during peacetime, he cannot tell whether Odin's story is "legend" or history. The blonde, Thor, asks nothing. Instead, he asserts that when he becomes king he will, "hunt the monsters down and slay them all." Unconcerned about the plausibility of what he has heard, young Thor completely lacks Loki's curiosity. Instead, he is assured by his ability to retaliate no matter what. The boys' temperaments, like their hair colors, differ radically.

As the Frost Giants invade the Asgardian homestead, the differences between the boys become a matter of practice instead of theory. In the next scene, the attack halts Thor's coronation, causing political disorder. If Thor is not yet king, does that mean Odin still is? And what about Loki? This uncertainty is significant because each person could apply his approach to the attack to differing outcomes. Thor responds heavy-handedly (and eventually illegally) to the breach of his home and realm. Again, before he knows any details about the attack, he labels it "an act of war" and asserts in Bush-like fashion that the enemy needs to be taught a lesson. He reasons the Frost Giants' attempt to reclaim their weapon, housed in Asgard's vaults, must signal Laufey's belief in the "weakness" of Odin's house. Thor wants to send a message of his own and argues that attacking the Frost Giants' home is "the only way to ensure the safety of [Asgard's] borders." Odin reproves his impetuousness, however, calling the attack "an act of but a few, doomed to fail." Focusing on the invasion's small scale and the success of Asgardian defenses, he resists escalating the violence. Having just reworded his tenets of kingship during Thor's coronation to include avoiding ambition, Odin's refusal to go to war becomes a sign of his good leadership. Odin's time-tested approach to war and kingship denounces the retaliatory response that most directly corresponds to the Bush administration's as impractical, childish, and dangerous. So far, the film criticizes the American response to terror of the last decade by associating it with a naiveté that threatens more than it protects.

But this criticism will soon recede as the film draws attention away from the intergenerational rupture that pits father against son, refocusing it on an alien intruder. Loki could reconcile Odin's inaction and Thor's foolhardiness. However, he remains silent during the exchange. He does not go unnoticed, though. The camera glances at him as the others spar verbally; his lean angular face and dark hair does not resemble the aged Odin or Odin's firstborn and so he stands outside of their dyad visually. Slithering up to Thor after the altercation, Loki supports Thor's fears about the Frost Giants and points to a possible future invasion. Voicing his reluctance to defy Odin, Loki nonetheless stokes his brother's anxieties about Asgardian security, propelling him to ignore Odin's advice and rally his warriors for a counterattack. It seems the younger generation has now united against the older. But, the audience eventually discovers that Loki anticipated this situation. Using the enemy to create a rift between Thor and Odin, Loki expected his brother's recklessness would earn his father's disfavor and make him the heir instead of the spare. As the action shifts from Asgard to its antipodes, we learn that Heimdall, Asgard's border patrol agent, had not seen the enemies enter Asgard, an unprecedented event since he began "his watch." Then, Loki alone of Thor's warrior band is unharmed by the touch of the Frost Giants. When Laufey proclaims that Odin's house is "full of traitors," he activates several interdependent metaphors: someone within the physical house had to provide access so as to avoid Heimdall's notice; Odin's household is fractured (suggesting the united scheming of Thor and Loki responsible for this encounter might be suspicious); the metaphorical household, Asgard as a political entity, is, by extension, unstable. The audience pieces together that the Frost Giants had not *intuited* anything about Asgard, endeavoring to send a message. Rather, Loki used them as blunt instruments in his plan to take the throne. When it is revealed he too is a Frost Giant, the attack, reframed through the house metaphor, becomes tethered to a malevolence marked as foreign.

By emphasizing Loki planned this attack before *he* knew he was an alien, the film validates perceptions of foreigners as inherent evildoers. As is suggested in *Thor* and explained in its sequel, Loki had been exploring the secret pathways to other realms since youth, motivated by curiosity about the world. This is why he could elude Heimdall when he planned the invasion. Loki seems unable to suppress the evil that lies within his "blood," leading him to aid his "people" unknowingly. Thus, what could have just been chalked up to "personality" is now laden with concerns about the foreign versus familiar. Moreover, Odin endangered his homeland because he had been lenient with his foreign adversaries, allowing one of them into the homestead. His mercy, once a sign of good kingship, can now be rewritten as folly, as naïve and as dangerous as Thor's rampage in the Frost Giants' realm. With Loki on the throne as Odin sleeps, Asgard becomes as imperiled as Earth was in the montage that began the aged king's narrative. For these reasons, strong-armed retaliation against alien others appears less blameworthy, if not necessary.

While Loki's otherness is thus villainized, Thor's otherness plays out across a set of romantic comedy episodes on Earth. The oversized, strange talking demi-god throws things in disarray when he escapes a hospital, interrupts breakfast, or even breaks into a maximum security area. However, the plot rapidly dismisses this commotion as the physicist Jane Foster begins to fall for him. Portman's diminutive size and Hemsworth's beefed-up physique respect America's Eurocentric standards of beauty, gender, and heterosexuality so that their mutual attraction seems natural although any relationship between the two could also be considered miscegenation. Whereas we are told the Frost Giant's weapon could destroy everything if used, we witness humans happily barbecuing around Thor's hammer, unharmed as they try to wield it. Loki as alien leads to mayhem, death, and exile; Thor as alien leads to picnics.

As the film disassociates the threat of otherness from Thor and Earth, it also handles the infringement of civil liberties light-heartedly. Out there in space, Heimdall's surveillance problematizes Loki's otherness for the domestic space and will eventually come to Asgard's rescue. Here S.H.I.E.L.D.'s surveillance attempts to brand Thor's foreignness dangerous for America/Earth but eventually forges an alliance with him. Jane Foster's romantic feelings for Thor allow her to ignore her reservations about the foreigner. However, the United States government sees him as a potential threat initially. As its name in the MCU makes clear, the agency known as S.H.I.E.L.D., the Strategic *Homeland* Intervention, Enforcement and Logistics Division, is a thinly veiled avatar for the DHS and CIA: it sponsors espionage to protect the homeland and responds to alien attacks through extrajudicial and clandestine means.[16] S.H.I.E.L.D. commandeers Jane Foster's belongings during an exchange that brings the legality of the U.S. government's post–9/11 data mining into view:

> AGENT COULSON: We are investigating a security threat. We need to appropriate your records and all your atmospheric data.
> JANE FOSTER: By "appropriate" do you mean steal?
> AGENT COULSON: [*Handing her a check*] Here this should more than compensate you for your trouble …
> JANE FOSTER: … I can sue you for violating my constitutional rights!
> AGENT COULSON: I am sorry, Ms. Foster, but we are the good guys.
> JANE FOSTER: So are we!

Foster remarks that the agency's rhetoric sidesteps her constitutional rights in the name of security. However, because Phil Coulson (the loveably unintimidating agent who anchors the first TV project of Marvel's transmedia enterprise) perpetrates the illegal seizure in public and claims impersonal data instead of her private correspondences, the entire scene loses much of its critical bite. Suspense will continue to surround the agency, but Coulson's easy mannered style and unwavering goodness gives S.H.I.E.L.D. credibility with the audience. This goodwill will increase when the agency not only returns Foster's equipment but also supports her research as she must be relocated for her own safety in between films.

The movie's conclusion further sublimates the various legal quagmires involved with domestic surveillance in response to terrorism, folding the

DHS-like agency within the narrative arc of the American monomyth.[17] This distinctive narrative pattern in American popular culture "secularizes Judeo-Christian dramas of community redemption … combining elements of the selfless servant who impassively gives his life for others and the zealous crusader who destroys evil."[18] In the myth's superhero iteration, the hero's origins outside of the community make him a loner, like a vigilante, but his superhero abilities (both physical and emotional) removes notions of lawlessness. As a non-citizen, the superhero can be impartial, not threaten political order, and has no need for due process.[19] So it happens in *Thor*. As Loki tries to destroy him once and for all, the exiled Thor decides to fight on behalf of the small New Mexico town as a "mere mortal" and dies doing so. Because of his sacrifice he is resurrected as a superhuman and successfully defeats Loki's weapon. Though he and Foster are romantically linked, he resists fulfilling his own sexual desire to sort out the problems within his family, chastely kissing her hands as he prepares his journey homeward. S.H.I.E.L.D. makes a show of trying to bring him into the U.S. legal system. Thor then assuages Coulson's concerns: "Know this, son of Coul. You and I, we fight for the same cause, the protection of this world. From this day forward, you can count me as your ally."

As with the Fourth Amendment concerns, the film does not ignore the political problems of Thor's actions. The dangers Thor brought with him threatened American lives and destroyed property. Inquiries should be undertaken, arrests made. However, we are simultaneously reminded of his otherness and told to ignore it. Thor authoritatively dismisses those considerations, making his outsider vigilante justice subservient to the United States. Moreover, by addressing Agent Coulson by "son of Coul," Thor mistakes his surname for a Scandinavian patronymic: as Thor is Odinsson, he believes Phil is the son of Coul. Americans do not recognize such naming conventions, so the "mistake," nonetheless accurate, outs him as "foreign." The misunderstanding also reveals that Thor thinks Agent Coulson and through him, S.H.I.E.L.D., are just like him. These similarities lead the audience to discard its fears. If he is on our side, what problem could we have with him?

Thor also endorses American exceptionalism here. He assumes that S.H.I.E.L.D. and Coulson fight for Earth in its entirety. Because of that shared mission, Thor does not view the agency with much suspicion, though he is careful to broker the exchange of Foster's materials. A non-citizen, Thor need not worry about which nation-state he is in or which laws to obey. His assumption that this land represents all lands thus reads more as good-hearted ignorance than jingoism. However, the underlying framework that both fails to correct him and, as happens in the following films, supports his assumptions counteracts such charity.

The Avengers *(2012) and* Thor: Dark World *(2013)*

Having laid out the rationale of the first film in great detail, briefer notes on how domestic space overlaps with political and ethnic boundaries via terrorism should suffice for its sequels.

The narrative logic and commercial pull of *Avengers* depended on the recognizability of characters developed in (e.g., *Thor*) and across media franchises (e.g., Agent Coulson). In this film, Thor's adopted brother becomes a menace to Earthlings and not just his family: terrorism has moved from a domestic problem that merely touches Earth to Earth's problem in the first instance. *Thor* had already problematized the Frost Giants' otherness, aligning Loki's biological origins with evil and violence. *Avengers* cashes in on that deposit, having this not *truly* white assailant bring an army of non-humans onto American/human soil. The villainization of Loki's biological identity, when coupled with his rhetoric, portrays him as an anti-democratic terrorist, a non-state actor using violence against civilians to upend political order. Furthermore, with a battle scene culminating in and around a New York City skyscraper, *Avengers*, of all the MCU films produced so far, most directly restages the World Trade Center attacks. In its response to Loki's terrorism, the film grants the aforementioned qualities of desirable otherness to its heroes while simultaneously diffusing concerns about legality, propriety, and racial stereotyping.

Though Loki's desire for power will affect Earth, his rhetoric more clearly signals an attack on the Bush administration's version of America. Recall that in Bush's rhetoric, the September 11th attacks were perpetrated and supported by those who hated freedom and, most often, were brown-skinned followers of Islam. In *Avengers*, we never see Loki's blue skin, as we saw in *Thor*, so the film avoids directly stereotyping his villainy.[20] Nevertheless, Loki's otherness is discussed and he is singled out as a non-state actor with an anti-freedom agenda. When he first appears in the film, he enters a S.H.I.E.L.D. bunker through a portal that the agency had assumed was an energy source. Arriving "burdened with glorious purpose," Loki declares his desire to bring about "a world made free from freedom." Later, when he demands the obeisance of humankind in Stuttgart, the resistance of an elderly man with a German accent who saw a similar man "once" likens Loki's ambitions to Adolf Hitler's. However, the racial component of Nazism has been replaced by anti-humanism. Alongside Loki's downplayed racial origins, Earth's political, ethnic, and religious diversity has once again become a monolith. As Nick Fury, the director of S.H.I.E.L.D. will declare, the fight against Loki will determine the "fate of the human race." Therefore, when that American agency leads the charge against Loki, America becomes humankind's defender, protecting freedom writ-large and ensuring Earth's security.

Loki's methods communicate his terrorist identity as much as his anti-freedom agenda. As Hagley and Harrison have argued and Iron Man says explicitly, Loki loves to pontificate.[21] He wants an audience, enjoys giving speeches, and owns the havoc he wreaks. This is an aspect of terrorism the American public and the rest of the world has grown used to, with messages of beheadings or that take credit for bombings regularly dispatched through various media outlets. In addition, Loki finds acolytes and, literally, touches the heart of humans in order to control their minds. His magic brainwashes, winning over the "vulnerable" to do his bidding. This is exactly the kind of terrorist recruitment counterterrorist intelligence agencies track. In this regard, Loki's entrance has relevance: the mystical portal is a porous boundary, like the internet, that allows quick access from one side of the world to the other. He dare not use the official paths from Earth to the realms because, as we learned in the first film, Heimdall surveys them at all times. Loki, with access to a stealthier gateway, is exactly who post–9/11 rhetoric needs him to be.

This film haphazardly defines the boundaries between foreign and familiar as well. Within the first fifteen minutes, S.H.I.E.L.D.'s director declares, "we are at war." It's unclear which "we" he is talking about and much of film's charm will work around the dynamics of the superhero team fighting on behalf of "us." Thor's role in the team is particularly fraught because he is not human. In a humorous scene, the demigod can be heard mocking humans as "petty ... and tiny." In fact, when he enters the film to apprehend Loki, who went missing at the end of *Thor*, he ends up battling Tony Stark/Iron Man instead. Iron Man, a reluctant G-man but a G-man nonetheless, views Loki as quarry for United States' justice and has made no Asgardian alliance himself. Later, Thor's uncertain status rears its head again when Bruce Banner maligns Loki. Thor warns Banner to "have care how [he] speak[s]" because Loki is still "of Asgard and [his] brother." When reminded Loki has murdered civilians, Thor adds that Loki "is adopted," disowning his negative character traits. The point is, and will be made again, that Thor has a different stake in the danger *and* its architect than all the other Avengers.

Like surveillance in *Thor*, *Avengers* topicalizes S.H.I.E.L.D.'s methods for global protection to give the film a more serious, suspenseful bent. The team learns that S.H.I.E.L.D. had been developing its own weapon of mass destruction after Thor landed in New Mexico. His appearance put Earth on high alert about what else could be out "there." But S.H.I.E.L.D.'s participation in an arms race causes the heroes to question the agency's motivations and legality. In one scene, the camera rotates 360 degrees with overlapping voices and Black Widow defends the agency that "monitors potential threats" even if that threat includes its star-spangled hero, Captain America. However, the plot quickly reasserts that Loki, the foreigner, is the problem instead of S.H.I.E.L.D. when Loki's converts attack S.H.I.E.L.D.'s base and Loki kills Agent Coulson. Coulson's death galvanizes the once feuding heroes and they unite, less for country than for friendship. Since Coulson dies immediately *after* citing Loki's lack of conviction for his inevitable demise, his death reorients what surely had been a discussion about global diplomacy and politics (e.g., nuclear proliferation, jurisdiction, alliances) into something moral and interpersonal.

The film's dénouement plays out the American monomyth arc once more. The superheroes manage to defend the world/U.S./New York City. Iron Man learns to sacrifice himself for the team, sublimating his ego and putting questions about law and jurisdiction aside. Indeed, he too dies momentarily. Resurrected, he returns to civilian mode. As the film ends, news programs show shots from around the world praising the Avengers and the heroes eat quietly at a diner amidst the rubble of an almost obliterated New York. The N.Y.P.D. and F.D., the U.S. Army, and the minor character Erik Selvig all help them fight the aliens along the way. Once again, Thor has had to learn that Loki has no love for their homeland because Loki tries to kill him when offered a means of ending the attack. In the end, no *human* has to punish Loki for he will be dealt with on Asgard. Addressing geopolitical problems has been suspended in favor of sanitized saviors and equally sanitized modes of heroism.

After these two films, the moves of *Thor: Dark World* should be familiar. A threat from less fair-skinned and less human looking aliens than those of Asgard throws Thor's homeland into chaos. A voiceover tells us these aliens, Dark Elves, are power hungry darkness dwellers that the house of Odin had to suppress. Thor and Odin disagree about the proper response to a Dark Elf attack and Thor circumvents Asgardian law to protect his homeland. Loki's role seems to have changed—he helps Thor defeat the Dark Elves out of love for his mother. But the closing scene reveals that he has not become a monomyth hero, putting aside his own desires. Instead, he manipulates Thor's sentimentality to claim Asgard's throne. His character remains antithetical to the kind of sacrifice Asgardian kin(g)ship and the American monomyth require.

The film changes trajectory slightly by moving the romance between Thor and Foster from Earth to Asgard. We become aware that Thor's love interest is in danger when Asgard's surveillance, Heimdall, can't find her. By then the Dark Elves' weapon has literally taken over Foster's body, turning her into a bomb. In the previous film, heroic violence sublimated the romance between Thor and Foster and comedy displaced the connotations of miscegenation that could have characterized their sexual relationship. This installation in the franchise once again dangles the possibility of Thor and Foster's sexual relationship in front of the audience only to delay such contact by using Foster's body as contested space in the cosmic struggle between good and evil. Instead of exploring dangers of interspecies intercourse, the movie generates crisis by having the Dark Elves' energy threaten to rip Foster's body apart, like a suicide bomber. Furthermore, their weapon's power turns Foster into a zombie, her mind controlled by their malevolent energy. These two aspects of the danger to Foster in tandem, brainwashing and suicide bombers, resemble stereotypes of women in Islamic countries. President Bush and many others used these women who needed American democracy to "free them" from oppression as a means of legitimizing war post–9/11 and vilifying the "East."[22] Moreover, when the Dark Elves attack Thor's home world, the Dark Elves' leader makes for the women's chambers. Thor's mother, Frigga, is killed protecting Foster. Between her death and Foster's possession, the fight for universal peace now uses the female body as symbolic capital.

In these ways and others, Marvel's cinematic adaptations of comic books reflect anxieties about otherness without resolving them or challenging conventions, just as their source texts did with other socio-cultural problems. With very minor tweaks—a black Heimdall or white Dark Elf—Marvel Studios' *Thor* franchise and the crossover film *Avengers* depend on images of good and evil and threats of spectacular violence found in the post–9/11 American imaginary. MCU heroes might be extraordinarily strong, wealthy, and/or smart, but they encounter the same problems facing regular humans in contemporary history. Likewise, MCU villains share objectives and characteristics with the U.S. government's characterizations of villainy in its response to terrorism. Thus, whereas the *Thor* franchise dramatizes crises generated by familial betrayal within Asgard overtly, closer scrutiny proves the boundaries of that domestic sphere and its interests are as conveniently elastic as those of the exceptional American homeland.

NOTES

1. Blake, sometimes referred to as "the lame physician" (e.g., Stan Lee and Jack Kirby, *The Mighty Thor* #143, August 1967 [New York: Marvel]), carries a cane, pines unsuccessfully for Jane Foster, and often laments his inabilities. He thus resembles physically and socially enfeebled Clark Kent or even Bruce Banner, Hulk's alter *ego*. For discussion of these characters and anxieties about masculinity, see Robert Genter, "'With Great Power Comes Great Responsibility': Cold War Culture and the Birth of Marvel Comics," *Journal of Popular Culture* 40 (2007): 953–978, and Julian C. Chambliss and William L. Svitavsky, "The Origin of the Superhero: Culture, Race and Identity in U.S. Popular Culture, 1890–1940," in *Ages of Heroes, Eras of Men*, eds. Julian C. Chambliss, William L. Svitavsky, and Thomas Donaldson (Newcastle upon Tyne: Cambridge Scholars Publishing, 2013), 20.

2. Julian C. Chambliss and William L. Svitavsky, "The Origin of the Superhero: Culture, Race and Identity in U.S. Popular Culture, 1890–1940," in *Ages of Heroes, Eras of Men*, eds. Julian C. Chambliss, William L. Svitavsky, and Thomas Donaldson (Newcastle upon Tyne: Cambridge Scholars Publishing, 2013), 6.

3. Simon Cooper and Paul Atkinson, "Graphic Implosion: Politics, Time, and Value

in Post-9/11 Comics," in *Literature After 9/11*, eds. Ann Kenniston and Jeanne Follansbee Quinn (New York: Routledge, 2008), 60.

4. Terry Kading, "Drawn into 9/11, but Where Have All the Superheroes Gone?," in *Comics as Philosophy*, ed. Jeff McLaughlin (Jackson: University of Mississippi Press, 2007), 214.

5. George W. Bush, "Remarks at the Swearing-In Ceremony for Tom Ridge as Director of the Office of Homeland Security" in *Public Papers of the Presidents of the United States: George W. Bush, 2001–2002*, 4 vols. (Washington, D.C.: Government Printing Office, 2001–2003).

6. Amy Kaplan, "Homeland Insecurities: Reflections on Language and Space," *Radical History Review* 85 (2003): 86.

7. *Ibid.*, 85.

8. *Ibid.*, 88.

9. Michele Mittelstadt, Burke Speaker, and Doris Meissner, *Through the Prism of National Security: Major Immigration Policy and Program Changes in the Decade Since 9/11*, accessed March 13, 2015, http://www.migrationpolicy.org/research/post-9-11-immigration-policy-program-changes.

10. Kim Rygiel, *Globalizing Citizenship* (Vancouver: University of British Columbia Press, 2010), 80. PRISM, a program affiliated with the Protect America Act of 2007, gained attention for also gathering civilian data in the name of counterterrorist intelligence. See Timothy B. Lee, "Everything You Need to Know About the NSA's Phone Records Scandal," June 6, 2013, *Washington Post*, www.washingtonpost.com/blogs/wonkblog/wp/2013/06/12/heres-everything-we-know-about-prism-to-date and James Bamford, "They Know Much More Than You Think," *New York Review of Books*, August 15, 2013, http://www.nybooks.com/articles/archives/2013/aug/15/nsa-they-know-much-more-you-think/.

11. Ronald Reagan, "Remarks at a Spirit of America Rally in Atlanta, Georgia, January 26, 1984". *The Public Papers of President Ronald W. Reagan*. Ronald Reagan Presidential Library. www.reagan.utexas.edu/archives/speeches/1984/12684g.htm.

12. Ronald Reagan, "Farewell Address to the Nation, January 11, 1989." *The Public Papers of President Ronald W. Reagan*. Ronald Reagan Presidential Library. http://www.reagan.utexas.edu/archives/speeches/1989/011189i.htm.

13. *Ibid.*

14. Leti Volpp, "The Citizen and the Terrorist," 49 *UCLA Law Review* 1575 (2002): 1576.

15. Volpp, "The Citizen and the Terrorist," 1590; cf. Nick Carbone, " Timeline: A History of Violence against Sikhs in the Wake of 9/11," *Time*, Aug. 6, 2012, http://newsfeed.time.com/2012/08/06/timeline-a-history-of-violence-against-sikhs-in-the-wake-of-911/.

16. For Marvel's renaming of the agency to include "homeland," see Darren Franich, " S.H.I.E.L.D: 10 Important Facts About Marvel's superspy organization," *Entertainment Weekly*, September 24, 2013, http://www.ew.com/article/2013/09/24/shield-agents-marvel.

17. For the term, see Robert Jewett, *The American Monomyth* (Garden City, NY: Anchor Press, 1977). For its application to comic book narratives, see John Shelton Lawrence and Robert Jewett, *The Myth of the American Superhero* (Grand Rapids, MI: W.B. Eerdmans, 2002).

18. Lawrence and Jewett, *The Myth of the American Superhero*, 6–7.

19. Jewett, *The American Monomyth*, 194–195.

20. Cf. DC's treatment of Superman's alien identity. See also Chambliss and Svitavisky, "The Origin of the Superhero," 21.

21. Annika Hagley and Michael Harrison, "Fighting the Battles We Never Could: The Avengers and Post-September 11 American Political Identities," *PS: Political Science & Politics* 47, no. 1 (January 2014): 121.

22. Cf. President Bush's description of women in Afghanistan as the beneficiaries of the War on Terror in the 2002 State of the Union Address: "Today women are free, and are part of Afghanistan's new government." For a discussion of post–9/11 Orientalizing gender stereotypes, see Nadine Naber, "Introduction," in *Race and Arab Americans Before and After*, ed. Amaney Jamal and Nadine Naber (Syracuse, NY: Syracuse University Press, 2008), 1–45; Susan Faludi, *The Terror Dream: Fear and Fantasy in Post-9/11 America* (New York: Metropolitan Books, 2007), esp. Chs. 1 and 4.; and Volpp, "The Citizen and Terrorist," 1586–1588.

More Than a Shield

Security and Empire Building
in Captain America: The Winter Soldier
and Vergil's Aeneid

JENNIFER A. REA

Introduction

In his article on post–9/11 scenarios in the *Captain America* comics, scholar Jason Dittmer argues, "a conceit of the American geopolitical narrative is that America only acts in the name of security, not Empire." Dittmer further asserts that Captain America acts as a "reluctant warrior"[1] who is willing to die for his country rather than an aggressor who seeks out the enemy. His analysis of Captain America's "narrative of identity"[2] has much in common with the ongoing scholarly dialogue on identity and security in Vergil's *Aeneid*, an epic poem about the founding of Rome.[3] I chose Captain America as the Avenger whose narrative most closely intersects with that of the epic hero Aeneas's for the following reason: Captain America's narrative has maintained a long-standing political relevance that allows for critical reflection on war's effects on a society. My study will focus on the question of why Captain America puts down his shield to fight in *Captain America: The Winter Soldier*.[4] In particular, I will concentrate on the final fight scene between the Winter Soldier and Captain America where the Captain fights without his shield. A close reading of the significance of the shield in Vergil's *Aeneid*, I argue, will offer a context for Captain America's reasons for putting down his shield.

The connection between classics and science fiction has been well established through, for example, the recent publications of *Classical Traditions in Science Fiction*[5] and *L'Antiquité dans l'imaginaire contemporain: Fantasy, science-fiction, fantastique.*[6] Both collections invite their audiences to see the relationship between the past and the present as dynamic and ongoing: new traditions and trends in SF challenge us to consider many of the same ethical questions that the ancients did. Rogers and Stevens specifically establish the connection between ancient and modern questions about humanity's future and above all, "ways of knowing and being human":

> … modern SF has, from its very beginning, as it were, looked forward to the future and around at the present in part by looking farther back: to Greco-Roman mythology, to the literature of classical antiquity, to the images of ancient history. As a locus of classical receptions, modern SF has engaged in historically and formally complex negotiations, not to say contestations, between pre-modern ways of knowing and being human, on one hand, and on the other hand, then-emergent and now-ascendant technoscientific thinking and practice.[7]

Thus, science fiction can explore the ethical consequences of living in our modern "technoscientific world." While I am not suggesting that the film *CA:TWS* is science fiction, I am noting that the movie's plot contains science fiction elements due to the weaponry featured in the film. The questions that the film's science fiction elements raises about the ethics of a centralized, imperial control that can develop from such weaponry are not far removed from the questions posed by ancient epics such as the *Aeneid*, which grapples with similar issues of imperial dominance, despite differences in time, location, and technology.

Both the *Aeneid* and *CA: TWS* share several characteristics in common, such as the theme of sacrifice, an issue which is at the heart of the debate on imperial dominance and the sacrifices one makes for one's country. Aeneas' *pietas*, or the value of piety, requires him to put Rome's communal needs before his individual ones and can be compared to Captain America's self-sacrificing deeds done on his country's behalf. Robert Jewett discusses the American fascination with "community impotence and superhero redemption," further arguing that the culture of fear created by the enemy encourages passivity except by the superhero. The hero Captain America is distanced from the rest of the populace by his active rescue of the society, much like Aeneas. A further point that could be made in reference to both heroes, Aeneas and Captain America, is that they are given "unlimited powers to accomplish the impossible task of restoring paradise."[8] Both Aeneas and Captain America come to terms with the future of their society—in Book VIII of the *Aeneid*, Aeneas gets to see how the Roman Empire will function as a result of his actions. And Captain America gets to experience how the American Empire functions as a result of his being missing in action because he wakes up in the future. Finally, each character has a shield as his primary weapon.

My essay examines war and its moral consequences in *CA: TWS*. In doing so, I will look at the intersection of science fiction and non-fictional current predictions of what the future of war will look like, followed by a discussion of *CA: TWS* and finally, Vergil's *Aeneid*. My methodology will employ Antulio Echevarria's description of the future of war, which he argues has evolved in modern society into an anticipation of the "war after next." He defines a "war after next" situation as one where the technology remains incipient, such as a Nano War, but the military has already initiated response strategies.[9] I argue that a similar preoccupation with the future of war and security is also found in the Roman epic the *Aeneid* as it deals with a society that is recovering from a brutal civil war, but anticipating future conflicts with non–Roman parts of the world. While I am not suggesting in this essay that direct allusions to particular passages in Vergil's *Aeneid* can be found within the film, I maintain each work compels its hero to come to terms with the cost of living in an age when freedom and personal liberty are not valued as highly as security. The concept of a "war after next" asks the question: "How do you guarantee long-term success against the enemy?" *CA: TWS* and Vergil's *Aeneid* share concerns about the loss of individual freedoms that this preoccupation brings.

Defining Empire and Defensive Imperialism

The *Captain America* comics have always been known for stressing the clash between the idealized American (as represented by Captain America) and the values of the narrative world in which he exists:

> Thus, *Captain America* not only defines what America is, but it also firmly ensconces the reader within its geo-graph. The reader, tacitly assumed to be American, is reminded of his or her identity as an American and is told what that means in relation to the rest of the world.

The post–9/11 Marvel Comics and Marvel Cinematic Universe's portrayal of Captain America highlights the tension between feeling secure while in one's homeland and accepting the consequences of living in a global economy: "Security requires understanding political connections to distant events; politics is also about obligations to distant strangers."[10] The right to personal freedom is no longer as valued as living in a secure society.

The post–9/11 setting of Captain America's world in *CA: TWS*, therefore, offers the audience critical treatment of events that involve America's foreign policy. Post–9/11, *Captain America* has constructed a space for the debate on what defines American foreign policy as imperialistic:

> … the myth of American exceptionalism and its consequent power to structure the earth's surface geopolitically requires a script of equal and mutually exclusive states.

This script needs to be, literally, narrated through comic books. While the example of Captain America *shows how that reading is possible from the text, it also shows the importance of dissident geopolitical narratives in what originated as a comic book proxy for American foreign policy.*

Captain America's post–9/11 narrative, Dittmer argues, generates debate on how to define the "American Empire" and how imperial policy operates within "the construction of a dominant American geopolitical narrative." Captain America's "ideal American" values—which include his dedication to justice— then clash with "the effects of American geopolitical activities."[11] In *CA: TWS*, the Captain will inevitably be at odds with the government and military when security is defined as keeping the world safe through the use of high-tech surveillance. By making American military operations global, the American government gets to define which cultures and values are incompatible with its own and eliminate them without any opposition. The "American Empire," therefore, is one in which war is not optional, but justice might be. The film stresses that any distance between ordinary everyday life in America and remote foreign military operations is gone. Since the action takes place following the Battle of New York in the film *The Avengers*, the way of life for Americans has forever been changed as their sense of security about their homeland[12] has been challenged.

Both the epic and the film depict Aeneas and Captain America confronting the responsibility that comes with what scholar Eric Adler refers to as "defensive imperialism." "Defensive imperialism" can be characterized as similar to Captain America's defensive approach to foreign aggression. Adler's study defines "defensive imperialism" as the premise that Rome rose to power as an enormous empire somewhat reluctantly and as a consequence of the threat posed by the enemy.[13] As both the *Aeneid* and *CA: TWS* demonstrate, a policy of defensive imperialism requires the hero to face the consequences of eliminating potential threats to the future of their society.

Future Wars

In David Seed's edited collection of essays, *Future Wars*, Echevarria affirms that "anticipating the future has become both a practice and a culture" and that both science fiction literature and military studies of "the emerging security environment and armed conflict" can tell us much about the basic depictions of war that keep repeating.[14] Concerns about the use of technology in future wars have been an on-going literary theme for the past century. Echevarria points out that public fears about safety mirror the concerns expressed by the military, which manages defense.[15] The preoccupation in our society with the complex relationship between privacy, security and technology has led to apprehension about the ways in which an "info-war" might be the next real threat we have to fear.

Echevarria argues that while it used to be that the perceived threat came from whoever possessed the best technology in regards to weapons. In the information age, things are regarded as very different: much more weight is being given to social media's ability to influence audiences: "Power, it seems, is no longer the ability to get things done, but the perceived impact of images and words, of messaging." But this idea, he argues, does not take into account the transient nature of the image, and that it is constantly being replaced by the next new visual.[16] This is not to say that an "info war" would not have very real and lasting consequences for the U.S. It is highly plausible that any attacks on our technology could have lasting, large-scale consequences for both civilian and military populations.[17] Preventing counter-attacks and eliminating possible terrorist threats requires the use of satellites, drones, and other weapons that can target the enemy with a much more sophisticated level of precision than previous weapons. So are our ethics keeping pace with technology?

Like the fictional world of *CA: TWS*, we are, Echevarria argues, in a time where the conditions are highly suited to hypothesizing about how to ensure long-term success against terrorists and insurgents: "Of particular concern is how to manage such conflicts within the West's moral and legal parameters, and under what circumstances it might be appropriate to adjust those parameters."[18] And that, in the words of *CA: TWS*'s Alexander Pierce, require us to consider how "to build a really better world sometimes means having to tear the old one down. And that makes enemies." This is exactly the moral and ethical struggle about which both *CA: TWS* and Vergil's *Aeneid* pose critical questions. Discord arises when "mutually exclusive"[19] views on the value of freedom coexist in the narrative.

Adaptation and Anticipation in Captain America: The Winter Soldier

Captain America was originally a civilian named Steve Rogers whose body was unfit for World War II military service.[20] His willingness to serve his country, however, made him qualify for a secret U.S. Army experiment that transformed him into a super soldier. But the "American standard" of fitness, according to John Richards, has become outdated and Steve Rogers proves this with his fervent patriotism that allows him to succeed despite not meeting the military's requirements at first. Richards has argued that the Captain's pro–American stance is an essential part of the comic series, especially in the context of issues that related to World War II events: "… a recognition of the war, as well as the youth's place within a mobilizing American landscape were important inclusions in *Captain America* comics that represented the thoughts and opinions of the comic book industry's young readers and creators."[21] Captain America's sense of identity and patriotism will evolve as the times change and the wars change, but the idea persists that he represents what it means to be an American.

Since Professor Erskine (Reinstein in the comics), the scientist who invented the serum that transformed the strength and physique of ordinary humans into extraordinary physical specimens, was killed by Nazi gunfire, Captain America remains the United States' only "Super Soldier." He is given a red, white and blue uniform to wear and a shield that cannot be destroyed: "While the colorful uniform is somewhat self-explanatory, it is worth considering the symbolism of the shield, as it constructs a narrative of America as fundamentally innocent and the victim of foreign aggression (much like the name of the US Department of Defense—formerly known as the Department of War—does)."[22] Captain America often uses his shield to defend himself or others, although he does sometimes throw it at the enemy offensively. As I will discuss later in this essay, Aeneas's shield will serve a different function and its primary use will be offensive.

Comic book representations of Captain America prior to *CA: TWS* tend to place Steve Rogers in situations where he is the unmistakable defender of the American home front against the clearly delineated enemy attack, such as the Japanese assault on Pearl Harbor, which brings harm to his country. The character Captain America, therefore, enables his audience to define what American values should be and therefore classify as the enemy anyone who does not uphold them: "In the pages of *Captain America Comics*, there can be no doubt that the enemy is among "us" and that they mean us harm."[23] Thus Dittmer sums up the *Captain America* comic book series as one in which the hero's actions invoke our nostalgia for conflicts such as World War II, in which there is no moral ambiguity about American involvement in the war, and the enemy of both America and American values can be clearly defined:

> This leadership comes easily to him, as he is driven to uphold American values, and others (even the occasional villain) find his moral claim to authority to be compelling. In addition, it is notable that Captain America's one weapon is a shield, which makes certain claims about the type of hero that he is: although he often has to resort to violence, he is armed only for defensive action.[24]

CA: TWS focuses on Steve Rogers' attempt to adjust to a society where the chief concern is no longer a world war "breaking out on the European continent,"[25] but rather how to stop potential terrorists and insurgents. This focus on preemptive, targeted strikes against possible terrorists in *CA: TWS* is in part influenced by post–9/11 anxiety. *CA: TWS* asks us to consider the moral and ethical costs of living with the high-tech weapons of which Echevarria spoke.

Captain America: The Winter Soldier

In *CA:TWS* we see Captain America struggling to justify not only his involvement in international politics, but also attempting to come to terms with his role as a hero whose actions now by necessity have to be more on the offensive, since his definition of the enemy has had to change in order to keep up with the times. But there are several episodes during the film when Captain America puts down his shield before a fight. The first occurs near the film's opening when he is on the counter-terror mission with Natasha. He is confronted by a terrorist: "I thought you were more than just a shield," he offers as a challenge to Captain America. The Captain responds, "Let's see," and he puts the shield on his back before defeating the enemy. His decision to do this early on in the film establishes his character's unwillingness to hide behind the shield and the values it represents[26] in order to justify his actions.

The second time that Captain America puts down his shield is during the final fight with Bucky Barnes. This also shows how he is questioning or challenging what is to be done with his childhood friend. When Captain America is forced to face the "World Assassin," the Winter Soldier, who used to be his chief companion Bucky, he remains hesitant to finish him off:

> STEVE ROGERS: You know me.
> THE WINTER SOLDIER: No, I don't! [He punches Steve].
> STEVE ROGERS: Bucky, you've known me your whole life. [They continue to fight].
>   Your name is James Buchanan Barnes—
> THE WINTER SOLDIER: SHUT UP! [He hits Steve again].
> STEVE ROGERS: I'm not gonna fight you. [He drops his shield]. You're my friend.
> THE WINTER SOLDIER: [Charges at Steve and repeatedly strikes him]. You're my
>   mission! YOU ARE MY MISSION!
> STEVE ROGERS [banged-up and bleeding as the Winter Soldier is about to deliver a
>   last punch]. Then finish it. 'Cause I'm with you 'til the end of the line. [The
>   fight ends as Steve falls from the plane].

Once again, Captain America puts down the shield as a way of stating that he understands that America as an "innocent" party and as a "victim of foreign aggression" does not apply uniformly to all situations. So why is it that the Captain cannot kill the Winter Soldier? Barnes was an unwilling prisoner of war and he has not been given a fair trial or even a chance to see if he can be rehabilitated.[27] Captain America will not leave any soldier behind. While it may seem like his actions were personal, since Bucky was his childhood friend, killing him would demonstrate that Captain America approves of "Project Insight," which gives machines the responsibility for deciding who lives and who dies.

Central to the theme of *CA: TWS* is the moral concern about what happens when we program machines to identify and eliminate potential terrorist threats through preemptive strikes. Steve Rogers is now living in Washington, D.C., and working for S.H.I.E.L.D. under the supervision of Nick Fury. After being sent on a counter-terrorism mission to free hostages that are being held aboard a S.H.I.E.L.D. ship, he sees Natasha Romanov gathering data from the ship's computers. When he confronts Nick Fury about why this mission was compartmentalized and not all of the operatives knew about it, Fury tells him about "Project Insight" which involves three spy satellites that have the potential to eliminate terrorism before it happens. But when the data Romanov claimed from the ship about these satellites proves to be encrypted, Captain America begins questioning the mission. He then learns about HYDRA, an organization that since World War II has created chaos worldwide in the hopes of convincing people to willingly give up their freedoms in order to live in a more secure society. This is certainly a reminder to the audience that they dwell in a post–9/11 culture, one in which the next terror attack is supposed to be identified and eliminated before it happens. Reoccurring anxiety, therefore, is generated by a need to anticipate where the next threat is brewing so that society does not break down into chaos and disorder due to an unanticipated attack.

The culture of fear that *CA: TWS* warns its audience about is not one that Captain America wishes to perpetuate. His dialogue with Nick Fury after learning about "Project Insight" offers some perspective on why he resists following orders:

> NICK FURY: We're gonna neutralize a lot of threats before they even happen.
> STEVE ROGERS: I thought the punishment usually came AFTER the crime.
> NICK FURY: We can't afford to wait that long.
> STEVE ROGERS: Who's we?
> NICK FURY: After New York, I convinced the World Security Council we needed a quantum surge in threat analysis. For once, we're way ahead of the curve.
> STEVE ROGERS: By holding a gun to everyone on earth and calling it protection.

Steve is confronted throughout the film with the idea that chaos and turmoil will result if preemptive measures against the enemy are not taken. But as he tells Nick Fury at the end of their conversation about "Project Insight," at S.H.I.E.L.D. headquarters, this new method of going to war takes away freedom, instead of securing it": This isn't freedom, it's fear."

Furthermore, the head of HYDRA, Dr. Arnim Zola, is all too happy to share with Steve his insight that "people will fight for their freedom if people try to take it away from them. But if you cause enough trouble, people will willingly give up their freedom for a more secure world." Zola describes for Captain America a world where HYDRA has deliberately created conflicts in order to generate terror and emphasize the need for restricted freedoms:

> Dr. Arnim Zola: HYDRA was founded on the belief that humanity could not be trusted with its own freedom. What we did not realize was that if you tried to take that freedom, they resist. The war taught us much. Humanity needed to surrender its freedom willingly. After the war, S.H.I.E.L.D. was founded, and I was recruited. The new HYDRA grew, a beautiful parasite inside S.H.I.E.L.D. For seventy years, HYDRA has been secretly feeding crises, reaping war. And when history did not cooperate, history was changed.... HYDRA created a world so chaotic that humanity is finally willing to sacrifice its freedom, to gain its security.

CA: TWS creates a culture of fear around the need to identify and eliminate the potential enemy preemptively, because if you do not, then you are not protecting yourself adequately. Jasper Sitwell informs Steve Rogers that HYDRA even claims to be able to calculate future threats: "The 21st century is a digital book. Zola taught HYDRA how to read it. Zola's algorithm evaluates people's past to predict their future."

When Steve challenges HYDRA's policy in the film, he is once again standing up for freedom over fear:

> Steve Rogers: Attention all S.H.I.E.L.D. agents, this is Steve Rogers. You're heard a lot about me over the last few days. Some of you were even ordered to hunt me down. But I think it's time you know the truth. S.H.I.E.L.D. is not what we thought it was. It's been taken over by HYDRA. Alexander Pierce is their leader. The S.T.R.I.K.E. and Insight crew are HYDRA as well. I don't know how many more, but I know they're in the building. They could be standing right next to you. They almost have what they want. Absolute control. They shot Nick Fury. And it won't end there. If you launch those helicarriers today, HYDRA will be able to kill anyone that stands in their way. Unless we stop them.... I know I'm asking a lot. But the price of freedom is high. It always has been. And it's a price I'm willing to pay. And if I'm the only one, then so be it. But I'm willing to bet I'm not.

In the above scene, where Steve calls upon the agents of S.H.I.E.L.D., the film is cautioning against giving up all rights to a higher authority who promises security but in reality is simply using that authority to eliminate any possible threats to their supremacy.

But the film also gets at the moral issue of waging war against humanity based on an algorithm capable of "evaluating people's past to predict their future." Captain America objects to this idea. When he says the "price of freedom is high" he is warning his fellow Americans that there will be risks and new threats will emerge, but that this is still a better way of life than living under Project Insight, which will give the order to kill millions to prevent a future war. Captain America knows that this kind of violence will not stop the endless cycle of hostility. And the theme of defensive violence that preserves the law, versus aggressive violence that establishes new martial law, is the same theme that Vergil's *Aeneid* will also address.

Justifying the Imperium Romanum

The *Aeneid* was published in 19 BCE after the poet's death and at a time when Rome was recovering from a bloody civil war. Aeneas, the epic's hero, is required to make the ultimate sacrifice on behalf of his new country: he must leave his homeland of Troy and his old identity as a Trojan behind in order to establish a new city,[28] one that will eventually lead to the establishment of the mighty Roman Empire. While the epic's story is drawn from myth, and the events place in Rome's distant and legendary past, the depictions of post–Trojan war Aeneas's suffering and his conflict over how to create a new life for himself would not have seemed that far removed from life in newly-imperial Rome. Vergil's audience was a post–civil war society that was under the rule of Rome's first emperor, Augustus. The community of Augustan Rome was in the process of rebuilding and determining how to reconstruct their identity following the aftermath of brutal conflict. Vergil's narrative on war and its moral consequences has inspired authors of science fiction and fantasy and other forms of popular media to include allusions to the epic and/or directly reference the epic in their works.[29] The questions Vergil is asking about what constitutes a civilized society[30] and the steps a society needs to undertake to recover from war still resonate with audiences today.

Aeneas is presented in Book VIII of the *Aeneid* with a shield crafted by Vulcan, the Roman god of the forge. Aeneas's mother, the Roman goddess Venus, requests that her husband, Vulcan, make a new weapon for Aeneas. The action in the epic stops when Aeneas receives it and the narrative pause[31] allows Vergil to offer a detailed look at Rome's policy when it comes to dealing with the enemy (*Aen.* 8.626–728). Prior to receiving the shield, Aeneas sees the sky flash with thunder and lightning (*Aen.* 8.523–527) and he knows war will soon follow. Lyne argues that Aeneas has, during his trip to the underworld, already viewed key moments in Rome's history as a sort of "spectacle of cost"—of war and its consequences—rather than as a vision of "splendor," so that when he receives the shield he is assuming the responsibility on behalf of his people: "With war imminent, he receives these splendid arms—and finds the shield inscribed with a majestic revelation of the destiny for which he is struggling."[32] The scenes depicted on the shield, then, come at a pivotal point in the action; after Aeneas has realized the cost to humanity of past conflict, but as he is just beginning to prepare himself for war.

The shield will be used in an epic battle between Aeneas and his archrival Turnus,[33] just before the epic comes to an abrupt end following Turnus's death. The duel between Turnus and Aeneas will confirm Aeneas's right to establish the Roman race: "Turnus and the city he embodies must be annihilated."[34] Aeneas will not put down his shield—and at first look, the shield's scenes of conflicts between opposing factions resulting in the enemy's death could appear to justify his actions, or at least offer some context for his actions.

The shield consists of scenes depicting Rome's legendary foundations,[35] key episodes from the Roman Republic in which Romans fought the enemy for their freedom and culminates in the Emperor Augustus's victory at the battle of Actium, which appears as the shield's central scene. The shield highlights various scenes from Roman military history in which the Romans either incorporated or eliminated threats to their city: "the shield represents the hard-fought but continued military success of Rome … but represents it from the particular angle of the preservation of the city and/or its local or international supremacy in moments of acute danger."[36] Casali puts the shield into an epic context, taking into account comparisons between Homer's Achilles and Vergil's Aeneas, since Aeneas will kill Turnus just as Achilles slays Hector. Consequently, the shield appears at a critical part in the epic storyline when Aeneas is poised to become the "next avenger."[37] But as Smith, notes, while the scenes on the shield may provide an opportunity for the audience in Vergil's time to "rejoice in the glorious victories … that have wrought peace and new hope," Aeneas cannot "predict or appreciate" what the future will bring from the scenes on the shield.[38] Instead, he will, as the bearer of the shield,[39] create the future.

In her work on the *Aeneid*, Michele Lowrie argues that, in the case of the *Aeneid*, the "pity" for the offender Turnus "masks a yearning for a credible threat to the order that will soon be established" when Aeneas kills him and obtains the right to rule.[40] The shield, according to Lowrie, offers in fact some justification for Aeneas's killing of Turnus. She categorizes the various scenes as follows: Lupercal (foundational), the war following the rape of the Sabines (law-making), Mettius Fufetius's punishment (law-preserving) and the appearance of Catiline (paying the price for crime) but in the end she argues that they all anticipate the re-foundation of Rome via civil war, just as Turnus' death anticipates the foundation of Rome. The new order, or *imperium Romanum*, is established with each act, from the rape of the Sabine women to the civil war following the death of Catiline.[41] Lowrie raises the question of whether or not Aeneas is justified in killing Turnus—who does the sanctioning of this act? The gods or the audience?[42] Aeneas's motivations for killing Turnus in the ancient epic are complicated because he is overcome with rage.[43] In the epic's final scenes, Aeneas takes the offensive tactic when he kills Turnus:

Aeneas, hesitating, brandishes the deadly weapon against him,
choosing fortune with his eyes, and with his whole body
he hurls it from a distance. Rocks moved violently from a war engine
never resound thus, nor have such great clashes burst forth from thunder.
The spear, bearing fearful destruction, flies like a black whirlwind
and pierces the edges of his cuirass, and the extreme layers of his sevenfold shield.
    Hissing it passes through the middle of his thigh.
Proud Turnus struck falls to the ground with bended knee[44] [*Aen.* 12.919–27]

The final scene in the *Aeneid* shows that Aeneas is not willing to put down his weapons, which include his shield and a sword, and establishes that Turnus, despite begging for mercy, will be killed.

Through the scenes on Aeneas' shield we come to see how Turnus' death is legitimized, according to Lowrie. Although the story takes place in a time before laws have been established for the society, Aeneas kills him because he poses a threat to establishing a peaceful existence:

Since the treaty that was ratified depended on the resolution of conflict by a duel between Turnus and Aeneas, it makes sense for Turnus to pay for the treaty's dissolution not just with defeat—that, according to the terms agreed upon, would indicate the Trojans had won, but with his life.[45]

Thus, Aeneas is justified in killing Turnus, as Turnus has proven that he has no place in the new world order. Even once law and order are established in Rome, the scene on the shield that depicts Catiline, who was killed without a trial as an enemy of Rome, appears to justify offensive tactics. As Galinsky notes, in the *Aeneid*, once it is determined that Turnus cannot be integrated into society, there is a reason for killing him.[46] But Lowrie argues that Aeneas's violent act of killing Turnus can be seen as exceeding the legal realm and the realm of reason due to divine intervention.[47] Aeneas acts outside of the law, but he can also be understood as stamping out potential violence and future threats to Rome's safety.

To return to the question of who is sanctioning the violence, fantasy authors who have written works inspired by Vergil's *Aeneid* would appear to suggest it *is* the guy with the shield, Aeneas, and that he will live long enough to see the consequences of his actions. In Jo Graham's *Black Ships*, Aeneas is in full control of his mind when he battles the Rutulians (Turnus was their king), and in Ursula K. Le Guin's *Lavinia* the audience learns that he regrets killing Turnus and gives serious consideration to the moral consequences of his act.[48] Captain America will not make that mistake of lifelong regret in the film when he fights Bucky. He puts down his shield instead.

When we think of Vergilian sentiments on violence in relation to *CA: TWS*, I argue that we can conclude that just as in the *Aeneid*, it is not productive to look for one uniform solution for dealing with the enemy in the film. Unlike what Alexander Pierce tells us, that a high tech info-war could end all of our troubles, the film suggests that Captain America and the rest of the Avengers should spend more time "thinking the unthinkable" rather than just assuming that this kind of technology would be a game-ender.[49] The lesson learned from Vergil that "attempts to tame violence fail, and fail spectacularly,"[50] can be applied to the film as well and Captain America demonstrates his knowledge of this when he refuses to act as the innocent victim of foreign aggression, and asks his fellow Avengers to follow his lead. He is again refusing to hide behind his shield in the way Alexander Pierce wants the U.S. to hide behind high-tech weapons to decide who lives or dies. He would be no better than HYDRA if he were to support Alexander Pierce or kill the Winter Soldier. Thus, Aeneas's motivations for picking up the shield to fight in the *Aeneid* offer critical insight into Captain America's motivations for putting his shield down before fighting in *Captain America: The Winter Soldier*. Understanding Aeneas' motivations in the final battle with Turnus as desiring to cut off any future threats before they can occur, can also clarify our understanding of the complex relationship between Captain America and his childhood friend Bucky Barnes.

Conclusion

I would like to end with a discussion of the 9/11 memorial.[51] It seems that for the commemoration of the 9/11 attacks on U.S. soil, Vergil's text has become our guide to post-war existence, just as he was Dante's guide in the *Inferno*.[52] On the 9/11 memorial, on the repository for unidentified remains, there is a quote from Vergil, "No day shall erase you from the end of time." This quote was taken from the Nisus and Euryalus episode in Book Ten of the *Aeneid*, which relates the story of Aeneas' comrades, two young Trojan men whose enthusiastic attack against the enemy ends up costing them their lives. There has been much controversy over this use of the quote on the monument, and what meaning we are to derive from it.

Is the quote more likely to remind us of the aggressors or the victims? I would suggest that the quote serves as a powerful reminder that, like the character Captain America, we can never return to the way things were before the attacks on American soil. We return to Vergil or Vergilian allusions in times of post-war reflection and anxiety, I believe, because of what Ursula K. Le Guin tells us is the essential difference between Homer and Vergil. In Vergil, the violence means something far more significant: "Homer seems to enjoy it [the violence] and Vergil does not."[53] Vergil's epic words on the 9/11 memorial remind us, in the same way Captain America's actions in the film do, that to allow aggressors to scare us into giving up essential freedoms and rights, is to give up on an critical part of our humanity. Taken out of context,

I suggest, the use of the quote leads to the conclusion that its presence on the monument speaks to our anticipation of future wars.

In quoting Vergil's *Aeneid*, are we being too passive about how to commemorate the past, or is the message active and calling us to think about the aggressor and who the "you" in the line of Latin really is?[54] Don't forget their anger; don't forget the violence and the devastating consequences of their actions for 9/11.[55] I suggest the monument is a call to action, for viewers to ask themselves, as Vergil's audience no doubt was also doing thousands of years ago, does war ever make the world a better place in which to live? The endings of *CA: TWS* and the *Aeneid* provide multiple perspectives on the consequences of war and the lasting effects of vengeance. And *CA: TWS* also shares this in common with the *Aeneid*—a brave yet enigmatic look at what would make the world a better place.

The *Aeneid* and *Captain America: The Winter Soldier* engage their audiences in complex questions about defensive imperialism as the key to successful rebuilding of a post-war society. In part, the film argues that America must be perpetually on the defensive. "Society is at a tipping point between order and chaos," Alexander Pierce warns the Winter Soldier, when he needs him to help make sure that "Project Insight" is initiated. The film also contends that maintaining a constant vigilance against the twin menaces of tyranny and oppression requires Americans to accept significant cultural and military changes. A discussion of similar themes of defensive imperialism in the *Aeneid* that will protect the future of Rome can lead to much more nuanced and exhaustive understanding of Captain America's actions in the film as they relate to his heroic identity as a defender of America.[56]

NOTES

1. Jason Dittmer, "Captain America's Empire: Reflections on Identity, Popular Culture, and Post 9/11 Politics," *Annals of the Association of American Geographers* 95, no. 3: (2005): 630. For the purpose of this article, I am using Simon Dalby's definition of geopolitics. Simon Dalby, "Calling 911: Geopolitics, security and America's new war," in *11 September and Its Aftermath; The Geopolitics of Terror*, edited by S. Brunn: 61–86. (London: Frank Cass, 2004), 62–63, argues that geopolitics is not only the spatial division of the world by hierarchy but that "geopolitics is also about the performance of political acts, the specification of friends and enemies, the designations of spaces as theirs and ours, the distinction between hostile and friendly places and peoples."

2. Jason Dittmer, *Captain America and the Nationalist Superhero: Metaphors, Narratives, and Geopolitics* (Philadelphia: Temple University Press, 2013), 63–66, defines Captain America's narrative of identity as the aspects of his origin story which can be explained through his participation in the development of an American national narrative. Thus, a story in which Captain America defends the U.S. against the Nazi's tells an audience a key detail about his identity—What are his moral values?—while also establishing that American morality requires U.S. involvement in World War II.

3. Michèle Lowrie, "Vergil and Founding Violence," Cardozo Law Review (2005): 949, argues that the understanding Roman identity in the *Aeneid* is tied closely to understanding the role violence played in the foundations of the city: "At stake are questions of not only

justice, but also of national identity, not just Roman, but the model of identity the *Aeneid* sets for being European, and in turn for being American."

4. *Captain America: The Winter Soldier*, directed by Anthony and Joe Russo (2014; Walt Disney. Studios Home Entertainment, Burbank, CA, 2014), DVD.

5. Brett M. Rogers and Benjamin Eldon Stevens, eds., Oxford: Oxford University Press, 2015.

6. Mélanie Bost-Fiévet and Sandra Provini, eds., Paris: Classiques Garnier, 2014.

7. Brett M. Rogers and Benjamin Eldon Stevens, "The Past Is an Undiscovered Country," in *Classical Traditions in Modern Science Fiction and Fantasy*, edited by Brett M. Rogers and Benjamin Eldon Stevens (Oxford University Press, 2015) 5.

8. R. Jewett and J.S. Lawrence, *Captain America and the Crusade against Evil: The Dilemma of Zealous Nationalism* (Grand Rapids, MI: Wm. B. Eerdmans, 2002), 40–41, determine that Captain America is given this "impossible task." Karl Galinsky, *Augustan Culture: An Interpretative Introduction* (Princeton: Princeton University Press, 1996) 123, notes, however, that Aeneas eventually comes to realize that he cannot return to the past: "Vergil deliberately presents Aeneas initially as someone who, like many a good Roman, is trying to seek recourse in the past, only to wean him away from it—Aeneas literally cannot go home again— and have him develop an existential ideal, which, like the revised Golden Age ideal in the *Georgics*, is far more trying, more challenging, and ultimately far more meaningful."

9. Antulio Echevarria II, "The War After Next: Anticipating Future Conflict in the New Millennium," in *Future Wars: The Anticipation and the Fears*, edited by David Seed (Liverpool: University of Liverpool Press, 2012) 248–251.

10. Dalby, "Calling 9/11," 83.

11. Dittmer, "Captain America's Empire," 641–642.

12. Marvel has extended the theme of security to the Netflix *Daredevil* Series.

13. Eric Adler, "Post 9/11 Views of Rome and the Nature of Defensive Imperialism," *International Journal of the Classical Tradition* 15, vol. 4 (2009): 595, notes that political associations that connect modern America to ancient Rome are fraught with complications. But he asks us to consider if we can selectively accept some parts of the Roman Empire as influencing our modern foreign policy and conveniently dismiss others.

14. Echevarria II, "The War After Next," 248.

15. *Ibid.*, 247–250.

16. *Ibid.*, 256–257.

17. *Ibid.*, 265.

18. *Ibid.*, 247.

19. Christopher Nappa, *Reading After Actium: Vergil's Georgics, Octavian and Rome* (Ann Arbor: University of Michigan Press, 2005), 18, argues for reading Vergil's text with an awareness of how often the poet presents opposing worldviews: "... a central strategy of Vergil's art consists of identifying and exposing the often irreconcilable tensions between incompatible perspectives." See also Galinsky, *Augustan Culture,*149 on the complexity of imagery in the Augustan Age.

20. The *Captain America* comic was invented by Joe Simon and Jack Kirby in the late 1930s. Jack Kirby speaks in a 1990 *TCJ interview* about the fear that Hitler generated and the fact that his generation "had to confront Adolf Hitler." Gary Groth, "The Jack Kirby Interview," *TCJ*, last accessed July 20, 2015, http://www.tcj.com/jack-kirby-interview/

21. John Richards, "Smashing Thru! The Story of Captain, America, Comic Books, and the Evolution of AmericanYouth," (MA thesis, Sonoma State University, 2011), 25.

22. Jason Dittmer, *Popular Culture, Geopolitics and Identity* (Lanham, MD: Rowman & Littlefield, 2010) 81.

23. Jason Dittmer, "Fighting for Home: Masculinity and the Constitution of the Domestic in *Tales of Suspense* and *Captain America*," in *Heroes of Film, Comics and American Culture: Essays on Real and Fictional Defenders of Home*, edited by Lisa M. DeTora (Jefferson, NC: McFarland, 2009), 101.

24. *Ibid.*, 102.

25. Echevarria II, "The War After Next," 247.

26. This is not to say that Captain America is never compelled by the events that occur

in the film to go on the offensive. The elevator scene in the film demonstrates this. When he finds himself in a small moving box filled with soldiers, Steve Rogers asks in advance of the fight, "Before we get started, does anyone want to get out?" And he remains determined to finish the fight on his own terms.

27. This is unlike Vergil's *Aeneid*, where Catiline, who was killed after Cicero brought charges against him of plotting to have the Senate killed and takeover the city of Rome, appears on Aeneas's shield. Thomas Habinek, *The Politics of Latin Literature: Writing, Identity and Empire in Ancient Rome* (2001) 86, considers the Catiline-Cicero conflict essentially a story of "Roman anxiety over identity and legitimacy."

28. Galinsky, *Augustan Culture*, 246–247, maintains that the work overall represents the Roman ethos of *labor* as the central idea: "Worthwhile achievement comes at a price." But Galinsky also emphasizes that there is "social responsibility" that goes along with the choices and sacrifices a leader must make.

29. Two recent examples of fantasy works inspired by Vergil's *Aeneid* are Ursula K. Le Guin's *Lavinia* (San Diego: Harcourt, 2008) and Jo Graham's *Black Ships* (New York: Hatchette, 2008). See Jennifer A. Rea, *Pietas* and Post-Colonialism in Ursula K. Le Guin's *Lavinia*," *Classical Outlook* 87, vol. 4 (2010): 127–132 for an analysis of *pietas*, post-colonialism and the cost of establishing civilization through violence in Le Guin's *Lavinia*. Another recent SF work that has received comparisons to the *Aeneid* is *Battlestar Galactica*. Corinne Pache, "'So Say We All'—Reimagining Empire and the *Aeneid*," *Classical Outlook* 87, vol. 4 (2010): 132–136, argues for allusions to Vergil's foundation story within the 2004–2009 television series *Battlestar Galactica*. See also Vincent Tomasso, "Classical Antiquity and Western Identity in *Battlestar Galatica*," in *Classical Traditions*, 245, who defines allusions to classical antiquity within the *BG* series as "positioned in a complex way as both a source of salvation through its myths, and a source of destruction through ancient Greece's cognitive inquiry and Rome's decadence. This attitude reflects uncertainties about the Western tradition and its future role in the formation of identity."

30. See Eve Adler, *Vergil's Empire: Political Thought in the* Aeneid (Lanham, MD: Rowman & Littlefield, 2003) 178, for the argument that the second half of the *Aeneid* (Books 7–12) demonstrates "the roots of Rome's ability to impose the custom of peace."

31. Horatio Vella, "Vergil's *Aeneid* VIII and the Shield of Aeneas: Recurrent Topics and Cyclic Structures," *Studia Humanoria Tartuensia* 5, vol. 1 (2004): 7, considers the scenes on the shield to be indicative of the "concepts of society the poet has in mind." For more on the selection of scenes in the shield see G. Ravenna, "Scuto di Enea," in *Encyclopedia virgiliana* IV, edited by Francesco Della Corte (Roma: Istituto della Enciclopedia italiana, 1988): 739–742.

32. R.O.A.M. Lyne, *Further Voices in Vergil's* Aeneid (Oxford: Oxford University Press, 1987) 210–211.

33. Although it will be Aeneas's *hasta*, or spear, that will deliver the final death blow to Turnus.

34. Andreola Rossi, *Contexts of War: Manipulation of Genre in Vergil's Battle Narrative* (Austin: University of Texas Press, 2004) 196.

35. The shield depicts Aeneas' ancestor Romulus founding the city of Rome. Further discussion of Rome's foundations by Romulus and in particular, the use of the Romulus and Remus myth in the time of Augustus, can be found in Jennifer A. Rea, *Legendary Rome: Myths, Monuments and Memory on the Palatine and Capitoline* (London: Duckworth Academic, 2007) 38–43.

36. Steven J. Harrison, "The Survival and Supremacy of Rome: The Unity of the Shield of Aeneas," *Journal of Roman Studies* 87 (1997): 70–71. Harrison, 70, argues for a unity of the scenes on the shield based on "the stress on the survival and continued supremacy of the immutable sacred city of Rome." R. Aldon Smith, *The Primacy of Vision in Vergil's* Aeneid (Austin: University of Texas Press, 2005) 58, notes that it is Augustus as "victor and the one who preserves his people, the heir of Aeneas" that Turnus spots on the center of the shield.

37. Sergio Casali, "The making of the shield: inspiration and repression in the *Aeneid*," *Greece and Rome* 53, vol. 2 (2006): 187. The shield also functions as a vehicle for establishing Aeneas's motivations for seeking a new homeland. Yasmin Syed, *Vergil's* Aeneid *and the*

Roman Self (Ann Arbor: University of Michigan Press, 2005) 70, notes that when Aeneas views the scenes on the shield, he is able to put a "positive interpretation on the spectacles of his and his people's past and future fame gives him the strength to pursue his destined course." Vergil's audience would have also been well aware of the *clupeis virtutis*, or the "golden shield" that the Emperor Augustus received in 27 BCE. The shield was inscribed with four virtues: *virtus, clementia, iustitia* and *pietas*. For more on how the virtues on the shield of Augustus were associated with the moral leadership of their owner see Galinsky (1996) 80–90.

38. Lee Fratantuono, *Madness Unchained: A Reading of Vergil's* Aeneid (UK: Rowman & Littlefield, 2007) 250.

39. Yet Aeneas is unable to comprehend scenes on the shield which refer to a future he has not yet experienced (*Aen.* 8.730–31). Denis Feeney, "The Taciturnity of Aeneas," *The Classical Quarterly* 33, vol. 1 (1983): 215, notes the silence of Aeneas when he views the shield as "strange reticence."

40. Lowrie, "Vergil and Founding Violence," 953. See also Adler, *Vergil's Empire*, 193 who discusses the Roman need to rule over all the nations: "As the poem unfolds, it becomes clear why there must be a single ruler over the nations ... and universal peace can be achieved only through the unification of all the nations under a single regime."

41. Lowrie "Vergil and Founding Violence," 254.

42. Lowrie, "Vergil and Founding Violence," 950.

43. While the scope of this essay does not allow for a more thorough discussion of Aeneas's reaction to the death of Pallas at the hands of Turnus, the young prince that King Evander entrusted to Aeneas, Aeneas turns to Turnus just before he kills him and says, "Pallas, Pallas sacrifices you with his wound and exacts this penalty from your profaned blood," which indicates that Aeneas is overcome with rage when he kills Turnus (*Aen.* 12.948–949).

44. All translations are my own.

45. Lowrie, "Vergil and Founding Violence," 955.

46. Galinsky, "The Anger of Aeneas," 343.

47. Lowrie, "Vergil and Founding Violence," 964.

48. There has been much recent scholarly interest in the significance of Turnus's death. See, for example, Craig Kallendorf, *The Other Virgil* (Oxford: Oxford University Press, 2007) 216, whose survey of the reception of Vergil in early modern culture discusses receptions of Turnus's death as necessary "for the new Roman state to rise." See also Richard F. Thomas, *Virgil and the Augustan Reception* (Cambridge: Cambridge University Press, 2005) 278–296, who includes debate on whether or not the poem's ending offers closure.

49. Echevarria II, "The War After Next," 257.

50. Lowrie "Vergil and Founding Violence," 970.

51. Caroline Alexander, "Out of Context," *The New York Times*, Last accessed, July 20, 2015, http://www.nytimes.com/2011/04/07/opinion/07alexander.html?_r=0.

52. David Dunlap, "A Memorial Inscription's Grim Origins," *The New York Times*, last accessed July 20, 2015, http://harvardmagazine.com/2014/01/a-poet-s-march-of-ages.

53. Ursula K. Le Guin, "The Age of Saturn," *Locus Magazine*, last accessed March 15, 2013, www.locusmag.com/2008/Issue10_LeGuin.html.

54. D. Dunlap, "A Memorial Inscription," questions who the "you" is in the quotation to those who view the memorial, as it could be seen as fitting the aggressors more that the victims. Caroline Alexander, "Out of Context," observes that this quote commemorates how the circumstances of the two companions' deaths could be considered fortunate, since they were killed at the same time: "The central sentiment that the young men were fortunate to die together could, perhaps, at one time have been defended as a suitable commemoration of military dead who fell with their companions. To apply the same sentiment to civilians killed indiscriminately in an act of terrorism, however, is grotesque." See also *The Virgil Encyclopedia*, 1st ed., s.v. "September 11th Memorial and Museum."

55. Dunlap, "A Memorial Inscription" interviews classicist Helen Morales who notes that there is a possibility that informed viewers may wonder about the young attackers' motivations for such a violent and chaotic act: "the quotation might also productively encourage

some visitors to "wonder, as might Virgil's readers have wondered of Nisus and Euryalus, what drives young men to commit such atrocities."

56. I would like to thank the editors of this volume, Julian Chambliss, Bill Svitavsky and Tom Donaldson and, in particular, Julian for his thoughtful critique of certain aspects of my argument. Warm thanks also go to Avery D. Cahill, Vince Tomasso and Velvet Yates for their insightful comments on drafts of this essay.

Acting with Limited Oversight

S.H.I.E.L.D. and the Role of Intelligence and Intervention in the Marvel Cinematic Universe

Jennifer Beckett

"While insecurity is not a new phenomenon, the context of the 'war on terror' expands external threats to universal proportions"[1]

There's a lot to love about an hour or two spent at the cinema absorbed in the fast-paced action and explosions of a superhero film or an afternoon spent flicking through the pages of the latest installment of something on your pull list. At their very best superheroes and the worlds they inhabit, filled with dangerous but ultimately manageable threats and villains, offer us a securitized reflection of the world around us. There is something comforting in the idea that while buildings may explode and aliens can swoop down and invade there is always someone better, a team of someones, there to save the day. So its not surprising that during times of political or social unrest or all out war we find superhero narratives particularly evocative and potent.[2] So of course, in the era of the global war on terror, superheroes are once again at the forefront of the popular imagination.

From Christopher Nolan's *Dark Knight* series to the Wachowskis' adaptation of Alan Moore's *V for Vendetta* and the films of the Marvel Cinematic Universe discussed in this volume, they have spoken to our deepest fears and concerns in a post–9/11 world. Concerns that extend beyond the fear of attacks on home soil and abroad to encompass growing unease with the power wielded by military and intelligence organizations. Although there remains a long-held view that comic books, and by extension the films based on them, are for children or adults trapped in some kind of adolescent homeostasis, the truth of the matter is that comic books have long co-opted social concerns into their storylines. In some instances, such as Marvel's introduction of a Hitler punching Captain America in *Captain America #1* on the eve of America's entry into the European campaign in World War II, bringing them to the fore before they were part of our general thinking on an area. In line with its primary source material, *The Ultimates (Earth—1610)* imprint, the MCU in general is highly critical of America's response to the war on terror, taking particular aim at the seemingly unchecked power of the military industrial complex in a post–9/11 environment.[3] Not that Marvel as a brand has ever steered clear of engaging directly with political movements, in fact *Iron Man's* origin story in the current MCU is essentially an updated version of his first appearance in print, replacing the battlefields of Vietnam with those of the Middle East. It could be said that the MCU in some respects functions as a reminder of Marvel's earlier critiques of the American military establishment—*plus ça change, plus c'est la meme chose* as the saying goes.[4]

Indeed there is perhaps no better space in which to examine the underpinnings of today's war on terror than in the pages and across the screens of a superhero dominated transmedia universe. Writing in the recent collection *What Is a Superhero?* Robin Rosenberg and Peter Coogan make the point that the genre has moved into the space previously occupied by the Western. A genre, they note, was a "useful metaphorical way of discussing immigration, Americanization, urbanization, America identity, changing modernism, and so many other central concerns."[5] If the western provided a neat Us vs. Them approach to Cold War politics though, the modern superhero genre, particularly Marvel's approach to it, is more concerned with trying to unpack the "end of American exceptionalism" in an age of heightened security concerns and in the face of an ephemeral, ever changing enemy.[6] Superheroes, as Dittmer notes, provide us with a "a crucial resource for legitimating, contesting, and reworking states' foreign policies"[7] while at the same time proffering "a certain level of wish fulfillment for audiences [that are] anxious about threats to their personal and national security."[8]

Anxious we certainly are; in the context of the "global war on terror" we have seen an intensification of security measures in the public sphere and an unprecedented rise in mass surveillance the world over. Paradoxically, the very events that have led us here—9/11, the London Terror Attacks, and the rise of ISIS—have brought with them questions about the efficacy of the very agencies we trust to give prior warning of and to thwart security threats. Since 2010, leaks from Chelsea (Bradley) Manning through Wikileaks and Edward Snowden have thrown a harsh light on the operations of these intelligence agencies. In combination with the damning report of the U.S. Senate Select Committee on Intelligence into allegations of the CIA's use of torture, and the mostly flawed intelligence it garnered, this has led to a worldwide conversation and questioning not just about the perceived lack of oversight as to what these agencies do and whether or not they have over-extended their reach, but to some extent whether it has been worth it.

In what feels like an increasingly unstable world, these are important discussions to be having. In line with fine work already done by the likes of Jason Dittmer, Rafiel and Chris York, and Marc diPaolo[9] this essays considers the ways in which Marvel's Strategic Homeland Intervention, Enforcement and Logistics Division (S.H.I.E.L.D.) acts as a touch-point for these debates. It argues that as the Marvel Cinematic Universe (MCU) has moved through Phases One and Two, and as we move into Phase Three, the trajectory of S.H.I.E.L.D. is providing a performative space in which to question the present, understand the past, and reframe the future of America's intelligence and security agencies.

The Rise of S.H.I.E.L.D. as an Organizing Unit in the MCU

> MARIA HILL: What does S.H.I.E.L.D. stand for Agent Ward?
> GRANT WARD: Strategic Homeland Intervention, Enforcement and Logistics Division.
> MARIA HILL: And what does that mean to you?
> GRANT WARD: It means someone really wanted our initials to spell out "shield."

Initially imagined by Stan Lee and Jack Kirby as an international espionage and law-enforcement agency, S.H.I.E.L.D.'s role has always been as a kind of CIA/NSA that deals with threats to the Marvel Universe. Throughout its history in the broader Marvel Multiverse its writers have directly aligned its operations with those of America's intelligence organizations and the greater military industrial complex. In line with the post–9/11 world where such organizations are enjoying greater power and visibility, S.H.I.E.L.D. has become a prominent part of the MCU. It is not a stretch to suggest that S.H.I.E.L.D acts as a binding agent keeping the whole universe together, particularly if you consider the way it weaves the narratives of the tie-in TV shows *Marvel's Agents of S.H.I.E.L.D.*, now about to commence its third season, and *Agent Carter*, which is set for a second, into the tent pole films. These shows give S.H.I.E.L.D. an always in the background, always around element independent of the cinema franchises (the critical incidents) that is in keeping with the position of its real-world counterparts. It's also telling that the organization is no longer known as the Strategic Hazard Intervention Espionage and Logistics Division (its title since 1991 in the print world) in the MCU. A change that reflects the current language, environment and extended powers of its real world counterparts along with their increased emphasis on "'critical infrastructure protection' and 'all-hazards management.'"[10]

So, in much the same way as recent events have placed the operations of the CIA and the NSA and their increasing militarization under scrutiny, so too has the MCU put S.H.I.E.L.D. under the microscope. Questions have been raised as to its ability to uncover, contain and control threats despite its powers (*Avengers Assemble*—a.k.a. *Marvel's The Avengers* in the United States release, *Thor: The Dark World*, the initial Chitauri invasion and the position of Thanos as an "invisible" off-world terrorist mastermind), its real plans for the alien technologies it captures (*Avengers Assemble, Marvel One Shot—Item 47, Captain America: The Winter Soldier, Avengers: Age of Ultron, Agents of S.H.I.E.L.D.*), and finally, over the accountability and oversight of the organization itself (*Captain America: The Winter Soldier, Agents of S.H.I.E.L.D., Avengers: Age of Ultron*).

While each film of show within the MCU appears as an organic narrative, separated out from the whole, they are in fact interlaced with the broader narrative direction of the universe. S.H.I.E.L.D. functions as a touch point within this larger universe particularly through its appearance in devices such as the end credit spots, Marvel One Shots and in crossover events. All of these are designed to bring the MCU together, forecasting upcoming films and providing opportunities for fan surveillance.[11] The most recent example of this has been the Inhumans storyline in season two of *Agents of S.H.I.E.L.D.* Going into season three the marketing campaign for the show has deliberately engaged with the notion of fan surveillance through the use of hidden messages in Instagram posts, which when decoded signal the arrival of Secret Warriors into the MCU. This poses an interesting question, and one that we can see being played out in the real world as well as we called upon to remain alert and aware during heightened times of security, how complicit, active even, are we in our own surveillance? It is an idea worth holding in the back of our minds as we consider how Marvel is using S.H.I.E.L.D. to critique the state of intelligence and security services within our own world.

Phase One: Fury's "fine line between the world and the even weirder world"

The CIA was, of course, a publicly known agency whose operations were secret. The Office of Policy Coordination's operations were not only secret, the existence of the organization itself was also secret. It was, in fact, for its first years [...] the *most* secret thing in the US Government after nuclear weapons [*James McCargar, ex-OPC*[12]].

STEVE ROGERS: You think Fury's hiding something?
TONY STARK: He's a spy. Captain, he's *the* spy. His secrets have secrets.
Avengers Assemble [*Marvel's The Avengers*].

The point of covert intelligence is not that we don't know that the agencies behind them exist but rather that we don't know what it is specifically that they do or have done, or perhaps even all of the levels of operation within the parent organization. Their role, ostensibly, is to work behind the scenes in order to keep us safe from potential threats to civil security. As long as they are doing their jobs well there is, for the most part, a tacit acceptance of them as a necessary evil. As the MCU commences this is the position that S.H.I.E.L.D. occupies. It is the most secret thing within the government's covert intelligence and security organizations.

While the rest of the MCU operates within the prevailing climate of the war on terror, the MCU being an overlaid secondary world,[13] the S.H.I.E.L.D. narrative, taken as a standalone, reflects that of a pre–9/11 intelligence and surveillance agency. Operating in the shadows, its role within Phase One remains to ensure that the weird world of the MCU is contained. It is also tasked with bringing together the Avengers Initiative. S.H.I.E.L.D's actions within Phase One are thus positioned as both necessary and unobtrusive. Despite their more significant role in *Iron Man 2*, where we are introduced to Black Widow or at the site of Mjölnir's[14] coming to earth, it is not until *Avengers Assemble* that we are made aware of the full extent of their capabilities. Taking this out of sight, out of mind approach allows Marvel to explore and question the historical understanding of the actions and role of intelligence agencies and how they have changed in the context of the war on terror. It positions us as viewers in the familiar context of the Cold War spy thriller.

In keeping with this, as we start out in the MCU, S.H.I.E.L.D. operates within the context of what Tim Weiners in his history of the CIA has called the "fiction of a golden era"[15] of espionage in which agencies are fighting the "good war" against easily identifiable bad guys, stepping in only when external events force their hand. While Nick Fury may be at the head of the agency, however, it is Agent Phil Coulson (Gregg Clarke) who acts as the quintessential "good spy." Calm, collected, and immaculately suited he is the model of efficiency and, importantly, we are never given cause to question his actions and by extension those of S.H.I.E.L.D. itself. If S.H.I.E.L.D. is the structural underpinning of the MCU then Coulson, as Clarke points out, is its "glue,"[16] acting as a moral and emotional touch-point for the volatile Avengers team across their personal franchises and into *Assemble*. It is Coulson's death at the hands of Loki after all that provides the impetus for the previously warring Avengers to come together and save New York from the Chitauri.

Phase One also the introduction of the Marvel One-Shots, a series of short films created as features for the Blu-Ray releases of key Phase One films.

The One Shot storylines take us behind the scenes with the agency, expanding the position of S.H.I.E.L.D. across the universe. In doing so they create a narrative framework for the MCU with the agency at its center, and Coulson at its core. Commencing with 2011's *The Consultant,* the "One Shots," in the words of co-producer Brad Winderbaum, "paint a picture of S.H.I.E.L.D. pulling the strings and being responsible for some of the events we've seen in the films."[17] While the notion of a secret organization "pulling strings" behind the scenes seems like something to be concerned about given, within the Phase One timeline the One-Shots frame such actions as essential to continued security. They also serve to make S.H.I.E.L.D.'s downfall in Phase Two an even more pointed critique of the contemporary position of their real-world counterparts.

Taking place after the events of *Hulk* and *Thor, The Consultant* is a particularly good example. Going behind the scenes with Agents Coulson and Sitwell it shows them conspiring to counteract an attempt by the World Security Council to release the imprisoned Emil Blonsky/Abomination[18] into S.H.I.E.L.D. custody for inclusion in The Avengers initiative. Not only is it a storyline that plays directly into what Stan Taylor[19] considers to be a prevailing theme in espionage-centered films that position attempts at oversight as "meddling" it also foreshadows some of the concerns about the limited or ineffective oversight of the CIA's role leading up to September 11 raised by members of Congress during their inquiries. Given what we know about the extent of Blonsky's mania, this blatant (and ultimately successful) attempt to derail the plans of an oversight agency seems to play into the idea of surveillance and intervention, whether sanctioned or not, as a necessary evil. In hindsight, given Sitwell's Hydra leanings, one can't help but wonder whether Blonsky was considered too much of a liability for either side.

As Phase One closes, however, we begin to question our assumptions about S.H.I.E.L.D. as their behind the scenes attempts to harness the Tesseract brings about a Chitauri invasion of the earth; an invasion that brings the organization and the "even weirder world" to light. The events in *Avengers Assemble* leading up to the Battle for New York—a stand in for the 9/11 attacks—force the viewer to confront not just the operational failings of S.H.I.E.L.D. in pre-empting such an attack, but the very duality of the nature of espionage and security agencies whose own actions may in fact be at the root of the problem. As Annika Hagley and Michael Harrison point out, *Avengers Assemble* in many ways destroys the myth of the good spy, and not just through the literal "death" of Coulson.[20]

Moving into Phase Two, the tensions created between the obvious need for increased security and this duality become even more obvious. Indeed, the One-Shot *Item 47* included on the Blu-Ray release for *Avengers Assemble* points to an agency that has no intention of moving away from its preoccupation with harnessing alien technologies, despite recent events. Mopping up after the Battle for New York, S.H.I.E.L.D. are made aware of a couple—Claire and Benny—using a Chitauri weapon to rob banks. Upon recognizing Benny's obvious abilities to work with alien weapons technology, rather than imprisoning the outlaws upon their capture they offer them employment instead. Is this an agency doomed to repeat the mistakes of the past?

Phase Two: Counter Terrorism, Trust and the Lessons of History

Responses to 9/11 betray an *intensification* of security practices that were already under way [...] And although civil defense originated with the Cold World, it has shifted somewhat to emphasize "critical infrastructure protection" and "all hazards management" [Torin Monahan[21]].

> NICK FURY: ... These new long-range precision guns can eliminate a thousand hostiles a minute. The satellites can read a terrorist's DNA before he steps outside his spider hole. We gonna neutralize a lot of threats before they even happen [....] After New York, I convinced the World Security Council we needed a quantum surge in threat analysis. For once we're way ahead of the curve [*Captain America: The Winter Soldier*].

The events of *Avengers Assemble* change the narrative surrounding S.H.I.E.L.D. in much the same way that September 11 signaled a change in how American surveillance was viewed. Although S.H.I.E.L.D. is notably absent from *Iron Man 3*, which kicks off Phase Two, fans have theorized that this is because they have been called in to face the World Security Council after the Battle of New York.[22] The agency is not gone for long, however, and in fact in Phase Two we get an expansion of S.H.I.E.L.D.'s narrative arc with two small-screen spin-offs: *Agents of S.H.I.E.L.D.* (2013–present), featuring a newly-revived Coulson and his handpicked team of agents, and; *Agent Carter* (2015), which provides a look back at the initial formation and work of the agency.

In the environment of increased security within the MCU after the revelation that there are stranger things "than a man in a flying tin suit" S.H.I.E.L.D. takes on a far more visible role. Indeed in *Thor: The Dark World*, their presence is a bone of contention for scientist Jane Foster, getting in the way of her ability to research a time/space rift. But, as Fury's explanation of the formation of Operation Insight to Steve Rogers in *Winter Soldier* indicates, not only has S.H.I.E.L.D. been granted enhanced powers and a greater budget at a time of heightened security risk, its powers also stem from an increased governmental and tacit civilian support for counter-terrorism measures. These expanded powers mirror those afforded to the CIA and NSA in the post–9/11 world, including the formal ability to "spy inside the borders of the US" as we see in *Winter Soldier*.[23] As events unfold, however, we find ourselves calling into question the organization's true motives. It's a move that deals directly with previous findings about the ability of real-world security agencies to police themselves and the need for greater transparency and oversight.

Phase Two provides us with a comprehensive interrogation of current discussions around security and intelligence agencies in the real world. It brings us face-to-face with three thorny real-world questions: just how much have intelligence and "security" operations long-term had the opposite of their desired effect, destabilizing the world we now live in? Understanding that there is a necessary role for them, what kind of security and intelligence agencies should we have? Finally, in the wake of Snowden's revelations about mass-surveillance tactics, should we be more cautious about giving up our civil liberties for the promise of civil security? The first of these questions acts as a theme throughout Phase Two, though it is most obviously played out in the events of the first season of *Agents of S.H.I.E.L.D.*, *Captain America: The Winter Soldier* and *Avengers: Age of Ultron*.

With the world still reeling from the events of *Avengers Assemble* the introduction of hacktivist organization The Rising Tide in *Agents of S.H.I.E.L.D.* directly references the operations of groups such as Anonymous and WikiLeaks and nods to the figure of Chelsea (Bradley) Manning. As a key member of the organization Skye is bent on uncovering and unmasking the truth about the "weirder world" she now lives in. It's an activism born both out of a distrust of government agencies post–*Avengers*,[24] but it also comes from a place of frustration and confusion and a desire for clarity in the form of transparency.[25] The questions that she asks are not dissimilar to those posed following the terror attacks in both New York and London—how much did security organizations really know and given what happened can we really trust them to act in our best interests? In her own words: "S.H.I.E.L.D. Government. Scary men in dark suits who go after guys like you [Mike Peterson/Deathlok]. They knew about the battle of New York before it even happened and then cleaned it up before anyone could ask any real questions."

Skye's inclusion as a "consultant" on Coulson's newly revived team provides us with a touchstone to the WikiLeaks affair and pre-empts the Snowden leak. She is also a stand-in for our own questions and ambivalence around the work of intelligence and security agencies. Where Coulson provided a moral center during Phase One, Skye's role is then somewhat more subversive. Coulson may be the glue but Skye is what Luis M Garcia-Miller would call "a people's secret agent," her role is precisely to mirror our own concerns and to act as an inroad into the workings of the security agency and its activities.[26]

Throughout the first half of the season then, Skye rails against the prevailing order, questioning S.H.I.E.L.D.'s tactics, purpose, agenda, and motives. Through her, for example, we come to question the ability of an agency that, despite its access to "billions of dollars of equipment,"[27] can still fail to uncover the existence of a real threat, Project Centipede,[28] while a girl "with a laptop [she] won in a bet" can. A question that mirrors the findings of Judge Silberman who, in his 2005 report on the CIA after the 9/11 inquiry into its operations, found that it was "fragmented, loosely managed and poorly coordinated" and "unable to gather intelligence on the very things we care most about."[29]

At the same time as Skye's season one arc effectively familiarizes us an audience with the internal workings of S.H.I.E.L.D. it raises some serious questions about accountability, and not just that of the agencies themselves. Her role in the episode *Girl in the Flower Dress*, directly engages with contemporary discussions around disclosure of material via security leaks under a "public good" argument. In this episode Skye is forced to question the ramifications of her hacktivism when a Rising Tide leak leads to the abduction and death of a S.H.I.E.L.D. monitored "enhanced" individual Chan Ho Yin (aka Scorch). More disturbingly, his capture is what ultimately provides the missing ingredient for Centipede's super soldier serum.

While the Scorch episode causes some soul searching for Skye, it does not prevent her from pushing back against the compartmentalization of information within the agency, particularly when it puts her colleagues in direct danger. Similarly, Coulson comes to have serious concerns of his own about the inner workings of S.H.I.E.L.D. as he comes up against brick walls in his search for answers about his miraculous return from the dead. These culminate in his (re)discovery of Project T.A.H.I.T.I.,[30] the alien biology that underpins it and his own part in leading it before ultimately recommending its immediate cessation. While this can be seen as part of the MCU's broader questioning of the ethical issues raised by militarized science, it also feeds into the idea that the agency, despite its causal role in the Chitauri invasion, is still operating unchecked. As we move into the events of *Captain America: The Winter Soldier*, Coulson is showing signs of deep distrust of the organization and its leadership with, as it turns out, good reason.

It is to the events of *Winter Solider* that we now turn, and the question they raise in the second half of Phase Two: is S.H.I.E.L.D. itself really what it seems?

It is [the CIA] an organization that thrives through deception. How do you manage an organization like that? [John Hamre, former deputy secretary for defense, Center for Strategic and International Studies, Washington]

And so the new Hydra grew, a beautiful parasite within S.H.I.E.L.D. [Armin Zola, *Captain America: The Winter Soldier*]

The events of *Winter Soldier*, which spill over into *Agents of S.H.I.E.L.D*, are a direct interrogation of both the history of the CIA and the NSA and their potential role in fomenting global insecurity. They also feed into growing anxieties about taking a reactive approach to increased threat by unquestioningly handing greater powers to security agencies. The use of Captain America as a proxy for the nation in these arguments is fitting. He is a nationalist superhero and as such is intrinsically linked to the nation's idea of itself, its highest values and sense of honor. His shaken faith in the institutions charged with protecting these values in this new era reflects the deeply held concerns and fears of many regarding the implications of America's ongoing security actions. At the same time he operates as a "source of wisdom from a golden era" harking back to the time of a "just war,"[31] in doing so he serves in many ways as a guiding light in times of uncertainty. Rather than providing a means for the acceptance of measures such as the USA PATRIOT Act as Francisco Veloso and John Bateman argue,[32] the Captain America of *Winter Soldier* holds a position far closer to that of the Cold War/post–Watergate era iteration of the print character who "seemed to be sending a message of wariness of the government."[33]

This position is cemented in the first key action sequence in *Winter Soldier* which pits the moral position of "just war" security activities and interventions of *Captain America: The First Avenger* against the modern era's war on terror. Nick Fury, playing on Cap's World War II–era moral certainty, uses the rescue of S.H.I.E.L.D. agents held hostage by terrorists as cover for Natasha Romanov/Black Widow—a character who personifies the moral ambiguity of espionage—to download the ship's files.

It is of course this very moral ambiguity that ultimately leads to the downfall of S.H.I.E.L.D. Infiltrated by Hydra at high levels as a result of employing former Hydra members in the post-war environment, the actions of the agency, past and present, are called into question. It's a storyline that draws on the history of the CIA in recruiting NAZI scientists post–World War II (code-named Operation Paperclip in the MCU) and instances of infiltration by the KGB at high levels. The latter calls to mind the William Wolf Weisband affair in particular, which directly led to the creation of the NSA,[34] a point which will become important during the latter half of Phase Two and in particular during Phase Three. The revelation that Hydra has been "secretly feeding crises, reaping war" in the guise of national security in the years following World War II echoes popular concerns about the influence of the CIA in assisting leaders such as Saddam Hussein into power.

While the rise of Hydra offers us a critique of the ability or even willingness of security agencies to police themselves, the Inhumans storyline in season two of *Agents of S.H.I.E.L.D.* and the backstory of twins Wanda and Pietro Maximoff (aka Scarlet Witch and Quicksilver) in *Avengers: Age of*

Ultron takes this question into the realms of the military industrial complex and discussions around the security threats posed by pre-emptive measures, and in particular drone strikes. While the twins develop their powers courtesy of Hydra's experimentation with the infinity stone in Loki's scepter, they side with Ultron as a result of the loss they encountered after an American drone strike on their hometown. It's a direct critique of the measures taken by the axis powers' military action in the war on terror, and how this may be responsible in part for the rise of militant organizations such as IS and the ease with which they are able to recruit. The story is more subtly explored through the Inhumans storyline, when Skye's mother Jiaying uses S.H.I.E.L.D.'s history of taking disproportionate action in the past as a means to foment a war between the Inhumans and S.H.I.E.L.D.

As we close out Phase Two, then, we find the heroes of the MCU battling against enemies of their own creation. Forget Hydra, in this situation the supervillain is now the military industrial complex.[35] With this in mind and given Zola's admission that Hydra's aim all along was to create "a world so chaotic that humanity is finally ready to sacrifice its freedom to gain its security" we turn now to our second question: should we be concerned about giving up our civil liberties for civil security?

In an attempt to commence a new era of agency transparency and oversight following the rise of Hydra in *Winter Soldier*, Black Widow releases S.H.I.E.L.D.'s files to the world. Although it is tempting to see this as a direct response to Edward Snowden's NSA leaks and in the contemporary context it was certainly seen that way, the inclusion of this scene actually pre-empted Snowden according to directors Anthony and Joe Russo Amongst the disclosures in those files is the evidence that Hydra/S.H.I.E.L.D. had used mass data collection as a means to single out *potential* threats for elimination prior to any actual wrongdoing, it's a direct critique of the American government's "kill list."[36] It's a revelation that goes against the superhero code where "because superheroes operate outside the law, they need to be sure their actions are just."[37] Similarly, if agencies are to be trusted operating on the very fringes of the law for the sake of our security agencies, surely there must be just cause.

This critique is taken up in *Age of Ultron* as events ask us to consider not only the ramifications of pre-emptive measures but also the potential for either deliberate or unintentional misinterpretation and misuse of mass collected data. Ultron's existence is partly the result of the mass production of drone-like Iron Man units for use in combat situations and partly the result of Tony Stark's continued hubris when he decides to use the powers of the infinity stone in Loki's scepter to create Artificial Intelligence able to determine and eliminate threats remotely. Though his intentions are pure, the result is an AI with access to all of our data via both the collection of metadata for security purposes, what we willingly give away online along with the available news and commentary online. Ultron's decision based on this data—that the world would in fact be better off if humans were made extinct—explicitly problematizes arguments around the security benefits of mass data collection. These discussions will come to the fore in Phase Three, particularly in relation to the *Civil War* storyline, which will see S.H.I.E.L.D. under even greater government control.

While Phase Two is certainly critical of the history of American surveillance and intervention and the current regime, however, it does not conclude, nor does the wider MCU, that we should do away with security organizations. Indeed as Black Widow's statement to the Congressional Inquiry notes, "Yes, the world is a vulnerable place, and yes, we helped make it that way. But we're also the ones best qualified to defend it." So what should the security agency of the future look like? That's the question currently under scrutiny as we come to the end of Phase Two.

S.H.I.E.L.D.'s storyline continues on to the close of season one of *Agents* as we find Nick Fury providing Coulson and his team with "a toolbox" to rebuild the agency, admittedly in the shadows, and this time to "do it right." Season Two finds a smaller, consolidated S.H.I.E.L.D. that consistently checks itself and questions any lack of transparency within the organization. It's a reflection of CIA agent turned KGB spy, Aldrich Ames' view that in order for effective monitoring and oversight to take place an organization such as S.H.I.E.L.D. "has to be small."[38] In this environment of greater mistrust about the internal withholding of information, Fury and Coulson's belief in the "compartmentalization" of intelligence has led to a split S.H.I.E.L.D. in which Coulson's "good spy" persona has come under increasing scrutiny.

In a Marvel One-Shot around the same time, *Agent Carter* takes viewers behind the scenes of S.H.I.E.L.D.'s foundations as the Strategic Scientific Reserve (S.S.R.). In taking on the birth of the agency, *Agent Carter* performs much of the same functions as the character of Captain America in the modern world. Its narrative acts as a form of retrospective wisdom about the right way to do intelligence work. Notably, by focusing on Peggy Carter, the show appears to decry the overtly masculinized space of the modern security and intelligence complex by making her the most effective member of the team. The majority of the male S.S.R. agents who make up her team are shown as either lazy or hotheaded and anxious to move up the ranks. As a result they miss crucial evidence and fail to connect or misconnect events, ultimately leading to the death of their commander, Roger Dooley.[39]

The show also offers a glimpse at an agency that considers the maintenance of security to be more important than the push to develop greater arms capacity. Indeed, the first season narrative in some ways echoes that of *Iron Man*, in that Howard Stark is forced to confront the potential for his weapons to move beyond his sphere of control and into the hands of organized criminals. Interestingly, too, where Tony Stark commences *Iron Man* reveling in the destructive power of his weapons and is happy to work with the military to create even more powerful artillery, Howard Stark is by contrast more circumspect. When asked why he hadn't handed over his inventions to the government he explicitly makes the point that some "inventions [are] too dangerous for anyone."[40]

Given that the S.S.R. is still effectively an arm of military intelligence it will be interesting to see what ultimately causes Howard Stark to form S.H.I.E.L.D. with Peggy at the helm. One can only surmise that a key element will be the need to separate intelligence agencies from military ones to prevent the latter from driving intelligence gathering for the purposes of greater power. Certainly that's a question that was raised repeatedly during the Bush administration, and has been a matter of concern as America has stepped up its drone strikes under Barack Obama.

Unlike the espionage narratives we have seen before the constant internal and external questioning of S.H.I.E.L.D. within the MCU provides a more nuanced picture of the role of security and surveillance. While not accepting of behaviors that appear to go beyond the scope of their work, and casting a critical eye over some of the shadier aspects of their past, as well as the increased militarization of security agencies, the MCU's positioning of S.H.I.E.L.D. does not advocate that it be cast aside entirely. Instead it comes to the same conclusion we most often do in discussions of intelligence and security agencies: we may not like what spies do, but we need them.

By breaking down and rebuilding S.H.I.E.L.D. alongside the *Agent Carter* narrative the MCU appears to be pointing to the possibility of a real rather than a fictional "golden era" of espionage. One in which a balance between civil liberties and civil security is met through a combination of increased cooperation with external oversight committees along with greater internal policing; a culture of "need to share" rather than the prevailing "need to know"; and, a more sensible approach to analyzing and understanding the potential risks of both general operations and pre-emptive measures.

NOTES

1. Torin Mohanan, *Surveillance in the Time of Insecurity* (New Brunswick: Rutgers University Press Language, 2010): 1.
2. Marc diPaolo, *War, Politics and Superheroes: Ethics and Propaganda in Comics and Films* (Jefferson, NC: McFarland, 2011), 1.
3. Richard J Stevens, *Captain America, Masculinity, and Violence: The Evolution of a National Icon* (New York: Syracuse University Press, 2015), 233.
4. Aldo J. Regaldo, *Bending Steel: Modernity and the American Superhero* (Jackson: University Press of Mississippi, 2015): 199, 203.
5. Peter M. Coogan and Robin S. Rosenberg, *What Is a Superhero?* ed. Peter M Coogan and Robin S. Rosenberg (New York: Oxford University Press, 2013), xvii.

6. Jason Dittmer, *Captain America and the Nationalist Superhero* (Philadelphia: Temple University Press, 2013) Kindle Edition, n.p.

7. *Ibid.*

8. Richard A. Schwartz, *Cold War Culture: Media and the Arts 1945–1990* (New York: Facts on File, 1998), n.p.

9. Dittmer, op.cit.; diPaolo, op. cit; and Chris York and Rafiel York, *Comic Books and the Cold War, 1946–1962: Essays on Graphic Treatments of Communism, the Code and Social Concerns*, ed. Chris York and Rafiel York (Jefferson, NC: McFarland, 2012.)

10. Torin, op. cit., 5.

11. Mark Andrejevic, *iSpy: Surveillance and Power in the Interactive Era* (Lawrence: University Press of Kansas, 2007); Henry Jenkins, "Transmedia Storytelling and Entertainment: An Annotated Syllabus," *Continuum: Journal of Media & Cultural Studies* 24, no. 6 (2010), 943–958.

12. Quoted in: Tim Weiner, *Legacy of Ashes: The History of the CIA* (New York: Doubleday, 2007): 34.

13. Mark J.P. Wolf, *Building Imaginary Worlds: The Theory and History of Subcreation* (Hoboken, NJ: Taylor and Francis, 2014) Kindle Edition, 28.

14. Aka Thor's hammer.

15. Tim Weiner, op cit., 513.

16. *Marvel Studios: Assembling a Universe* (ABC Studios, 2014) TV Film.

17. Marc Strom, "Marvel One-Shots: Expanding the Cinematic Universe," Marvel.com, last modified 11 September 2011, http://marvel.com/news/movies/16398/marvel_one-shots_expanding_the_cinematic_universe#ixzz1XWSoJ8UQ.

18. Interestingly, in the MCU Blonsky is far removed from his original communist character. No longer an evil "Red," he now represents the worst excesses of an over zealous military. For a reference to Blonsky's original character and story arc please see DiPaolo, op cit., n.p.

19. Stan Taylor, "The Depiction of Congressional Oversight in Spy Film and Fiction: Is Congress the New Meddler?" *Intelligence and National Security* 23, no. 1 (2008), 61–80.

20. Annika Hagley and Michael Harrison, "Fighting the Battles We Never Could: *The Avengers* and Post–September 11 American Political Identities," *PS: Political Science & Politics* 1 (2014), 120–124.

21. Torin Mohanan, op. cit, 5.

22. See comments on *The Escapist Portal* from May 2013 at www.escapistmagazine.com/forums/read/18.407369-Where-were-the-Avengers-SHIELD-in-Iron-Man-3.

23. Weiners op cit., 483.

24. As we later learn, Skye's motives are not born solely out of a desire to expose the underbelly of intelligence agencies, but also to access their information about her past.

25. Dittmer op cit., n.p.

26. Luis M. Garcia-Mainar, "The Return of the Realist Spy Film," *Cineaction* 88 (2012), 12–19.

27. *Marvel's Agents of S.H.I.E.L.D.* (Hollywood: ABC Studios, 2013–present) TV series, S1.01.

28. This storyline follows on from the Extremis narrative that formed much of the basis for *Iron Man 3*.

29. Quoted in Weiner, op cit., 506.

30. Terrestrialized Alien Host Integrative Tissue I.

31. Stevens op cit., 84, 218 and 234.

32. Francisco Veloso and John Bateman, "The Multimodal Construction of Acceptability: Marvel's Civil War Comic Books and the PATRIOT Act," *Critical Discourse Studies* 19, no. 4 (2013), 433.

33. Arnold T. Blumberg, *Espionage, Spies, and Skullduggery: Comic Book Counterintelligence* (Salem Press, Inc. 2013), 138.

34. Weiner op. cit., 51.

35. Frank Verano, "Superheroes Need Supervillains," in *What Is a Superhero?* ed. Peter M. Coogan and Robin S. Rosenberg (New York: Oxford University Press, 2013), 86.

36. Asawin Suesbsaeng *"Captain America: The Winter Solider* Is About Obama's Terror-Suspect Kill List, Say the Film's Directors," *Mother Jones* April 14 2014, www.motherjones.com/mixed-media/2014/04/captain-america-winter-soldier-obama-kill-list-politics-drones-nsa.

37. Stevens op cit., 220.

38. Quoted in Weiners op cit, 449.

39. As an aside, the show also deliberately challenges the notion of the popular damsel in distress role given to women in espionage films, highlighting the disjuncture between Peggy's real experiences alongside Captain America in the war with those of her radio play counterpart Betty Carver. For a fuller discussion of this see Jennifer K. Stuller, "What is a Female Superhero?" in *What Is a Superhero?* ed. Peter M. Coogan and Robin S. Rosenberg (New York: Oxford University Press, 2013).

40. *Agent Carter* (Hollywood: ABC Studios, 2015) TV series, S1.01.

"To be the shield"

American Imperialism and Explosive Identity Politics in Agents of S.H.I.E.L.D.

Samira Shirish Nadkarni

Introduction

In 2013, Marvel Television, ABC Studios, and Mutant Enemy Productions launched *Marvel's Agents of S.H.I.E.L.D.*, a television series based on the Marvel Comics organization, The Strategic Homeland Intervention, Enforcement and Logistics Division, or S.H.I.E.L.D., which is congruous with the Marvel Cinematic Universe (MCU) film franchise. Focusing on a small group of S.H.I.E.L.D. agents, headed by Agent Phil Coulson (Clark Gregg), the show foregrounds forthcoming MCU films within its own production timeline, while simultaneously providing the viewer with its own parallel accounting of HYDRA infiltration. Opening with Coulson's resurrection after the events of 2012's *The Avengers*, the series positions itself within the MCU's established framework of a technocratic, post–9/11 America that hearkens back to its triumphant role in World War II, making concrete the media rhetoric that linked these two events in the aftermath of September 11, 2001.[1] Yet this premise is eventually undercut (in a manner of speaking) by the events of *Captain America: The Winter Soldier* (2014) that parallels contemporary American foreign policy within the MCU with the fundamentalist imperialism of the Third Reich at its climax.[2] This provides the basis of a critique wherein S.H.I.E.L.D.'s self-appointed role as global protector is revealed as ruse by HYDRA, having played upon the colonial myth of protection for the purpose of resource gathering and war-mongering. This revelation consequently acts as justification for the continued presence of S.H.I.E.L.D. and indeed, further militarization in order to combat various global threats under the implication that once these threats are dealt with, the American imperial force that is S.H.I.E.L.D. will no longer be necessary. The series appears to posit the assumption that by virtue of being disenfranchised, the agents under Director Coulson no longer embody militarism, while continuing to repeat the same patterns of positioning themselves as American saviors and gathering resources within their control. The viewer is assured that this continued militarism is a necessity in the war against HYDRA, and that the team, the only ones that see HYDRA's continuing threat, are the world's only defense. This echoes the rhetoric of historical and contemporary U.S. foreign policy with regard to its use of seemingly humanitarian militarism regarding the necessity of armed force and the withdrawal of troops after the purported end of terrorism.[3]

Agents of S.H.I.E.L.D. thus begins by repeating American imperialist policies that conflate militarism with global security and protection, and presupposes U.S. imperialism within a system of what might be termed "consensual empire." That is, (1) on the basis of trade agreements the Global South has been made to "consent" to the imperatives of free trade markets that are themselves largely controlled by and functioning in the interest of the United States, (2) through the creation of wars billed as humanitarian intervention (notably the American "good war" of World War II) that emphasize the military might of the U.S., and (3) through a certain level of dominance within intergovernmental organizations such as the United Nations, the United States has positioned itself as a "new" empire that disguises its own authoritarianism (badly) as consent.[4] Representations of the World Security Council in *The Avengers* and *Captain America: The Winter* Soldier mirror the United Nations by purporting to be global and representing multinational and multiethnic voices, yet each depiction mirrors the reality of U.S. global hegemony. The American military (as S.H.I.E.L.D.) enacts this in the name of moral justice, and although the events of *Captain America: The Winter Solider* seem to problematize its intentions somewhat, little has been done to indicate any change to the status quo.

The MCU, and *Agents of S.H.I.E.L.D.* in particular, repeat propagandistic cultural discourse that repeats the claim of American exceptionalism—that the U.S. is distinct in its creation, settlement, and mission in regard to itself and the world.[5] This claim draws upon a history of European settler colonialism and the continued theme of the European "civilizing mission" seemingly made invisible through the myth of multicultural neoliberal personhood. As a result, the MCU participates in contemporary and historical propaganda that positions the United States and its allies as performing humanitarian militarism from what Feldman and Ticktin recognize as a notable position of power—that of speaking for and acting in service of an oppressed portion of humanity—and therefore recasting the performance of violence upon the other seemingly in service of rehumanizing an other. As Atanasoski notes:

> The predominant fiction of the United States as a multicultural haven, which morally underwrites the nation's equally brutal war making and peacemaking meant to facilitate the spread of liberal democracy and free markets after the fall of communism, conceives parts of the world still subject to the violence of U.S. power as being permanently in need of reform as they are homogenous and racially, religiously, and sexually intolerant.[6]

In essence, the cultural presumption that paints this humanitarian militarism as morally multicultural both rewrites the violence of its incursion as American exceptionalism while recasting those that it opposes as unjust and inhumane in a manner that is often quite specific to historical racial or global hierarchies.

Given the MCU's attempt to contextually locate itself within a narrative frame that is recognizable to its viewers, drawing upon contemporary events and historical allusions, the series' reliance upon historic cultural prejudices and persisting neo/colonial and imperial hierarchies implicitly reproduces these structures despite their seeming disavowal by the show's protagonists. *Agents of S.H.I.E.L.D.* deliberately locates itself within a transnational context, implicitly indicating a plurality of ethnicities, nations, and cultures who will therefore be affected by the various threats that exist whether within the global landscape or outside of it. As a result, transnational landscapes could potentially interact in different, competing ways, resisting the smooth operation of single narratives of ethnic, social, classed, sexed, or nationalized power, and/ or pre-existing structures that create and reinforce colonial and imperial systems of power; creating what Anna Tsing has termed "friction." Tsing's use of friction is distinct from resistance, suggesting merely that hegemony is created as well as undone within the space of friction, allowing for competing narratives to form and be recognized.[7]

However, despite the presumption of the global and the potential for these complexities, *Agents of S.H.I.E.L.D.* has created what is largely a specific hierarchy wherein (1) U.S. hegemony is a dominant force, (2) American militarism is created as distinct from the state yet functioning on its behalf and validated multiple times within the narrative, and (3) this power is white male led. It echoes what John Carlos Rowe asserts with regard to U.S. cultural production renders global differences as simply aspects of the U.S. nation itself so as to internalize and hypernationalize transnational issues.[8] As a result, not only does Tsing's concept of friction fail to give rise to competing narratives despite the show's frequent depictions of multiple nations, ethnicities, and cultures, but the singular narrative produced is inevitably a reassertion of American exceptionalism and reliant upon the historical systems of prejudices and hierarchies that allowed for its creation. That is, European colonizers perceived themselves as bastions of morality, justice, and culture and perceived those with ethnic, cultural, and racial difference as savage and inferior, and these hierarchies of prejudice continue to underlie contemporary assumptions regarding "true" Americana.⁹

This essay explores the complicated racial and national politics evoked within the series, suggesting that while *Agents of S.H.I.E.L.D.* is arguably the best representation of racial diversity within the MCU, its use of tropes and stereotypes to advance its storyline within its limited frame is particularly problematic. That is, while the inclusion of multiple instances of racial and national diversity within the narrative, whether as members of the main cast or as episode elements, can be seen as a step towards transnational inclusion and visibility of narratives framed by raced and/or sexed differences, the text itself fails to challenge any of the dominant narratives of American imperialism. This critique therefore acknowledges the high visibility of multiple characters of both sexes, different ethnicities and nationalities within the series, but argues that their inclusion facilitates the problematic manner in which American exceptionalism promotes itself. As Ananya Mukherjea has noted: "When there are relatively so few minority characters on television, those that are present bear a representational burden that might be out of proportion to their intended role as a character."¹⁰ Multi-national or multi-ethnic representation thus, while a step in the right direction, cannot be seen to be enough, particularly since these tropes, stereotypes, or historical allusions are often used in problematic ways to reinforce a social and cultural hegemony that continues to see the U.S. as largely white male led while simultaneously reinforcing American global dominance.

American Exceptionalism and Race

Dawson and Schueller link white hegemony and the export of American imperialism within the cultural market to multiple events, notably the theorized reluctant U.S. as "empire by invitation" during World War II, the war in Vietnam, the U.S.'s subsequent anti-communist stance in the Cold War, and the more recent wars in Afghanistan and Iraq following 9/11.¹¹ The resultant globalization of American culture and its exported propaganda of American exceptionalism creates its national concerns as global ones while simultaneously expanding the borders of its imperialist "protection" to encompass the global. The MCU's multiple references to historical events (for example, Captain America's (Chris Evans) link to World War II, Black Widow's (Scarlett Johansson) evocation of Cold War ethos, Iron Man's (Robert Downey, Jr.) links to Afghanistan) reiterate this seeming history of "empire by invitation." Given this constant threat of attack made concrete, the MCU plays out fantasies of American saviors where the whole world is positioned as a battlefield. The United States acts as a first and only line of defense, implicitly positing U.S. supremacy and the world itself as a playing field for American politics. This is particularly the case in *The Avengers*, with distinct links made between the technocratic, post–9/11 United States and the mythologized and "good" America arising from World War II, repeating real world media propaganda that linked these two events during the supposed "War on Terror." Victory at the film's close thus not only functions as a nationalistic reframing of American history, but also implicitly positions this war to underscore American forces having saved the world from the threat of terror while stripping it of any of the real world consequences of the aftermath of these wars (most recently in Iraq and Afghanistan).

The continued call to arms that forms the basis of the MCU's narrative in both its films and *Agents of S.H.I.E.L.D.* draws on the war film genre and specifically evokes the platoon narrative. Richard Slotkin suggests that the creation of the World War II combat film marked a general shift in the perception of America as essentially a white man's country to that of a multiracial and multiethnic democracy while maintaining racial inequalities. The platoon narrative therefore presents an idealized image of American soldiers at war who are multi-racial, female-inclusive, united by a common purpose, and lead by a white male, and whose internal racial and ethnic difference does exist in a hierarchy with whiteness at its head, and is largely tolerated on the basis of the presence of a dehumanized external enemy.[12] The contrast of seeming rationality on the one hand (S.H.I.E.L.D.) and outright violence, slavery, and compelled body modification on the other (HYDRA) encourages the audience to invest in S.H.I.E.L.D.'s more assimilative imperialism instead of HYDRA's more visibly violent colonialism. Moreover, the events of *Captain America: The Winter Soldier* having resulted in the disavowal of S.H.I.E.L.D. and a manhunt for its personnel by the "official" American military (led by General Talbot [Adrian Pasdar]), resulting in the reinforcement of the platoon narrative wherein they are effectively surrounded by potential enemies, whether considered unfriendly (HYDRA, Calvin Zabo, Raina, or a rogue "gifted" individual) or friendly (the American military seeking to prosecute them).

Yet even when officially disavowed and on the run, S.H.I.E.L.D. continues to reinforce American military might by not only continuing to function with enough access to funds and technology to continue operations, run their base, but also construct what is clearly a multi-billion dollar helicarrier ("Scars" [2.20]) to evacuate the citizens of Sokovia during the events of *Avengers: Age of Ultron* (2015). The series prefaces and mirrors *Avengers: Age of Ultron*'s attempt to return to the status quo where S.H.I.E.L.D. is publically once more perceived as a morally just military unit, as Director Coulson maintains an agreement with Talbot regarding the American military's seeming inability to handle alien artifacts, the Inhumans, or anyone on S.H.I.E.L.D.'s gifted index. As such, Coulson's team come to embody a "true" United States—diverse, female-inclusive, and led by a white heterosexual male—in contrast to the hapless formal military who are constrained by rules, regulations, and rationality.

Additionally, the superhero narrative indicates that the MCU is concerned with both, individual and collective cultural trauma. Superheroes are often created or originated as the outcome of individual trauma that often sees them placed in situations that then combat or help resolve the effects of collective cultural trauma.[13] Open-ended collective trauma built on fears of attack and eradication are inscribed in the superhero genre, and have become more strongly linked to themes of global terrorism in the aftermath of the September 11th attacks. In the MCU, these threats take the form of forces within (HYDRA, the Inhumans) or without (the Chitauri, the Kree, the looming threat of Thanos) in such a way that the trauma and its corresponding fear of future attack is always inevitable and seemingly insurmountable.

Slotkin notes that military narratives within popular culture are crucial to the work of nation as they depict people involved in the territorial and cultural defense of the state against the claims of others.[14] The nation itself is concerned with its people, and more specifically with its cultural invocation of the primacy of the nuclear family unit. The depiction of the platoon narrative in *Agents of S.H.I.E.L.D.* draws on both these aspects, creating the system of a found-family with Coulson in the role of patriarch, and group bonds largely forged through the shared political ideology of moral justice conflated with military intervention. The MCU's creation and presumption of S.H.I.E.L.D. as a global policing military (in both, the films and *Agents of S.H.I.E.L.D.*) and its use of the Avengers as agents of global protection that are U.S. led therefore indicates not only the propaganda of American imperialism as the first and only line of defense against any global threat, but assumes the concerns of an American public as representative of the needs of the world as a whole through the use of its pseudo-family structure. Notably, although multiple episodes of the show are situated in nations that are not under U.S. control, the only presumed nation and laws that seem to be of interest or concern to S.H.I.E.L.D., even when on the run in the show's second season, are those of the United States. In effect, this emphasizes to the viewer that the U.S.' global mandates are the only ones that truly matter.

For example, the *Agents of S.H.I.E.L.D.* episode "0-8-4" involves members of S.H.I.E.L.D. locating an alien object of significance in an Incan temple in Peru. Entering the country without initiating any formal diplomatic or immigration procedures, they intend to remove it without the Peruvian government's sanction, as they believe it to be too dangerous to be under any control other than S.H.I.E.L.D.'s. The episode depicts not only a confrontation with the Peruvian national military, but also an altercation with a group of local rebels led by Camilla Reyes (portrayed by Chilean actress Leonor Varela), a former associate of Coulson's who contests S.H.I.E.L.D.'s right to any device found on Peruvian soil. Coulson's insistence that the device is safest in S.H.I.E.L.D.'s hands enacts American exceptionalism with its subtext of racially and socially coded presumptions wherein the Peruvians would be unable or unwilling to control access to power within their own country, and extending an unwanted mantle of American moral protection. Reyes' refusal to accept American imperialism in Peru and its guise of protection is then punished within the narrative, signifying to the viewer that sole access to a means of power is the prerogative of the American military, respect for American global dominance is essential, and that rebellion will be coded as betrayal. The viewer is provided with no contradiction within the narrative, nothing to enact Tsing's theory of "friction" as Reyes' attempt at a competing narrative that challenges S.H.I.E.L.D. and U.S. hegemony results in the death of the entirety of the group.

Moreover, the use of ethnic and sexual stereotypes wherein Reyes relies on seduction for the purposes of betrayal reinforces Coulson's status as an everyman-hero[15] and simplifies any complexities associated the S.H.I.E.L.D.'s actions. This pattern of affirming American global hegemony through conflict, revised as nominally preventative measures ensuring access to power remains solely in U.S. hands, continues to repeat throughout the show. The result is an affirmation of the historically persisting geopolitical systems made further visible in the aftermath of 9/11 that insist groups or individuals, whether state sponsored or otherwise, are enemies of the U.S. unless they demonstrate their allegiance outright by acceding to the U.S.' "consensual" empire under the guise of accepting protection (in this case, from themselves).

Fears of the Inhuman and the Global South

Feldman and Ticktin note that as a universal subject, the claims of humanity are inevitably positioned as paramount, but this stance is inevitably complicated by contradicting bases of assumptions. They cite, for example, the preservation of ecology in developing countries as essential to continued human survival, which then does act against the interests of local communities who may be forced into poverty and starvation as a result.[16] These contradictions in this claim of humanity as paramount are similarly evident within the Inhumans storyline within *Agents of S.H.I.E.L.D.* The series changes from its initial stance wherein any person with superhuman abilities would be immediately controlled and indexed by S.H.I.E.L.D. for the protection of humanity in its first season, to the second season's recognition of the presence of multiple Inhumans and their society, Afterlife. The character of Skye/ Daisy Johnson/ Quake (played by Chinese-American Chloe Bennet) forms the center of these contradictions as she functions both, as a member of S.H.I.E.L.D. and as an American, therefore largely within its field of protection and specifically under the protection of its Director and pseudo-father figure, Coulson, while her roots are traced to the Inhuman city of Afterlife under the control of her mother, Jiaying (played by Tibetan-Australian Deichan Lachman). Skye's narrative positions her as (protected) inhuman threat that has her leave S.H.I.E.L.D. for Afterlife and consequently return following the events of Afterlife's seeming declaration of war on S.H.I.E.L.D., depicting multiple subtextual markers that not only repeat American propaganda regarding the moral right of the U.S. but also the inevitable "betrayal" and falsity of a communist Asian country (i.e., China.)

To clarify: Afterlife, a haven for Inhumans, has narrative parallels to the floating cities of Tian in the Marvel Comics. In the reality of a globalized world, the notion of a mysterious Asian city in the mountains whose inhabitants must be categorized by S.H.I.E.L.D. so as to assess the nature of their threat reinvents spaces of colonial enterprise for the U.S.[17] The lack of specific cultural markers or linguistic use within the show provides no cultural specificity to the depiction of Afterlife, creating it within the space of multiple Orientalist stereotypes. Additionally, its seeming use of common ownership of means of production, no formal social classes, no money, and a lack of formal hierarchy (aside from the single figure of Jiaying) suggests that Afterlife is coded as representative of communism. The Inhumans that live in Afterlife are therefore immediately introduced as an unknown threat, both ideologically and nationally, existing outside of the structures of S.H.I.E.L.D.'s "consensual" empire. S.H.I.E.L.D.'s response to this situation is to leverage their contact with Skye in order to insist that their people be made available for indexing, thereby placing themselves within structures controlled by S.H.I.E.L.D. in case of the need for humanitarian military intervention against them.

The connotations are clear: whether with regard to their risk of being captured, used and/or tortured by HYDRA or their own role as Inhumans which make them alien and unknown, their only possible responses are a willingness to consent to S.H.I.E.L.D.'s demands or the threat of brutal retaliation. They are created simultaneously as victims or threats, either devoid of agency or threatening in their agency respectively. This recreates the realities of U.S. imperialism as consent is couched in humanist rhetoric and enforced with the threat of militarism; no option outside of this control is available and the citizens of Afterlife are not afforded the courtesy of continuing to exist as uninvolved political outliers. They are effectively positioned as the equivalent of paroled criminals without having committed any crime other than existing outside of U.S. control and culturally influenced perceptions of normativity

As a result of this purported act of diplomacy, Jiaying attempts to instigate an Inhuman war against S.H.I.E.L.D., killing S.H.I.E.L.D.'s ambassador, Robert Gonzales (Edward James Olmos) and pretending to wound herself. Her ruse is intended to repeat the U.S.' traditional stance of moral justice and humanitarian militarism, mobilized this time in the name of (in)humanity. Yet this act is immediately construed as treasonous within the show, Skye and Calvin Zabo working with S.H.I.E.L.D. to stop her and seemingly killing her to accomplish this. The citizens of Afterlife are caught up within this conflict: either forced into a war for their independence on the one hand (with the likelihood of a high death toll) or treated as largely sub-human and "tagged" by a secret organization publicly disavowed by its own government whose individuals have already displayed markedly xenophobic tendencies towards the Inhumans. Given Jiaying's apparent death, the likelihood of them being forced to accede to S.H.I.E.L.D.'s demands seems high, and given Coulson's creation of an Inhuman team with Skye as its leader, some of their number has likely been mobilized in favor of S.H.I.E.L.D.'s continued imperial agenda.

The choice to elide the brutality hidden behind the acts of "consensual" empire as depicted by S.H.I.E.L.D. not only reiterates the show's own blindness to the complexity of the systems involved, but omits the creation of their own narrative regarding Jiaying's complex backstory and the specific cultural markers that have been introduced throughout the series. The first season saw her forcibly captured twice by agents of HYDRA and her organs harvested by Dr. Reinhardt/Daniel Whitehall ("The Things We Bury"). Reinhardt's repeated statement that "discovery requires experimentation" and his willingness to harvest her organs in order to further his own interests evokes historical associations with Nazi scientists who performed experiments on racial and ethnic minorities in concentration camps, therefore implicitly continuing to reassert S.H.I.E.L.D.'s role as humanitarian military intervention as per the "good war" rhetoric of Americana following World War II.

However, Lachman's visible ethnicity as Asian also brings to the forefront contemporary real world contexts in which Asians are among groups most at risk for trafficking, slavery, and illegal organ harvesting, as per the 2012 Global Report on Trafficking in Persons compiled by the United Nations Office on Drugs and Crime. Originally introduced to the narrative as a largely silent and mysterious Chinese woman who dies nearly immediately, Jiaying's role for the majority of the first season saw a combination of the tropes of the damsel in distress, the dead mother/wife, and the mysterious Asian. Her death served as a tool by which to resolve four pivotal issues within the series—(1) Skye's heritage as a Human-Kree hybrid, (2) the reasoning behind Calvin Zabo's rage at S.H.I.E.L.D., (3) the massacre in the Hunan province in China, and (4) Reinhardt's survival and transformation into Daniel White-hall. The visible exploitation of Jiaying's body is thus simultaneously produced within a set of tropes and real world associations that sees her reduced to a prop within the narrative, with no agency of her own and her body is located as the site of struggle for two white men (Renhardt/Whitehall and Zabo). In consequence, her return in the second season as the scarred leader of Afterlife and mother figure to the Inhumans returned some of this agency to her, only to shortly have it be revealed as treasonous and necessitating her death once more, this time at the hands of Zabo.

In effect, Jiaying's narrative of capture, torture, her body's use as a com-modity, the loss of her child, her resurrection following only upon the death of her community ties, is then narratively followed by a demand from the Global North that the people she represents as a member of Afterlife and the Inhuman community would need to subjugate themselves to a global protocol instigated by people who have previously depicted prejudice towards their people without any consultation regarding these protocols with the people they intend to force these protocols upon.

Each of these markers on their own suggest specific stances with regard to human rights in the global state, and Jiaying's refusal to comply with what is essentially the threat of compliance or attack by S.H.I.E.L.D. is stripped of its complexity with regard to the plight of less developed nations within global frameworks in favor of a narrative that privileges the morality of the Amer-ican imperialism embodied in Coulson's division of S.H.I.E.L.D. Jiaying's act of resistance/terrorism, only glancingly situated within the historicity of her narrative's racial socio-cultural markers, is re-appropriated to signal the importance of S.H.I.E.L.D. as a source of protection, and results in the cre-ation of an Inhumans force mobilized under the control of S.H.I.E.L.D. to police its people. ("S.O.S." [2.21]). This narrative framing seems to explicitly argue that resistance that locates itself outside of U.S. constructs is inevitably misguided, thereby once more indicating a global hierarchy in which the U.S. retains its significance and the resistance to this framing is discredited.[18]

As a result, while her Jiaying's act of resistance is informed by her nar-rative and her understanding of the realities of empire, insofar as she repeats them as proof of her reasoning, their validity is ignored in favor of Skye's role (as inhabiting dual roles as a member of S.H.I.E.L.D. and an Inhuman) in insisting that participating within S.H.I.E.L.D.'s indexing (and its consequent promise of control as protection) intends no harm, despite all historical evi-dence to the contrary.

It is worth noting that nearly all of the Inhumans presented up to the mid-season finale of the second season of *Agents of S.H.I.E.L.D.* are played by women of color, and the eventual interplay of allegiances and distrust between Raina, Skye, and Jiaying informs much of the end of the second season. Notably, each of these characters depicts particular subsets of racially motivated Asian stereotypes. While Skye's portrayal largely informed by her assimilation into S.H.I.E.L.D. and Coulson's pseudo-family platoon, as well as a submissiveness to the American imperial ideology it promotes, Jiaying's depiction within the series moves from silent victim that is a mere commodity in the first season as her body is literally preyed upon by a white man, to the stereotypical image of the Asian dragon lady in the second. As Fong, Soe, and Aquino note, the Asian dragon lady is typically portrayed as sneaky, untrustworthy, devious, and willing to use her sexuality to deceive unfortunate men[19] and is often punished by the narrative. The use of this stereotype as per Jiaying's supposed manipulation of Calvin Zabo and the murder of Gonzales thus implicitly reinforces anti-communist propaganda and a history of racist portrayals of Asian characters arising in the aftermath of the Vietnam war. Additionally, the same is used to reintegrate and retrospectively rewrite white American patriarch Calvin Zabo's narrative, whose sudden assimilation into a weapon for S.H.I.E.L.D. sees him rewarded with a happy ending.

To be more specific, Calvin Zabo's narrative has seen him perform multiple acts of what could be construed as terrorism. Not only has he attacked S.H.I.E.L.D. multiple times, seemingly working with and against HYDRA, murdered multiple random individuals in "A Hen in the Wolf House" (2.5) seemingly only due to their angering him, recruited Raina to manipulate events, as well as multiple other people from S.H.I.E.L.D.'s index in "One of Us" (2.13) in the effort to regain his daughter against her will and to attack S.H.I.E.L.D. without any regard for casualties or civilian life. Yet this narrative is retrospectively forgiven and its basis rewritten on the assumption that Jiaying, after having recovered from her horrific ordeal, had manipulated him into performing these acts. As a consequence, white American male Calvin Zabo, despite his acts of terrorism is reintegrated into society and provided with resolution, while Asian female Jiaying is retrospectively further vilified, her own torture discounted within her unwillingness to comply with S.H.I.EL.D.'s demands, and killed by Zabo in order to facilitate his reassimilation. Both Jiaying and Zabo claim to be acting in aid of their community (in Zabo's case, on behalf of his daughter, and in Jiaying's case, on behalf of Inhumans at large) yet only Zabo's narrative is validated. The racial, national, and political context is clear and as, in reality, it skews strongly in favor of white American men.

In a similar manner, Raina also inhabits the dragon lady stereotype for much of the first and second seasons before shifting more firmly to the mystic stereotype after her conversion to what she perceives as a hideous Inhuman in "Aftershocks" (2.11). Despite being played by Irish-Ethiopian Negga, Raina is strongly coded by Asian signifiers in the series, most notably her insistence upon silk dresses covered in flowers which is repeatedly emphasized in the course of the first season, and discarded in the second season in order to dress drably as a mystic stereotype in Afterlife. Raina's use of deviousness and sexuality is depicted more overtly in the course of the series, and is paired in large part with a theme of bodily harm and exploitation, usually at the hands of a white male. Her shifting allegiances result in mistrust and threats from each group as her assimilation remains uncertain. During her time with HYDRA, she is threatened by Daniel Whitehall with slow, painful mutilation while being tortured ("Face My Enemy" [2.4]), is physically attacked and nearly choked to death by Calvin Zabo, and has a tracker forcibly imbedded in her thigh without her consent by Lance Hunter in order for S.H.I.E.L.D. to use her as a lure ("A Hen in the Wolf House" [2.5]). Threats against Raina before her conversion are therefore focused on her willingness to shift allegiances instead of her potential as an Inhuman.

In the aftermath of her conversion and having been discarded by Zabo, she attempts to integrate herself into Afterlife through the continued use of manipulation and seeming deceit, creating a format wherein two Asian-coded dragon ladies (Jiaying and Raina) vie for dominance. Raina's eventual choice to inhabit only the mystic stereotype sees her discard even this attempt at assimilation, and her eventual death is positioned in the narrative as a means by which Skye is fully reintegrated into S.H.I.E.L.D.'s assimilative imperialism as a consequence of Jiaying's more violent refusal and counterattack ("The Dirty Half Dozen" [2.19], "S.O.S." [2.21–22]). Raina's prescient assertion that Skye will understand the significance of what is occurring only upon witnessing Raina's death is set up within the show's storyline as a means by which to avert a coming war, yet little is made of the fact that averting this war occurs only as a result of the Inhumans being forced to accede to the global authority of a government organization that in reality has no jurisdiction over them.

In contrast to Jiaying and Raina, Skye's willingness to assimilate quickly to S.H.I.E.L.D.'s American imperial agenda is largely reinforced and rewarded through the length of the show. Originally a part of the hacktivist collective, the Rising Tide (which has clear parallels to real world hacktivist organization Anonymous), Skye shifts rapidly from a socialist worldview that emphasizes the democratization of knowledge and anti-military anti-neoliberal rhetoric (a rhetoric that is itself openly vilified and declared a falsity in the episode "The Girl in the Flower Dress" [1.5]) to assimilation as an agent of S.H.I.E.L.D. in pursuit of global authority under the guise of humanitarian intervention. These distinct allegiances and assimilation into the S.H.I.E.L.D. team affords her certain protections that the show reinforces by the repeated instances of bodily threats against her largely focused around her Human-Kree heritage.

The issue of her mixed race forms the basis of much of the show's storyline, and Chloe Bennet's own Chinese-American and European-American heritage appears to inform this, as her fears in the first season revolve around Calvin Zabo's insistence upon her undergoing the ritual in which she will be "awakened" to her Inhuman heritage despite her repeated wishes for the undertaking not to occur, and Reinhardt/Whitehall threatening her with bodily harm in order to ascertain the powers she might have yet to manifest.

As a result, upon being awakened, the very nature of her heritage and the unknown nature of her allegiances sees the section of S.H.I.E.L.D. under the control of Robert Gonzales view her as a threat to be contained or eradicated, and her only protection at the time appears to be specifically linked to the family-platoon led by Coulson. The finale of the second season demands she acknowledge the allegiance of either her Inhuman roots in the Asian female-led Afterlife (which is strongly conflated with racist Orientalist stereotypes and communism) or her life amidst the American white male-led S.H.I.E.L.D. Skye's eventual choice ensures her safety within the parameters of the show, and her Inhuman heritage is purposed to lead a team under S.H.I.E.L.D.'s guidance which will likely continue to enact American imperialism. The implication seems clear: power within global systems will only be tolerated when acting on behalf of an American imperial agenda.

Narratives of Slavery Amidst Contemporary Imperialism

Aside from the historical reference of militaristic propaganda, "empire by invitation," and anti-communist neoliberal propaganda within the show, a further system of discourse politic emerges as a secondary narrative as names become markers of identity that indicate eventual allegiances and outcomes. That is, *Agents of S.H.I.E.L.D.*'s construction of naming repeatedly continues a pattern of competing imperialist sides while also re-appropriating problematic historical legacies in order to reaffirm the team's role as heroes and saviors. The naming of allies and antagonists permits and excludes modes of engagement, and this functions as appropriative or combative within colonial contexts. Michael V. Bhatia draws on Dale Spencer when speaking on the nature and authority of name-giving, arguing that the conditions of a name highlight what the giver feels is important in terms of their own experiences and constructs the world by virtue of this chosen pattern of naming. Function is defined by this re-naming and previous identity is erased (as is its consequent social, geographical, and cultural markers) and a new identity is created within the parameters of this function. Those marginalized by systemic forces rarely are in a position to use this system of name giving, and are consequently subordinated in this linguistic ordering of the world.[20]

For example, in the episode "Girl in the Flower Dress," Raina's (played by Ethiopian-Irish Ruth Negga) manipulation of Chan Ho Yin (played by Louis Ozawa Changchien of Japanese and Taiwanese descent) repeats the colonial act of compelled naming and re-naming, functioning as a "a symbolic and literal act of mastery and control."[21] Displaying her own appropriation of this systemic form of oppression, Raina subordinates Yin's experiences and world-view as Scorch to that of John Garrett (played by Bill Paxton) and HYDRA. Thus, the control of name-giving and its subsequent effects are underscored as when Agents Coulson and May attempt to reason with Yin regarding Project Centipede's likely motives and outcomes, Yin declares that while "poor, little Chan Ho Yin may have believed [their] lies," Scorch would not. This distinguishes both personas from each other while also indicating Yin's understanding of the situation—his own name with its distinct Chinese linguistic signifiers is presumed inadequate and his new name is Anglicized, displaying a distinct cultural hierarchy wherein Yin's "hero" name is deliberately not drawn from his own dialect. His very personhood is stripped from its ties to his first language and its associated culture for the assumption that upon a global stage, recognition can only be achieved by playing to the presumed cultural dominance of an English-speaking audience. Agent May's attempts to reconnect with Yin by using Cantonese fail as Yin asserts his knowledge that both sides would seek to use or oppress him, stating that he has been kept a prisoner "by you, by them, it makes no difference," and choosing agency or death instead. From his position as outlier, he recognizes that the reality of the narrative play between the HYDRA team and S.H.I.E.L.D. is not one of colonist and liberator, but rather of a choice of colonists.

Noting that Yin has now been given a new name, Coulson immediately accedes to the significance of the name giving. By accepting the reduction of Yin to the persona of Scorch, Coulson not only indicates to the viewer that this is not the first time such an event has occurred, but also codes the narrative situation with regard to the eventual explosive outcome of Yin's inability to overcome this naming. Yin's submissiveness to this renaming is, in large part, a consequence of S.H.I.E.L.D.'s forcible insistence upon his obedience to their dictates regarding his use of his own powers. The show's hubris of American imperialist militarism is underlined through the manner in which S.H.I.E.L.D. has inferred hidden jurisdiction in China and interfered with Yin's ability to earn as per his abilities. Yin's barely willing submission to American imperialist militarism and his coerced conversion to Scorch exhibits all the hallmarks of an established colonial and imperial legacy wherein he functions under presumption that this conversion to an Anglicized framework will finally grant him agency and freedom. Yet even the adoption of the dominant cultural discourse and his renunciation of his previous identity results in him subordinated and reduced to the narrative coding of his new name. The show fails to challenge to its own American imperialist subtext, instead reasserting itself through the implicit suggestion that Yin's own disobedience of S.H.I.E.L.D.'s orders and his unwillingness to submit to their claim of humanitarian military intervention has led to both, his original discovery by Raina as well as his eventual death. Scorch, trapped into his role as a pawn by competing imperialist sides and stripped of agency regardless of his attempt at integration, can do nothing else but explode.

In another example, S.H.I.E.L.D. agent Akela Amador (played by African American actor Pascale Armand) is also captured, her left eye modified without her consent, and forced into obedience with the threat of death ("Eye-Spy"). Michael Peterson (played by African American actor J. August Richards) is repeatedly re-named through the course of the show as The Hooded Hero ("Pilot") and Deathlok ("T.R.A.C.K.S."), while periodically returning to his own name. Peterson's body, while first modified with his consent, was subsequently modified without; episodes detailing changes to his right leg and left eye without his consent, both of which were used to compel him into obedience. While Amador isn't re-named, both Peterson and Amador's narratives display contextual links to the historical issue of slavery wherein the stripping of an original identity and non-consensual body modification played a major factor in the way in which colonial slave owners would assert dominance and superiority (Wood, 2005: 29). The show's specific focus on black bodies used to repeat these narratives reinterprets historical structures of slavery while updating them with contemporary concerns linked to terrorism. That is, while both Amador and Peterson are both reduced to simply bodies or tools on behalf of HYDRA, this compelled allegiance nearly resulting in their death at the hands of S.H.I.E.L.D., their bodies are modified in ways specific to their roles as weapons and sleeper agents to be activated. Both Peterson and Amador's narratives display forced displacement, separation from family and community, coercion, threats of death or torture, and control that insisted on absolute obedience, and these factors overlap in terms of slavery and contemporary fears regarding a forced conversion to a terrorist agenda. In effect, this combines traditional slavery narratives with contemporary fears regarding terrorism, and focuses on black bodies as simultaneously most vulnerable to attack as well as most threatening.

Problematically, their freedom from slavery comes at the hands of the S.H.I.E.L.D. team, led by a white male, and their agency and original names are granted to them once more (with seeming repercussions in Amador's case, as Coulson assures her the circumstances will be taken into account as she is taken to stand trial for her crimes). This play of historical allusions not only situates the S.H.I.E.L.D. team as liberators and reaffirms their role as protectors, but it also disguises the re-assimilation that occurs due to the consequent claim of gratitude and loyalty. This is made clear in the episode "Afterlife" (2.16) that re-introduces Michael Peterson and reveals that he has spent his time continuing to work for S.H.I.E.L.D. while receiving upgrades to his bio-technology, effectively becoming a literal weapon in S.H.I.E.L.D.'s arsenal and subordinate to Coulson's directives. The series itself is not unaware of its evocation of modern weaponized slavery as the recognition of his status as both weapon and the contemporary equivalent of chattel is underlined in the episode "The Frenemy of My Enemy" (2.18) as Grant Ward openly indicates that the upgrades to his weapons and indicated subservience makes Peterson a valuable commodity. The threat Peterson embodies is therefore undercut by his willing subservience to a white man (Coulson) in favor of an American imperial agenda, and any own agency outside of this role is left unrepresented after this return so as to emphasize his position as tool of the state. Although this is posited within the series as genuine choice, it remains that the likelihood of any other option that would see Michael Peterson marshal these bio-technological changes in favor of any agenda other than that of the U.S. would have harsh repercussions, most likely amongst which would be his death. Therefore, while Peterson regains his name in the course of the show, his displacement from his family and community, the modifications to his body, his creation and role as a weapon, and his obedience all function as subtextual markers of contemporary slavery within a neoliberal militarized state.

Conclusion

The pattern that emerges within *Agents of S.H.I.E.L.D.* does indicate repeated instances wherein people of ethnicities other than white are produced as stereotypes or tropes, and/or reduced to narrative props by which white male power is confirmed. That this is then used to further a systemic bias wherein power is notably located in the hands of white men, revealing and reproducing racial and cultural hierarchies that invest and associate systems of whiteness with power, continues to reinforce presumptions of American exceptionalism used to justify imperialism. With the repeated calls for more diversity and representation in the media in general, and the MCU film and television franchise in particular, the problematic issues of representation on *Agents of S.H.I.E.L.D.* are of particular importance to discussion and critique of the MCU.[22] As Andrew Martin notes:

Popular culture in the United States is where war comes from and where it is made possible—even desirable—and it is where it ends up, as the lived experience of war is fed back to us in displaced forms and narratives. It is one of the key sites where social

234 Section III: "Provide for the common defense"

norms and identities are constructed and valorized; it is where culture in all its complex tangles of residual, dominant and emergent forms overlaps and is enfolded back into structures of authority and control. It is through this process that the lived experience of insecurity, of uncertainty about the motives and aims of outsiders (the possible evil ones), are best viewed both as constructs and as constructed.[23]

Representation by itself cannot be seen as enough if this representation is in service of reinforcing systems of white hegemonic power that privilege American imperialism without engaging with or critiquing the larger issues of global identity politics at stake.

NOTES

1. See Ensley F. Guffey, "Joss Whedon Throws His Mighty Shield: Marvel's *The Avengers* as War Movie," in *Reading Joss Whedon*, edited by Rhonda V. Wilcox, Tanya R. Cochran, Cynthea Masson, and David Lavery (Syracuse: Syracuse University Press, 2014), 280–293; Susan Faludi, *The Terror Dream: Myth and Misogyny in an Insecure America* (New York: Picador Books, 2007); *Exceptional State: Contemporary U.S. Culture and the New Imperialism*, edited by Ashley Dawson and Malini Johar Schueller (Durham: Duke University Press, 2007).

2. Although the film nominally links American imperialism with the historicity of the Third Reich, it does so in such a way as to distinguish overt American militarism from "real" American heroes such as the Avengers and the remnants of S.H.I.E.L.D.. In doing so, the film acknowledges the reality of the political critique of current U.S. foreign policy, yet at the same time it undercuts it by insisting on the continued importance of what might now be seen as "independent" yet truly American secretive military strength which continues to be posited as essential for global protection.

3. Neda Atanasoski, *Humanitarian Violence: The U.S. Deployment of Diversity* (Minneapolis: University of Minnesota Press, 2013).

4. Dawson and Schueller, 1–36.

5. See Deborah L. Madsen, *American Exceptionalism* (Edinburgh: Edinburgh University Press, 1998); William V. Spanos *American Exceptionalism in the Age of* Globalization (New York: SUNY Press, 2008).

6. *Ibid.*, 3.

7. Anna Tsing, *Friction: An Ethnography of Global Connection* (Princeton: Princeton University Press, 2005), 1.

8. John Carlos Rowe, "Culture, U.S. Imperialism, and Globalization" in *Exceptional State,* edited by Ashley Dawson and Malini Johar Schueller (Durham, NC: Duke University Press, 2007), 37–60.

9. Richard Slotkin, "Unit Pride: Ethnic Platoons and the Myths of American Nationality," *American Literary History*, Vol. 13, No. 3 (2001): 470–476.

10. Ananya Mukharjea, "Somebody's Asian on TV: Sierra/Priya and the Politics of Representation, " in *Joss Whedon's Dollhouse: Confounding Purpose, Confusing Identity*, edited by Sherry Ginn, Alyson R. Buckman, and Heather M. Porter (Lanham, MD: Rowman & Littlefield, 2014), 65.

11. *Ibid.*, 1–10.

12. *Ibid.*, 476.

13. See *Comic Books and American Cultural History: An Anthology*, edited by Matthew Pustz (Bloomsbury Academic, 2012); Christopher Murray, *Champions of the Oppressed: Superhero Comics, Propaganda and Popular Culture in America During World War Two* (New Jersey: Hampton Press, 2010).

14. *Ibid.*, 471–472.

15. Guffey, 289.

16. Ilana Feldman and Miriam Ticktin, "Government and Humanity," in *In the Name*

of Humanity: The Government of Threat and Care, edited by Ilana Feldman and Miriam Ticktin (Durham, NC: Duke University Press, 2010), 2.

17. Samira Nadkarni, "I Believe in Something Greater Than Myself": What Authority, Terrorism, and Resistance Have Come to Mean in the Whedonverses," *Slayage: The Journal of Whedon Studies*, 13.2 [42], Summer (2015), np.

18. Nadkarni, n.p.

19. Timothy P. Fong, Valerie Soe, and Allan Aquino, "Portrayals in Film and Television," in *Encyclopedia of Asian American Issues Today: Volume 2*, edited by Edith Wen-Chu Chen and Grace J. Yoo (Greenwood, 2009), 644.

20. Michael V. Bhatia, "Fighting Words: Naming Terrorists, Bandits, Rebels and Other Violent Actors," *Third World Quarterly*, 26.1 (2005): 9.

21. Bill Ashcroft, Gareth Griffiths, and Helen Tiffin, *Key Concepts in Post-Colonial Studies* (USA and Canada: Routledge, 1998, 2001), 32.

22. See Abraham Reisman, "Marvel's Diversity Issue: Screen Output Doesn't Reflect Open-Minded Comics," *Vulture* (October 9, 2013), np; James Whitbrook, "When Will the Marvel Cinematic Universe Become More Diverse?," *io9* (July 17, 2014), n.p.

23. Andrew Martin, "Popular Culture and Narratives of Insecurity," in *Rethinking Global Security: Media, Popular Culture, and the "War on Terror,"* edited by Patrice Petro and Andrew Martin (New Brunswick: Rutgers University Press, 2006), 108.

Bibliography

Abbott, Stacey. "'Can't stop the signal': The Resurrection/Regeneration of *Serenity*." In *Investigating* Firefly and Serenity: *Science Fiction on the Frontier*, edited by Rhonda V. Wilcox and Tanya R. Cochran, 227–238. London: Tauris, 2008.

Adler, Eve. *Virgil's Empire: Political Thought in the Aeneid*. Lanham, MD: Rowman & Littlefield, 2003.

Agamben, Giorgio. *Homo Sacer: Sovereign Power and Bare Life*. Stanford: Stanford University Press, 1998.

Alaniz, José. *Death, Disability, and the Superhero: The Silver Age and Beyond*. Jackson: University Press of Mississippi, 2014.

Altman, Rick. "Cinema and Popular Song: The Lost Tradition." In *Soundtrack Available: Essays on Film and Popular Music*, edited by Pamela Robertson Wojcik and Arthur Knight, 19–30. Durham: Duke University Press, 2001.

Andrejevic, Mark. *iSpy: Surveillance and Power in the Interactive Era*. Lawrence: University Press of Kansas, 2007.

Arnaudo, Marco, and Jamie Richards. *The Myth of the Superhero*. Baltimore: Johns Hopkins University Press, 2013.

Ashcroft, Bill, Gareth Griffiths, and Helen Tiffin. *Key Concepts in Post-Colonial Studies*. London: Routledge, 1998.

Askwith, Ivan, and Jonathan Gray. "Transmedia Storytelling and Media Franchises." In *Battleground: The Media*, edited by Robin Andersen and Jonathan Gray, 519–527. Westport, CT: Greenwood, 2008.

Atanasoski, Neda. *Humanitarian Violence: The U.S. Deployment of Diversity*. Minneapolis: University of Minnesota Press, 2013.

Bainbridge, Jason. "'Worlds Within Worlds'—The Role of Superheroes in the Marvel and DC Universes." In *The Contemporary Comic Book Superhero*, edited by Angela Ndalianis, 64–85. New York: Routledge, 2009.

Bamford, James. "They Know Much More Than You Think." *New York Review of Books*. August 15, 2013. http://www.nybooks.com/articles/archives/2013/aug/15/nsa-they-know-much-more-you-think/.

Barthes, Roland. *Camera Lucida*. New York: Hill and Wang, 1981.

Barton, David. *Literacy: An Introduction to the Ecology of Written Language*. Malden, MA: Blackwell, 1994.

Bazin, André. "Adaptation, or the Cinema as Digest." In *Film Adaptation*, edited by James Naremore, 19–27. New Brunswick, NJ: Rutgers University Press, 2000.

Beaty, Bart. "The Blockbuster Superhero." In *The Wiley-Blackwell History of American Film*, edited by Cynthia Lucia, Roy Grundmann, and Art Simon, 236–240. Chichester, UK: Blackwell Publishing, 2012.

Blake, William. *The Complete Poetry and Prose of William Blake*, Revised ed. Edited by David Erdman. New York: Anchor Books, 1982.

Blum, Elizabeth. *Love Canal Revisited: Race, Class, and Gender in Environmental Activism.* Lawrence: University Press of Kansas, 2008.
_____. "Save the Whales and Beware Wilderness: Star Trek and Reflections of the Modern Environmental Movement." In *The Influence of Star Trek on Television, Film and Culture (Critical Explorations in Science Fiction and Fantasy)*, edited by Lincoln Geraghty, 82–99. Jefferson, NC: McFarland, 2007.
Blumberg, Arnold, T. *Espionage, Spies, and Skullduggery: Comic Book Counterintelligence.* Ipswich, MA: Salem Press, 2013.
Bongco, Mila. *Reading Comics: Language, Culture, and the Concept of the Superhero in Comic Books.* New York: Garland Publishing, 2000.
Bourdieu, Pierre. "Cultural Reproduction and Social Reproduction." In *Knowledge, Education, and Cultural Change*, edited by Richard Brown, 56–68. London: Tavistock Publications, 1973.
Brandt, Deborah. *Literacy in American Lives.* Cambridge: Cambridge University Press, 2001.
Brooker, Will. *Batman Unmasked: Analyzing a Cultural Icon.* New York: Continuum, 2000.
_____. "We Could Be Heroes." In *What Is a Superhero?*, edited by Robin Rosenberg and Peter Coogan.
Bukatman, Scott. *Matters of Gravity: Special Effects and Supermen in the 20th Century.* Durham: Duke University Press, 2003.
_____. "Secret Identity Politics." In *The Contemporary Comic Book Superhero*, edited by Angela Ndalianis, 109–25. New York: Routledge, 2009.
Burke, Liam. *The Comic Book Film Adaptation: Exploring Modern Hollywood's Leading Genre.* Jackson: University Press of Mississippi, 2015.
_____. *Superhero Movies.* Harpenden, UK: Pocket Essentials, 2008.
Burroughs, Edgar Rice. *A Princess of Mars.* New York: Doubleday, 1970.
Campbell, Joseph. *The Hero with a Thousand Faces*, 3rd ed. Princeton: Princeton University Press, 1973.
Carbone, Nick. "Timeline: A History of Violence Against Sikhs in the Wake of 9/11." *Time.* Aug. 6, 2012. http://newsfeed.time.com /2012/08/06/timeline-a-history-of-violence-against-sikhs-in-the-wake-of-911/.
Chambliss, Julian C., and William L. Svitavsky. "The Origin of the Superhero: Culture, Race, and Identity in U.S. Popular Culture, 1890–1940." In *Ages of Heroes, Eras of Men*, edited by Julian C. Chambliss, William L. Svitavsky and Thomas C. Donaldson, 6–28, 2013.
Chambliss, Julian C., William L. Svitavsky, and Thomas C. Donaldson, eds. *Ages of Heroes, Eras of Men: Superheroes and the American Experience.* Newcastle upon Tyne: Cambridge Scholars, 2013.
Clarke, Arthur C. *Profiles of the Future: An Enquiry Into the Limits of the Possible.* New York: Harper and Row, 1973.
Cole, David R., and Darren L. Pullen. *Multiliteracies in Motion: Current Theory and Practice.* New York: Routledge, 2010.
Coleridge, Samuel Taylor. *The Collected Works of Samuel Taylor Coleridge.* London: Routledge, 1983.
Coltrane S., and R.D. Parke. *Reinventing Fatherhood: Toward an Historical Understanding of Continuity and Change in Men's Family Lives.* Philadelphia: National Center on Fathers and Families, 1998.
Comtois, Pierre. *Marvel Comics in the 1960s: An Issue-by-Issue Field Guide to a Pop Culture Phenomenon.* Raleigh, NC: TwoMorrows, 2009.
Coogan, Peter. *Superhero: The Secret Origin of a Genre.* Austin: MonkeyBrain Books, 2006.
Cooper, Simon, and Paul Atkinson. "Graphic Implosion: Politics, Time, and Value in Post 9/11 Comics." In *Literature After 9/11*, edited by Ann Keniston and Jeanne Follansbee Quinn, 60–81. New York: Routledge, 2008.
Curtin, Michael, and Jane Shattuc. *The American Television Industry.* London: Palgrave Macmillan, 2009.
Dalby, Simon. "Calling 911: Geopolitics, Security and America's New War." In *11 September and Its Aftermath; The Geopolitics of Terror*, edited by S. Brunn, 61–86. London: Frank Cass, 2004.

Daniels, Les. *Marvel: Five Fabulous Decades of the World's Greatest Comics*. New York: Harry N. Abrams, 1991.

De Kosnik, Abigail. "Fandom as Free Labor." In *Digital Labor: The Internet as Playground and Factory*, edited by Trebor Scholz, 98–111. New York: Routledge, 2013.

Derrida, Jacques. "Force of Law: The 'Mystical Foundation of Authority.'" In *Deconstruction and the Possibility of Justice*, edited by Drucilla Cornell, Michael Rosenfield, and David G. Carlson, 3–67. New York: Routledge, 1992.

_____. *Specters of Marx*. Translated by Peggy Kamuf. London: Routledge, 1994.

DiPaolo, Marc. *War, Politics, and Superheroes: Ethics and Propaganda in Comics and Film*. Jefferson, NC: McFarland, 2011.

Dittmer, Jason. *Captain America and the Nationalist Superhero: Metaphors, Narratives, and Geopolitics*. Philadelphia: Temple University Press, 2013.

_____. "Fighting for Home: Masculinity and the Constitution of the Domestic in Tales of Suspense and Captain America." In *Heroes of Film, Comics and American Culture: Essays on Real and Fictional Defenders of Home*, edited by Lisa M. DeTora, 96–116. Jefferson, NC: McFarland, 2009.

_____. *Popular Culture, Geopolitics and Identity*. Lanham, MD: Rowman & Littlefield, 2010.

Doloughan, Fiona. *Contemporary Narrative: Textual Production, Multimodality and Multi-literacies*. New York: Continuum, 2011.

Dudley, Andrew. *Concepts in Film Theory*. Oxford: Oxford University Press, 1984.

Dugall, Robin J. "Running from or Embracing the Truth Inside You? Bruce Banner and the Hulk as a Paradigm for the Self." In *The Gospel According to Superheroes: Religion and Popular Culture*, edited by B.J. Oropeza, 145–154. New York: Peter Lang, 2005.

Duncan, Randy, and Matthew J. Smith. *The Power of Comics: History, Form and Culture*. New York: Continuum, 2009.

Echevarria, Antulio II. "The War After Next: Anticipating Future Conflict in the New Millennium." In *Future Wars: The Anticipation and the Fears*, edited by David Seed, 246–266. Liverpool: University of Liverpool Press, 2012.

Evans, Elizabeth. *Transmedia Television: Audiences, New Media and Daily Life*. New York: Routledge, 2011.

Eyerman, Ron. *Cultural Trauma*. New York: Cambridge University Press, 2002.

Faludi, Susan. *The Terror Dream: Myth and Misogyny in an Insecure America*. New York: Picador Books, 2007.

Feldman, Ilana, and Miriam Ticktin. "Government and Humanity." In *In The Name of Humanity: The Government of Threat and Care*, edited by Ilana Feldman and Miriam Ticktin, 1–26. Durham: Duke University Press, 2010.

Ferri, Anthony J. *Willing Suspension of Disbelief: Poetic Faith in Film*. New York: Lexington Books, 2007.

Fitzpatrick, Peter. *Modernism and the Grounds of Law*. Cambridge: Cambridge University Press, 2001.

Flanagan, Martin, Andrew Livingstone, and Mike McKenny. *The Marvel Studios Phenomenon: Inside a Transmedia Universe*. New York: Bloomsbury Academic, 2016.

Fong, Timothy P., Valerie Soe, and Allan Aquino. "Portrayals in Film and Television." In *Encyclopedia of Asian American Issues Today: Volume 2*, edited by Edith Wen-Chu Chen and Grace J. Yoo, 644. Santa Barbara, CA: Greenwood, 2009.

Foresta, Ronald A. *The Land Between the Lakes: A Geography of a Forgotten Future*. Knoxville: University of Tennessee Press, 2013.

Frank, Jerome. *Courts on Trial: Myth and Reality in American Justice*. Princeton: Princeton University Press, 1949.

Fratantuono, Lee. *Madness Unchained: A Reading of Virgil's Aeneid*. Lanham, MD: Rowman & Littlefield, 2007.

Freud, Sigmund. *Totem and Taboo*. Translated by J. Strachey. New York: Norton, 1950.

Gaines, Elliot. *Media Literacy and Semiotics*. New York: Palgrave Macmillan, 2010.

Galinsky, Karl. *Augustan Culture: An Interpretive Introduction*. Princeton: Princeton University Press, 1996.

Gee, James Paul. *Situated Language and Learning: A Critique of Traditional Schooling*. New York: Routledge, 2004.

Geltzer, Joshua A. *US Counter-Terrorism Strategy and al-Qaeda: Signaling and the Terrorist World-View*. London: Routledge, 2010.

Genter, Robert. "'With Great Power Comes Great Responsibility': Cold War Culture and the Birth of Marvel Comics." *The Journal of Popular Culture* 40 (2007): 953–78.

Gilmore, James N., and Matthias Stork. "Introduction: Heroes, Converge!" In *Superhero Synergies: Comic Book Characters Go Digital*, edited by James N. Gilmore and Matthias Stork, 1–10. Lanham, MD: Rowman & Littlefield, 2014.

Goggin, Joyce, and Dan Hassler-Forest. *The Rise and Reason of Comics and Graphic Literature: Critical Essays on the Form*. Jefferson, NC: McFarland, 2010.

Gordon, Ian. *Comic Strips and Consumer Culture, 1890–1945*. Washington, D.C.: Smithsonian Institution, 1998.

Gottlieb, Robert. *Forcing the Spring: The Transformation of the American Environmental Movement*. Washington, D.C.: Island Press, 1993.

Graham, Jo. *Black Ships*. New York: Hachette, 2008.

Gray, Richard J. II, and Betty Kaklamanidou, eds. *The 21st Century Superhero: Essays on Gender, Genre and Globalization in Film*. Jefferson, NC: McFarland, 2011.

Guffey, Ensley F. "Joss Whedon Throws His Mighty Shield: Marvel's *The Avengers* as War Movie." In *Reading Joss Whedon*, edited by Rhonda V. Wilcox, Tanya R. Cochran, Cynthea Masson, and David Lavery, 280–295. Syracuse: Syracuse University Press, 2014.

Habinek, Thomas. *The Politics of Latin Literature: Writing, Identity and Empire in Ancient Rome*. Princeton: Princeton University Press, 1998.

Hagley, Annika, and Michael Harrison. "Fighting the Battles We Never Could: The Avengers and Post–September 11 American Political Identities." *PS: Political Science & Politics* 47, no.1 (January 2014): 120–24.

Hassler-Forest, Dan. *Capitalist Superheroes: Caped Crusaders in the Neoliberal Age*. Croydon, UK: Zero Books, 2012.

Hayles, N. Katherine. *How We Became Posthuman: Virtual Bodies in Cybernetics, Literature, and Informatics*. Chicago: University of Chicago Press, 1999.

Heath, Shirley B. *Ways with Words: Language, Life, and Work in Communities and Classrooms*. Cambridge: Cambridge University Press, 1983.

Hess, Stephen, and Martin Kalb. *The Media and the War on Terrorism*. Washington, D.C.: Brookings Institution Press, 2003.

Hoeveler, Diane. *Romantic Androgyny: The Women Within*. University Park: Penn State University Press, 1990.

Howe, Sean. *Marvel Comics: The Untold Story*. New York: HarperCollins, 2012.

Hutcheon, Linda. *A Theory of Adaptation*. New York: Routledge, 2006.

Jamal, Amaney, and Nadine Naber, eds. *Race and Arab Americans Before and After 9/11: From Invisible Citizens to Visible Subjects*. Syracuse: Syracuse University Press, 2007

Jay, Martin. "Must Justice Be Blind?" In *Law and the Image: The Authority of Art and the Aesthetics of Law*, edited by Costas Douzinas and Lynda Nead, 19–35. Chicago: Chicago University Press, 1999.

Jenkins, Henry. *Convergence Culture: Where Old and New Media Collide*. New York: New York University Press, 2006.

_____. *Fans, Bloggers, Gamers*. New York: New York University Press, 2006.

_____. *Textual Poachers: Television Fans & Participatory Culture*. New York: Routledge, 1992.

_____. *The Wow Climax: Tracing the Emotional Impact of Popular Culture*. New York: New York University Press, 2007.

Jenkins, Henry, Sam Ford, and Joshua Green. *Spreadable Media: Creating Value and Meaning in a Networked Culture*. New York: New York University Press, 2013.

Jewett, Robert. *The American Monomyth*. Garden City, NY: Anchor Press, 1977.

Jewett, Robert, and J.S. Lawrence. *Captain America and the Crusade Against Evil: The Dilemma of Zealous Nationalism*. Grand Rapids, MI: Erdmanns Publishing Co., 2002.

Johnson, Derek. "Will the Real Wolverine Please Stand Up?" In *Film and Comic Books*, edited by Ian Gordon, Mark Jancovich, and Matthew P. McAllister, 64–85. Jackson: University Press of Mississippi, 2007.

Kading, Terry. "Drawn into 9/11, but Where Have All the Superheroes Gone?" in *Comics as Philosophy*, edited by Jeff McLaughlin, 207–27. Jackson: University Press of Mississippi, 2007.

Kallendorf, Craig. *The Other Virgil.* Oxford: Oxford University Press, 2007.

Kaplan, Amy. "Homeland Insecurities: Reflections on Language and Space." *Radical History Review* 85 (2003): 82–93.

Keniston, Ann, and Jeanne Follansbee Quinn, eds. *Literature After 9/11.* New York: Routledge, 2008.

King, Stephen. *Danse Macabre.* London: Futura, 1986.

Kress, Gunther. *Literacy in the New Media Age.* London: Routledge, 2003.

_____. *Multimodality: A Social Semiotic Approach to Contemporary Communication.* London: Routledge, 2010.

LaFeber, Walter. *America Russia and the Cold War 1945–1992, 7th Edition.* New York: McGraw-Hill, 1993.

Lawrence, John Shelton, and Robert Jewett. *The Myth of the American Superhero.* Grand Rapids, MI: Wm. B. Eerdmans, 2002.

Lear, Linda. *Rachel Carson: Witness for Nature.* New York: Henry Holt, 1997.

Lee, Stan, and Don Heck. *Marvel Masterworks: The Incredible Hulk, Volume 1.* New York: Marvel Worldwide, 2010.

_____. *Marvel Masterworks: The Invincible Iron Man, Volume 1.* New York: Marvel Publishing, 2009.

_____. *Marvel Masterworks: The Mighty Thor, Volume 1.* New York: Marvel Worldwide, 2013.

Lee, Stan, and Jack Kirby. *The Mighty Thor #143.* New York: Marvel, 1967.

Lee, Timothy B. "Everything You Need to Know About the NSA's Phone Records Scandal." *Washington Post.* June 6, 2013. www.washingtonpost.com/blogs/wonkblog/wp/2013/06/12/heres-everything-we-know-about-prism-to-date.

Lefèvre, Pascal, "Incompatible Visual Ontologies: The Problematic Adaptation of Drawn Images." In *Film and Comic Books*, edited by Ian Gordon, Mark Jancovich, and Matthew P. McAllister, 1–12. Jackson: University Press of Mississippi, 2007.

Le Guin, Ursula K. *Lavinia.* San Diego: Harcourt, 2008.

Lévy, Pierre. *Collective Intelligence: Mankind's Emerging World in Cyberspace.* Cambridge, MA: Perseus Books, 1997.

Litowitz, Douglas E. *Postmodern Philosophy and Law.* Lawrence: University Press of Kansas, 1997.

Lyne, R.O.A.M. *Further Voices in Virgil's Aeneid.* Oxford: Oxford University Press, 1987.

Lyotard, Jean-Francois. *Just Gaming.* Translated by Wlad Godzich and Jean-Loup Thebaud. Minneapolis: University of Minnesota Press, 1985.

Madsen, Deborah L. *American Exceptionalism.* Edinburgh: Edinburgh University Press, 1998.

Manovich, Lev. *The Language of New Media.* Cambridge, MA: MIT Press, 2002.

Martin, Andrew. "Popular Culture and Narratives of Insecurity." In *Rethinking Global Security: Media, Popular Culture, and the "War on Terror,"* edited by Patrice Petro and Andrew Martin, 104–116. New Brunswick: Rutgers University Press, 2006.

Martin, Geoff, and Erin Steuter. *Pop Culture Goes to War: Enlisting and Resisting Militarism in the War on Terror.* Lanham, MD: Rowman & Littlefield, 2010.

McEniry, Matthew J., Robert Moses Peaslee, and Robert G Weiner, eds. *Marvel Comics into Film: Essays on Adaptations Since the 1940s.* Jefferson, NC: McFarland, 2016.

McLaughlin, Jeff, ed. *Comics as Philosophy.* Jackson: University Press of Mississippi, 2007.

Meehan, Eileen. "Holy Commodity Fetish, Batman!: The Political Economy of a Commercial Intertext." In *The Many Lives of the Batman: Critical Approaches to a Superhero and His Media*, edited by Roberta E. Pearson and William Uricchio, 47–65. New York: Routledge, 1991.

Merchant, Carolyn. *The Death of Nature: Women, Ecology and the Scientific Revolution.* New York: HarperCollins, 1980.

Mills, Anthony R. *American Theology, Superhero Comics, and Cinema: The Marvel of Stan Lee and the Revolution of a Genre*. London: Routledge, 2014.

Mittell, Jason. *Complex TV: The Poetics of Contemporary Television Storytelling*. New York: New York University Press, 2015.

Mittelstadt, Michele, Burke Speaker, and Doris Meissner. *Through the Prism of National Security: Major Immigration Policy and Program Changes in the Decade Since 9/11*. http://www.migrationpolicy.org/research/post-9-11-immigration-policy-program-changes.

Mohanan, Torin. *Surveillance in the Time of Insecurity*. New Brunswick, NJ: Rutgers University Press, 2010.

Moskowitz, Sam. *Explorers of the Infinite: Shapers of Science Fiction*. Cleveland, OH: Meridian Books, 1963.

Mukharjea, Ananya. "Somebody's Asian on TV: Sierra/Priya and the Politics of Representation." in *Joss Whedon's Dollhouse: Confounding Purpose, Confusing Identity*, edited by Sherry Ginn, Alyson R. Buckman, and Heather M. Porter, 65–80. Lanham, MD: Rowman & Littlefield, 2014.

Murray, Christopher. *Champions of the Oppressed: Superhero Comics, Propaganda and Popular Culture in America During World War Two*. New Jersey: Hampton Press, 2010.

Naber, Nadine. "Introduction." In *Race and Arab Americans Before and After*, edited by Amaney Jamal and Nadine Naber, 1–45. Syracuse: Syracuse University Press, 2008.

Nappa, Christopher. *Reading After Actium. Virgil's Georgics, Octavian and Rome*. Ann Arbor: University of Michigan Press, 2005.

Naremore, James. *More Than Night: Film Noir in Its Contexts*. Berkeley: University of California Press, 2008.

Nash, Roderick. *Wilderness and the American Mind*. 3rd ed. New Haven, CT: Yale University Press, 1982.

Neal, Arthur G. *National Trauma and Collective Memory: Major Events in the American Century*. New York: M.E. Sharpe, 1998.

Newman, Michael Z., and Elana Levine. *Legitimating Television: Media Convergence and Cultural Status*. London: Routledge, 2012.

Nietzsche, Friedrich. *The Will to Power*. Translated by R.J. Hollingdale and Walter Kaufman. New York: Vintage, 1968.

Nilges, Mathias. "The Aesthetics of Destruction: Contemporary U.S. Cinema and TV Culture." In *Reframing 9/11: Film, Popular Culture and the War on Terror*, edited by Jeff Birkenstein, Anna Froula, and Karen Randell, 23–34. New York: Continuum, 2010.

Nyberg, Amy. *Seal of Approval: The History of the Comics Code*. Jackson: University Press of Mississippi, 1998

Pedler, Martyn. "Morrison's Muscle Mystery Versus Everyday Reality ... and Other Parallel Worlds!" In *The Contemporary Comic Book Superhero*, edited by Angela Ndalianis, 250–269. New York: Routledge, 2009.

Potter, W. James. *Theory of Media Literacy: A Cognitive Approach*. Thousand Oaks, CA: SAGE Publications, 2004.

Public Papers of the Presidents of the United States: George W. Bush, 2001–2002, 4 vols. Washington, D.C.: Government Printing Office, 2001–2003.

Pustz, Matthew. *Comic Book Culture: Fanboys and True Believers*. Jackson: University Press of Mississippi, 1999.

Pustz, Matthew, ed. *Comic Books and American Cultural History: An Anthology*. New York: Continuum International, 2012.

Ravenna, G. "Scuto di Enea." In Encyclopedia Virgiliana IV, edited by Francesco Della Corte, 739–742. Roma: Istituto della Enciclopedia Italiana, 1988.

Ray, Robert B. "The Field of Literature and Film." In *Film Adaptation*, edited by James Naremore, 38–53. New Brunswick, NJ: Rutgers University Press, 2000.

Rea, Jennifer A. *Legendary Rome: Myths, Monuments and Memory on the Palatine and Capitoline*. London: Duckworth Academic, 2007.

Reagan, Ronald. "Farewell Address to the Nation, January 11, 1989." The *Public Papers of President Ronald W. Reagan*. Ronald Reagan Presidential Library. http://www.reagan.utexas.edu/archives/speeches/1989/011189i.htm.

Regaldo, Aldo, J. *Bending Steel: Modernity and the American Superhero*. Jackson: University Press of Mississippi, 2015.

Reynolds, Richard. "Heroes of the Superculture." In *What Is a Superhero?*, edited by Robin Rosenberg and Peter Coogan, 51–58. New York: Oxford University Press, 2013.

Ring, Robert C. *Sci-Fi Movie Freak*. Iola, WI: Krause Publications, 2011.

Roach, Joseph. *Cities of the Dead*. New York: Columbia University Press, 1996.

Rogers, Brett M., and Benjamin Eldon Stevens. "The Past Is an Undiscovered Country." In *Classical Traditions in Science Fiction*, edited by Brett M. Rogers and Benjamin Eldon Stevens, 1–26. New York: Oxford University Press, 2015.

Rogers, William. *Interpreting Interpretation: Textual Hermeneutics as an Ascetic Discipline*. University Park: Penn State University Press, 1994.

Romagnoli, Alex S., and Gian Pagnucci. *Enter the Superheroes: American Values, Culture, and the Canon of Superhero Literature*. Lanham, MD: Scarecrow Press, 2013.

Rome, Adam. *Bulldozer in the Countryside: Suburban Sprawl and the Rise of American Environmentalism*. New York: Cambridge University Press, 2001.

Rose, Frank. *The Art of Immersion: How the Digital Is Remaking Hollywood, Madison Avenue, and the Way We Tell Stories*. New York: Norton, 2011.

Rossi, Andreola. *Contexts of War: Manipulation of Genre in Vergil's Battle Narrative*. Ann Arbor: University of Michigan Press, 2004.

Rothman, Hal. *The Greening of a Nation? Environmentalism in the United States Since 1945*. Fort Worth: Harcourt Brace, 1998.

Rovin, Jeff. *Return of the Wolf Man*. New York: Berkley Boulevard, 1998.

Rovira, James. *Blake and Kierkegaard: Creation and Anxiety*. New York: Continuum, 2010.

Rowe, John Carlos. "Culture, US Imperialism, and Globalization." In *Exceptional State*, edited by Ashley Dawson and Malini Johar Schueller, 37–60. Durham: Duke University Press, 2007.

Runte, Alfred. *National Parks: The American Experience*. 3rd ed. Lincoln: University of Nebraska Press, 1987.

Rushkoff, Douglas. *Media Virus: Hidden Agendas in Popular Culture*. New York: Random House, 1994.

Rygiel, Kim. *Globalizing Citizenship*. Vancouver: University of British Columbia Press, 2010.

Sarup, Madan. *Identity, Culture and the Postmodern World*. Edinburgh: Edinburgh University Press, 1996.

Saunders, Ben. *Do the Gods Wear Capes? Spirituality, Fantasy, and Superheroes*. New York: Continuum, 2011.

Schatz, Thomas. *The Genius of the System: Hollywood Filmmaking in the Studio Era*. Minneapolis: University of Minnesota Press, 2010.

Schwartz, Richard A. *Cold War Culture: Media and the Arts 1945–1990*. New York: Facts on File, 1998.

Sconce, Jeffrey. "What If? Charting Television's New Textual Boundaries." In *Television After TV: Essays on a Medium in Transition*, edited by Lynn Spigel and Jan Olsson, 93–112. Durham: Duke University Press, 2004.

Scott, Suzanne. "Who's Steering the Mothership? The Role of the Fanboy Auteur in Transmedia Storytelling." In *The Participatory Cultures Handbook*, edited by Aaron Alan Delwiche and Jennifer Jacobs Henderson, 43–52. New York: Routledge, 2013.

Slotkin, Richard. *Gunfighter Nation: The Myth of the Frontier in Twentieth Century America*. New York: Macmillan Publishing Company, 1992.

Smith, Aldon R. *The Primacy of Vision in Virgil's Aeneid*. Austin: University of Texas Press, 2005.

Spanos, William V. *American Exceptionalism in the Age of Globalization*. Albany: State University of New York Press, 2008.

Spears, Ellen Griffith. *Baptized in PCBs: Race, Pollution, and Justice in an All-American Town*. Chapel Hill: University of North Carolina Press, 2014.

Sprengler, Christine. *Screening Nostalgia: Populuxe Props and Technicolor Aesthetics in Contemporary American Film*. Oxford: Berghahn Books, 2009.

Stahl, Roger. *Militainment, Inc.: War, Media and Popular Culture*. New York, Routledge, 2010.

Stevens, Richard J. *Captain America, Masculinity, and Violence: The Evolution of a National Icon.* Syracuse: Syracuse University Press, 2015.

Stork, Matthias. "Assembling the Avengers: Reframing the Superhero Movie Through Marvel's Cinematic Universe." In *Superhero Synergies: Comic Book Characters Go Digital*, edited by James N. Gilmore and Matthias Stork, 77–96. Lanham, MD: Rowman & Littlefield, 2014.

Stork, Matthias, and James Gilmore. *Superhero Synergies: Comic Book Characters Go Digital.* Lanham, MD: Rowman & Littlefield, 2014.

Street, Brian. *Cross-Cultural Approaches to Literacy.* Cambridge: Cambridge University Press, 1993.

_____. *Literacy and Development: Ethnographic Perspectives.* London: Routledge, 2001.

Syed, Yasmin. *Virgil's Aeneid and the Roman Self: Subject and Nation in Literary Discourse.* Ann Arbor: University of Michigan Press, 2005.

Thomas, Richard F. *Virgil and the Augustan Reception.* Cambridge: Cambridge University Press, 2005.

Thomas, Roy, and Peter Sanderson. *The Marvel Vault.* Philadelphia: Running, 2007.

Tolkien, J.R.R. *The Tolkien Reader.* New York: Ballantine, 1966.

Tomasso, Vincent. "Classical Antiquity and Western Identity in *Battlestar Galactica*." In *Classical Traditions in Science Fiction*, edited by B. Rogers and B. Stevens, 243–59. Oxford: Oxford University Press, 2015.

Truffaut, François. "A Certain Tendency of The French Cinema." In *Movies and Methods: An Anthology Vol. 1.*, edited by Bill Nichols, 224–237. Berkeley: University of California, 1976.

Tryon, Chuck. *Reinventing Cinema: Movies in the Age of Media Convergence.* New Brunswick, NJ: Rutgers University Press, 2009.

Tsing, Anna. *Friction: An Ethnography of Global Connection.* Princeton: Princeton University Press, 2005.

Tushnet, Mark. "Class Action." In *Legal Reelism: Movies as Legal Texts*, edited by John Denvir, 244–260. Chicago: University of Illinois Press, 1996.

Verano, Frank. "Superheroes Need Supervillains." In *What Is a Superhero?*, edited by Robin S. Rosenberg and Peter Coogan, 83–88. New York: Oxford University Press, 2013.

Wandtke, Terrence R. *The Meaning of Superhero Comic Books.* Jefferson, NC: McFarland, 2012.

Weber, Max. *Protestant Ethic and the Spirit of Capitalism.* Translated by Talcott Parsons. London: HarperCollins Academic, 1991.

Weiner, Tim. *Legacy of Ashes: The History of the CIA.* New York: Doubleday, 2007.

Weisberger, Bernard, A. *Cold War, Cold Peace: The United States and Russia Since 1945.* New York: American Heritage Publishing Co., 1984.

Wells, Paul. *Animation: Genre and Authorship.* London: Wallflower Press, 2002.

Whelehan, Imelda. "Adaptation: The Contemporary Dilemmas." In *Adaptations: From Text to Screen, Screen to Text*, edited by Deborah Cartmell and Imelda Whelehan, 3–19. London: Routledge, 1999.

Wilcox, Rhonda V. "Introduction: Much Ado about Whedon," in *Reading Joss Whedon*, edited by Rhonda V. Wilcox, Tanya R. Cochran, Cynthea Masson, and David Lavery, 1–16. Syracuse: Syracuse University Press, 2014.

Williams, Bronwyn T., and Amy A. Zenger. *Popular Culture and Representations of Literacy.* New York: Routledge, 2007.

Winograd, Morley, and Michael D. Hais. *Millennial Momentum: How a New Generation Is Remaking America.* New Brunswick, NJ: Rutgers University Press, 2011.

Wolf, Mark J.P. *Building Imaginary Worlds: The Theory and History of Subcreation.* Hoboken, NJ: Taylor and Francis, 2014.

Wood, Betty. *Slavery in Colonial America 1619–1776.* Lanham, MD: Rowman & Littlefield, 2005.

Wright, Bradford W. *Comic Book Nation: The Transformation of Youth Culture in America.* Baltimore: Johns Hopkins University Press, 2001.

Contributors

Jason **Bainbridge** is chair of media and communication at Swinburne University of Technology in Melbourne, Australia. He has published widely on screen culture, comic books and popular culture more generally.

Jennifer **Beckett** is a lecturer in the School of Culture and Communication at the University of Melbourne, Australia. She is a researcher, writer and social commentator who works in the fields of public communication, social media, cinema, and the psychology of trauma.

Elizabeth D. **Blum** is a professor of history and the associate chair at Troy University in Alabama. She is at work on her second book, tentatively titled "Growing Up Green."

Liam **Burke** is a lecturer and researcher in media and communications at Swinburne University of Technology in Melbourne, Australia. His research areas include cinema, comics, adaptation studies, and new media and migration. He is the author of *The Comic Book Film Adaptation*.

Julian C. **Chambliss** is a professor of United States history at Rollins College in Florida. His research examines race, identity, and community in real and imagined spaces. His work on comics has appeared in numerous edited collections and journals. He is a coeditor and contributor to *Ages of Heroes, Eras of Men*.

Perry **Dantzler** is an assistant professor at Georgia Gwinnett College. She completed a doctorate in rhetoric and composition from Georgia State University. Her research has focused on literacy and technology in the college classroom and the evolution of Batman.

Sasha-Mae **Eccleston** is an assistant professor of classics at Pomona College in California. Her research interests include Latin literature, intellectual history, and classical reception. She is also writing about Platonist narrative ethics in the works of the Roman North African, Apuleius.

Daniel **Fandino** is a history graduate student at Michigan State University. His academic interests include American and Asian pop culture, as well as the virtual histories of multiplayer online games.

246   About the Contributors

Masani **McGee** is a doctoral student and writing instructor at the University of Rochester in New York. Her research interests include horror and fantasy film and portrayals of masculinity. She has also written on Joss Whedon in *Race and Ethnicity in the Works of Joss Whedon*.

Antony **Mullen** is a Ph.D. student at Durham University in England where he is a teaching assistant in the department of English studies and a Pemberton Scholar at University College. His research includes 1980s fiction and he has published on that, as well as literature and film more broadly.

Samira Shirish **Nadkarni** is a researcher in postmodern poetry and performance, pop culture, hermeneutics, ethics, fan studies, and digital texts. A contributor to the digital poetry project *i <3 e-poetry*, she has also published creative writing and is coeditor of a forthcoming essay collection on the Whedonverse.

Lisa K. **Perdigao** is the humanities program chair and a professor of English at Florida Institute of Technology. She is the author of *From Modernist Entombment to Postmodernist Exhumation* and coeditor of *Death in American Texts and Performances*. She has published articles on numerous films and television series.

Jennifer A. **Rea** is an associate professor of classics at the University of Florida. Her research focuses on the intersections between ancient Rome and modern science fiction and fantasy.

James **Rovira** is the department chair and an associate professor in the English department at Mississippi College, where he teaches British literature, creative writing, and theory. He is the author of *Blake and Kierkegaard* and has been published in academic journals.

William L. **Svitavsky** is an associate professor and emerging services librarian at the Olin Library of Rollins College in Florida. His research interests include American comic book history, the work of M.P. Shiel, and geek culture. He previously coedited and contributed to the *Ages of Heroes, Eras of Men*.

Derek R. **Sweet** is an associate professor of communication studies at Luther College in Iowa, and his research includes the intersection of rhetoric, popular culture, and politics. He is also interested in *Star Wars, Iron Man, Buffy the Vampire Slayer*, and female fronted punk.

Sarah **Zaidan** is an assistant professor of visual and media arts at Emerson College in Boston, where she teaches game design. She is a scholar and creator of video games and comics, including the feminist superhero series *My So-Called Secret Identity*. Her research interests include narrative, gender and gameplay.

Index